DATE			

CHEKHOV

OTHER BIOGRAPHIES BY HENRI TROYAT IN ENGLISH

Firebrand: The Life of Dostoyevsky
Pushkin
Tolstoy
Divided Soul: The Life of Gogol
Catherine the Great
Alexander of Russia: Napoleon's Conqueror
Ivan the Terrible

HENRI TROYAT
CHEKHOV

Translated from the French by Michael Henry Heim

E. P. DUTTON | NEW YORK

Passages from Chekhov's correspondence originally published
in *Letters of Anton Chekhov,* translated from the Russian
by Michael Henry Heim in collaboration with Simon Karlinsky,
selection, introduction, and commentary by Simon Karlinsky.
Copyright © 1973 by Harper & Row, Publishers, Inc.,
reprinted by permission of Harper & Row, Publishers, Inc.,
and The Bodley Head, Ltd.

First published in the United States in 1986 by
E. P. Dutton, a division of New American Library,
2 Park Avenue, New York, N.Y. 10016.

Library of Congress Cataloging-in-Publication Data
Troyat, Henri, 1911–
Chekhov.
Translation of: Tchekhov.
Bibliography: p.
Includes index.
1. Chekhov, Anton Pavlovich, 1860–1904. 2. Authors,
Russian—19th century—Biography. I. Title.
PG3458.T7613   1986   891.72′3 [B]   86-8897
ISBN: 0-525-24406-9

Published simultaneously in Canada by
Fitzhenry & Whiteside Limited, Toronto

W

Designed by Mark O'Connor

10 9 8 7 6 5 4 3 2 1

First American Edition

Contents

Eight pages of illustrations follow page 166.

Translator's Note

Henri Troyat's *Chekhov* contains many quotations from Russian sources. The large majority come from Chekhov's letters. When the excerpts quoted by the author appear in *Anton Chekhov's Life and Thought: Selected Letters and Commentary* (University of California Press, Berkeley, 1975 [originally published as *Letters of Anton Chekhov* by Harper & Row, New York, 1973]), translated by myself in collaboration with Simon Karlinsky, I have reproduced them here. I gratefully acknowledge the permission of Simon Karlinsky and the publishers to do so. Otherwise I have translated them from the Russian for the present volume.

Most of the other quotations come from the correspondence and memoirs of Chekhov's relatives and friends. When a standard English translation exists, I have used it and cited it in the end notes. Otherwise I have wherever possible translated the passages myself from the Russian.

Translated passages include a number of ellipses. When *bracketed*, they indicate editorial omissions; when *unbracketed*, they reproduce ellipses in the original.

CHEKHOV

I

The Family Circle

"**M**y father began my education or, to put it more simply, began to beat me, before I reached the age of five," wrote Anton Chekhov of his earliest memories. "Every morning as I awoke, my first thought was, 'Will I be beaten today?'" When a schoolfriend happened to mention that he was never beaten at home, the young Chekhov called him a liar. After a thrashing, his behind smarting, he was required by custom to kiss the hand that had punished him so harshly.

Chekhov's father, Pavel Yegorovich, convinced that his every action conformed to the will of a God with whom he was on special terms, ruled his family with an iron hand. His wife, the gentle and rather conventional Yevgenia Yakovlevna, his sons, Alexander, Nikolai, Anton, Ivan, and Mikhail, and his daughter Maria*—all trembled the moment he raised his voice in their presence.

Yet Pavel Yegorovich meted out punishment with little anger and no malice. He loved the children in his own way and believed he was helping them by treating them harshly. Carried away by high-flown principles, he neglected to separate morals from the cane. The method he chose to inculcate the sacred truths in his witless progeny was one of shouting and beating. "That's how I was brought up," he would say to his wife to justify his violence, "and look how I've turned out!" Later Chekhov would say on a melancholy note, "Our grandfather was beaten by his masters, and the lowest of officials could smash his face in. Our father was beaten by our grandfather, and we by our father. What sort of nerves, what sort of blood have we inherited?" And elsewhere: "When I was a child I had no childhood."

Yevgenia Yakovlevna would try to ward off her husband's fury, but lacking all force of character and worn down by six closely spaced childbirths, she was incapable of reasoning with him. In fact, the self-important paterfamilias was not above treating her like a servant girl. "Let me ask you to recall," Anton wrote as an adult to his elder brother Alexander, "that it was despotism and lying that ruined your mother's youth. Despotism and lying so mutilated our childhood that it's sickening and frightening to think about it. Remember the horror and disgust we felt in those days when Father threw a tantrum at dinner over too much salt in the soup and called Mother a fool. [. . .] It's better to be the victim than the hangman."[1]

Whenever he thought of his mother, Anton saw her bustling about in the kitchen or hunched over the sewing machine. Hadn't she six children to feed and clothe? She grieved at the thought of how fast they wore things out, how fast they grew; she was obsessed by the problem of keeping them in clothes. Lengthening a coat, patching a pair of trousers—it was all so

---

*Alexander was born in 1855, Nikolai in 1858, Anton in 1860, Ivan in 1861, Maria in 1863, Mikhail in 1865.

expensive. She constantly added up kopecks in her head, afraid that her husband would scold her for being a poor housekeeper.

Young Anton, too, was forever plagued by the fear of reprimand. Poring over his Latin grammar, he would pray for the day to end without incident. But soon he heard the sound of steps moving up to the door, and in would come Father— heavy, broad-shouldered, dark-bearded, bushy-browed—an overbearing look in his eye, a thick winter coat on his back, and leather boots up over his calves.

"I have some business to attend to, Antosha. Run along to the shop and make sure things are going smoothly."

"It's cold in the shop," Anton protested with tears in his eyes. "I've been shivering since the minute I left school."

"That doesn't mean anything. Dress properly and you won't be cold."

"I have a lot of homework for tomorrow."

"You can do it in the shop. Go on, now, and take care of things. Quickly! No dillydallying!"*

Ever docile, Anton laid down his pen, pulled on his quilted school coat and a pair of cracked boots, tucked the Latin grammar under his arm, and followed his father into the icy darkness of the street. The temperature was arctic. Andryushka and Gavryushka, the two small Ukrainian peasants who waited on customers in the shop, were stamping their feet and rubbing their blue faces to keep warm. At the sight of their boss they drew themselves to attention. Pavel Yegorovich ordered Anton behind the counter and, crossing himself several times before the shop's guardian icon, clumped out of the shop.

Snuffling back a combination of tears and mucus, Anton perched on a Kazan soapbox and opened the Latin grammar on the counter, bravely determined to resume his assignment. But when he tried to dip his pen in the inkpot, the steel nib met a film of ice. The two little shop assistants had started jumping up and down again and were soon chattering away, laughing

---

*This dialogue as well as the scene that follows come from the *Memoirs* of Chekhov's elder brother Alexander.

up their sleeves. Customers came and went, their voices reverberating loudly from the low ceiling. The hubbub made it impossible to dream, much less study, and Anton knew he was confined to the shop for a good several hours: whenever his father went out to visit friends or pray at church, he would forget his son's very existence. And so, pulling his arms inside his sleeves and curling his toes inside his boots, Anton thought of the bad marks he would get in class the next day, and felt himself going numb with misery and fear.

The dark and dirty shop stocked all sorts of articles. Groceries, of course, but also oil, lamps, wicks, penknives, tobacco, nails, and laxatives. Boxes of tea were shelved next to bags of candles; sacks of flour leaned against sacks of sunflower seeds; a string of sausages and sticky sweets hung down over the counter. The merchandise gave out a composite odor: the coffee smelled of oil, the rice of suet. TEA, SUGAR, COFFEE, AND OTHER GROCERIES—TO TAKE HOME OR DRINK ON THE PREMISES, read a black, gold-lettered sign over the door, the tag end inviting patrons to stop off for a vodka or two in a small room adjoining the shop. A few habitués had turned the dusty, foul-smelling place into a sort of club. At nightfall they gathered round small carafes, and before long, faces would light up, tongues loosen. When his father was away, Anton would descend into the cellar to replenish the supply of vodka; he would wait on customers, make out their bills, take their money. Vodka was not expensive in Russia; several kopecks' worth could make one drunk. The tipplers would exchange crude jokes. Every time one of them had a particularly risqué story to tell, he would call out to the boy, "Don't you listen, Antosha! You're too young!" But little Anton heard all, guessed all, grasped all. Despite his age he had firsthand experience with misery, ugliness, torpor, stupidity.

The shop was open from five in the morning to eleven at night. To get to the privy, which was located in a plot of unused land, Anton had to walk a verst.* "There were times," he wrote, "when, making my way in the dark, I would come face to face

*A verst is 1,067 meters or about two-thirds of a mile.

with a tramp who had taken refuge there for the night. The terror that gripped us then, the two of us!"

At last one of the shop assistants ran in from his outdoor post shouting, "Papa's coming!" Anton straightened his back, rubbed his sleep-filled eyes, and, his heart in his mouth, steeled himself for a reprimand. Pavel Yegorovich inspected the shop with an eagle eye, then leaned over the accounts. Anton held his breath. Woe unto him if he got a sum wrong! Back at home, exhausted and chilled to the bone, he was comforted by his mother. From time to time she dared to suggest, respectfully, that the work was perhaps more than the child could manage.

"He'll just have to get used to it!" was Pavel Yegorovich's response. "I work! Why shouldn't he? Children are supposed to help their fathers."

"But he's spent all week in the shop. At least let him rest on Sunday!"

"Instead of resting he makes a fool of himself running around outside with a bunch of brats. If the children aren't in the shop, the help will start filching sweets, and the next thing you know they'll be at the cash desk!"

If Anton so much as peeped about not being able to learn his lessons for the cold and the customers, Pavel Yegorovich would growl into his beard, "I find time to read two psalms in the Bible every day, and you can't even learn one lesson!" His favorite saying was, "Wares without owners go weeping." Yet he himself was rarely to be found behind the counter. Wasn't that what sons were for?

In Anton's mind the nightmare of the shop went hand in hand with the nightmare of the church. Pavel Yegorovich had such a passion for religion that he spent most of his time praying and reading devotional literature. What attracted him in the practice of his faith was not so much Christian precepts as the slow and mysterious beauty of the rites, the glitter of icons and their gilded frames, the pageantry of the chasubles, the searching melody of the hymns, the repeated calls to kneel and make the sign of the cross, the heady fragrance of incense. He required his sons to accompany him to the main services of the day.

Since Orthodox churches have no seats, the children would stand for hours, dazed by the solemn progress of the liturgy.

Soon, however, he found even this diligence insufficient. Possessed of a pleasant voice and a good ear, he decided to form a church choir. Rehearsals took place from ten to midnight in a room off the shop. Most of the choristers were blacksmiths with powerful rib cages, and to counterbalance the effect of their cavernous basses and manly baritones, the choirmaster recruited his sons. He gave Alexander and Nikolai the first and second soprano parts and Anton the alto. They would sit on soapboxes around a table, singing the glory of God to Pavel Yegorovich's fiddle. "Novices," he would say, "recite prayers and sing hymns for nights on end, and it does them no harm. Church singing strengthens the children's chests. I've sung since I was a child, and I'm in fine health, thank God. Making an effort for God is never amiss!"

Thanks to connections in church circles he was offered frequent singing engagements, which, while tickling his vanity, plunged his children into despair. Anton especially dreaded Sundays and holidays, when services started early in the morning. Pavel Yegorovich would wake him and his brothers two or three hours ahead of time to enable them to prepare both body and soul for the divine liturgy to come. Although they returned home exhausted, he would impose his own reenactment of the service on them, pompously swinging a censer back and forth in front of the icons and ordering the family to accompany him as he intoned the hymns. Mother, father, and children would lie prostrate, beating their heads on the floor and raising their voices in a pious tribute to God until it was time for the last morning mass. When the bells began to chime again, they would all march back to church. It was with these trials in mind that Chekhov wrote to his friend Ivan Leontyev-Shcheglov on March 9, 1892: "In my childhood, I received a religious education—choir singing, reading of the epistles and psalms in church, regular attendance at matins, altar-boy and bell-ringing duty. And the result? When I think back on my childhood it all seems quite gloomy to me. I have no religion now. You know, when my two brothers and I would sing the "Let My Prayer Arise" trio or "Archangel's Voice," everyone looked at us and was moved. They envied my parents, but we felt like little convicts . . . For us childhood was sheer suffering."

Despite Pavel Yegorovich's narrow mind and coarse ways he did have a certain taste for art. Not only had he taught himself to play the violin; he painted icons with a kind of fumbling veneration.* "Our talent," said Chekhov, "came from our father, our soul from our mother."

All the prayers, all the candles burned before sacred images, did not keep Pavel Yegorovich's shop from going downhill. Customers were put off by his abrupt manner, his petty outlook, his parsimony. His goods were of decidedly poor quality. When a rat drowned in a barrel of oil one day, he could not bring himself to sacrifice the contents. How to reconcile the honesty required of a Christian with the desire to avoid a painful outlay? Enlightened by the Almighty, Pavel Yegorovich sent for a priest and had him recite the purification ritual over the desecrated oil. Although the ceremony took place in the utmost privacy, word of it leaked out to an indignant community. Even after its exorcism the oil found no buyers. Moreover, a trace of contamination spread to everything in the shop. Only the bibulous remained faithful.

Regularly unhinged by the combination of despotism and devotion, Pavel Yegorovich left much to be desired as a tradesman, but he was still a member of the Second Merchants' Guild of Taganrog. With naïve satisfaction he would sport the association's insignia on a chain, and he never set foot out of the house on Sundays in anything but a top hat and white shirt. Looking back on the milieu he had come from, he could indeed be proud of how far he had risen in the world.

His father, Anton's paternal grandfather, Yegor Mikhailovich Chekh, had been born a serf. Clever, hardworking, and thrifty, he managed to have himself appointed manager of his

---

*Chekhov was careful to preserve some of these icons, and they are now in the Chekhov Museum in Yalta.

master's sugar-beet refinery. He had learned to read, write, and reckon, and expected the same of his children. In 1841 he was able to buy his own liberty and the liberty of his wife and three sons at the substantial price of seven hundred rubles a head. And though his money had run out by the time he came to his only daughter, she was given to him as a bonus by his generous owner, Count Chertkov.* Once Yegor Mikhailovich was freed, his reputation of being strict but honest landed him the position of steward on the Countess Platova's immense estates between Taganrog and Rostov-on-Don. Nor did he go by the scornful-sounding Chekh any longer; he had become Chekhov.

In the hope of assuring his family's future, he apprenticed Mikhail to a bookbinder in Kaluga, Mitrofan to a shopkeeper in Rostov, and Pavel to the rich merchant mayor of Taganrog. As a bookkeeper Pavel had a good deal of responsibility, but he knuckled down through ten years of bad pay and bad treatment, champing secretly at the bit. Then, on October 29, 1854, Pavel married Yevgenia Yakovlevna Morozova, like himself from a serf background.

Yevgenia's father, a cloth merchant in Morshansk, had died in a cholera epidemic during a business trip to Novocherkassk. His wife, who received news of his death while visiting a relative at the other end of Russia, in the province of Vladimir, hired a carriage and set off on an endless and perilous journey to locate her husband's grave. Yevgenia loved to tell her son Anton the tale of the journey they made across plains and through forests, of the barren splendor of the countryside, of encounters with wandering holy fools, of nights spent at sinister inns where the fear of highwaymen led them to barricade the doors. As they moved southwards, the fears and strains of the journey were tempered by its poetry. Freed from earlier anxieties, the family occasionally slept out in the open under a transparent sky, with only the chirping of crickets or the piercing cry of a nocturnal bird to disturb the stillness. Anton remembered his mother's stories all his life, and the several incidents he incorporated into

---

*Grandfather of the future disciple and executor of Lev Tolstoy.

"The Steppe" are so full of feeling that he seems to have experienced them himself. The whereabouts of Grandfather Morozov's grave forever remained a mystery, and for want of anything better his widow and two daughters settled in the port town of Taganrog. There Pavel Yegorovich met his future wife.

Married life proved difficult at first. The Crimean War paralyzed activity in the port, and soon Taganrog itself was bombarded by the Franco-British fleet. Yevgenia, pregnant at the time, took refuge with her husband on the outskirts of town. Ten months after the wedding she gave birth to her first child, Alexander. As soon as the war was over, the couple and their baby moved back into town, setting up house in a hovel bought for them by Pavel Yegorovich's father. In 1857, after several years of scrimping and saving, Pavel Yegorovich could at last afford to make his dream come true and buy his own grocer's shop. There, in the heart of Taganrog, in Gnutov House, Police Street, on January 17, 1860, Anton Chekhov was born.* A small one-story structure with green shutters and a zinc roof, it soon grew too crowded, and the family moved twice more until coming to rest in Moiseev House, Monastery Street, on the outskirts of town, in 1869.

Chekhov's memories of his successive childhood abodes are nothing if not dismal. "On meat days," he wrote in the story "My Life," "the houses smelled of borscht, on fast days of sturgeon fried in sunflower oil. The food was unsavory, the water unhealthy. [. . .] I did not know a single honest man in the whole town." And in a letter to his family: "I am in Taganrog. [. . .] It gives the impression of a Herculaneum or a Pompeii. [. . .] All the houses look flattened and haven't been stuccoed in ages; the roofs have no paint on them, the shutters are closed . . . Starting at Police Street the road is filled with mud that dries and then turns sticky and blisters. [. . .] Making my way across the New Bazaar, I came to realize how dirty, empty, lazy, illiterate, and boring Taganrog really is. No sign is without a spelling error—I even saw a 'Rusha Tavern.'

*The house still exists at 47 Chekhov Street.

The streets are deserted but for some self-satisfied stevedores and fops in caps and long coats. [. . .] There is a prevailing idleness, the skill of being content with a few kopecks and an uncertain future."[2]

In another letter, dated the same day and addressed to the journalist Nikolai Leikin, he expanded on the point. "Everything around me is so Asiatic I can't believe my eyes. Sixty thousand inhabitants and all they do is eat, drink, and reproduce; they have no other interests . . . No matter where you go, all you see is *kulich* [a cylindrical cake traditionally made in Russia for Easter], eggs, Santorini [a Greek wine], and babies; no newspapers, no books. [. . .] There are no patriots, no businessmen, no poets, or even decent bakers . . ."

During the period in question Taganrog, a town on the northeast shore of the Sea of Azov, was in fact all but moribund. The port, created by Peter the Great, had once known a certain prosperity. A number of foreign merchants, Greeks for the most part, had settled there and virtually taken over the exportation of agricultural products. They set up a kind of moneyed aristocracy and assumed dominion over the native population, promptly reducing them to clerks and jobbers. The opulent overlords, the Taganrog millionaires, had names like Valiano, Scaramanga, Kondoyaki, Moussouri, Sfaello, with nary an Ivanov or Petrov among them. They built their houses in a special residential area and were at home only to their own kind; they lived high off the hog, sporting the latest in Parisian fashions, supporting the local theater, and having marble brought in from Paros or Carrara for the monuments they erected to themselves and their families in the Greek cemetery. The town enjoyed a glimmer of celebrity when Tsar Alexander I died a mysterious death there in 1825,* but it soon fell back into oblivion. The bay began silting up, and larger ships were forced to lie at anchor farther and farther out. Meanwhile, the neighboring munici-

---

*Legend has it that the death was a sham, that the coffin contained the corpse of a soldier, and that the Tsar fled to Siberia to live a holy life under the name of Elder Fyodor Kuzmich.

pality of Rostov-on-Don began to grow, modernize, and take over as a trading center.

By midcentury Taganrog had turned into a ghost town. Chekhov was both repulsed by its inertia and affected by its morbid charm. Unlike the foreign population, which still strutted about like turkey-cocks, the Russians—unskilled workers, stevedores, shopkeepers, and petty clerks—eked out a miserable livelihood. In autumn and spring, pedestrians sank ankle-deep in the mud-filled potholes that riddled the unpaved streets; in summer the road disappeared under a tangle of weeds. Only the two main arteries were lit, and they but poorly; the town's inhabitants were forced to carry lanterns while abroad at night. When from time to time a girl was reported missing, she was commonly believed to have been sold into a Turkish harem. Prisoners from the municipal jail pulled carts with sacks of flour through the streets or wandered through the marketplace in search of stray dogs, which they massacred with clubs and spiked sticks in full sight of the passersby. Water was scarce and polluted. Every Saturday the town crier would saunter up and down the streets, wielding a large straw broom and shouting, "To the baths! To the baths! To the public baths!"

Buried deep within that godforsaken outpost, a "deaf town," as Russians would call it, young Anton felt a combination of disgust and affection, revolt and resignation. How well he knew that ill-favored corner of the earth. All he saw around him were people like his parents who lived in small, broken-down wooden houses with awnings for summer relief and dingy little gardens. He knew the names and quirks of all the neighbors; he knew their dogs' names and how many chickens they had. Every illness, every death, every marriage, birth, and ceremonial meal was everyone else's business. They all spied on one another, envied one another, but stood by one another.

Chekhov felt very much a part of provincial Russia's gentle inertia. Yet he also suffered from belonging to a community so listless that its members had lost all faith in a better tomorrow. For despite his youth he felt a driving need for hope. Early in life he knew he would not live out his days in Taganrog. Sitting in his father's shop among the sacks of flour and clusters of sausages, he would dream of a journey like the one his mother had told him about—a long, fearsome, but exciting journey across the length and breadth of Russia. Would he, too, be able to break away and find new horizons, new faces? Until that time came, the best he could do was keep his nose to the grindstone and sigh away his boredom.

II

Schools
and
Escapes

Disappointed by the meager returns from his shop, Pavel Yegorovich decreed one day that his sons should rise above the station of greengrocer. Since in Taganrog the rich Greek merchants held sway, he would beat them at their own game. Instead of placing Anton and Nikolai in a Russian school, as his wife had timidly advised, he would send them to a Greek one, where they would learn the language of trade. Later, their knowledge of the language would gain them admission to an import-export firm, where they would rise to the upper echelons step by step.

A teacher at the Greek church school, Nikos Voutsina by name, a large man with a red beard, loose tongue, and hazy past, supported the idea. He was so persuasive, in fact, that he argued the tightfisted Pavel Yegorovich into paying a twenty-five-ruble advance on the yearly school fees. And so the hopes of the family, Anton and Nikolai, set off for the establishment where, according to Voutsina, the commercial elite of the town received its education.

What they found was a building consisting of a single drab and decrepit room crowded with seventy Greek "youths"— aged six to twenty. The room was divided into five rows of desks numbered I, II, III, etc., each of which corresponded to a class. The pupils in the first row recited, "*Alpha, beta, gamma, delta*," while the pupils in the fifth row—strapping young fellows with striped sailors' jerseys stretched against muscular chests—stumbled through Greek history. Voutsina was the only teacher, and he taught all subjects with equal aplomb. Having sat Anton (then age seven) and Nikolai (then age nine) on the "preparatory bench," he handed each of them a pamphlet entitled *The New Alphabet* and told them, "You will bring me twenty-five kopecks for each book tomorrow."

From the outset the newcomers were terrorized by this band of squabbling youths, who spoke a language they did not understand, and by their tawny-bearded teacher, who went from row to row berating his charges and inflicting a variety of sophisticated punishments on them: rapping them on the knuckles or the head with a ruler, making them kneel on coarse salt, depriving them of the noonday meal. As soon as he saw that, despite his admonitions, the Chekhov boys had failed to master their primers, he ceased to bother with them. Relegated to the dunces' corner, Anton and Nikolai sat with their arms crossed over their chests from nine in the morning to three in the afternoon. At least it was better than being in the shop or at church! Anton's only fear was that his father would be informed of his lack of progress. But several weeks later, when Pavel Yegorovich asked Voutsina what he thought of his sons, a beaming Voutsina replied that his teaching had begun to bear fruit. To back up his claim, he awarded the brothers certificates of excellence or *brabea* (prizes in the games). Nikolai's *brabeion* spoke of him as *eusebes* (pious), while Anton's called him *epimeles* (attentive).

During the Christmas holidays Pavel Yegorovich invited a few Greek friends to his house to show off his sons' skill in the language of Homer. Unfortunately, neither Nikolai the Pious nor Anton the Attentive could come up with more than a few words. Pavel Yegorovich, the laughingstock of the evening, threw an Olympian tantrum. But since he had paid the fees in advance, he sent the two culprits back to Voutsina for the rest of the school year.

Not until August 23, 1868 did Yevgenia Yakovlevna see her wish come true. On that day Anton donned the official navy-blue uniform of the Taganrog Russian Gymnasium and entered the preparatory class. At the time he was pale and pudgy with a round face, bushy hair, and large brown, dreamy eyes. Though shy, modest, and distant, he could burst into fits of gaiety and would make his school friends laugh by seizing on the absurdities around them. After Voutsina's one-room schoolhouse the Russian gymnasium seemed enormous. The white flaking walls, green zinc roof, and long squalid corridors made it look like an army barracks. The door of each room contained a porthole-shaped peephole to enable proctors to watch the pupils without being seen. The curriculum lasted eight years and emphasized Latin, Greek, Church Slavonic, and Russian. After completing the course, pupils were automatically enrolled in the lowest of the fourteen divisions that made up the much-vaunted "Table of Ranks" instituted by Peter the Great a century and a half earlier; they were also ensured university admission.

The teachers and proctors entrusted with the task of educating this segment of provincial youth were for the most part mediocrities. Dyakonov, the teacher in charge of discipline, was nicknamed the "Centipede" by the pupils for the furtive way he had of sneaking up on them; he would torture his victims with moral exhortations. Kramsakov, who taught history and geography, insulted his pupils in appallingly coarse language. Urban, the Czech Latin master, spied on his pupils, sniffing out political plots and sending off letters of denunciation to the police; nor did he stop at attacking his fellow teachers. One of his reports reads: "My colleagues smoke during staff meetings. Little do they care that there is an icon and a portrait of His Majesty the Emperor hanging on the walls of the room."

Doubtless these are the hidebound, provincial schoolmasters Chekhov had in mind when he makes a character in "The Man in the Case" exclaim: "So you think you're pedagogues, teachers? You're a bunch of pen pushers! And this is no temple of learning, it's a local church office with a sour police-station smell."

Of all the teachers at the school only Father Pokrovsky, who taught religion, found grace in his eyes. Father Pokrovsky, a cultured man who loved literature and did not hesitate to speak of Shakespeare, Goethe, or Pushkin in class, was quick to notice Anton's comic talent. He gave him the jocular nickname Chekhonte and advised him to read Molière, Swift, and the Russian satirist Saltykov-Shchedrin. Anton's schoolmates, too, appreciated his ability to tell story after funny story. But even while delivering a joke that unleashed roars of laughter, he remained apart. If he thought up a good prank, he would leave it to others to act out. His irony was light and frothy, completely free of malice. Besides, he knew how to make fun of himself. Father Pokrovsky's encouragement notwithstanding, his marks hovered near the zero level, but there was always the excuse that between waiting on customers in the shop and singing in the church choir he had precious little time to study.

To put the finishing touches on his sons' education, Pavel Yegorovich had them given French lessons by a certain Madame Chopet and music lessons by a bank clerk who read music. When he realized that the lessons' practical value was basically nil, he enrolled the boys in a course designed to turn them into budding young tailors. Nikolai and Ivan were soon expelled for "unruly conduct and slow progress," but Anton persevered. When he felt he had acquired the requisite skill, he fashioned a pair of trousers for Nikolai, but they turned out so tight that the family dubbed them the "macaroni trousers."

Shop, church, school, sewing—despite all his obligations Anton found ways to run off from time to time and wander through the streets. Everything he saw made him laugh: a dog sauntering along with a turned-up tail, a funeral with the family in tears behind the coffin, an argument among stevedores—

they all made memorable events. He paid frequent visits to graveyards, deciphering inscriptions on the tombs and dreaming of the fates of the myriad strangers resting beneath them. All his life, in fact, he was attracted by cemeteries. At the time he preferred the graveyards of the villages surrounding Taganrog, where the traditional cypresses had been replaced by cherry trees whose fruit left red specks on the slabs "very much like drops of blood."

Anton also enjoyed playing with his brothers. They would ambush goldfinches in a bramble patch and sell them for a kopeck apiece. They would spread out in Elizabeth Park* and play cowboys and Indians, scalping one another à la James Fenimore Cooper and Mayne Reid. Or, taking Police Street down to the port, they would fish for hours and go for a quick dip in the sea. One morning Anton came up from a dive with a deep gash in his head; the scar remained with him for the rest of his life. If only for fear of Pavel Yegorovich, the Chekhov progeny became a close-knit clan with its own rites, secrets, and language. All its members had a sense of humor, but more often than not Anton was the one who set the tone. No matter how poor and poorly treated they might be, the young Chekhovs had a need to laugh, and laughter always saved them from despair.

While Taganrog sweltered in the heat and dust of the long summer holidays, the children went barefoot and slept out in the garden in little shacks they put together themselves. Anton built his in the shelter of an arbor draped with wild vines. There he would scribble mischievous rhymes, styling himself "Job under his fig tree." A little girl who lived next door was so enchanted by him that she chalked a sentimental quatrain on the garden gate. Anton replied with a satirical quatrain of his own, admonishing the young poetess to play with her dolls rather than scrawl all over walls. And when in high dudgeon she called him a peasant, a *muzhik,* he clobbered her on the head with a dusty sack of charcoal. His first idyll had come to an

---

*It was named after the wife of Alexander I.

17

end. "I was initiated into the mysteries of love at the age of thirteen," he wrote ironically when asked some years later for biographical material.[1]

Anton was the son Yevgenia Yakovlevna sent to the market early each morning. Conscious of the responsibility involved, he did his best to look serious, and always clutched the money tightly in his pocket. His brother Mikhail would tag along. One day, after buying a duck, he tortured the poor animal all the way home, shaking and pinching it to make it squawk "and let everyone know we were having duck for dinner."

On some Sundays the Chekhov family would dine with Uncle Mitrofan, who, like his brother, had ended up a Taganrog grocer. His shop, however, was better situated, better stocked, and better run than Pavel Yegorovich's, and his business thrived. Deeply religious, he tended to dot his speech with biblical quotations. Yet unlike Pavel Yegorovich he was a Christian in deed as well as word. He made a point of condemning corporal punishment, showed respect for his wife, treated his children with concern, and had nothing but kindness for his nephews and niece. For Anton, each visit to Uncle Mitrofan's house was a holiday. He loved the man and enjoyed playing jokes on him. Once he decided to appear at his uncle's door dressed as a beggar. Mitrofan, taken in by his pitiful face, gave him three kopecks. The family had many a good laugh over Anton's innocent hoax.

But what were these trifling diversions compared with the summer visits the children would pay to their paternal grandfather, the Countess Platova's steward in the village of Knyazhaya, seventy versts from Taganrog in the Donets steppe? For the journey, which took several days, the family would hire a *telega,* a sturdy peasant wagon whose floorboards rested directly on the axles, and after Pavel Yegorovich, who fortunately remained behind to mind the shop, had delivered his exhortations and his blessing, Yevgenia Yakovlevna and her daughter and five sons would scramble in, laughing and squeezing together against the slatted sides. The *telega* made slow progress, bumping and creaking in its cloud of dust. The plain stretched out interminably under the harsh sun, the long, dry grass rippling at the slightest puff of wind. Thousands of midges quivered in the torrid atmosphere. Anton could not help recalling the journey his mother had recounted to him, the expedition across the great expanses of Russia in search of a grave. The memory of her story became one with his personal impressions. Without realizing it, he was storing up the images, scents, and sounds of his future masterpiece "The Steppe." At long intervals they would stop and picnic by the road, go for a swim in a pond, sprawl in a haystack. Nights they spent either at an inn or in the open, around a fire. Watching the flames, Anton felt his heart overflow with gratitude for the clear sky above, the fragrance of grass and smoke, the deep stillness, and his shivering kith and kin.

At Knyazhaya, Yegor Mikhailovich gave his grandchildren a hearty welcome. They had an abandoned house all to themselves and the run of the vast grounds; they could romp, climb trees, and swim to their hearts' content. Nikolai had unearthed an old opera hat somewhere and insisted on wearing it through all their games, until one day Anton managed to knock it off and it sank pitifully to the bottom of the ornamental lake. Even work was fun in the paradise of Knyazhaya. By order of Grandfather Yegor Mikhailovich, the Chekhov children were sent into the fields more than once during the harvest. Anton later remembered having to leave off his capers and spend a day tending the steam threshing machine and keeping track of the grain. Fifteen years later he would write to Alexei Suvorin, the editor of the journal *New Times*: "The whistling, the hissing, and the deep, toplike drone of the machine when work is in full swing, the creak of the wheels, the oxen's lazy gait, the clouds of dust, the black, sweaty faces of fifty or so men—it is all as engraved in my memory as the Lord's Prayer."[2]

Shortly after returning from Knyazhaya in the autumn of 1873, Anton received a shock that marked him for life: he discovered the theater. How many times had he passed the small municipal theater in Peter Street without feeling the slightest desire to go in? Then, when he was thirteen, he was taken to see a performance of Offenbach's *La Belle Hélène*. He was dazzled. The blue cloth representing the sky puckered badly and still showed its diagonal folds; the marble columns were of the consistency of cardboard; the singers got tangled in their grotesque and gaudy rags and acted abominably—and yet the whole had a magic effect on the boy. It offered him entrée into a world of illusion and masquerade, of tinsel and hocus-pocus, that made his head spin. Cowboys and Indians, goldfinch hunting, cemetery visits—he abandoned them all and gave himself up entirely to his new passion. He was equally enchanted by *Hamlet*, Gogol's *Inspector General*, Griboedov's *Wit Works Woe*, a stage adaptation of *Uncle Tom's Cabin*, and melodramas and frothy comedies based on French models.

Anton's infatuation with the stage was all the more exciting in that he had to resort to various ruses to indulge in it. A gymnasium student was allowed to attend theater performances only with the authorization of his headmaster. Anton and a few of his friends, including the future actor Alexander Vishnevsky and the well-to-do Andrei Drossi, tackled the problem by draping themselves in their fathers' coats and hiding behind blue spectacles. Thus disguised, and quivering all the while, they would manage to sneak past the gymnasium inspector in charge of preventing them from entering the den of iniquity.

For the best seats, up in "the gods," Anton would arrive at the box office two hours before curtain. Often he had no idea of what play he was going to see. Drama, comedy, opera, operetta—he was game. Perching at the edge of the abyss and greedily inhaling the smell of dust, makeup, and glue, he awaited the magic moment when the curtain would rise. Little by little the gallery came alive with a boisterous and unkempt crowd that talked, laughed, and cracked sunflower seeds with utter abandon. Then the expensive stalls and balcony seats began to fill up with local worthies: rich Greek shipowners and prosperous indigenous tradesmen with their brilliantly adorned wives. A hum of excited impatience made its way to the stage. The idea that all these different people had come to applaud the same play brought home to Anton the extraordinary power wielded by an actor over the common mortal. He saw the artist's life, with its surprises, its grandiloquence, its illusions, its peregrinations, as an exhilarating alternative to a staid, dreary family life. He, too, dreamed of joining a traveling company.

Nothing thrilled him more than dressing up as one or another local eccentric observed on the sly, and parodying his victim's mannerisms and verbal tics. With the help of his brothers and sister, themselves talented actors, he created his own theater company, which performed before a benevolent audience of relatives, friends, and neighbors. One evening he would transform himself into a dental surgeon and, armed with a pair of coal tongs and any number of grimaces, proceed to pull a recalcitrant patient's tooth. Or he was a benighted, decrepit priest being examined by his bishop—a skit that could only be performed in the absence of his father, who would never have tolerated watching the clergy made a butt for ridicule. Or else he would mimic the mayor of Taganrog presiding at a church ceremony or reviewing a detachment of Cossacks.

Later, his ambition growing, Anton tackled actual plays. A stiff neck, a cushion-swollen stomach, and a chest studded with cardboard medals made him so amusing as the governor in *The Inspector General* that the audience could not stop laughing. His next, and even greater, hit was as an old woman gossip in Grigoryev's *The Coachman, or A Hussar Officer's Prank*. According to his friend Andrei Drossi, "It is impossible to imagine the Homeric roars resounding each time Anton Pavlovich made an entrance. There can be do doubt but that he had a brilliant command of the role."

The actors most enjoyed performing at the home of Drossi's amiable and well-to-do parents. They would divide the living room in two by means of a curtain decorated with a multicolored firebird. One side of the curtain was the stage, the other the auditorium with several rows of seats. The actors had a wardrobe all to themselves, and they crammed it full of costumes, props, makeup, and wigs. Soon, encouraged by success, Anton ventured to put on his own playlets, which mocked the failings of his fellow citizens. The texts went into exercise books and were destroyed after each performance. None has come down to us.

Meanwhile, the Chekhovs had moved into a new house. It was built by Pavel Yegorovich on a piece of land his father had given him in Office Street. Despite the most stringent of budgets all the family savings were eaten up by the undertaking, and in 1874 Pavel Yegorovich had to take out a loan for five hundred rubles from the local credit institution to complete it. Since any source of income was welcome in those hard times, he rented a part of the house to a minor court official, Gavriil Parfentievich Selivanov.

In June 1875, on the way to spend the holidays with Selivanov's brother, who had come into a country estate by dint of a good marriage, Anton stopped in the boiling sun for a dip in an icy river. After a torturous night at a coaching inn he was sent back to Taganrog with acute peritonitis, the illness that caused the hemorrhoids he would suffer from for the rest of his life. The gymnasium physician, a Doctor Strempf, treated him with such care and devotion that Anton decided to become a doctor. His inborn generosity thrilled at the idea of one day offering to others the relief he himself had been given. But a medical career required many years of study, and his end-of-term report was so poor that he had to repeat the fifth year. Nor did the family milieu foster rigorous thinking.

Disgusted by their father's iron hand, Anton's elder brothers, Alexander and Nikolai, could think of nothing but breaking away. Alexander, who tended to be unstable and violent, severed his connections with the family when he was nineteen and went to live in the house of the gymnasium's headmaster as tutor to his children. Pavel Yegorovich viewed the move as an act of insubordination and personal insult and upbraided him for it in a letter: "I am sorry that you have begun at such an early age to forget your father and mother, who love you with all their hearts and have spared neither their money nor their health to give you a decent upbringing. Henceforth, I have but one thing to ask of you: that you change your character and be good to us and yourself."

Alexander turned a deaf ear to his father's admonitions. After scoring brilliantly on his final examinations, he resolved to go to Moscow and study mathematics at the university there. He did not consult his parents. Nikolai, who was only sixteen at the time and had not yet completed his studies, decided to go with him; he had an aptitude for painting and wished to enroll in the Moscow School of Fine Arts. The two rebels departed Taganrog in August 1875, leaving Pavel Yegorovich crushed by their audacity.

The temporary loss of his two elder and much-loved brothers made his father's tyrannical powers all the more onerous for Anton. In reaction against the stifling atmosphere at home, he took to editing a single-copy, handwritten journal that he called *The Stutterer*. It consisted of witty vignettes of Taganrog life and was an immediate success. His fellow students looked forward to each issue. As soon as it had gone the rounds at school, it would be sent on to Alexander and Nikolai in Moscow. Alexander proved a severe judge, writing back the following to his parents about the September issue: "Tell the author of *The Stutterer* that his rag is less interesting than it used to be. It lacks spice." These harsh words induced Anton to discontinue his journalistic activities.

Besides, he found it harder and harder to muster a playful mood. Pecuniary difficulties haunted the family on a daily basis. Pavel Yegorovich ran the shop with no regard for common sense, and it brought in almost nothing. He could not even pay the interest on the amount he had borrowed to build the house. "My profits plunge from day to day," he wrote to Alexander. "I am in the doldrums, losing heart. I don't know what your mother and I are going to do. Oh, money, money! How hard to earn it honestly!" Alexander, however, was annoyed by his lamentations and responded that he and his brother deserved even more pity: they went hungry and wore rags.

Pavel Yegorovich's fears were justified. He came so close to ruin that he could not afford to keep the children in school. "Antosha and Vanka have not been to school for a week," Yevgenia Yakovlevna wrote to her sons in Moscow. "The school demands its fees, and we haven't got money enough to pay them. Yesterday, October 9, Pavel Yegorovich went to see the headmaster. He agreed to take Vanka back without payment, but Antosha is still at home, and we owe forty-two rubles for him and Masha. How can I help being upset?"

But Alexander and Nikolai were not to be moved. Alexander was slaving away at his degree in mathematics, supporting himself and his brother with exhausting copy work; Nikolai, who spent all his time painting, kept assuming a miracle would come along and rescue them from their squalor, and never regretted having fled Taganrog. "When you have a heavy heart and a head full of bleak thoughts, you expect a word of good cheer, of sympathy," Alexander wrote to his father, "and what we get instead is an exhortation to go to church."

What with one misfortune and another, Pavel Yegorovich was eventually forced to declare himself bankrupt, and on April 3, 1876, afraid of being thrown into prison for his debts, he sneaked out of the house and out of Taganrog to a neighboring town where he would not be recognized, and caught the train to Moscow. After years of dreaming about social success, he had ended up in a third-class carriage, alone, humiliated, stigmatized, and exhausted, fleeing the town he had meant to dazzle. What would his abandoned Taganrog children and wife think of him? How would his elder Moscow sons receive him, this graying failure of a father who had once taken them to task so overweeningly?

Of the children remaining behind, only Anton was capable of standing up for his mother. Shattered by the calamity, she sent him to a moneylender in the hope of selling or mortgaging the house. The moneylender showed no interest. She turned to various members of the family for temporary relief. They all refused. Even kind Uncle Mitrofan pleaded lack of funds. And then Selivanov, their boarder, intervened, hand on heart. Wasn't he a friend of the family? As an official at the court where Pavel Yegorovich's case was to be tried, he could settle everything in a jiffy. And settle everything he did: after paying back the credit institution the five hundred rubles Pavel Yegorovich had borrowed, he took advantage of a loophole in the law and assumed ownership of the house. To make matters worse, the court ruled that the interest which had accrued on the loan was to be paid by the sale of the family's furniture at public auction.

Without a roof over her head, without a stick of furniture, Yevgenia Yakovlevna left for Moscow on July 23, 1876, to join her impoverished husband, bringing Mikhail and Maria with her. Ivan, who had been taken in by his maternal aunt, remained in Taganrog several months before going on to Moscow himself. After all, living in other people's homes was not such a tragedy for a Russian. In Russia hospitality was generous and took many forms. If you needed a place to sleep, you could be certain to find an obliging friend. And if your friend went off to stay with friends of his, you simply and very naturally tagged along. The result was that Russian homes were full of boarders with greater or lesser family ties, that is, full of indispensable parasites and amiable spongers who were permanently woven into the fabric of the clan.

Anton, however, was left alone with Selivanov in what had once been the family home. The new owner, brazenly preening himself on his victory, offered him a corner (not even a small room) to sleep in and a plate at his table. In exchange for room and board, Anton was to give lessons to Selivanov's nephew, the young Pyotr Kravtsov, who had come to live with his uncle and was studying for his military-school entrance examinations. "I need you and you need me," Selivanov told him with a cynical smile. Anton would have been only too glad to turn down the hospitality of the man who had ruined his parents, but he was so destitute he had to pocket his pride. Swallowing all Selivanov's affronts, he lived only for the day when he would be ready to leave school. If all went well, he could set off for Moscow, diploma in hand, in three years. Meanwhile, he was on his own.

III

The
Allure
of
Moscow

After the breakup of the family Anton felt even more alone and vulnerable. True, he had been freed of all the burdens weighing on him—no more keeping an eye on the shop or waiting on customers, no more singing in the church choir or deferring to his father's wild, tyrannical ideas—but the new freedom had its bitter side: at the age of sixteen he was left to provide for all his own needs. To earn a few rubles, he turned to tutoring. He would race across town from one pupil to the next, shivering his way through the winter in a flimsy, threadbare coat. Since he could not afford galoshes, he would hide his muddy, down-at-heel shoes well under the table during lessons, thankful for the cups of sweet tea the more thoughtful of the parents offered him. Later, as an adult, he said that the poverty he suffered in his adolescence was like a "never-ending toothache." Yet he had a friend more destitute than he, a lively and intelligent young Jew by the name of Isaak Srulev, who often went hungry. Anton suggested they should take turns at tutoring one of his pupils, who lived at a great distance, beyond the railway tracks. They were paid three rubles a month for the lessons and shared the meager salary like brothers.

Shortly before leaving Taganrog, Anton's mother instructed him to sell the few objects she had left—a chest of drawers, some broken chairs, some old clothes, a number of pots and pans—and to send her the proceeds along with whatever else he could scrape together. When he failed to do her bidding immediately, she complained to him in naïve, poorly spelled, and poorly punctuated letters. What annoyed the poor woman most of all was that her son responded in a jocular, playful tone. She was incapable of comprehending that his irony, coming as it did from the depths of despair, was a form of dignity. "We received two of your letters full of jokes and puns," she wrote on November 25, 1876, "at a time when we had only four kopecks for food and candles. We had been expecting you to send us money, it was very hard on us, though you probably don't believe it, and Masha has no cloak, I have no fur-lined boots, so we stay at home, I have no sewing machine to earn a bit of money, and you haven't even told us when you're going to send us our due, we're in dire straits, write quickly, for the love of God, send me the money quickly. [. . .] Don't let me die of grief." Alexander put it differently: "We're in a bad way. [. . .] We've eaten up all our money. It's nothing new. The same old story. There's nothing left to hock."

Anton, however, never complained. To an outsider his life might have seemed a bed of roses. From the summit of his adolescent experience he would give the family lessons in moral behavior. "There is one thing I don't like [in your letter]," he wrote to his younger brother, Mikhail. "Why do you refer to yourself as my 'worthless, insignificant little brother'? So you are aware of your worthlessness, are you? Not all Mishas have to be identical, you know. Do you know where you should be aware of your worthlessness? Before God, perhaps, or human intelligence, before beauty or nature. But not before people.

Among people you should be aware of your worth. You're no cheat, you're an honest man, aren't you? Well then, respect yourself for being a good honest fellow. Don't confuse 'humility' with 'an awareness of your own worthlessness.' "[1]

Brimming over with enthusiasm, generosity, and affection, Anton decided to seek the friendship of a Moscow cousin, Mikhail Chekhov, who was ten years older than he and whom he had never met. A warm and intimate correspondence resulted, and Anton soon thought of him as a brother, a "*Bruder* once removed." He requested a photograph and all kinds of information on Mikhail's way of life: "Write me whether you smoke or not. I very much need to know."[2] He also asked him to look after Yevgenia Yakovlevna: "Could you continue to comfort my mother? She is physically and morally crushed and has found in you much more than merely a nephew. My mother's nature is such that she has a very strong positive reaction to any kind of moral support coming from another person. [. . .] In this ever so malicious world we have nothing dearer than our mothers, and therefore you will much oblige your humble servant by comforting his semi-moribund one."[3] Then, two months later, again to Mikhail Chekhov: "My father and mother are the only people on the face of the earth for whom I will never spare anything. If anything ever comes of me, it will be their doing. They are such fine people. The boundless love they bear their children is beyond praise and enough to obliterate all the shortcomings their hard life may have engendered."[4]

Despite the many faults he found with his parents, Anton felt he had no right to judge them; he forgave them everything for the memory of a few hours of family bliss. His desire to rush off to Moscow was partly a desire to see his loved ones. "There's nothing new in Taganrog," he wrote to Mikhail Chekhov. "It's deadly dull."

Ignoring an empty stomach and the endless worries vying for his attention, Anton pushed forward doggedly with his studies. A lazy daydreamer in his early years, he now proved himself capable of serious work. His marks improved from month to month. The prospect of the diploma and the promise of medical school it held out for him became his obsessions. On Sundays and holidays he would take refuge in the newly opened public library, reading indiscriminately in Harriet Beecher Stowe, Schopenhauer, Humboldt, Victor Hugo, Cervantes, Goncharov, Turgenev, Belinsky. The very smell of print excited him. There were times when he forgot to eat. He began to encourage his brothers to set their thoughts on higher things. When his younger brother Mikhail wrote him that he had very much enjoyed *Uncle Tom's Cabin,* he responded in no uncertain terms, "So Madame Beecher Stowe brought tears to your eyes? I thumbed through her once and read her straight through for scholarly purposes six months ago, and when I'd finished I experienced that unpleasant sensation that mortals are wont to feel when they've eaten too many raisins or dried currants. [. . .] Have a look at [. . .] *Don Quixote* (complete, in all seven or eight parts). It's a fine work written by Cervantes, who is just about on the level of Shakespeare."[5] Schopenhauer produced so strong an impression that at times he felt on the brink of despair—and life in Taganrog provided little enough antidote. To counteract his morose thoughts, he took to reading such Moscow and Petersburg humor magazines as *Dragonfly, Alarm Clock,* and *Fragments.* Sitting next to Andrei Drossi in the reading room, he would laugh so loudly at the biting articles and jokes that the other readers complained.

Andrei Drossi had a young and flirtatious sister, Marina, to whom Anton was attracted. He would go walking with her in the local park and ply her with sweets, in exchange for which she granted him entrance to her room. It was only a passing fancy, however. Yet as he later told his friend Suvorin, he did have moments of unforgettable passion during adolescence. One day he was staring down a well when a fifteen-year-old peasant girl came up beside him to draw water. She was so beautiful that he put his arms around her, and instead of pushing him away she yielded to his caresses. How far did they go in their awkward embrace? Anton, as always discreet, refused to say more. He once told his younger brother Mikhail that he had had several delightful romances in Taganrog, and his elder brother

Alexander, when apprised of his amorous hopes and disappointments, wrote, "There is no need to put girls on a pedestal, but there is no need to run after them either." In fact, Anton's crushes were more a matter of admiration and affection than of sensuality. His feelings were skin-deep, thoughts of feelings. Perhaps he was still too young to feel a desire for carnal union.

In 1877 Alexander sent Anton a train ticket to Moscow for the Easter holidays. He set out on the long, twelve-hundred-kilometer journey wondering with a mixture of joy and fear what he would find at the other end. The letters he had received from his mother and brother had prepared him for a difficult situation; the reality far surpassed anything he could have imagined.

The Chekhovs were living in a furnished room with a mattress spread on the floor. Every night the entire family lay down side by side on the mattress. Nikolai and a painter friend stole wood from carts to light the stove. Yevgenia Yakovlevna, wearing a ragged men's overcoat, got up before dawn to do the sewing she had taken in. Pavel Yegorovich, who had worked for a while as a manual laborer, was once more unemployed, and although he claimed to spend his days looking for work he was actually out drinking with friends. Gentle Maria, fourteen at the time, cleaned house and did the cooking and washing. There was no money to send her to school. In addition to her household duties she knitted woolen shawls at fifteen or twenty kopecks apiece. The two elder brothers brought in some money by giving lessons, copying lecture notes, and contributing illustrations to minor magazines. But Alexander also had to maintain a woman whom he had seduced and who had just left her husband for him, and Nikolai was more likely to be found tippling at a local tavern than painting at the School of Fine Arts. The family was sinking deeper and deeper into fatalism and decay. Its Taganrog existence seemed the height of luxury and elegance by comparison.

What surprised Anton most upon his arrival was his father's attitude. Bankruptcy had done nothing to impair his self-assurance: in spite of the hard blow he had received he continued to play the divinely inspired autocrat. He would deliver sermons at the drop of a hat, purchasing the texts from the beadle of a neighboring church. If one of his sons dared to interrupt his pious rantings, he shouted, "Quiet, you pagans!" And at the close of each session he would hang the sermon on a nail and give it a number, date, and the inscription "Price: one silver kopeck. God Be Praised!" Under the icons Pavel Yegorovich had also posted a list of handwritten rules and regulations bearing the solemn heading "Schedule for the Family of Pavel Chekhov in Moscow." It told each of the children—with the exception of the oldest—when he was to rise, go to bed, eat, go to church (matins every day at seven and, on holidays, mass at half past six and at nine). The paternal edict concluded with the following admonition: "Those who fail to carry out these duties will be first strictly reprimanded and then thrashed. No shouting will be permitted during the thrashing." It was signed: "Pavel Chekhov, Father."

First to be thrashed was twelve-year-old Mikhail: he had woken up eight minutes late. Shortly thereafter, the sixteen-year-old Ivan shouted so loud during a beating that the neighbors complained. Pavel Yegorovich's only response was to mutter that people in the big city had forgotten the necessity for domestic discipline. He saw nothing wrong with what he had done.

When called upon to justify his lack of employment, he would gaze off into the distance and drop a few well-chosen words from the Gospel: "Consider the ravens: for they neither sow nor reap; which neither have storehouse nor barn; and God feedeth them." Then, coming back down to earth, he would proclaim in a loud voice, "Father and Mother must eat!"* He felt he had done enough for his children to expect them to care for him and respect him till the end of his days. It was a matter of family solidarity, he told them. And in preparation for the exquisite, euphoric state of idleness, he drank.

On the evenings when the miserable flat served as a gath-

*Chekhov often repeated his father's maxim, with irony, in his letters.

31

ering place for his friends, bottle followed upon bottle in quick succession: vodka and Crimean wine. No sooner did they take effect than the guests started philosophizing—as only Russians can do—on the meaning of life, the immortality of the soul, proofs of the existence of God. Next they would launch into a chorus of church hymns. By the time they went their separate ways, tongues were heavy, eyes moist.

Filled with dismay at how low his parents had sunk, Anton felt more keenly than ever that he was the only one who could save them. He would use work and love. His elder brothers— wild, unstable, indolent—could hardly be counted on for assistance in such an undertaking. Not that he condemned them. As was his wont, he accepted them for what they were, deploring only their bad luck.

In an effort to overcome his sorrow, he went sightseeing with his younger brother Mikhail. Unlike the rest of the family, which missed Taganrog, Anton was thrilled with the metropolis. He admired everything he saw: the busy, noisy streets where men in European dress, officers in high-ranking uniforms, and elegant ladies rubbed shoulders with peasant women in scarfs and muzhiks in badly patched sheepskin coats; the coachmen calling out to their prospective customers or haggling with them over the price of a ride; the sober buildings and the delicate colors in which they were painted; the windows of the shops selling luxury goods. . . . In Red Square he was taken first with the Kremlin walls and the extraordinary combination of bells, cupolas, and gilt crosses rising up behind them; then, at the far end of the square, with Saint Basil's, a cathedral in motley, absurd and joyous, an assortment of toys piled high at the edge of a table. He dreamed in front of the imposing façade of the Bolshoi Theater, lost his way in the narrow streets leading down to the Moscow River. He met his cousin, the Mikhail Chekhov with whom he had corresponded regularly, and noted with satisfaction how right he was to have placed his confidence in him. Mikhail Chekhov was friendly, levelheaded, and well-read. He had a budding career with one of the city's major merchants and was devoted to his uncle's family. Aware of

Anton's passion for the stage, he made certain they went to the theater.

Back in Taganrog, Anton realized that after breathing the air of the metropolis he could never be content with provincial pleasures. The moment he thought of Moscow, his head would spin. "I went to the Taganrog theater the other day," he wrote to Cousin Mikhail, "and compared it with your theater in Moscow. What a difference! And what a difference between Moscow and Taganrog! As soon as I finish school, I'll fly to Moscow on wings. I do so love Moscow!"[6] Only one thing kept him from returning for the summer holidays: "The Minister of Finances will explain," he wrote with sad irony. But fearing that his correspondent would tire of reading one plaint after another on the subject of his parents' destitution, he assured him that he envisaged making a fortune in trade: "I think we'll have to put up with things for some time yet. But when I'm rich—and that I shall be rich is as certain as two times two is four—and my head reaches the ceiling, I'll feed you nothing but white bread and honey and treat you to the best of wines for the brotherly love with which you have repaid our respect and affection. You're a fine chap in many respects. I say so with no intent to flatter, as a brother. May you live a hundred years and then some!"[7] The ambition to become a merchant rolling in riches lasted about as long as it took to write the letter.

Whenever he felt the need for a break from his studies, he would go to a seaside village known as "The Quarantine," several versts from Taganrog. The name came from an outbreak of the plague, which, many years before, had forced the local population into evacuation there. It had since turned into a dacha colony, and young people enjoyed gathering there once the weather grew warm. Anton would meet his classmates at a small columned pavilion on the water. Most of them were fascinated by politics, and some had even read the incendiary tracts of Alexander Herzen, the foremost Russian liberal of the nineteenth century. With the urgency that comes with adolescence they criticized the government of Tsar Alexander II and dreamed of overthrowing the existing order. The recent terrorist assassinations had led them to believe that a ground swell of support for their cause would soon spread throughout Russia. Liberal opposition was all the rage. Anton would listen, but refused to take part. Unlike his friends, he had qualms about discussing issues that fell beyond the scope of his knowledge.

More than the interminable discussions of "The Quarantine," he enjoyed the holidays he spent with the parents of his pupil Pyotr Kravtsov, who owned a farm in the Don steppes. There he found a way of life in tune with nature, the kind of life that had so appealed to him at his grandfather's house on the Countess Platova's estate. At first the immensity of the steppe gave him a feeling of total freedom, but in the end the sight of flat, empty space, with neither forest nor hill to catch the eye, proved oppressive. Fortunately, the farm provided any number of distractions. Coached by his pupil, Anton learned to ride, shoot, and hunt. The dogs, not fed at home, were as hungry as wolves on the trail. Even in the farmyard brutality was the rule. When a chicken was needed for the table, it was killed on the spot with a well-placed bullet—for practice, for the sport of it. Training wild horses was also a matter of sport. Anton kept his eyes open, taking everything in, storing images.

For he had begun dreaming of a literary career. Nothing serious yet, merely a means for bringing in a little money. As early as November 1877 he had sent his older brother Alexander some "bagatelles," which Alexander then offered to various Moscow humor magazines. In vain. The following year he sent his brother a farce (*Why the Hen Clucked*), a satirical comedy (*He's Met His Match*), and a drama with horse thieves, a train robbery, and abducted damsels.* Alexander, always a severe critic, pronounced the latter "an inexcusable, if innocent, fabrication." But when he read the comedy to a group of friends including a playwright by the name of Solovyov, the reaction was quite favorable. In the oracle's words: "The style is excellent, the play itself intelligent, but it shows little observation of

*The manuscripts of these juvenilia have been lost.

life and a total lack of experience. In time, *qui sait,* he may make a skillful writer."

Temporarily, however, the "skillful writer" was completely engrossed in examinations. "Do be quick about finishing up," his mother wrote to him on February 29, 1879, "and come and join us soon. I can hardly wait. And if you have any respect for me, apply to the School of Medicine. Medicine is the best career. Remember, Antosha, if you work hard, you will always be able to earn a living in Moscow. [. . .] I can't help thinking that things will be better for me once you are here."

Four months later Anton took his last set of examinations. Russian came first. Topic: "There is no worse calamity than anarchy." Anton was forced to expound his views on the issue for three full hours. The result was satisfactory enough: four out of five. And since his marks in the other subjects were comparable, he obtained the much-coveted diploma, imperial eagle and all: "Deportment: Excellent; Punctuality: Very Good; Effort: Very Good; Written Work: Very Good."

His joy knew no bounds. Despite all the memories binding him to Taganrog, he could not wait to break away from its small-minded, tedious atmosphere. He was enthralled by Moscow and its glitter. He would study, write, make new friends, go to the theater. The only shadow on the horizon was his father's authoritarianism. But he would take it in his stride. Living on his own in Taganrog, he had acquired a wisdom beyond his years. Serious and aloof, modest yet far from innocent, he had learned to value freedom of action and thought above everything.

"Moscow! Moscow! Moscow!"—a cry of hope. How often he had uttered it in his native Taganrog before putting it in the mouths of his heroines in *Three Sisters*! Even after the examinations were over, he had to stay on into the summer to negotiate a town-sponsored scholarship of twenty-five rubles a month. He also persuaded two classmates who intended to enroll in medical school with him to take board and lodgings with his mother, promising them "divine cooking."

Everything was settled at last, and on August 6, 1879, all three boarded the Moscow train together. The official permit required of all Russians wishing to change residence characterized Anton as follows: "Age: nineteen; Height: two arshins, nine vershoks [about five feet, eleven inches, or 181 centimeters]; Hair and Eyebrows: light brown; Eyes: brown; Nose, Mouth, Chin: average; Face: elongated; Complexion: fair; Distinguishing Features: scar on forehead under hair."

In Moscow Anton took a hackney and gave the driver his parents' new address. His friends would join him after he had had time to hug his family and settle in. No sooner had he dismissed the cab in front of the house than he found himself face to face with his younger brother, Mikhail, who was sunning himself on the threshold. Anton had changed so much the child failed to recognize him. In two years the pie-faced adolescent had turned into a tall, thin young man with finely chiseled features and pale cheeks. He wore a threadbare suit and a round hat too small for his head. His hair was long. The shadow of a mustache stretched across his upper lip. He looked like a Christ with deep, gentle eyes, but a Christ not beyond a wry smile. Whom did it mock, himself or others? "How are you, Mikhail Pavlovich?" he said in a velvet bass. Only then did Mikhail realize he was looking at his brother. "Anton!" he whooped with joy, and rushed into the house.

The entire family descended in tears on the traveler. After hugs and shouts and the requisite signs of the cross before the icons Yevgenia Yakovlevna sent Mikhail to dispatch a telegram to his father, who was employed as a ledger clerk on the other side of the river in the warehouse of a rich cloth merchant. Local telegrams cost only a kopeck a word. Soon the whole Chekhov clan was reunited, including Yevgenia Yakovlevna's sister, mild-mannered Aunt Fedosia, who, constantly afraid of being surprised by a fire, wore her galoshes to bed. Then the two new lodgers made their appearance: Zembulatov, small, pudgy, and more interested in finding a rich match than doing well in his studies, and Savelyev, quiet, serious, and good-looking. Every-

one laughed and talked at once under the arched ceiling, celebrating the reunion with wine and vodka. Next Pavel Yegorovich made a speech laced with biblical quotations. And by the
time they had moved to the table, they were all so merry that
Anton forgot the many troubles awaiting him in his new existence.

IV
A New Clan Leader

Once the initial joy had flown, Anton gave his new quarters a thorough inspection. He was filled with dismay. As a result of the move, their twelfth since Taganrog, the Chekhovs were now living in the basement of a dark Grashovka Street tenement belonging to the Church of Saint Nicholas and situated in the middle of the red-light district. Wet laundry, perpetually hanging on clotheslines, made for a humid, acrid atmosphere, and the tiny windows showed nothing but passing feet. The street was a spectacle of crumbling façades, sordid little shops, and women of the night loitering in doorways. Everything exuded indigence and corruption. But what an observation post for a man who would one day depict the sufferings of mankind!

Ten people lived crammed together in the poorly ventilated room. A young medical student, Korobov by name and "gentle as a virgin," had latched on to the other two lodgers. Pavel Yegorovich boarded at his employer's, but returned home every Sunday. His meager thirty-ruble-a-month salary did not go far in meeting the family's expenses. Alexander, like his father, lived away from home. Brilliant and erratic, ambitious and irresolute, cultured and idiosyncratic, he wrote for various magazines but received little recognition and drowned his disappointment in alcohol. Nikolai, who was weak, generous, and wonderfully talented in both art and music, squandered his gifts in a combination of lethargy and drunkenness that was driving him slowly but surely to the depths of self-debasement. He rarely got up before noon and routinely forgot to wash, but he did sell a canvas now and then and earned a bit of money giving drawing lessons. The future schoolmaster Ivan, unlike his elder brothers, was a taciturn fellow, assiduous but lacking in imagination, and of limited intelligence. "He is one of the most acceptable and solid members of the family," Anton would say of him ironically. Clearly he preferred the scintillating imp Mikhail. As for Maria, she enchanted him with her practical yet highly sensitive spirit. He made up his mind that no matter what the expense both she and Mikhail would pursue their education. Moreover, instead of following Alexander's lead and moving away from the family's squalor, he found it the most natural thing in the world to take his place at the center of their universe of desolation and idleness and try to save them. His twenty-five-ruble scholarship—plus the sixty rubles a month brought in by the lodgers, plus Pavel Yegorovich's contribution, plus a few extra kopecks garnered here and there—would suffice to secure the tribe's subsistence, he maintained, provided it was all well managed. Yevgenia Yakovlevna, trained as she was in the ways of domestic servitude, did not dare take over the family affairs, yet her husband's appearances had been growing more and more infrequent. Anton stepped into the breach with a calm authority. Pavel Yegorovich felt a certain bitterness. This enterprising son of his had robbed him of his prerogatives. Even when home for a visit, he was no longer consulted on decisions that needed to be taken. He pouted at first, but eventually resigned himself to the situation, especially since Anton continued to treat him with great deference.

Under the energetic but tender new leadership of the nineteen-year-old Anton the atmosphere in the tenement flat began to change. No more rules on the wall, no more corporal punishment, no more outbreaks of hysteria. Anton preferred persuasion to threat and his own good example to persuasion. He announced that he would do the housework on such and such a day and that his brothers and sister would take turns on the other days. He gently advised the young Mikhail to dress properly, give up prevaricating, and act fairly in every situation. Little by little his quiet superiority impressed even those who at the outset had been inclined to cast doubts upon it. Alexander dubbed him "Papa Antosha." As soon as a family problem cropped up, the family asked ritualistically, "What does Anton say?" "What does Anton think?" His *idée fixe* was to reinculcate in them a taste for moral purity and hard work. Even while readying himself for the long ordeal of medical school, he tried to come up with ways to pay the school fees for his younger brothers and sister, make the most of his elder brothers' talents, free his father from a humiliating job, and lighten his mother's exhausting domestic burden. No sacrifice was too great if it could help to pull them out of the quagmire they were in.

A month after his arrival Anton took the initiative and moved the family a thirteenth time. Gathering up the rags, the Chekhovs left the dark, dank cellar for a flat located in the same ill-famed street but more spacious—Anton, Nikolai, and Mikhail had a room to themselves—and three flights up. It was a first step towards the light. "Who knows what would have happened to the family if Anton hadn't arrived from Taganrog in time," Mikhail wrote many years later. "It was a touching alliance, with Anton at the center."

And indeed, within weeks the situation had improved: Mikhail and Maria, who had long since spent their time hanging around the house, went off, one to a gymnasium, the other to the Raevsky Institute for Girls; Ivan returned to his teacher training college; and Anton enrolled in the first year of medicine at the University of Moscow.

He had pictured the university as a sort of Greek temple basking in the sun of knowledge, and was amazed to find an unprepossessing jumble of dark, dilapidated buildings. The small, low-ceilinged room in which the registration procedure took place was jammed with long-haired, slovenly-looking students smoking cheap tobacco and arguing in loud voices. Anton, who could not bear disorder or discourtesy, had no desire to make friends with them. Attending the first classes only increased his disillusionment. "We're just like schoolboys," he wrote, "regurgitating what we memorize and forgetting it as quickly as possible."

Despite his disenchantment he studied hard. Lectures and laboratories kept him busy from early morning until three in the afternoon. Most of his professors were renowned scholars, and listening to them brought home to him the depths of his ignorance. He wondered if he would ever acquire the knowledge necessary to practice his chosen profession. Though originally attracted by the doctor's philanthropic role in society, he now also dreamed of the security and respect that came with the career. No more odd jobs to pay the rent or have a pair of shoes resoled. No more blushing at the family's decrepitude. A chance for a regular income!

Of course his fellow students looked forward to success as much as he did. But they protested against their temporarily inferior status by criticizing the Tsar's oppressive policies. In their associations and cafés the more fanatic among them talked and plotted and wrote seditious pamphlets. Here, as at school in Taganrog, Anton refused to make common cause with them. Polite yet distant, he had entered the university to learn to care for the sick, not overthrow the regime. He did not see how anyone could be a doctor and a revolutionary at the same time. Besides, he found the student unrest vain and theatrical. He harbored an instinctive aversion to crowds and crushes, to the sheeplike reactions that allowed the critical faculties of the one to be diluted by the hysteria of the many. Too individualistic to submit to the pressure of a clique, he sided with no one and refused to sign any manifesto.

On March 1, 1881, Tsar Alexander II was assassinated, ripped to pieces by a terrorist bomb. Chekhov was stupefied: not only did he abhor violence; he could not comprehend why the group of fanatics had felt the need to do away with a liberal sovereign, who had emancipated the serfs, instituted trial by jury, abolished corporal punishment, and promised Russia her first constitution. And even if the revolutionaries were primarily interested in destroying the symbol rather than the man, their deed turned against them. The Tsar's successor, his son Alexander III, immediately inaugurated a policy of all-out repression, executing the regicides, brushing aside the draft constitution, increasing the number of searches and arrests, stepping up censorship, and tightening police surveillance on students. After a short period of perturbation Anton's comrades returned to their indignant protests against the government. He tried hard to understand them, but kept a cool head and a still tongue. A close friend, Grigory Rossolimo, had this to say in his *Reminiscences*: "While Chekhov did sometimes attend the rallies held at the university, he attended them as a spectator. During our second year of medical school, in 1880–81, at the time of the disturbances preceding and following the event of March 1 [the assassination of Alexander II], he went along with the majority of students who, though far from indifferent, could not be considered active revolutionaries."

Anton was not insensitive to the misery of the poor; his compassion could hardly have been greater. But he felt that Russians should try to pull themselves up by their own bootstraps instead of yielding to their inborn tendency to self-pity; he believed in the possibility of social progress based on the will and education of the individual. His medical studies only reinforced his faith in the edifying power of knowledge.

For pecuniary reasons he continued to send stories to various humor magazines. The editors required them to be short and snappy—anecdotes, sketches, quickly spun yarns peopled with such stock characters of farce as cuckolds, scatterbrains, lying officials, crooked tradesmen, officers on a spree, butterfingered dentists, faded old maids. . . . Under Alexander's guidance he stuck to the rules. After several rejections he found the following in the *Dragonfly* "Letter Box" column among the notes directed at its aspiring authors: "Not bad at all. We shall publish what you have sent. Our blessings on your future work." Shortly thereafter he received a letter from the magazine informing him he would be paid five kopecks a line,* but he had to wait two months before he saw the story, "Letter to a Learned Neighbor," in print. It was signed ". . . V." Nothing more. Anton had no literary ambitions. All he cared about was making some easy money with his pen. The family celebrated his success with an enormous cake, which he bought with his first earnings. Little did he dream then, at twenty, that his true career had just begun.

Encouraged by a fortunate debut, he started to devote most of his free time to writing. His only requirement was to please the editor in chief, and since the stories were short and the remuneration low he had to publish a good many to keep the family solvent at the end of the month. He sent *Dragonfly* story after story, anxiously awaiting the response. In 1880 he placed nine of them, in 1881, thirteen; by 1883 he had reached a total of 129 stories and articles. He wrote with intoxicating ease. He had a good laugh giving a good laugh. But it never occurred to him to sign his own name to the "twaddle." Indeed, he used any number of pen names: "The Man with No Spleen," "My Brother's Brother," "Ulysses," "Antosha," and, most often, the nickname given to him as a child by Father Pokrovsky, his religion teacher: "Antosha Chekhonte." Some of his manuscripts were rejected with uncomplimentary remarks in the "Letter Box": "A few witty words cannot obliterate such woefully

---

*At the end of the nineteenth century a kopeck was worth approximately one-half of an American penny or one-quarter of a British penny.

insipid verbiage" or "We cannot publish 'The Portrait.' It is not for us. You obviously wrote it for another magazine" or "Very long and colorless, like the white paper streamer a Chinaman pulls out of his mouth." His last submission to *Dragonfly* for 1880 elicited the following comment: "You have ceased to flower; you are withering. A pity. But no one can write without maintaining a critical attitude to his work." Anton was so upset he resolved never again to submit a story to the *Dragonfly*'s finicky editors. At least one of the staff members, a man by the name of Soimonov, regretted his colleagues' move. "The *Dragonfly*'s stupid editorial board," he said, "has rejected a story by a certain Antosha Chekhonte when nothing of comparable worth has yet appeared in these columns."*

As difficult as it was to have a story published in a humor magazine, it was nothing compared with exacting payment. More often than not Mikhail, whose task it was to collect the money due his brother, would be told that the coffers were momentarily empty, unless, that is, he was offered theater tickets instead or informed that the managing editor had just slipped out the back door.

In July 1880, his first-year examinations out of the way (he did well in all subjects but anatomy), Anton left Moscow to spend the summer with his friend and lodger Zembulatov at the country house of Zembulatov's parents. In affirmation of his medical calling he moved a skull into his room and assigned his host's young brother to keep him in frogs and rats, which the two students, surrounded by fearful peasants, dissected in the garden.

Back in Moscow Anton took a sudden renewed interest in the theater, and during a winter-long burst of enthusiasm wrote a long, confused, four-act play that he neglected to title. After Mikhail had made a clean copy, he delivered it, in person, to a famous actress of the Maly Theater, Maria Yermolova. As was to be expected, it went no further. The rejection hit him hard and he destroyed the manuscript, but a first sketch in his own

*The stories that were rejected have not come down to us.

hand was discovered in 1920 in his archives and published under the title *Platonov*.*

For all its melodrama, chaos, and verbosity this immature work contains all the great Chekhovian themes in embryo. The tone is present from the very first lines: "Nothing . . . We're quite bored . . . We're bored, dear Nikolai . . . It's no good . . . Depression . . . Bleak thoughts . . . What to do with myself . . ." A country setting, sultry provincial boredom; idle, weak-willed characters yawning as they dream of a better life and doing nothing to shake off their drowsiness; the new generation, realistic, grasping, willing to go to any lengths to take over; a family estate about to be sold to pay off debts; vodka flowing like water, drunkenness and stupor, empty but stentorian speeches, and the sighs of beautiful, underloved ladies. Platonov, the hero, casts a spell over his female entourage, a spell he cannot control. Sapped by lethargy and depression, he seeks distraction in erotic entanglements. Intruding in the life of every woman he meets becomes an obsession with him. All he really craves is a chance to destroy the women physically and morally and then lose himself in them. He is a combination Don Juan and sponger or, as one of his victims puts it, an "all-round swine." Yet in a moment of repentance he shows signs of despair. "Crushing, smothering weak, innocent women . . . I'd have no regrets if I'd done away with them differently, in the grip of wild emotion, like a Spaniard, but I did it all so . . . stupidly, like a Russian . . . [. . .] I was hungry, cold, worn out, done for; I'd used up every trick in the book. I came to this house . . . They gave me shelter, clothes, affection . . . And this is how I've repaid them!" The unwilling or unwitting seducer reappears in other Chekhov plays. So do his accomplices. The gallery is complete, but the portraits are still caricatures, all in black. With time Chekhov lightened the dialogue, toned down the effects, refined the intentions, brightened

---

*Performed in its entirety it would last more than seven hours. Numerous abridged versions have been staged throughout Europe and the United States. The first Soviet production did not take place until 1959.

the palette, but the gift of bringing a situation to life is there, the art of drawing original characters, the dramatic intuition.

Rejection by the Maly Theater led Chekhov to set aside his dramatic pursuits and return to the humor magazines. Having fallen out with *Dragonfly,* he entered into an agreement with two of its competitors, *Alarm Clock* and *The Spectator.* The pay was six kopecks a line. Already a protean writer, he moved from the comic story to the serial and from the serial to the detective story. In 1882, on a bet with the editor in chief of *Alarm Clock,* he published a serialized novel in eight parts called *A Useless Victory,* which was in fact a pastiche of the famous Hungarian writer Mór Jókai. The imitation was so skillful that the *Alarm Clock*'s naïve readers wrote enthusiastic letters to the editor, one of which read as follows: "How interesting! Can you publish something else by the same author? And why not give his real name? Could it be Mór Jókai?"

Along with this fiction—more or less long, more or less well received—Chekhov would dash off accounts of the latest in local events. A cross between a cub reporter and a gossip columnist, he gathered as much material in courtrooms as at literary cafés or the stage door. The wide range of circles he traveled in enlarged his vision of the world. At twenty-two, he was intimately acquainted with all levels of Russian society, and his head swarmed with unusual specimens picked up in odd places and just waiting to come to life under his pen.

But he was also a demanding critic. When writing about the theater—his early failure as a playwright had not dimmed his love for it—he preached simplicity and sincerity in both acting and stage design. Annoyed by the tumultuous enthusiasm that greeted Sarah Bernhardt in Moscow at the end of 1881, he went to see her in *Camille* and *Adrienne Lecouvreur* at the Bolshoi Theater. He recorded his impressions in two *Spectator* articles. "More than anything in the world she loves publicity," he wrote curtly. And in the following issue: "Her sighs, her tears, her death agonies—everything she does onstage is nothing more than a perfectly and intelligently learned lesson. [. . .] She makes her heroines into women as exceptional as herself. [. . .]

It is not talent we see glowing in her stage presence; it is stupendously hard work. [. . .] Here and there we were touched almost to tears by her acting, and if the tears did not flow, it was only because charm was obliterated by artifice."

Nor was he any easier on Russian actors. After watching the famous Ivanov-Kozelsky interpret the role of Hamlet, he wrote in the journal *Moscow*: "It is not enough to transmit one's sentiments adequately on stage; it is not enough to be an artist; an actor must have a broad intellectual background. To play Hamlet, one must take the trouble to cultivate one's mind."

Chekhov's brothers, Alexander and Nikolai, also worked for humor magazines, the former as a subeditor, the latter as an illustrator. In their wake Chekhov entered a boisterous, sarcastic, hard-drinking, no-holds-barred bohemian world. Though remaining somewhat aloof, he enjoyed the company of the cantankerous and intemperate writers he found there. One of his favorites was the poet Liodor Palmin, a tattered but brilliant crank constantly surrounded by the pack of mangy dogs he cared for lovingly. Palmin lived in a hovel with his aged housekeeper, and when evening came on the two of them would drink themselves under the table. After downing his first few glasses of vodka, he would go into a trance and utter noble new ideas with brio. Wreck that he was, he spoke several languages, translated foreign classics into Russian, and professed liberal views that made him suspect to the authorities. "Chatting with him is never tiring. True, when you chat with him you have to drink a lot, but you can be certain that during the entire three or four hours of talk you won't hear a single lie or commonplace, and that's worth anyone's sobriety."[1]

Another remarkable rowdy among the bohemian fauna was Vladimir Gilyarovsky, a journalist with *Russian News* and a stocky, ruddy-faced, booming-voiced man who took great pride in his iron-man musculature, his faultless memory, and his diabolic dexterity in performing card tricks. At the drop of a hat he would proffer his biceps or smash a chair. He worked at a thousand and one occupations: he had been a Volga barge hauler, a stevedore, a factory worker, a circus acrobat, a horse trainer. . . . His head was full of salacious stories, which he accompanied with the guffaws of an ogre. He knew everyone in Moscow—he was as at ease in the salons of the English Club as in Khitrov Market flophouses—and kept his magazine supplied with local gossip and all sorts of sketches, news reports, and poems. To his friends he was "the king of journalists." He took a special liking to Chekhov and initiated him into Moscow's underground life, suggesting more than one idea for the articles Chekhov wrote for his daily bread.

The group also included Fyodor Popudoglo, a master stylist who was, however, far gone on alcohol and destined to an early grave, and Pyotr Sergeenko, a fellow graduate of the Taganrog Gymnasium who lived modestly by his pen and swore by the theories of Tolstoy. Nikolai, for his part, would bring home ragged artists who drank hard and argued feverishly over tradition and innovation in art. Towards the end of 1880 he introduced Anton to a shy nineteen-year-old Jew, Isaak Levitan, the future landscape painter. Such creative spirits attracted the friends of Mikhail and Maria, who also would join in the discussion and add to the general pandemonium.

Meanwhile, the family had moved again, this time to the Sretenka district, where they now had even more spacious rooms. Chekhov, a great lover of commotion and new faces, opened his door to all comers. Either the guests gathered round him to play a parlor game, or Nikolai sat down at the piano, someone picked up a balalaika, and the rest sang folk songs until throats went dry and needed some alcoholic lubrication.

There were times, however, when Chekhov complained that the constant jollity and commotion robbed him of a quiet corner in which to work. "I'm writing under abominable conditions. Before me sits my nonliterary work pummeling mercilessly away at my conscience, the fledgling of an itinerant kinsman is screaming in the room next door, and in another room my father is reading 'The Sealed Angel'* aloud to my

*A story by Nikolai Leskov depicting Russian sectarians, the so-called Old Believers.

mother . . . Someone has wound up the music box, and I can hear *La Belle Hélène* . . . It makes me want to slip off to the country, but it's one in the morning. It would be hard to think up a more abominable setting for a writer. My bed is occupied by the visiting kinsman, who keeps coming up to me and starts discussing medicine. 'My daughter must have colic. That's what's making her scream.' [. . .] I promise myself never to have children."[2]

Often the evenings shaded into drinking bouts. Once Alexander staggered home dead drunk, making crude remarks to his mother and sister and threatening to smash Anton's face in. Chekhov, highly indignant, wrote him forthwith to set the record straight: "Even if I love you a hundred thousand times over, I will not, on principle or on any grounds you may choose, tolerate insults from you. Should you wish to resort to your usual ruse, that is, to blame it all on 'not being responsible for your actions,' just remember I am perfectly aware that 'being drunk' does not give you the right to [. . .] on the head of another. As for the word 'brother' you used in order to scare me as I left the field of battle, I am ready to drop it from my vocabulary whenever necessary, not because I have no heart but because we must be ready for everything in this world. I fear nothing and advise my brothers to follow my lead."[3]

Doubtless Alexander apologized to Anton as soon as he was sober again, for the incident was soon forgotten. Chekhov was too closely attached to his family to allow something of the sort to rankle. Besides, his brother Nikolai caused him every bit as much trouble. A talented artist with a special gift for humor, he often illustrated Anton's stories and would have made a brilliant career in journalism if he could have been relied upon to get a drawing in on time. He had no concept of punctuality, working in fits and starts, letting the most urgent assignments slip his mind, and dropping out of sight for several days at a time to carouse with Moscow lowlife. He would return home at night, still vomiting, collapse fully dressed on the couch, pull a blanket over his head (so that all anyone could see of him was a pair of filthy, hole-ridden socks), and sleep off his vodka for a full twenty-four hours. Chekhov, who was extremely fond of him, never upbraided him for his antics, but he was appalled to see such talent ruined by such lethargy. "You must work constantly," he wrote to him, "day and night. You must never stop reading, studying in depth, exercising your will. Every hour is precious. [. . .] Smash your vodka carafe!"[4]

The brothers' slow decline brought out in him the need to restore their sense of human dignity. As always, however, he refused to cloak himself in conventional morality. Rather than preach, he wished to set an example, demonstrate by his own behavior that nothing was ever lost. Since he had no use for metaphysical or religious speculation, he never prayed to God for help; his battles were very much of this earth. He swore to improve his inner self and educate his family, and did so by love, patience, and will alone. Several years later he wrote to his friend Suvorin: "What aristocratic writers take from nature gratis, the less privileged must pay for with their youth. Try and write a story about a young man—the son of a serf, a former shopboy, choirboy, schoolboy, and university student, raised on respect for rank, kissing priests' hands, worshiping the ideas of others, and giving thanks for every piece of bread, receiving frequent whippings, making the rounds as a tutor without galoshes, brawling, torturing animals, enjoying dinners at the houses of rich relatives, needlessly hypocritical before God and man merely to acknowledge his own insignificance—write about how this young man squeezes the slave out of himself drop by drop and how one fine morning he awakes to find that the blood coursing through his veins is no longer the blood of a slave but that of a real human being."[5]

Chekhov did everything he could to persuade his brothers they had "real human blood." Contrary to appearances, the agnostic had ardent faith in the future, the skeptic believed in the intrinsic, almost divine value of the individual, no matter how lowly.

V

Journalism and Medicine

The sullen but sensible Ivan eventually landed a teaching position at the parish school of Voskresensk, a village not far from Moscow. The perquisites included a fair-sized house and a great deal of leisure time. Anton was overjoyed. In 1882, his third-year examinations out of the way, he decided to spend the summer in the country. The rest of the family followed suit.

At Voskresensk Chekhov divided his time between fishing and mushrooming on the one hand and the much more profitable hunt for usable characters and anecdotes on the other. Always on the alert, he would haunt the post office, the tavern under the sign of a gilt samovar, the dusty premises of the justice of the peace, the peasants' smoky *izbas,* the gentry's columned mansions, and the officers' mess of an artillery regiment billeted in the village. No matter what their station, the people he visited were flattered by the interest shown them by the tall young

Muscovite with the broad-brimmed black hat and good manners. They had not the slightest suspicion he was pumping them for all they were worth. Before coming to Voskresensk he had been willing to pay family and friends ten kopecks for an anecdote and twenty for a full-blown plot, and his brother Mikhail had taken advantage of the offer more than once. But in Voskresensk there were all kinds of ideas, faces, and situations for the taking. The windfall of village impressions served him in good stead back in Moscow, where he put them to use in story after story.

Even as he returned to his studies, he was obsessed by the need to maintain the family financially; even as he wrote, he thought more of pecuniary problems than art. Neither his professors nor his fellow students had an inkling of his literary activities. None of the uninitiated ever thought to connect the Chekhonte who published those funny stories in the weeklies with Chekhov, the quiet, gentle medical student. But happy as he was to maintain anonymity, he was furious at being so poorly recompensed for his efforts. His great dream was to part company with the short-lived, parsimonious Moscow magazines and gain entrée into the national Petersburg-based press. Then, he thought, he would be paid on time and in cash.

One brisk October day in 1882 he was out for a stroll with his brother Nikolai when a carriage pulled up beside them. Next to Chekhov's eccentric poet friend Palmin sat a potbellied gentleman with a bushy black beard. He was Nikolai Leikin, Petersburg writer and editor in chief of the famous humor weekly *Fragments*. Several moments earlier Leikin happened to have mentioned that he was on the lookout for gifted but undemanding staff writers, and Palmin had immediately pointed at the two passersby and exclaimed, "There are two brothers with talent! One writes, the other paints!" Palmin introduced him to Anton and Nikolai. Chekhov, who remembered having guffawed at the popular writer's stories in the Taganrog Public Library, was flattered by his attention, and telling him so only improved matters. As there was a nip in the air, they continued the conversation in the warmth and commotion of a nearby café. Chekhov was fascinated by the way Leikin's beard and ears moved as he ate his sausage and drank his beer: the whole of his heavyset face took part in the process. At last he lit a cigar and, engulfing himself in smoke, laid out his requirements. What he needed was short, colorful, light, funny stories. The first rule was to keep the censor in mind—in other words, avoid any topic that might make a disenchanted reader linger on the current hard times. Chekhov would earn eight kopecks a line, which came to four or five rubles a story. The pay scale was so superior to what any of the Moscow rags offered that Chekhov had trouble hiding his joy, especially since Leikin had promised to consider publishing Nikolai's drawings as well. Chekhov, for his part, promised to send *Fragments* his very best work.

He kept his word, working at fever pitch. The response of the editorial board to his first submission read as follows: "It is unfortunately too long, though the form is excellent. We have long been looking forward to working with you. Write more concisely and you will be paid more generously." Undaunted, he dispatched another parcel of manuscripts to the capital, and shortly thereafter, on November 20, 1882, his work, still signed Chekhonte, made its first appearance in the columns of *Fragments*.

From then on, story followed story in an ever-increasing rhythm. On Leikin's initiative Chekhov even agreed to write a regular column, "Notes of Moscow Life," consisting of candid vignettes of life in the city's streets, hospitals, courts, cafés, and theaters, combined with urbane chitchat and gossip of the literary, musical, and artistic worlds. As unfulfilling and exasperating as he found the work, he could not afford to be particular: he was compelled by the family's needs to push on with it. "Don't envy me," he wrote to Alexander. "Writing brings me nothing but twitches. The hundred rubles a month I get for it go right down the gullet. I can't even trade my drab, unseemly frock coat for something less ancient. I pay out to all and sundry and am left with *nihil*. The family alone squanders more than fifty. [. . .] If I lived by myself, I'd be a rich man."[1]

Money matters come up again and again in his letters of the period. Although he could not imagine a solitary existence, the family was a millstone around his neck. Several years later he explained the significance he accorded to money in the following terms: "I was terribly corrupted by being born and having grown up, gone to school, and started writing in an atmosphere in which money played a hideously large role."[2]

Under the stress of his forced literary labor he ran the risk of sinking into facile blather, of writing about everything and nothing. He was aware of the danger and would periodically rebel against Leikin's commercialism. What irritated him most was the ironclad rule of containing a story within a hundred lines. The *Fragments* staff seemed to consider no subject matter worthy of more. "I, too, am an ardent defender of miniature pieces," he wrote to his editor, "and if I published a humor magazine, I'd cut anything that got too long. [. . .] But at the same time I must confess that 'from-here-to-here' limits cause me no end of grief. [. . .] I have a subject. I sit down to write. The idea of 'one hundred' and 'no more' won't let go of me from line one. I condense insofar as I can, I filter, I cut—sometimes (or so my authorial sensibility tells me) to the detriment of both subject and (more important) form. Once I've finished condensing and filtering, I start counting . . . When I get as high as a hundred, a hundred and twenty, a hundred and forty (I've never written more for *Fragments*), I take fright and . . . decide against sending it. [. . .] Which brings me to a plea: extend my rights to a hundred and twenty lines!"[3]

In the long run, however, Chekhov was more disturbed by the obligation to make his readers laugh. Humble but insistent, he begged Leikin for authorization to slip in a melancholy note here and there: "A piece that is short and light can be serious too [. . .] and still be easy to read. [. . .] (And to tell the truth, chasing humor is hard work. There are times when you set out after something humorous and end up with something so stupid it turns your stomach. You can't help turning serious . . .)"[4]

It took a lot of persuading, but at last Leikin accepted a

few stories in a more minor key. And although he feared the reactions of his humor-hungry readers, he received no protests. Chekhonte charmed his public in the new register as well as in the old. But even his very limited success incited the animosity of certain colleagues. "Newspapermen," he wrote to his brother Alexander, "suffer from an illness called jealousy. Instead of rejoicing in your good fortune, they pour out their venom!"[5] It was one of the rare complaints he made in a letter.

Anton's reserve, his moral dignity, was totally lacking in Alexander, who, after landing a post in the Taganrog Customs Department, left Moscow with a married mistress whose intransigent husband would not hear of divorce. Scarcely had he settled in Taganrog with her and her son when he began plaguing Chekhov with desperate letters. Chekhov tried to talk long-distance sense into the eternal malcontent. "You snivel from one end of the letter to the other," he wrote at one point, and reproached him for laying into their brother Nikolai, who, fast sinking into dipsomania, deserved their pity and support. "A fine, powerful, Russian talent is going to waste, and for nothing . . . In another year or two his song will be sung." Nor would he countenance any abuse of their father for deploring his eldest son's liaison with a married woman. "What do you expect of Father, anyway? A sworn enemy of tobacco and illegal cohabitation. You want to change him? You may succeed with Mother and Aunt Fedosia, but not with Father. He's a rock, as firm as the Old Believers. [. . .] Everyone has a right to live with whomever he pleases and however he pleases. [. . .] How do you perceive your cohabitation? It's your nest, your warmth, your grief and joy, your poetry, and you treat your poetry like a stolen watermelon. You're suspicious of everybody ("I wonder what he thinks"); you keep bringing it up, moaning and groaning . . . If I were your family, I'd be hurt at the very least. Does it matter to you what I think or Nikolai or Father? What do you care? [. . .] Get on with your own life."[6]

His personal view of "getting on with life" at the time meant combining journalism, a temporary source of income, with medicine, his career. As he expressed it to Alexander: "I'm becoming popular and have read reviews of myself. My medicine has begun to *crescendo*. I can hardly believe how much I've got under my belt . . . You can't name a single illness I won't treat. We have exams soon. If I make it into the fifth year, it means *finita la commedia*. . . ."[7] Several months later, in another letter to Alexander, he wrote, "I'm a journalist because I write a lot, but it's only temporary . . . I won't die one. If I go on writing, it will be from afar, hidden in a crack somewhere." And convinced once and for all that his future lay with the stethoscope rather than the pen, he added, "I'll plunge into medicine, it's my salvation, though I still can't get over the fact that I'm a medical student."[8]

In fact he was deeply involved in his medical studies, visiting hospitals, attending operations, and giving free advice to penniless friends. He took devoted care of Popudoglo, who showed his gratitude by leaving him a sizable collection of books. "He died of encephalitis even though he had me for a doctor. True, he had twenty doctors before me and I was the only one who guessed the real malady while he was alive. May he rest in peace eternal. He died of alcohol."[9]

So carried away was he by his love of medicine that he thought of compiling a study of the relations between the sexes in the various animal families, *A History of Sexual Authority*. He soon abandoned the project, however; he was too anxious about the forthcoming examinations. "I've got to learn everything all over again," he wrote to Alexander in the same letter. "Besides the exams (which are still quite a way off) I have some dissecting, a few clinical exercises with the inevitable *historiae morbi*, and my hospital rounds . . . All that work makes me weak. My memory is no good at cramming anymore: I'm too old, too lazy, and then all the literature. [. . .] I'm afraid of flunking one of the exams."[10]

As a respite from his medical and literary efforts Chekhov was glad to return to Voskresensk. In nearby Chikino he made friends with the head of the country hospital, Dr. Arkhangelsky, whom he helped in his rounds. Sometimes he would stay the night, enjoying long talks with the doctor and the students in training there. They discussed politics and literature, quoting Turgenev and Saltykov-Shchedrin and declaiming the verse of Nekrasov; they sang old favorites. Time passed so swiftly that Chekhov forgot about his *Fragments* deadlines. "Excuse my sloth," he wrote to Leikin. "It's summer. There's nothing I can do about it . . . Only poets can combine scribbling with moonlit nights and love . . . They declare their love as they write their poems . . . Those of us who work in prose are not so lucky."[11]

The discreet hint at an affair of the heart did not go any further. As usual Chekhov kept his emotional life to himself, and if he did bring it up he invariably made a joke of it. Sources close to him maintained that he had been on intimate terms with a ballerina and with a French actress from Lentovsky's theater, and he himself admitted he enjoyed a certain Moscow café with a reputation for attracting officers on the loose and girls of loose morals, who made him laugh and drink. "By the will of the fates I stayed up all night playing cards with the ladies. I played straight through to Mass and was so bored I kept drinking vodka, which I do drink from time to time, though only when bored. My head's full of fog."[12]

If he conformed at all to the rules of gallantry, he did so without passion. He tended to treat women as objects of curiosity or persiflage. Here he is at his most whimsical in a letter to the wife of his friend Savelyev: "I shall be visiting Taganrog at the end of June in the hope of finding the fiancée you promised me. My conditions are as follows: beauty, grace, and, alas! a small matter of twenty thousand. Today's youth is terribly mercenary."[13]

Even though he vowed he was only an occasional writer, condemned to mediocrity, Chekhov dreamed of having a collection of his best stories published. In the end he published one himself, at his own expense. *Tales of Melpomene,* a small, ninety-six-page volume of six stories, sold for sixty kopecks and bore the name of Chekhonte. Alexander, who had left his post at the Taganrog Customs Department and returned to Moscow, took charge of persuading bookshops to stock it. But because of the title—the Russian word for 'tales,' *skazki,* refers normally to *fairy* tales—booksellers placed it in the children's book section, where potential readers never saw it. Unsold copies were sent back to the author en masse. Alexander responded with irony: "Russia shall hear of you yet, Antosha. Die young so you may witness her wails from the north, from the west, from beyond the seas. Your glory shall grow, but in the meantime people are very reluctant to buy your book."

The literary and commercial failure of the book was largely offset for Chekhov by the successful outcome of the last round of medical examinations in June 1884. Gloating over his new social status, he wrote to Leikin, "I currently reside in the New Jerusalem . . . I am perfectly poised because I can feel the documents entitling me to practice medicine in my pocket." And he signed the letter "Doctor and District Practitioner A. Chekhov."

Chekhov returned to the Chikino hospital that summer as an attending physician. His first fees had the following unlikely sources: five rubles for failing to cure a young lady of her toothache, a ruble for curing a monk of dysentery, and three rubles for soothing the capricious stomach of a Moscow actress on holiday in the region. "I was so elated by my success in my new career that I gathered up all the rubles and sent them off to Bannikov's Tavern, whence I receive vodka, beer, and like medicines for my table."[14]

Hearing that a murder had taken place near Voskresensk, he obtained permission to be present at the autopsy. The operation took place out of doors in the shade of a young oak alongside a country road. "The corpse, in a red shirt and new trousers, was covered by a sheet . . . On the sheet lay a towel with a small icon. We asked the *desyatsky** for water . . . There was water in a nearby pond, but no one would give us a pail: they were afraid we'd defile it."[15] This scene inspired the story "The Corpse," in which the main characters are neither victim

*A peasant elected by his peers to serve as a policeman.

nor murderer but the two peasants charged with watching over the body in the woods at night.

When the director of the country hospital at Zvenigorod took two weeks' leave, Chekhov offered to step in for him. It was a spontaneous move and a bold one for a young doctor so poor in experience. As it happened, his first operation, a routine matter on a child, nearly ended in disaster. The small patient wriggled and wailed so much that Chekhov lost his head and had to call in a Chikino colleague, who immediately set things right for him. Otherwise, his hospital duties were painfully monotonous. With thirty to forty patients to examine a day he saw case after case of suppurating wounds, diarrhea, chest colds, and tapeworms. He was struck by the general physical decrepitude of the peasants, their filth, ignorance, and drunkenness. Where was Tolstoy's openhearted, earth- and God-inspired muzhik? Between patients Chekhov would stare out of his office window at the rain pouring down on the chief of police's house across the road. He found relief from provincial misery and narrow-mindedness in dreams of a project of major proportions, a *History of Medicine in Russia*. He conceived of it as an academic thesis that would secure his fame in scholarly circles, but after reading and annotating a good hundred works on the subject he lost interest. Such an enterprise could scarcely have engaged an imagination and sensitivity like his for long.

Back in Voskresensk his spirits failed to improve. The weather was "foul" and, as he liked to put it, "diphtherial." So on September 3 he returned to the city. He found himself growing more and more attached to Moscow and declared he would "belong to it forever." Soon a copper plaque engraved with the words "Anton Chekhov, Medical Doctor" appeared on his door. A perusal of the accounts for the next few months led him to the conclusion that medicine was a surer source of income than writing.

Then, on December 7, 1884, in the midst of the exhausting battle to deliver copy and treat impecunious patients, came a warning he pretended to take lightly: a dry cough, a bitter taste in the mouth, spasms of blood-spitting. "It's not tuberculosis," he hastened to tell his friend Sergeenko. And on December 10 he opened a letter to Leikin: "For three days now I've had blood coming out of my throat. It keeps me from writing and will keep me from going to Petersburg . . . I must say I never expected it! For three days I've had no clear spittle, and when the medicines my colleagues cram me with will take effect I can't say. My general state is satisfactory . . . The whole thing is probably due to a ruptured blood vessel . . ." At the end of the letter he added some thoughts concerning his practice: "Wouldn't you know it—I've got patients now . . . I ought to go and see them, but I can't . . . I don't know what to do with them . . . It would be a shame to hand them over to another doctor. Money is money, after all!"

As soon as he recovered, he went back to his practice. Though rejecting the possibility of tuberculosis, he toyed with the idea of traveling to a warm climate—to the Crimea, the Caucasus, or abroad—for treatment. Then he rejected that very wise idea as well. "My medical career is chugging along nicely," he wrote to his Uncle Mitrofan. "I've got a busy practice. Every day I spend more than a ruble on cab fare. I have a lot of friends and therefore quite a few patients. Half of them I treat free of charge; the other half pays me three or five rubles. (In Moscow doctors are paid no less than three rubles a visit. Everything has a higher price here than in Taganrog.) Of course, I haven't amassed any capital yet, nor shall I in the near future, but I live a decent life and want for nothing. If my health holds out, the family is *provided for*."[16]

Chekhov's financial situation improved from day to day. He was soon able to buy some furniture and a piano, hire two women to help with the housekeeping, and arrange some "intimate evenings of music." The middle-class comfort and the quiet respectability of it all were highly gratifying after years of hardship and humiliation. At the age of twenty-five he felt he had triumphed once and for all over the "slave" who had lived inside him since birth. Perhaps he did spit blood, but at least it was the blood of a free man. "I have no debts nor do I feel the need for any . . . Until recently we bought food (meat and groceries) on credit; now I've done away with that: we pay cash for everything."[17]

Clearly the optimism is a bit forced, of a kind to impress an uncle in the provinces, yet there is no question but that Chekhov was proud of the material improvements his work had brought about. For the time being his ambition was simply to live comfortably and honorably. He had entered literature by the back door and held the giants of Russian letters—Dostoevsky, Turgenev, Tolstoy—in awe. True, Dostoevsky had died in 1881, Turgenev in 1883, and Tolstoy, though still alive, was making a show of turning his back on art and playing the prophet, but their works were still foremost in everyone's mind and discouraged emulation on the part of the rising generation. How could anyone improve on such illustrious predecessors?

At first, the question did not even occur to Chekhov. Writing fast and furiously, meeting deadlines, he had no time to deal with the moral, religious, or social issues of the day, no time to preach. His only concern was to entertain his readers or give them something to dream about. Between 1880 and 1884 he published three hundred texts under various names and in various Moscow and Petersburg humor magazines. Among the hodgepodge of jests and japes a few stories—"The Daughter of Albion," "The Death of an Official," "Fat and Thin," "The Medal," "Surgery," "The Chameleon," "Promotion by Examination," "Appropriate Measures"—exhibit a subtle psychology and finely spun irony. As impressed as Leikin was by Chekhov's originality, he subjected each of his manuscripts to a form of pre-censorship, cutting shocking or dangerous passages out of hand. "Your description of Easter Eve, of sextons in belfries, is not bad at all," he wrote to Chekhov, "and I've sent the first half of the story to the typesetters. But I'm sorry, everything to do with the prosaic side of Easter—the drunkenness, the holiday visits—I've had to delete." And later in the same letter: "Your baubles are charming, but there's one I'm afraid won't pass through the crucible of censorship. It has been weighing heavy on us lately, crushing, stifling us."[18]

Leikin was not exaggerating: even after his preliminary

purge the censor would intervene with a blue pencil. Behind the most innocuous of words the guardian of civic honor spied offensive allusions to the Tsar, the Army, the Church, the family. Many of Chekhov's stories were either mutilated or rejected. With the reign of Alexander III Russia had entered an era of rigidity and suspicion. Under the influence of Konstantin Pobedonostsev, head of the Holy Synod and intimate of the Tsar, the intellectual life of the country soon congealed. Any personal opinion was considered subversive.

Chekhov, however, adapted quite well to the situation. He had never had the temperament of a rebel; he was more of a skeptical but kindhearted observer of human nature. Moving from story to story, he unconsciously painted a broad yet minute, humble yet faithful canvas of contemporary Russian life. There they were, side by side—the ordinary people he had caught unawares in both town and country: ignorant and brutal peasants, idle gentryfolk half ruined by the emancipation of the serfs, drunken students with grand but naïve ideas, disenchanted professors, unlucky doctors, shopkeepers chained to their accounts, corrupt officials. Society's loose change. To one and all he gave the pitiful misadventures befitting their pitiful characters, yet with a series of seemingly insignificant remarks he was able to hint at the mystery behind their gray exteriors. He made the absurdity of everyday life unmistakably plain without ever putting it in so many words. No speech for the prosecution, no speech for the defense. The raw truth. Photographic. Moreover, his bag of tricks seemed inexhaustible: there is no repetition whatever in the entire massive portrait gallery.

Leikin kept pushing Chekhov to write more ("Why waste time reworking your stories? Nobody bothers anymore"), but Chekhov turned a deaf ear to his plaints. As he grew more conscious of his art, he started attaching greater importance to form. He wanted his style to be sober, rapid, unaffected, as if there were only characters, characters without an author—yet another instance of his reluctance to put himself forward. In December 1881 he received an issue of the *Novorossiisk Telegraph* that carried a glowing review of his *Tales of Melpomene*: "The stories are short and make for fast, easy reading accompanied by an unwitting smile. They have a Dickensian humor to them: they are both funny and heartrending." The article was signed Iago. But Chekhov was well aware that Iago was a pen name of his faithful old classmate Sergeenko. He therefore put the praise down to their friendship and concluded without the slightest bitterness that his literary breakthrough was still a long way off.

VI

First Successes, First Failures

Following a rather complicated set of procedures Ivan was able to leave his Voskresensk post for the better-paying headmastership of a Moscow primary school. Although Chekhov had long wished to see the family reunited, the move had its bleak side: it meant the loss of the Voskresensk house for summer holidays. As soon as the weather improved, he yearned for the country. The shopkeeper's son, the small-time journalist down on his luck, still associated success with the vast estates described by Turgenev and Tolstoy, and the summers he had spent outside Moscow had whet his appetite for country living. So he went out on a limb and rented a house at Babkino, three versts from Voskresensk, an estate belonging to his friends the Kiselyovs, whose children had been Ivan's pupils. To finance the venture he was obliged to borrow a hundred rubles from the *Alarm Clock* editorial board.

Late in the night of May 6, 1885, the Chekhov tribe, divided between two carriages and loaded down with suitcases, trunks, bundles, books, papers, pots of jam, and pots and pans, passed the main house, where the Kiselyovs lay sleeping, and pulled up at the other end of the estate in front of the smaller house that was to be theirs for the summer. The doors were open. They lit the lamps. Chekhov was bowled over. "The rooms are enormous, the furniture more than we need," he wrote to his brother Mikhail. "Everything is extremely nice, comfortable, cozy. Matchbox stands, ashtrays, cigarette boxes, two wash basins and . . . heaven only knows what our kind hosts didn't think to put out for us. A dacha like this outside Moscow would go for at least five hundred rubles. You'll see when you get here. As soon as we were in, I unpacked my bags and sat down for a bite. I took a drink of vodka and . . . you can't imagine how nice it was to look through the window at the darkening trees and the river . . . I heard a nightingale sing and couldn't believe my ears."[1]

Next day Chekhov set out to explore the estate in earnest. It spread along a steep bank of the Istra and had an immense English garden, densely wooded areas, meadows, fish ponds, flower beds. . . . Reigning over this paradise of *dolce far niente* were the Kiselyovs and their two grown children, Alexandra (Sasha) and Sergei. Madame Kiselyova was an energetic, jovial soul with quite a reputation as a children's author. The house teemed with servants on errands for their masters. Every meal had its guests. The Kiselyovs seemed intent on squandering what was left of their fortune. Chekhov would remember them when he described the decline of a family estate in *The Cherry Orchard*.

At the time, however, he was more impressed by their friendliness and high spirits. Despite the temptation to give in to their idleness he had to work hard to pay for the luxury of being there. He would get up at seven with the intention of spending the morning writing at an old sewing-machine table, but was often interrupted by local peasants, who had heard there was a doctor at Babkino and came to him for advice. "My patients keep flowing in; they won't stop pestering me. I've seen several hundred of them this summer and earned a total of one ruble."[2]

In the afternoon he would fish and spread osier traps, marveling at the catch: "Yesterday there was a perch in one of them, and this morning we pulled out *twenty-nine* carp. Pretty good, eh? We're having fish soup, fried fish, and fish in aspic today."[3] Madame Kiselyova often went fishing with him, discussing literature as she dipped her line. Since she knew he was on the lookout for subject matter, she would retell him stories from old French magazines.

Home from fishing, he would return to his desk till evening. Now that he had stopped providing *Fragments* with Moscow prattle, he had more time to polish his stories, especially the ones for the *Saint Petersburg Gazette* with no length restrictions. After dinner, which was served at eight, everyone would retire to the Kiselyovs' sitting room for drink, talk, whist, chess, and, most of all, music. Madame Kiselyova had a delightful voice, and the governess was an excellent pianist. Chekhov particularly enjoyed Chopin's *Nocturnes*. At the end of the evening Madame Kiselyova extinguished the lights and the governess played Beethoven's *Moonlight Sonata*. Sitting alone on the terrace, Chekhov would feel his heart swell with peace and happiness. When the last notes had faded into the night, the guests departed in silence.

Several days after arriving at Babkino, Chekhov learned that his friend, the painter Isaak Levitan, had holed up in a neighboring village and was suffering from suicidal neurasthenia. He immediately went and gave him a talking-to, dragged him from his lair, and put him up in an outbuilding that went with the Chekhovs' dacha. "Poor Levitan is in a bad way. It looks like the beginnings of a psychosis. [. . .] He wanted to hang himself . . . I've taken him in with us and go for walks with him . . . He seems to be doing better. [. . .] What luxuriant nature! I could eat it . . ."[4]

During the long hikes the two men took through the fields and woods, Levitan gradually regained a taste for life. As for Chekhov, he became a more attentive observer of the landscape;

under the painter's tutelage he came to appreciate the smallest bush, the slightest puddle, the slimmest blade of grass, carrying them off in his head like so many bits of patiently collected treasure. Nothing of what he saw, nothing of what he experienced was lost to his art.

Unfortunately, Levitan's "cure" did not proceed smoothly; he would swing back and forth between rapture and deep depression. The moment he was in the presence of a young and passably attractive woman, he would fall in love with her and declare his passion, only to forget her the following day for another. With a shock of curly black hair, a large nose, burning eyes, and devilish eyebrows he was not what one might call handsome, but even women who criticized his extravagance found him engaging.

At Babkino he could not keep his eyes off Chekhov's sister. Maria had just turned twenty-two; she was a lively combination of dreamer and realist, trying her hand at painting while following the teachers' training course at the Raevsky Institute for Girls. Levitan's dark moods, his talent, his fiery speech made a deep impression on her: she took him for a romantic hero lost in a society unable to understand him. One morning, as they were out walking together in the Babkino woods talking amiably of this and that, he fell on his knees before her and swore he loved her and wanted to marry her. Utterly distraught, Maria ran off to the house, locked herself in her room, and cried there for the rest of the day. When she failed to appear for dinner, Chekhov went to her room and heard her confession. Sobbing, she told him of Levitan's declaration and her own state of confusion. He wisely counseled her to think things over. "Of course you can marry him," he said, "but keep in mind he needs women of a Balzacian age and not girls like you." Without quite understanding what he meant by "women of a Balzacian age," Maria realized he was disturbed at the thought of her being tied down to a man as unstable as Levitan. She therefore decided to discourage him. "I gave him no answer," she later wrote, "and he wandered about, dark and gloomy, for another week, while I kept to the house, to my room. [. . .] That was the end of our romance. But we remained good friends for the rest of his short life."[5]

As the summer wore on, Chekhov grew more worried about financial matters: he still had Babkino debts to take care of, to say nothing of the family's return to Moscow. By plaguing his editors with supplications, he managed to collect enough overdue payments to take the clan back to town in late September. As he walked the "infernally boring" streets of Moscow, he could not stop dreaming of Babkino's bucolic charm. "There is nothing yet in my poor soul but memories of fishing rods, ruffs, traps, that long, green thing for worms . . . [. . .] I'm still so much involved in summer that when I wake up in the morning I wonder whether we've caught anything or not."[6]

Yet the stay in paradise did little to improve his health, and he had resumed spitting blood. Soon after their return the Chekhovs moved again, this time to the other side of the Moscow River and a district that Chekhov described to Leikin as "the real provinces: clean, peaceful, cheap, and . . . rather stupid."[7] Also soon after their return Leikin invited Chekhov to Petersburg for a fortnight, all expenses paid. Chekhov had never been to the capital and jumped at the chance; he even went and bought a new overcoat and a new pair of trousers. On December 10, 1885, he took the train for the city of fog, bureaucracy, and literary greats, home of the leading writers of the day—Saltykov-Shchedrin, Grigorovich, Leskov, Uspensky, Pleshcheev—and the shades of the classics—Pushkin, Gogol, Dostoevsky, Nekrasov. . . .

Leaning out of the carriage that took him from the station to Leikin's house, Chekhov admired the broad, rectilinear avenues, the almond-green or yellow-ocher Italian façades of the buildings, the cold order, the decorous beauty that represented the antithesis of everything he loved in colorful, chaotic, common old Moscow. He had no idea yet that the stories he called "trifles" had begun to win him the reputation of a real writer, and was stupefied at the enthusiastic reception he got from the colleagues Leikin introduced him to. "People kept offering me invitations, singing my praises," he announced to Alexander, "and I began to feel bad about having written so sloppily, care-lessly. If I'd known I was being read like this, I'd never have written to order."[8] Two weeks later he told Victor Bilibin, a writer and editor at *Fragments,* "In the days when I didn't know people were reading and judging me, I wrote serenely, as if eating *bliny*; now I'm afraid when I write."[9]

The most important new acquaintance Chekhov made in Petersburg was the influential press magnate Alexei Suvorin, founder and editor in chief of the largest daily of the period, *New Times.* On the strength of a reading of "The Huntsman" he recruited Chekhov to contribute stories to his paper at twelve kopecks a line. Chekhov was delighted at the new source of income, and, more important, he immediately saw in Suvorin a man of great energy, loyalty, and culture. True, his staunch pro-government stance had earned him the reputation of an unscrupulous opportunist among liberals, but then Chekhov stood apart from politics and its passions.

From Moscow he hastened to send *New Times* a fresh story, "The Requiem." It was immediately published. "Thank you for writing such flattering words about my work and printing the story so promptly," he wrote to Suvorin. "You can judge for yourself what a refreshing and even inspiring effect the kind attentions of so experienced and talented a person as you have had on my ambitions as a writer."[10]

Chekhov's creative fervor was soon dampened, however, when a typhus epidemic broke out in the city. Like all doctors he was constantly on call, and he slept only a few hours a night. With his frail constitution he was more fearful of contagion than most. "I write and doctor," he wrote to Bilibin. "Moscow is a hotbed of typhus. I'm particularly afraid of it. I have a feeling that if I catch the foul thing I'll never shake it, and the risk of contagion is all around me."[11]

Even when he could grab a bit of time from his patients, he had trouble concentrating on the blank page. An entire floor of the building where he lived was occupied by a caterer, who used it for wedding receptions, funeral dinners, and guild ban-quets, and the shouting, the blare of music, the tinkle of dishes never seemed to end. To Bilibin he wrote, "There is a wedding orchestra playing over my head at the moment . . . Some asses are getting married and stomping away like horses";[12] and to Leikin: "I've been so exhausted, frenzied, and crazed these past two weeks that my head is spinning . . . The flat is constantly full of people, noise, music . . . The office is cold . . . The patients keep coming . . ."[13]

In spite of it all, however, he wrote not only a number of facile comic stories but also such masterpieces of tender humor as "The Criminal," "Sergeant Prishebeev," and, above all, "Sadness," the story of an old coachman who, having lost his son and tried in vain to confide his grief to one fare after another, turns in the end to his old mare. "Now say you've got a colt, you're the colt's mother . . . And suddenly, say, your colt, it ups and dies . . . Wouldn't you be sad?" And while the old coachman tells it the whole story, "the horse chomps away, listening and breathing on its master's hands. . . ."

Much as the readers of *Fragments, Saint Petersburg Gazette,* and *New Times* were dazzled by these stories, Chekhov still lacked self-confidence. He could not comprehend why Suvorin advised him to abandon his pseudonym and sign his works properly. When Bilibin, too, begged him to publish his forthcoming collection *Varicolored Stories* under his own name, Chekhov replied, "I've given my family name and coat of arms to medicine, which I won't abandon till the grave. Literature I shall have to abandon sooner or later. [. . .] I don't understand you. Why should the public find Anton Chekhov any more pleasing than A. Chekhonte?"[14]

In fact, however, the naturally shy Chekhov was reluctant to take off his mask and face the crowd; he feared throwing his name to the lions lest they growl or roar back at him. Moreover, by putting himself on display he would be putting his family on display. Had he the right? And finally, as he himself formulated it, "Medicine takes itself seriously; the game of literature requires nicknames."[15]

Then, on March 25, 1886, several weeks after asserting to Bilibin that his days on the literary scene were numbered, he received a letter from Petersburg that moved him to tears. The highly celebrated, highly venerable Grigorovich, to whom he had been introduced during his stay in the capital, had written a spontaneous hymn of admiration and praise. Forty years earlier the same Grigorovich had greeted the birth of Dostoevsky's genius with such a letter, a precedent that made it all the more valuable. "I have read everything signed *Chekhonte,* though inwardly annoyed with a man who has so poor an opinion of himself as to deem the use of a pseudonym necessary. [. . .] You have *real* talent, a talent which raises you far above the new generation of writers. [. . .] If I speak of your talent, I do so out of conviction. I am over sixty-five, but I still feel so great a love for literature and follow its progress with such great fervor, I am so overjoyed when I discover something alive and inspired that, as you see, I am unable to restrain myself and I hold my hands out to you." But the benediction from glorious master to most worthy successor was not without its benevolent advice: "Stop trying to meet deadlines. I do not know what your income is; if it is small, then starve, as we starved in our youth, but keep your observations for works you ponder, revise, works you write during the blissful hours of inspiration, not in one go. One such work will be valued more than a hundred perfectly decent stories scattered throughout the papers." Grigorovich also chided his young colleague for certain "pornographic" effects. Did he need to push realism so far as to speak of "dirty feet with twisted nails" or "a scribe's navel"? Finally, he was adamant about the necessity for the collection *Varicolored Stories* to appear under his real name. The letter ended with the words: "I write to you not as an authority of any kind but out of the simplicity of a pure heart."

After reading the long missive ten times over, Chekhov had the strange feeling of having been granted a wish he had never quite dared to put into words. It was as if by holding out his hand Grigorovich had helped him to cross the line separating the crowd of hack journalists from a small group of the elect. He immediately responded with gratitude and humility. "Your letter, my kind and dearly beloved bearer of glad tidings, struck me like a thunderbolt. I was so overwhelmed it brought me to the brink of tears, and even now I feel it has left a deep imprint on my innermost being. May God comfort your old age as you have befriended my youth. I can find neither words nor deeds to thank you enough. [. . .] If I do have a gift that warrants respect, I must confess before the purity of your heart that I have as yet failed to respect it. I felt I had one, but slipped into the habit of considering it worthless. [. . .] I have hundreds of friends in Moscow, about twenty of whom are writers, and I can't remember even one of them ever reading my things or considering me an artist. [. . .] In the five years I have spent hanging around newspaper offices, I have grown resigned to the general view of my literary insignificance; I soon took to looking down on my work, and kept plowing on. That is the first factor. The second is that I am a doctor and up to my ears in medicine. [. . .] I can't remember working on a *single* story for more than a day, and "The Huntsman," which you so enjoyed, I wrote while I was out swimming. [. . .] But there out of the blue was your letter. Please forgive the comparison, but it had the same effect on me as a governor's order to leave town within twenty-four hours, that is, I suddenly felt an uncontrollable urge to hurry and extricate myself from the spot where I was stuck."

Farther on, Chekhov explained that the collection had already been printed and it was too late for him to sign it with his real name. Besides, he wasn't happy with the book; it was a "hodgepodge, an indiscriminate conglomeration of the tripe I wrote as a student, plucked bare by the censors and humor-sheet editors. I'm sure many people will be disappointed once they've read it. Had I known that I was being read and that you were keeping track of me, I'd never have let it be published." In any case, he swore to be wary of "cynicism" and to devote his summer holidays to the noble and serious task ahead. He asked Grigorovich to send him a photograph of himself and closed in the following terms: "All my hope lies in the future. I am still only twenty-six. I may manage to accomplish something yet, though time is flying."[16]

Chekhov showed the Grigorovich letter to his parents and friends and copied out several passages for Uncle Mitrofan, but he was careful not to make too much of it. The tone he adopted to announce the event to Bilibin, for example, combines vanity and childish irreverence. "Suddenly, unexpectedly, in the form of a *deus ex machina,* a letter from Grigorovich came for me. [. . .] The handwriting is indecipherable, doddering; the old man commands me to produce something major and stop trying to meet deadlines. He argues I have *real* talent (emphasis his). [. . .] He writes with great warmth and sincerity. I'm happy, of course, though I feel he's gone overboard."[17]

He dreamed of returning to the capital, where so many highly respected people believed in his genius. "I'm the latest thing!" he told Alexander. But he had trouble raising the funds. Besides, he was exhausted from a new bout of blood-spitting. And while he suspected what was behind it, he refused to seek formal confirmation; he preferred living in a state of uncertainty, even if uncertainty meant anxiety. "I'm afraid to submit myself to my colleagues' examination . . . What if they discover prolonged expiration or numbness! . . . As I see it, it's not so much the lungs as the throat . . . I have no fever."[18] As soon as he felt better, he took the train to Petersburg.

For a fortnight, from April 25 to May 10, he enjoyed an uninterrupted display of friendship, society, and flattery. Grigorovich and Bilibin lauded and extolled him, and Suvorin, who had published three long stories by the young author ("The Requiem," "The Witch," and "Agafya"), considered himself his protector in the world of letters. Suvorin was rich and influential, and Chekhov recognized his extraordinary stature, but he also found his habit of playing lord and master slightly ridiculous. "He gave me a very pleasant reception and even let me shake his hand. 'Persevere, young man!' he said. 'I am satisfied with you, but be sure you go to church more often and give up vodka. Exhale!' I exhaled. Not smelling anything on my breath, he turned and called out, 'Boys!' A boy appeared. He was ordered to serve tea in the peasant fashion. Whereupon the esteemed Mr. Suvorin gave me some money and said, 'You must learn to economize. Tighten your belt!' "[19]

In the same letter Chekhov admitted to being rather taken with the young woman at *New Times* whose duty it was to send him his payments. He hoped to see her again. In fact, he never denied having a soft spot for the ladies. Maria's friends provided him with a kind of "posy of pretty misses": pleasant to see, pleasant to sniff, pleasant to tease. There were even times he dreamed of marrying one of them.

In January he met a new friend of Maria's, a rich young Jewess by the name of Dunya Efros, whose grace, intelligence, and vivacity immediately turned his head. Taking her home one evening, he unexpectedly proposed. "I'm jumping out of the frying pan into the fire," he wrote jokingly to his friend Victor Bilibin. But two weeks later he renewed his attack: the damsel was indecisive. The fact that she was Jewish complicated the issue, because to marry a Russian Orthodox she would, in principle, have to convert. Things quickly turned sour between the two of them, and Chekhov was horrified to discover how aggressive she was, this woman he considered his fiancée. "We've quarreled . . . Tomorrow we'll make it up, but in a week we'll quarrel again . . . She's so upset at the obstacle religion has caused that she snaps pencils and tears up photographs on my desk. That's typical of her . . . She's a terrible shrew . . . There's no doubt I'd divorce her after a year or two of marriage."[20] Four weeks later he announced a definitive rupture with the impetuous virgin. "I'm still unmarried. I've broken *once and for all* with my fiancée. That is, she's broken with me. But I haven't yet bought a revolver, and I'm not keeping a diary."[21] Then in two more weeks: "I won't speak to you of her again. Maybe you're right when you say it's too early for me to get married . . . I'm frivolous even though I'm only one (1) year younger than you . . . I still have dreams of being at school and afraid the teacher will call on me when I'm unprepared . . . In other words, a babe in arms."[22]

But though left without a bride, he was not left alone. And

for all his complaints about the racket in the new flat, Chekhov confessed he needed friendly faces and even a bit of hustle and bustle around him. "I absolutely can't live without company," he wrote to Suvorin. "When I'm alone, I feel a kind of anxiety, as if I were sailing solo in a frail bark at sea."[23]

Chekhov returned to Babkino that summer, to the Kiselyovs, Levitan, and the myriad regular guests. They spent their time in parlor games, practical jokes, and masquerades, all of which ended in wild laughter. The only sour note was the rather lukewarm reception given by the press to the recently published *Varicolored Stories*. The critic of *The News* called it "the delirium of a madman"; his colleague at the *Northern Herald* wrote that the Chekhonte book presented "the tragic spectacle of a young talent's suicide," and compared the author to "a squeezed-out lemon rotting under a gate." Although such attacks would have made no impression on him several months earlier, they wounded him now that he knew men like Grigorovich and Suvorin admired him. All at once he was ashamed of the slightest splash of public venom. His sensitivity was doubtless heightened by an attack of hemorrhoids and a series of excruciating toothaches. At the beginning of September he went back to Moscow for treatment.

The untimely return coincided with a new move. This time Chekhov had rented a whole house rather than a flat, a house in the elegant Sadovaya-Kudrinskaya Street near the center of town. The two-story building was painted red and had a double overhang in front that Chekhov said made it look like a chest of drawers. Rent: 650 rubles a year. To make the necessary down payment Chekhov was obliged to pawn his watch and borrow from Leikin.

Never before had he had such a luxurious place to live. The ground floor consisted of the study where he received patients, his own room, and the rooms belonging to Mikhail, the maid, and the cook. His mother and sister lived on the next floor, which also housed the dining room and a sitting room complete with aquarium and rented piano. The walls of the

75

study were lined with a wealth of photographs and shelves containing the books his friend Popudoglo had left him when he died.*

Despite all the new comforts Chekhov's mother, who had grown nervous and querulous with age, was apprehensive about the future and complained that Anton's success had robbed her of him. "He's no longer mine," she sighed to her guests. To her mind the best thing for Anton—and the best thing he could do for the family—was to marry a rich merchant's daughter. His father, who still lived away from home but paid the family frequent visits, took a more conciliatory attitude. He found the boy's growing fame flattering to himself. He admired Anton and took care not to reprimand him for his lack of interest in religion.

The move to the "chest of drawers" changed nothing in the Chekhov family's commitment to boisterous hospitality. Every evening a band of heterogeneous visitors crowded around Anton, who was unable to shut his doors to anyone. Young painter friends of Nikolai and Levitan, strangers bearing manuscripts, and the inevitable "posy of misses" invited by Maria— they would all end up at the samovar, talking more at than to one another in an atmosphere of artistic exhilaration.

One evening the well-known writer Vladimir Korolenko came to call. When he questioned Chekhov about his work, Chekhov replied that it was all merely a diversion for him. "You want to know how I write my stories?" he asked. "Here!" And looking over at the table, he picked up the first object his eye lit upon, an ashtray, laid it down in front of Korolenko, and said, "If you like, it will be a story tomorrow . . . 'The Ashtray.' " "His eyes suddenly sparkled with merriment," writes Korolenko in his memoirs, "as if vague images had begun to swarm above the ashtray, situations, adventures yet to take shape but already humorous in mood . . . When I look back on that conversation, the small sitting room where old Madame Chekhov presided over the samovar, the affectionate smiles of

*In 1954 the house was made the Chekhov Museum.

his sister and brothers, and the general atmosphere of a close-knit family revolving around a charming and talented young man with what seemed a joyous outlook on life, I have the feeling it was the happiest, the last happy period in the life of the family as a whole."[24]

Often the artists' wide-ranging discussions ranged deep into the night as well, disintegrating into song- or joke-fests by morning. One evening Grigorovich himself turned up at such a gathering—tall, elegant, and stately with diaphanous gray sideburns. At first the young people were paralyzed with respect before this statue out of the literary pantheon, but they soon resumed their tumultuous play, whereupon Grigorovich joined in and even flirted with the girls. Back in Petersburg he reported to Suvorin's wife, "If you only knew what goes on at the Chekhovs', my dear. Why, it's a bacchanalia, a veritable bacchanalia!"

Sometimes Chekhov had to drag his brother Nikolai home from a tavern where he had been sighted dead drunk. Nikolai was by then a confirmed alcoholic; he had given up painting and lived a vagrant's existence, trailing along after one prostitute or another. Undaunted, Anton did his best to treat him, but Nikolai was not about to take his advice. "As your brother and intimate, I assure you that I understand you and sympathize with you from the bottom of my heart. I know all your good qualities like the back of my hand. [. . .] You are kind to the point of fault, magnanimous, unselfish, you'd share your last penny, and you're sincere. Hate and envy are foreign to you, you are openhearted, you are compassionate with man and beast, you are not greedy, you do not bear grudges, and you are trusting. You are gifted from above with something others lack: you have talent. Your talent places you above millions of people." He implored his brother to respect that talent, to "sacrifice comfort, women, wine, and vanity to it." True artists "cannot bear to sleep fully dressed, see a slit in the wall teeming with bedbugs, breathe rotten air, walk on a spittle-laden floor, or eat directly from the stove. They try their best to tame and ennoble their sexual instinct. [. . .] What they look for in a woman is not a bed partner or horse sweat [. . .] but spontaneity, elegance, compassion, the ability to be a mother, not a whore. They don't guzzle vodka on any occasion, nor do they go around sniffing cupboards, for they know they are not swine."[25]

When all is said and done, what Chekhov really wanted was to make his brother into a "well-bred human being." The letter, which he must have written without much hope of bringing Nikolai around, is in fact something of a credo, a declaration of his own moral principles. At twenty-six he was an avowed Stoic: he believed in self-control, honor, and sobriety; he advocated moderation in all things, forcing himself to drink and smoke in small doses and following a milk diet to keep his weight down; he felt work to be the surest protection against an artist's tendency to excess.

While he had little chance of being heeded by Nikolai, he still hoped to rescue Alexander from his lethargy. Indeed, Alexander had quieted down considerably and was well on his way to embodying his brother's concept of the "well-bred human being." Anton had arranged for him to work as a reporter and proofreader on the *New Times* staff, and he was living in Petersburg. He also served Anton as a kind of agent, dunning tardy magazines for payment, delivering messages to editors and colleagues, and keeping an eye on the sale of books. That he both admired his younger brother and envied his success did not keep him from writing, and Chekhov gave him advice modeled on the exhortations he had himself recently received from Grigorovich. "Have some respect for yourself, for heaven's sake, and don't grab your pen when your brain's not working. [. . .] Watch every line as you write, and you won't botch so many."[26] He also let him in on some tricks of the trade. "In nature descriptions you must go after tiny details, grouping them in such a way that once you've read them you can close your eyes and see a picture. [. . .] In the domain of psychology, more details. But heaven keep you from clichés. It's best to avoid describing the characters' psychic states, which should be clear from their actions."[27]

Chekhov's approach appears full-blown in these recommendations, and still he denied he was destined to be a writer. "Besides a wife, medicine," he wrote to Alexander, "I have a mistress, literature. But I never mention her, for those who live outside the law shall perish outside the law."[28]

In fact, the "mistress" gave him more satisfaction than the "legal wife." His fame was spreading. He told friends about people pointing him out in restaurants. He also boasted to Madame Kiselyova that in one of the more fashionable of those establishments he had recently partaken, for the first time in his life, of a dish of oysters. "Not much of a taste. Take away the chablis and the lemon and they're positively disgusting."[29]

At the end of September he took his sister with him on a trip to Petersburg, intending to show her the capital and give her a chance to bask a little in his glory. Once more, the reception his admirers gave him surpassed his expectations. To Madame Kiselyova he complained that things had gone too far. "Alas and alack, I'm quite the rage in Petersburg, another Nana. Whereas Korolenko, a serious writer, is hardly known by the editors, the whole town is reading my rubbish. [. . .] It may be flattering to me, but it offends my literary sensibility . . . I feel embarrassed for an audience that courts literary lapdogs for want of an ability to recognize elephants, and I deeply believe that not a soul will have anything to do with me once I start doing serious work."[30]

All the periodicals were suddenly writing about Chekhonte. In an article for the journal *Russian Wealth* the eminent critic Obolensky placed him above Korolenko. And in a letter Chekhov received shortly after his return, Alexander mentioned all sorts of flattering rumors about him. "People speak to me as though they're convinced you have a divine spark in you, as though they expect something of you without quite knowing what."

When early in March 1887 Chekhov learned that Alexander had come down with typhus, he immediately took off for Petersburg. He had a bad journey, his only consolation being "dear, sweet Anna," *Anna Karenina,* which he read all the way there. Upon arrival he found Alexander in perfect health. Apparently in a moment of depression he had thought himself ill and sent off a telegram to Moscow forthwith. As it turned out, however, his wife had the disease, and Chekhov treated and cured her. Petersburg was in the midst of a typhus epidemic; the hospitals were full, the streets still, except for occasional funeral processions and groups in mourning on the way to church. Chekhov went to see Grigorovich, who was himself ill. The old man kissed him on the forehead, hugged him, and wept; indeed, he was so overcome with emotion that he had a bad attack of angina pectoris on the spot. The only ray of light during the gloomy trip was the conversation Chekhov had with Suvorin, a conversation lasting from nine in the evening until one in the morning and resulting in an offer from *New Times* to publish a collection of stories and an advance of three hundred rubles on future stories.

Chekhov was thrilled at this manna from heaven: he had been planning to take a trip south and now nothing stood in his way. As soon as he got back to Moscow, he settled the most urgent of his affairs, scribbled off a few stories—"Typhus," "The Weariness of Life," and "The Mystery"—made a list of the sixteen stories he wished to include in the collection, sent it off to Suvorin, and, with mixed feelings, abandoned his family for Taganrog and memories of youth.

Seeing his native town after an eight-year absence proved an experience both moving and distressing. Accustomed to the hustle of Moscow and Petersburg, he had the impression that people barely dragged themselves along, that even the air they breathed was thicker. They seemed to be living in another century and to have nothing but base, material interests. He was touched by his Uncle Mitrofan's warm hospitality, but could not stand his aunt's idle chatter, the servants' filth, the evil-smelling water in his basin, or the undersized bed and old pink quilt. The coarse cooking upset his stomach, and he was in constant need of the privy, which was out near the gate. The possibility of lurking street urchins made the trip dangerous as well as inconvenient. "I run out day and night. At night it's sheer torture: the darkness, the wind, the creaky, hard-to-open doors, the hike across the pitch-black courtyard, the suspicious silence, the lack of cut newspaper . . ."[31] But that was not all. "Yakov Andreich [the family nickname for a chamber pot] makes an appearance only in dreams and fantasies. Only two people in Taganrog can afford such a luxury: the lord mayor and Alferaki [one of the rich Taganrog Greeks]; everyone else must either piddle in bed or journey out to the back of beyond."[32]

Besides diarrhea Chekhov had bronchitis, phlebitis in his left leg, and, as always, hemorrhoids. Every street corner seemed to have an old acquaintance on it, and he was constantly invited to people's houses for questions and commentary. Since it was Eastertime, he went to church, and the odor of incense and glitter of candles reawakened in him bitter memories of his choirboy days. Everything in Taganrog displeased, annoyed, rebuffed him. He wondered what had made him undertake so long and arduous a journey. Yet he refused to depart for Moscow until he had a chance to see the steppe again.

The steppe, at least, did not disappoint him. At the sight of the bare, open spaces, the scorched grass, the vast sky broken only by an occasional sparrow hawk, he felt a complex mingling of joy and melancholy: the soul soared, the body could not follow. In Novocherkassk he attended a two-day Cossack wedding with earsplitting music, wild dancing, and much brotherly drinking. "I was so drunk I mistook the bottles for girls and the girls for bottles."[33] The newlyweds kissed as if there were no tomorrow, smacking their lips with great gusto. "Watching them brought the taste of oversweet grapes to my mouth and a spasm to my left calf. Their kisses aggravated the phlebitis there." Pretty provincial maidens flocked round him like flies round a bowl of honey. One of them, full of airs and graces, kept tapping his arm with her fan and saying, "Oh, you naughty boy!"

He also stayed with the Kravtsovs at the estate he had visited in his youth while tutoring their son Pyotr. Despite the uncomfortable lodgings, the garlic soup, and a series of hunts that turned into veritable massacres, he was delighted by their rustic hospitality. The magic propinquity of the steppe made up for any inconvenience.

From there he moved on to the Monastery of the Holy Mounts on the banks of the Donets, where fifteen thousand pilgrims had gathered to pay homage to Saint Nicholas. Chekhov found accommodation at the monastery: a mattress as thin as a pancake in a bare cell. He took part in a Procession of the Cross on the river and spent the rest of the time watching the comings and goings of the faithful—old women, for the most part—and listening to their prayers and lamentations. "I had no idea there were so many old women in the world," he declared to his sister, "and had I known, I'd have long since blown my brains out."[34]

After making a short stop in Taganrog to catch his breath, Chekhov took the train for Moscow. "I have all kinds of impressions and material," he wrote to Leikin, "and I don't repent having used up a month and a half on the journey. The only vile, foul thing is that I haven't a kopeck."[35] He could afford only a third-class ticket.

He spent only a day in Moscow before going off to Babkino. Once there, however, he missed the merriment and inspiration of the previous years: the house was poorly heated, the weather dismal. Chekhov's mood deteriorated from day to day. "If I haven't written anything for a while," he wrote, again to Leikin, "it doesn't mean I've plugged up the fountain. Alas, the fountain has shut off on its own! For three weeks I've yielded to a cowardly melancholy; I've had no desire to go outdoors, can't keep a pen in my hand—in a word, nerves, which you don't believe in. I've been so distraught I haven't been able to get a stitch of work done."[36] Two days later more of the same to Madame Kiselyova, "I've no new ideas and the old ones are all jumbled together in my head like worms in the green box after five days of exposure to the sun."

Chekhov's general malaise continued unabated despite the success of his new collection *At Twilight,* which had just come out. "Reading reviews, I can't for the life of me tell whether they're praising me or mourning the loss of my soul. 'Oh, the talent! The talent! But Lord, send peace to his soul!'—that's what the reviews come down to. The book is selling quite well.''

In a letter to the same correspondent he had bemoaned the vanity of earthly satisfactions the year before: "I'm leading a gray life, with nary a happy soul in sight. [. . .] Everybody has a hard life. Whenever I give it serious thought, I feel that people who have an aversion to death are illogical. As far as I can make out the order of things, life consists of nothing but horrors, squabbles, and banalities, one after the other and intermingled.''[37]

Then he hit upon the idea of writing himself out of his melancholy. Why not turn it into a play? He had long been attracted by the stage. A theater owner named Korsh had twice asked Chekhov to write something for him. At first Chekhov attached little importance to the request and even wrote to Madame Kiselyova, "Of course I won't write a play. [. . .] I'm in absolutely no mood for theaters or humanity . . . They can go to the devil!''[38]

For all that, the idea made fast headway. Three weeks later he announced to the novelist Yezhov, "My play is ready," then boasted to his brother Alexander of how smoothly the work had gone: "I'd finished it before I knew what was happening, after a single talk with Korsh. I went to bed, came up with a theme, and wrote it out. I spent two weeks on it, no, ten days, since there were days during the two weeks when I didn't work or was writing something else. I can't judge its merits. It has turned out suspiciously short. Everybody likes it. Korsh says I haven't broken a single rule of dramatic writing, which goes to show what fine, perceptive judges I have. It's my first play, ergo it has mistakes. The plot is complicated and rather clever. I finish every act as I do the stories: I keep the action calm and quiet until the end, when I smash the audience's faces in. I've put all my energy into a few really powerful, striking parts; the bridges connecting them are uninteresting, weak, commonplace. Still, I'm happy: no matter how bad the play is, I've created a type of some literary value and fashioned a role that only an actor of Davydov's stature will attempt, a role that will display the actor's talent, show what he can do."[39]

The play in question was *Ivanov*. In Chekhov's eyes the title character symbolized the helplessness of the intellgentsia when faced with a repressive government and a drastic decline in social values. Ivanov, unable to reconcile his generous dreams to the imperatives of reality, is consumed by guilt and despair. He is a negative hero lost in a web of humanitarian speculations, a landowner with no interest in his estate, which is going to seed, or his wife (the Jewess Sara, who has converted to Russian Orthodoxy and taken the name Anna Petrovna), who is seriously ill. Sasha, his neighbor's daughter, has fallen in love with him and tells him so. By thus defying convention, she believes she has proved her ability to save him from his depression. He is touched by her lack of guile and permits her to adore him, sighing, "Day and night my conscience tortures me; I feel profoundly guilty, but of what?" Anna Petrovna dies at last. The graying widower soon announces his marriage to the fresh, young Sasha. But when on the day of the wedding he is vilified in public by the young Doctor Lvov, Ivanov breaks with Sasha and shoots himself.

Three surely drawn characters come through the melodramatic framework of the play: Ivanov, the misfit, incurably tired of himself and the world; little Sasha, thrilled at the thought of using her love to save the passive Ivanov from sinking into the mire; and Doctor Lvov, an honest but narrow-minded young man, who aggravates Ivanov's problems even as he believes he is resolving them.

Thus, unlike the heavily ironic *Platonov, Ivanov* was meant to be a traditional, realist work based on the interplay of characters. Whereas in Chekhov's later plays—the theater of atmosphere—everything was semitones, allusion, and silence, here the colors were distinct and harshly lit, and a plot with spectacular ups and downs obliterated the humdrum details of life. Moreover, the dominating factor was not yet time and its gnawings but the personality of the hero, a sort of Russian

Hamlet trapped in his dreams, incapable of feeling true passion and morbidly ready to resume his inertia after each rare burst of enthusiasm.

There can be no doubt but that Chekhov's portrait of the passive seducer was inspired by traits of his brothers Alexander and Nikolai, but it also reflects some of his own. *Ivanov* dates from a time when Chekhov himself was going through a bout of depression, and certain of his hero's remarks express his personal bugbears. But Chekhov had too much dignity and loved his work too much to give in to despair. He felt a special, almost avuncular tenderness for Ivanov and clearly meant him to be loved. As he told Suvorin, "If my Ivanov comes across as a blackguard or superfluous man and the doctor as a great man, if no one understands why Sara and Sasha love Ivanov, then my play has evidently failed, and there can be no question of having it produced."[40] He went on to explain in great detail why Ivanov, who had no grounds for being unhappy, deserved every indulgence, why Lvov was little more than a virtuous imbecile, and why Sasha had fallen in love primarily under the illusion of doing a holy deed, that is, of saving Ivanov from going under.

After a public reading the play was accepted by Korsh without reservation. Chekhov immediately started calculating his profits. If, as promised, he could count on 8 percent of the box-office receipts, he stood to earn a good six thousand rubles. Extremely excited by the prospect, he spent hours discussing points of interpretation and staging with Davydov, his choice for the leading role. And not wishing to leave the play's commercial success to chance, he asked Alexander to have the following notice printed on the *New Times* theatrical page: "A. P. Chekhov has written a comedy in four acts entitled *Ivanov*. When read in a Moscow literary salon (or something like that), it made a powerful impression. The subject matter is new, the characters three-dimensional, etc."[41]

As soon as rehearsals were under way, however, he lost confidence. He suddenly saw that the author had precious little to say in the "collective enterprise" of putting on a play: the actors deprived him of his lines and the director of everything else. Of the ten rehearsals agreed upon, only four took place. It was painful for Chekhov, huddled in a seat in the auditorium, to hear the actors fumble through their lines with the aid of a prompter. They *played* their roles instead of *living* them. What is more, the actors had not the slightest idea what he was after; they were impervious to him, full of themselves. If he interjected a timid remark about the psychology of this or that character, he was ignored. "I've tried to be original," he wrote to Alexander. "I have not introduced a single villain or a single angel (though I haven't been able to abstain from fools); nor have I accused or vindicated anyone . . . Whether or not I've succeeded, I can't tell . . . Korsh and the actors are sure the play will work. I'm not so sure. The actors don't understand it and say the most ridiculous things, they're badly miscast—I'm constantly at war with them. [. . .] Had I known, I'd never have got involved in it."[42]

Opening night took place in Moscow on November 19, 1887. The poster gave the author's name as Chekhov, not Chekhonte. After weeks of nervous tension Chekhov was surprised to feel so calm. The family, half dead with anxiety, had squeezed into a box; Chekhov stood in a tiny cell-like room just off the stage. The actors paced back and forth in front of him, crossing themselves to drive away stage fright and bad luck. At last the curtain went up. The house was full.

Act One went off as well as could be expected, though one of the actors, Kiselevsky, had a tendency to stuff the holes in his memory with ad-libbing. The ad-libbing continued in Act Two, this time on the part of the supporting actors as well. But the audience did not seem to notice; at the end of Act Three it clapped and called for the author. Victory was in sight, or at least so Chekhov thought. Then came Act Four. The actors had taken quite a few nips by then and turned it into a clown act. Kiselevsky, "drunk as a cobbler," babbled, charged, made faces. Ivanov's suicide shocked some members of the audience and amused others. Their reactions grew louder and louder: hissing and applause, jeers and bravos; fistfights began to break out, and the police had to intervene. Chekhov's sister was so upset she nearly fainted. One of his friends "ran out of the theater with palpitations"; another took his head in his hands and moaned, "What am I going to do now?"

As for Chekhov, he remained cool, and although in a letter to Alexander he confessed to being exhausted and frustrated he went on to boast: "Theater lovers say they've never seen such ferment, such applausamento-hissing, or heard so many arguments as they saw and heard at my play."[43] And a few days later, joking about his "flop," he signed the next letter to Alexander: "Schiller Shakespearovich Goethe."[44]

The critic of the *Moscow News* wrote: "The play's many errors are due to the author's lack of experience and knowledge. I waited till the end for an explication of Ivanov's character. It never came." The *Muscovite Newssheet* declared *Ivanov* "a flippantly cynical piece of foolishness, foul and immoral." The next two performances took place under more serene circumstances. They were the last.

Chekhov took a philosophical attitude towards the failure. He bore no malice to Korsh, who had withdrawn the play prematurely, or to the actors, who had betrayed its main idea, or to the audience, which had failed to appreciate its characters. Once the storm had passed, he felt strangely relieved, as if the shock had helped him to regain his equilibrium. It was therefore with a light heart that he picked up his pen once more to write humorous stories under the name of Chekhonte.

VII

"My Life Bores Me"

Swear as he might that *Ivanov* had cured him forever of his mania for the stage, Chekhov was unable to forget the play: he had put too much suffering and hope into it. If by any chance it could be made to work in a Petersburg production, he would at last have some remuneration for his pains, a prospect that the poor sales of *Varicolored Stories* and *At Twilight* made particularly attractive. The first step was to find a theater willing to stage it. On November 29, 1887, he set off for the capital.

To save expenses he stayed with Alexander. He soon regretted it. Alexander lived in a hovel and was irritable, lazy, and hardheaded. Moreover, the woman he lived with was ill, and he never stopped complaining. "The filth, the stench, the tears, the lies," Chekhov wrote to Mikhail. "After a week of him you'd go out of your mind and feel as dirty as a dish rag."[1]

What a difference between the sordid, petty atmosphere at

Alexander's and the bright lights, suave manners, and intelligent conversation at the salons Chekhov frequented nearly every evening. Before leaving Moscow he had forwarded a copy of *Ivanov* to friends; by the time he arrived it was making the rounds. And by some miracle everyone who had read it was enthusiastic. "Suvorin is furious I gave my play to Korsh. He doesn't think Korsh or the Moscow audience (?) can understand *Ivanov*. The Moscow reviews make people laugh here. They can't wait for me to have it put on in Petersburg, and they're sure it will be a success."[2]

Delighted by the praise, Chekhov added that Petersburg was a wonderful city and he was in "seventh heaven." He gave a reading of the play to a literary circle and stared at his feet during the applause, savored a long and highly complimentary article about him in the *Herald of Europe,* went to suppers in his honor, met the famous painter Repin, and dined with the writer Leontyev-Shcheglov. Leontyev-Shcheglov introduced him to the aging poet Alexei Pleshcheev, who, thirty-eight years before, had been arrested as a member of the revolutionary Petrashevsky Circle and stood with Dostoevsky before a firing squad; at the last moment Nicholas I commuted their death sentences to forced labor in Siberia. Korolenko, after seeing Chekhov again in Petersburg, detected in him an odd blend of intellectual acumen and peasant innocence. "Even Chekhov's eyes," Korolenko wrote, "his sparkling blue,* deep-set eyes, would shine simultaneously with thought and with childlike ingenuousness. Simplicity of movement, manners, and speech dominated his person as it dominated his writings. [. . .] He struck me as a man with a deep-seated zest for life."

If Chekhov did have a "zest for life," it came in bursts and among friends, when he could forget the cares his family caused him, forget his financial worries, his loneliness. He returned to Moscow with the idea of reworking *Ivanov* before submitting it to a Petersburg theater, but another project soon claimed his attention. On January 1, 1888, he set to work on a major story,

*In fact, they were brown with flecks of blue.

"The Steppe." It was based on an idea he had been toying with for months, maybe years: his recent journey through the Don steppes had called up a series of shimmering childhood memories, and they begged to be turned into a story. In Petersburg the venerable Pleshcheev had urged him to put aside a serious piece for the *Northern Herald*; Grigorovich had recently written him from Nice, imploring him yet again to give up his humoresques and concentrate on a novel, even suggesting a topic he felt worthy and moving enough: the torments of a seventeen-year-old culminating in his suicide. Chekhov replied that it would doubtless make a fine work but that he had started in on something quite different: the evocation of a long journey through the steppe, a kind of "encyclopedia of the steppe."

He worked relentlessly, day in and day out: he wanted it perfect. He almost begrudged it the few hours he snatched to write the shatteringly simple and sensitive "Sleepy" for the *Saint Petersburg Gazette,* but he returned to it with renewed vigor. Of course he was used to dashing off several-page stories; now, without flagging or letting the reader's interest flag, he meant to bring alive a child's gradual discovery of the steppe in all its variety. The complete absence of plot complicated the issue: he needed to replace dramatic turns of events with descriptions of people and places both emotionally satisfying and psychologically convincing. "It's a good theme, and I enjoy writing about it," he noted to Korolenko, "but unfortunately, since I'm not used to writing anything long and am afraid of writing to excess, I've gone to the other extreme. Every page comes out as compact as a little story, and the scenes keep piling up, crowding one another out, getting in one another's way, and ruining the general impression. Instead of a scene in which all particulars merge into a whole like stars in the sky, I end up with an outline, a dry list of impressions. A writer, you for instance, will understand me, but the reader will be bored and drop the whole thing."[3] And to Leontyev-Shcheglov: "What's driving me crazy is that it hasn't got a romance. A story without a woman is like an engine without steam."[4] The further he advanced, however, the more he regained confidence. He confessed to writing "The Steppe" as "a gourmet savors a woodcock," slowly, with feeling. To Pleshcheev he remarked, "As I wrote, I felt summer and the steppe all around me." And to a fellow writer, Alexander Lazarev-Gruzinsky: "I consumed a lot of vital juices, energy, and phosphorus on my 'Steppe'; I wrote under tension, under strain, drained myself terribly, squeezed myself dry. Whether it's successful or not I don't know; in any case, it's my masterpiece, I can't do any better."[5]

It took a month to write and was immediately dispatched to Pleshcheev with a request for sincere, even merciless criticism: "For heaven's sake, don't stand on ceremony. Tell me it's bad or ordinary if that's what you think. I very much need to know the truth." The letter is signed: "Your sincerely devoted *débutant,* Antoine Chekhov."[6]

Five days later Chekhov received a wildly enthusiastic response: "I read your story eagerly. Once I had started it, I could not put it down. Korolenko agrees . . . It is so exquisite, such a mine of poetry that I can say nothing more and make no other comment than that I am in ecstasy. It is an absorbing piece, and I predict a great, a brilliant future for you."

Pleshcheev's encomium was particularly important because Chekhov considered "The Steppe" a much more intimate work than anything that had preceded it. He had nourished it with childhood memories and was gratified to learn that the images of his personal folklore could move strangers. He was also gratified at the fee the *Northern Herald* offered him for something that had taken him barely a month to write: a thousand rubles! He bragged to all his friends about it.

"The Steppe" appeared in the March issue of the *Northern Herald* and immediately had a warm reception from both critics and readers. Burenin, the critic for *New Times,* likened its author to Gogol and Tolstoy. Many important writers of the time showered Chekhov with praise: Leskov spoke of genius, Saltykov-Shchedrin and Ostrovsky went even further; the young and brilliant Garshin gave readings of the novella, proclaiming,

"A writer of the first order has just made his appearance in Russia . . . It's as if an abscess had burst and I suddenly felt better."

The all but unanimous infatuation with the work was justified by Chekhov's artistic feat: he had made a fascinating story out of the simple journey of a nine-year-old, Yegor, whom his merchant uncle is taking across the steppe in a cart to the town where he will go to school. Their ups and downs en route form a string of stories united by the personality of the young Yegor. Yegor is sad to leave his mother, uneasy about the new life awaiting him, and filled with wonder at the splendor of the countryside. Every turn of the wheels brings him more under the spell of nature. He watches it awaken in the morning dew, go numb in the shimmering noonday sun, rebel under sudden storms, and find peace in the cool, silent night. The monotony of the journey is broken only by brief encounters with strangers, minor incidents, scraps of conversation. Peasants, carters, merchants—steppe regulars all—turn up from time to time to distract little Yegor from his daydreams. All the portraits—Moses the innkeeper and his brother Solomon; Father Christopher; Uncle Kuznichov; Varlamov, the steppe moneybags; Dymov, the sly, hothead of a peasant—are both colorful and true to life. Dymov deserved a work to himself, said Pleshcheev, to which Chekhov replied: "Men like Dymov are created by life not for heresy or vagrancy or a sedentary existence but for revolution pure and simple . . . Yet there will never be a revolution in Russia, and Dymov will either drink himself to death or end up in jail. He's a superfluous man."[7]

Through it all, however, Yegor—shy, sensitive, melancholy Yegor—remains the axis around which they all turn. Everything he sees, everything he hears is engraved in his memory and enriches his spirit. He has left the house where he was born to discover the world outside, and for several days the steppe becomes his school of life. By the end of the journey, when he must bid his traveling companions farewell and enter the house where he will live while attending a more conventional school, he cannot hold back his tears: he feels his entire past being wrenched from his heart. "He fell back on the bench utterly exhausted and welcomed the mysterious new life opening up before him with bitter tears. What would that life be like?"

"The Steppe" was in a language so spare, so perfect, that, like many passages in Pushkin's prose, it simply cannot be told in other words. At first Chekhov intended to write a sequel to the adventures of young Yegor, but he wisely refrained. By taking his hero beyond childhood, he risked dispelling the freshness and charm that made "The Steppe" what it is. Would he not—after the fact, as it were—destroy its delicate balance in the reader's mind? He gave up the project.

Having worked longer and harder on "The Steppe" than on his regular stories, he felt written out. All he wanted to do was lie in bed and, as the Russian saying goes, "spit on the ceiling." For the fun of it he tossed off a one-act farce called *The Bear*. Then, heeding the call of glory, he left again for Petersburg.

This time he lived in Suvorin's luxurious flat rather than in Alexander's sordid one. He had two elegantly furnished rooms to himself, complete with grand piano, harmonium, padded couch, and private bath; he had a carriage ready to take him wherever he might want to go; and he had his own servant. "My Vasily is better dressed than I am," he wrote to Mikhail, "and has a dignified face. It's strange to have him tiptoeing respectfully in my proximity and trying to anticipate my wishes."[8] His hosts ushered him around to fashionable shops and champagne suppers, and everywhere they went he heard the most extravagant praise. It both cheered and annoyed, flattered and shamed him. "I felt a perfect scoundrel," he wrote to Madame Kiselyova.[9]

The most unpleasant part of it all was Madame Suvorin's blather. She would skip pell-mell from her horror of the human race to a jacket she had bought for 120 rubles to her migraines. Chekhov's response was strained but always courteous. On the other hand, he came to appreciate Suvorin's company more and more. The two men soon reached agreements on a new edition of *At Twilight* and on the publication of a new collection of stories. As a sign of confidence—and in all seriousness—Suvorin offered Chekhov the hand of his daughter, who "for the moment," Anton told Alexander, "can still walk upright under the table." He had his father-in-law's word that in a few years after the wedding he would enjoy one half the revenue of *New Times*. Chekhov merely laughed.

For all Suvorin's bluff and cynicism, however, Chekhov found much to admire in the man. There was a certain effervescence about him that Chekhov found invigorating. Little by little, their intellectual affinity grew into friendship. Twenty-six years older than Chekhov, Surovin could boast of a great deal more experience and of spectacular financial success. Yet both men descended from the peasantry. Suvorin's grandfather had been a serf, his father had fought at Borodino as a private, and he himself had begun his career as a country schoolmaster. From there he had gone into journalism, and his early columns had had a markedly liberal tone to them. But he was not long in realizing that if money, honor, and power were what he was after he would have to flatter the government. In 1876 he bought a minor Petersburg daily, *New Times,* for almost nothing and shamelessly took to defending the status quo. His about-face earned him the scorn of the intelligentsia and the protection of the authorities. Within ten years *New Times* had developed into Russia's largest daily. Soon Suvorin founded his own publishing house and obtained the bookstall concession for all Russian railway stations from the tsarist administration. He was a multimillionaire and led a sumptuous existence, but he liked to recall the time when his wife walked around their village barefoot so as not to wear out her shoes. The price of opulence in his case was a constant betrayal of his deepest sentiments: the despotism he so extolled in the pages of *New Times* he reviled in his diary. Like all self-made men, he was a confirmed skeptic; he had no use for idealism and judged men by what they did rather than what they said. His only consolation for the disappointments they caused him was a passion for art and literature.

Home in Moscow, Chekhov wrote to Alexander, asking

him to give his best to his generous hosts, and to Madame Kiselyova, joking as usual: "In my capacity as a great writer I constantly drove about Petersburg in a landau and constantly drank champagne. [. . .] For some reason they nicknamed me Potyomkin, though I have no Catherine. Obviously they consider me the favorite of the muses."[10]

The social butterfly had trouble readjusting to family life in the "chest of drawers." The household comprised eight members. Nikolai had returned and spent much of his time staggering drunk and half-naked from room to room. Ivan would come and hover over Anton from three in the afternoon until late at night. Pavel Yegorovich would drop by in the evening and start prophesying. "They're all perfectly nice and cheerful," he wrote to Alexander, "but selfish, pretentious, uncommonly talkative, noisy with their feet, and penniless . . . My head is spinning."[11] And to Leontyev-Shcheglov: "You have a *wife,* who pardons you if you have no money, but I have a *regime* that will collapse if I don't earn a given number of rubles a month, collapse and tumble down on my shoulders like a boulder."[12]

To flee the suffocating clanlike atmosphere, Chekhov took the advice of a friend, Alexander Ivanenko, and rented a dacha on the estate of the Lintvaryovs. The estate was in the Ukraine near the village Luka on the Psyol River. Even before setting off for the place, he invited Suvorin and Pleshcheev to come and stay with him, and he was worried he had acted too impulsively until, in May 1888, he actually arrived in the village. There he found a roomy, clean, well-furnished house, a gardenful of bucolic perfumes, and, in addition to the river, a verst-long pond teeming with fish. The silence immediately went to his head. He also reveled in the surrounding area: it reminded him of the even-then clichéd settings of the Russian novel with its "old, overgrown gardens, highly poetic and melancholy boarded-up manors where souls of beautiful women dwell, to say nothing of ancient moribund butlers, who look back fondly on their serf days, and of young ladies pining for the most stereotyped kind of love."[13]

Sociable as always, Chekhov was quick to make friends with the owners of the estate, the Lintvaryovs, who belonged to the fragile caste of semiruined gentry that lived as best as it could on what remained of its fortune, always putting on a brave face and keeping up its tradition of culture, hospitality, and courtesy. Madame Lintvaryova, a widow who enjoyed reading Schopenhauer in the original, was delighted to have a young and talented writer staying with them. The eldest daughter, Zinaida, was a doctor, and the peasants worshiped her as a saint. Owing to a brain tumor she was completely blind and suffered from epilepsy and constant headaches. She spoke serenely of her imminent death. The middle daughter, Yelena, was also a doctor. She was sweet, generous, and ugly, loved family life, and, according to Chekhov, "would never be happy for a moment." Natasha, the youngest and a tomboy ("bony, muscular, tan, and loud"), was a teacher with a passion for Ukrainian culture. She had built a school at her own expense and was teaching local children the fables of Krylov in Ukrainian translation. She would be happy with the most banal of loves "though she has read Marx's *Das Kapital*."[14] There were also two sons: Pavel, the elder, had been expelled from the university and led a quiet, modest life, apparently content with his lot; Yegor, the younger, followed the evangelical teachings of Tolstoy.

Chekhov was charmed by this family of high-minded individualists and their old-fashioned way of doing things; he was charmed by the cheerful, shrewd Ukrainian peasants and their quick tongues. He went for walks, bathed in the river, strolled through the bustle of local fairs, paid visits to neighboring estates, attended musical evenings, flirted with the girls, and fished for everything including crayfish.

Among Chekhov's visitors that summer the one who made the greatest impression on the Lintvaryov girls was the venerable Pleshcheev. They offered him flowers, invited him for boat rides, and sang him romances; they were touched to tears by the poems he recited to them in return. "He's the same sort of symbol here as he is in Petersburg, that is, an icon people worship because it is old and once hung side by side with won-der-working icons."[15]

Alexander, whose wife had just died, came to Luka with children in tow and immediately set to drowning his grief in vodka. He also courted Yelena Lintvaryova and even thought of asking for her hand. Chekhov went to great lengths to dis-suade him from the idea: the reckless Alexander was already considering a liaison with a certain Natalia Golden, whose mar-ried sister lived with his brother Nikolai. Everyone was im-mensely relieved when he left.

Soon Chekhov, too, would take leave of the Lintvaryovs. Despite the appeal of Luka he seemed compelled to make fre-quent changes of environment. It was as if the illness had created in him a need to see the world, convinced him that health and repose could be found only where he was not.

On July 10 he departed suddenly for Feodosia, in the Cri-mea, where the Suvorins maintained a sumptuous villa by the sea. There he spent two weeks in otiose bliss. Rising at eleven, retiring at three, and consuming only the finest of wines and delicacies in between, he managed to forget he was a writer. "I haven't written a line," he confessed to his family, "haven't earned a kopeck. If my vile languor lasts another week or two, I'll be flat broke, and the Chekhov family will have to winter in Luka."[16]

The heat was torrid. To keep cool Chekhov would bathe several times a day in the splendid—"as gentle as virgins' hair"[17]— deep-blue sea. His hostess, who had irritated him in Petersburg, amused him in Feodosia, prattling constantly, "like a canary," changing dresses by the hour, laughing in the morning, singing gypsy romances in the afternoon, and weeping on the deserted beach at night. As for Suvorin, he engaged his "protégé" in intense conversations on all kinds of topics. "I'm gradually turn-ing into a talking machine," Chekhov wrote to Leontyev-Shcheglov. "Now that we've solved all existing problems, we're starting in on problems never raised before. We talk and talk and talk; we may die of inflammation of the tongue and vocal chords." But, he added, "Suvorin is a great man. He is to art what a setter is to the hunt, that is, he has a remarkable flair and is always passionate. [. . .] Once you catch on to his way of talking and to his sincerity, which most talkers lack, the chats are almost a delight."[18]

Suvorin would have liked to keep his guest until September, but Chekhov was itching to move on. He pleaded, reasonably enough, the need to return to his work at Luka, yet with Suvorin's son, Alexei, he made a considerable detour—as far as the Caucasus. Boarding the steamboat at Feodosia, he visited the New Athos Monastery, Sukhumi, Batum, Tiflis, and Baku. Baku and its pervasive smells of oil and naphtha filled him with disgust.

By early August he was back in Luka with his friends the Lintvaryovs, and again he fell prey to the charm of the Ukrainian countryside. He even dreamed of buying a small estate in the area and setting up a small writers' colony there. But where could he find the money? The wisest plan was to return to Moscow. "Oh, how hard it is for me to leave here! Especially now, with the river more beautiful every day, the weather magnificent, the peasants bringing in the hay . . . The thought of Moscow with its cold climate, bad plays, snack bars, and Russian ideas makes my flesh creep. I wish I could spend the winter far, far away."[19]

He left for the Sadovaya-Kudrinskaya Street "chest of drawers" on September 2, weakened rather than fortified by the summer wanderings. No sooner had he returned to Moscow than he started hemorrhaging again. But if it were really consumption, he said, he would long be dead and buried. As usual, he played down the importance of the attacks. According to his own diagnosis, he displayed no other symptoms of the disease. "It scares me only when I see blood," he wrote to Suvorin. "There's something ominous about blood coming from the mouth like the glow of a fire. When there's no blood, I don't worry and don't threaten Russian literature with 'yet another loss.' "[20] Did this attitude, so strange on the part of a doctor, reflect fear of the truth or acceptance of the inevitable? One thing is certain: Chekhov refused to believe himself ill so as to savor the short time he had left to live. Without admitting it to himself, he knew that the only way for him to enjoy a semblance of happiness on earth was to live the lie of health. Only by closing his eyes to the symptoms could he maintain a desire for work, friends, success.

Once more the family's demands kept him from writing. Nikolai had no steady work or identity papers, and the police were after him for evading military service until Chekhov asked some highly placed friends to intervene on his behalf. As for Alexander, he had just had a run-in with Suvorin. When he signed a mediocre story in *New Times* as Al. Chekhov, Suvorin wrote him an indignant letter, accusing him of usurping and sullying a name worthy of respect. Since Anton stood to lose the most from it all, he too could have taken umbrage; instead, his only concern was to resolve the dispute. What is more, he sent the following melancholy message to his brother to balm his pathologically sensitive nature: "Since none of us can escape death or has long to live, I attach no serious importance to my works, my name, or my literary errors. I advise you to do the same. The simpler our view of the ticklish issues raised by Suvorin, the more straightforward our lives and relations will be. An. Chekhov or Al. Chekhov—what's the difference?"[21]

A few weeks later a drunken Alexander grossly insulted the members of the *New Times* editorial board. Anton, fearing his brother would be dismissed, wrote to Suvorin deploring the incident and trying to explain what lay at the bottom of it: "What can I do with my brother? The trouble he causes! When he's sober, he's intelligent, shy, upright, and gentle, but when he's drunk, he's impossible. [. . .] He's a heavy drinker—of that there's no doubt. But what does it mean? It's as much a psychosis as morphine addiction, onanism, nymphomania, and the like. It is usually passed on from the father or mother, grandfather or grandmother, but our line has no drunkards. Every once in a while my grandfather and father drank heavily with their guests, but it never kept them from attending to work or waking up in time for matins. Liquor made them equable and witty; it cheered their hearts and stimulated their minds. My teacher brother and I never drink solo; we know nothing about liquor and can drink as much as we please and wake up with a clear head. [. . .] Alexander and the artist are drunk out of their minds after two or three glasses, and there are times when they crave drink . . . Whom they take after, I don't know. I only know that Alexander always has a reason for drinking: he gets drunk when he's unhappy or discouraged about something. I haven't got his address. If it's not too much trouble, please send it to me. I'll write him a diplomatically-abusively-gentle letter. My letters have an effect on him."[22]

In the midst of these family worries Chekhov received an unexpected piece of good news. He had just sent off "a slightly tendentious" story ("The Name-Day Party") to the *Northern Herald* and was reworking *Ivanov* when, on October 7, 1888, he was amazed to learn that the Literary Section of the Academy of Sciences in Saint Petersburg had unanimously awarded him the Pushkin Prize for his collection *At Twilight*. He was overjoyed, "as if in love." The whole family was ecstatic. "Mother and Father are saying the most ridiculous things and are unutterably happy," he wrote to Suvorin. "My sister [. . .] is making the rounds of her friends to proclaim the news. [. . .] I feel so lucky that I'm beginning to squint guiltily at the skies. I think I'll run and hide under a table and sit there quietly, submissively, keeping my voice down. [. . .] I'm going to put the five hundred rubles aside for a farmstead in the Ukraine." In the same letter he wrote, "Everything I have written, everything I received the prize for, will live no more than ten years in people's memories."[23]

To Grigorovich, a member of the Academy and the man he felt beholden to for the prize, he poured out his gratitude like a novice. He promised to set to work on a novel, but made it clear that like the rest of his works it would not take a partisan position on the issues of the day. "I still lack a political, religious, and philosophical world view—I change it every month, so I'll have to limit myself to the description of how my heroes love, marry, give birth, die, and how they speak."[24]

In spite of the prize and the receptions, banquets, and speeches

that went along with it, Chekhov could not decide whether he
was a doctor or a writer. Referring to the comparison he liked
to make between his legal wife, medicine, and his mistress,
literature, he wrote to Suvorin, "When one gets on my nerves,
I spend the night with the other. It may be somewhat disor-
ganized, but it's less boring that way."[25] Besides, he found the
world of the other young writers distasteful. He hated their
clans, their intrigues, their fierce ambitions and bowing and
scraping; he felt they would go to any lengths to attract flattering
notices. How could they be so eager for fame when he, after
eight years of writing, was still unsure about what made him
write?

Far from joining a malevolent clique, Chekhov remained
independent, his own modest man. "Let's be ordinary people,
let's treat everybody alike," he wrote to Leontyev-Shcheglov,
"and there won't be any need for trumped-up solidarity."[26] And
to Pleshcheev, in stronger terms: "The people I fear are those
who look for tendentiousness between the lines and are determined to see me as either liberal or conservative. I am neither
liberal, nor conservative, nor gradualist, nor monk, nor indif-
ferentist. I should like to be a free artist and nothing else, and
I regret God has not given me the strength to be one. I hate
lies and violence in all their forms. [. . .] Pharisaism, dull-
wittedness, and tyranny reign not only in merchants' homes
and police stations; I see them in science, in literature, among
the younger generation. That is why I cultivate no particular
predilection for policemen, butchers, scientists, writers, or the
younger generation. I look upon tags and labels as prejudices.
My holy of holies is the human body, health, intelligence, talent,
inspiration, love, and the most absolute freedom imaginable,
freedom from violence and lies."[27]

Total independence—he not only advocated it to his fellow
writers, his critics, and the public; he also applied it to his
characters. Following the example of Pushkin and the pre-
conversion Tolstoy, he felt his place was to state problems, not
solve them. No veiled preaching. No message. No ulterior
motives. Just life. A writer was at the service of his characters

and not vice versa; he had to be brave enough to choose between their presence and his. By intervening to explain, judge, condemn, or absolve them, he overstepped his bounds as a writer. The more he hid behind them, the more likely they were to survive him. "In my opinion," he wrote to Suvorin, "it is not the writer's job to solve such problems as God, pessimism, etc.; his job is merely to record who, under what conditions, said or thought what about God or pessimism. The artist is not meant to be a judge of his characters and what they say; his only job is to be an impartial witness. [. . .] Drawing conclusions is up to the jury, that is, the readers. My only job is to be talented, that is, to know how to distinguish important testimony from unimportant, to place my characters in the proper light and speak their language."[28] A few months later he was still making his point to Suvorin: "It is bad for the artist to take on something he doesn't understand. We have specialists for dealing with special questions; it is their job to make judgments about peasant communes, the fate of capitalism, the evils of intemperance, about boots and female complaints. The artist must pass judgment only on what he understands."[29]

Chekhov's concern for objectivity in literature did not in the least imply a lack of concern for the choice of detail in a descriptive passage or in dialogue. But while Chekhov called himself a realist, he was actually moving in the direction of impressionism, of light touches, airy dabs, evanescent hints. He wrote to Lazarev-Gruzinsky to avoid the conventional: "You do too much polishing and furbishing, and you make sure to put everything you think daring and harsh in parentheses and quotation marks. [. . .] You don't give your temperament free rein. That's why your devices lack originality. You must describe your women in such a way that the reader feels your tie is off and your waistcoat open. Women and nature both. Let yourself go."[30]

The freedom to let oneself go, the refusal to preach politics or philosophy or to give in to the constraints of literary schools, the willingness to make one's own steadfast yet modest way— such was the catechism of the true writer according to Chekhov.

His reserve and utter lack of preconceived notions come across clearly in a letter to Pleshcheev about his story "The Name-Day Party": "The way I see it, I can be accused of gluttony, drunkenness, frivolity, coldness—of anything at all rather than wishing to seem or not to seem. I've never been secretive."[31]

While defending the principle of nonengagement for the novelist and short-story writer, Chekhov never forgot his allegiance to the theater. There, too, nonengagement was the golden rule. Much as he cursed the state of the theater, he could not escape the lure of the greasepaint. "We must do whatever we can to see that the theater passes from the hands of the grocers to the hands of writers and critics. Otherwise it is doomed,"[32] he wrote to Suvorin. And to Leontyev-Shcheglov: "Contemporary theater is a rash, a serious disease of the cities. It must be done away with; loving it is unhealthy."[33]

For all that, he was never anything less than an assiduous playgoer, and enjoyed spending evenings with actors. He continued to write hilarious curtain raisers like *The Swan Song* and *The Proposal,* and even dusted off *Ivanov,* hoping to clarify its meaning with each new variant. "My Mr. Ivanov is much more comprehensible now,"[34] he wrote to Suvorin. The revised little Sasha, he claimed, was an entirely new character, one of those women "who love men as they are about to go under." As for Ivanov, he now killed himself not so much because he had been publicly slandered and insulted as because he had "reached the end of the road." Furthermore, Chekhov saw Ivanov's character as quintessentially Russian. "Lethargy, heightened excitability, and a feeling of guilt are purely Russian traits," he wrote to Suvorin. "Germans never get excited, so Germany has no disappointed, superfluous, or lethargic people . . . The excitability of the French remains at the same level, never rising or falling abruptly, so the Frenchman remains his usual excited self quite into senility."[35]

When the revised *Ivanov* entered the repertory of the prestigious Alexandrinsky Theater in Petersburg, Chekhov went to the capital to attend rehearsals. All his doubts, anxieties, and anger immediately returned. Again he deplored the actors' approach. To make matters worse, Davydov, in the title role, kept complaining of last-minute changes and threatening to resign. Chekhov made desperate attempts to reason with him, to explain the motivating forces behind his character. The two men quarreled and made peace ten times a day. But Davydov remained so full of himself that Chekhov feared the worst. The evening before opening night he wrote to Mikhail that as far as he could tell the play was doomed.

But not only was *Ivanov* far from doomed, it turned out to be a smashing success. At the end of the premiere, knees weak, heart pounding, Chekhov joined the actors to the ovation of the audience. Next day there was a banquet in his honor, and the host, raising his glass, compared him to the immortal playwright Griboedov. Flustered by the unexpected triumph, Chekhov left immediately for Moscow. He felt like hiding in a hole, he claimed. "As for the success and applause," he wrote to Leontyev-Shcheglov, "it's so noisy and unsatisfying that it only wears you out and makes you want to run and run . . ."[36]

Even so, he perused the reviews avidly. On the whole, the press agreed with the public and praised the play. Only the leftist critics—Mikhailovsky, Korolenko, Uspensky—made negative comments, upbraiding him for failing to make a social statement. The accusation did not in the least upset him; indeed, it confirmed him in his belief that art and politics must remain separate. Besides, people who had seen the play sent letters congratulating him on having created real characters, characters who reflected the sensibility of the times. Leskov noted in his diary: "An intelligent play. A great dramatic talent."

The play grew daily in popularity. The house was full night after night—sweet revenge after the recent Moscow failure. *Ivanov* was a must, "a colossal, phenomenal success," as Chekhov put it in a letter to Madame Kiselyova. "Petersburg has two current heroes: Semiradsky's *Phryna Naked** and me dressed. We're all the rage."[37]

*A painting on exhibit at the Academy of Fine Arts in Petersburg.

But the jaunty tone masked a desire to flee the vain glamour of the moment for a place in the country where he might spend as much time as he liked at his favorite sport: fishing. "A sprawl in the hay and a perch on the line give me much more palpable satisfaction than reviews and applause,"[38] he wrote to Leontyev-Shcheglov. More and more his letters showed signs of disenchantment and bitterness. "Whom and what do I write for? The audience? But I don't see my audiences and believe in them less than I believe in spirits: they are uneducated, ill-mannered, and even their finest elements are unscrupulous and insincere in their dealings with us. Does the audience need me or not? I can't make it out. [. . .] All in all, my life bores me, and I'm beginning to develop aversions, which is new for me. The long, stupid talks, the guests, the suppliants, the handouts of one, two, and three rubles, the cab fares for patients who never pay a thing—in short, a mess that makes me want to chuck it all and run. People borrow money without paying it back, go off with my books, waste my time . . . All I need is an unhappy affair."[39]

At the time Chekhov showed little inclination towards affairs, happy or unhappy. Attentive as he was to the friends his sister Maria brought home, he never allowed his courting to take a serious turn. He was charmed, for example, by the pretty Lydia Mizinova, known as Lika, a buxom eighteen-year-old with a fair complexion, blond hair, and bright gray eyes, a teacher's assistant at the school where Maria taught geography and history. Chekhov won her over by his talent, regular features, and gentle smile, but the more interest she showed in him, the more evasive and mocking he became. Then there was Maria's mathematician friend, the remarkable Olga Kundasova, who had an attractive—though slightly heavy and mannish— face and paid no attention whatever to fashion, always wearing the same black, white-collared dress pulled in at the waist with a wide leather belt. She had a passion for astronomy—Chekhov called her "the astronomer"—and was passionate and sincere by nature. At the first hint that she felt something more than friendship for him, he withdrew. Women frightened him or, rather, he feared increasing his already numerous worries by latching on to one of them.

Scandalous rumors about him began circulating in Moscow and Petersburg. They insinuated that he had sold out to Suvorin, the aristocracy's henchman, that is, had promised to marry Suvorin's daughter—she was still only ten—and was soon to sit on the editorial board of Suvorin's *New Times*. Pleshcheev, alarmed by what he heard, warned Chekhov that collaboration with a paper so intimately associated with the powers that be would place him squarely and permanently in the camp of the reactionaries. "I'm annoyed at the gossip," Chekhov replied, "not because *you* write to me about it but because *everybody* is writing about it and the students repeat it: they're all going on about my marrying into millions. Pure depravity!"[40]

Nor did his family give him any respite. The turbulent Alexander, now well into his thirties, refused to mend his ways. During his December visit to Petersburg Chekhov had been horrified to see him parade half-drunk and in his underwear before the cook and hurl filthy abuse at his new mistress in front of the children. "Pardon my saying so, but treating women like that, no matter who they are, is unworthy of a decent, loving human being. What heavenly or earthly power has given you the right to make them your slaves? Constant profanity of the most vile variety, a raised voice, reproaches, sudden whims at breakfast and dinner, eternal complaints about a life of forced and loathsome labor—isn't all that an expression of blatant despotism? No matter how insignificant or guilty a woman is, no matter how close to you she is, you have no right to sit around without trousers in her presence, be drunk in her presence, utter words even factory workers don't use when they see women nearby. You think of decency and good breeding as prejudices, but you have to draw the line somewhere—at feminine frailty perhaps, or the children, or the poetry of life if there's no prose left. [. . .] Children are sacred and pure. [. . .] You must not make them playthings of your moods, tenderly kissing them one minute and frenziedly stamping at them the next. It is better not to love at all than to love with a despotic love."[41]

Nikolai, the likable drunkard, presented an even greater problem. The family had long been anxious about his health, but it took a sudden turn for the worse in March 1889: he contracted typhus. Chekhov immediately treated him but, after curing him of the typhus, found him to be tubercular. When consultations with colleagues confirmed his findings, he decided to try a rest cure, and set off with his patient for the Luka dacha, which he had rented again from the Lintvaryovs. There he was happy to find spring at its height—the apple and cherry trees in blossom, the nightingales and cuckoos in voice—and his dear friends overjoyed to see him.

The cheerful mood did not last long. Nikolai grew weaker and more feverish from day to day; soon he was unable to lie down, and had to sleep in an armchair. Watching him waste away, Chekhov could not help contemplating his own case. His capricious, irascible brother gave him a lugubrious premonition—or prefiguration—of his own end. "Nikolai has a chronic pulmonary process, an incurable disease," he wrote to Alexander. "There are temporary improvements, deteriorations, and in situs, but the real question is not so much 'When will he recover?' as 'How long will the process last?' "[42] And a week later to Suvorin: "My painter will never recover. He has consumption. The only question is how long the disease will go on."[43]

Confined to his brother's bedside, Chekhov tried to forget his anguish by reading. Goncharov's *Oblomov* disappointed him, larger-than-life Gogol was a "sheer delight," and *The Disciple* by the contemporary French novelist Paul Bourget seemed interesting and intelligent in its way, yet false and harmful. He could not understand the need for its "pretentious crusade against materialist doctrine." "Prohibiting materialist doctrine is tantamount to preventing man from seeking the truth. Outside of matter there is no experience or knowledge, and consequently no truth. [. . .] It seems to me that when a corpse is being dissected even the most inveterate spiritualist must *necessarily* come up against the question of where the soul is."[44]

Nikolai grew more affectionate and more resigned as his strength failed him. But while Chekhov pitied him with all his heart, he suffered greatly from being nailed to the spot, and dreamed guiltily of a change of scene, a chance to put spittoon and dirty linen behind him. "I'd be glad to run off to Paris and have a look at the universe from the height of the Eiffel Tower," he confessed to the writer Vladimir Tikhonov, "but alas, I'm bound hand and foot."[45]

In mid-June Alexander joined him at Luka. Ivan had preceded him. Assured of regular relief, Chekhov felt free to take a break, and left for Poltava to spend four or five days with his friends the Smagins. He ran into a bad storm on the way—a celestial punishment for having deserted his post, he said—and the day after he arrived a peasant delivered a dripping-wet telegram from town with the message "Kolya deceased." Although the news of Nikolai's death came as no surprise, he was shattered. He set out immediately, in the rain, for the nearest railway station. The cold and windy trip back was extremely unpleasant. He had to change trains, and waited from seven in the evening until two in the morning for the connection, exhausted and chilled to the bone, sitting in a park and listening to a group of actors rehearse a melodrama on the other side of a wall.

When he arrived at last in Luka, he found his brothers grief-stricken. "We are crushed," Alexander wrote to his father on June 19, "and choked with tears. Everyone is weeping. Only Anton's eyes are dry. It's a bad sign." Chekhov, for his part, wrote to Pleshcheev, "Our family has never known death before; it's the first time we've seen a coffin at home."[46] Though still exhausted, Chekhov saw to all the formalities. According to local custom, Nikolai's body was carried to the village church and from there to the cemetery, where it was buried "under the honey-scented grass." "Whatever faults he may have had," Chekhov wrote to a close friend of Nikolai's, "he expiated them by the sufferings [of his last days]."[47]

Meditating on the void left by his brother, Chekhov felt

both shamefully relieved and deeply despondent. "I felt so miserable that I couldn't stand summer, the dacha, or the river."[48] Yet he also felt bad about leaving the family in mourning and put off departure until July 2. Departure for where? He needed to get away, but could not decide on a destination. The Caucasus? France? Austria? (The Suvorins had invited him to Vienna.) In the end, he went to Odessa, where an actor friend Alexander Lensky was on tour with the Maly Theater. As it turned out, the carefree and rather harebrained group of actors helped to put him back on his feet. He took a room in their hotel, bathed daily in the sea, ate huge amounts of ice cream, and, after attending the evening performance, stayed up until two talking to his friends. One of the actresses was amazed that a man like Chekhov, who wore a gray suit and boasted such fine manners, could munch away at sunflower seeds like the lowest peasant. After about ten days, however, he grew tired of the cackling in even this most pleasant of coops and decided to move on to Yalta. The Maly company saw him down to the boat and gave him two neckties for a farewell present.

Once actually in Yalta, Chekhov could not fathom why he had come. The heat was smothering, and he was besieged by admirers. "I swim in the morning, die of heat in the afternoon, drink wine in the evening, and sleep at night," he wrote to Pleshcheev. "The sea is magnificent, the vegetation pitiful. The place is full of Jews. Every day I plan to leave and can't seem to. But I must. My conscience is bothering me. I'm a little ashamed of playing the sybarite when things are bad at home."[49]

The heat and the fascination of an endless stretch of blue sea did not keep him from writing the major part of a curious work, "A Dreary Story." "It's a weighty piece, weighty enough to kill a man," he announced to the writer Vladimir Tikhonov from Moscow on September 13, "but with the quality not quantity of pages. It's awkward and clumsy. I touch on a new theme." The "new theme," as he informed the editor in chief of the *Northern Herald,* was the "miserable state of mind I couldn't shake off all summer." But when writing to Suvorin, he maintained with the same conviction that he shared no part of his hero's ideas: "If someone serves you coffee, don't try to look for beer in it. If I present you with the professor's ideas, have confidence in me and don't look for Chekhovian ideas in them. No, thank you. In the whole story there is only one idea that I share, the idea that obsesses the professor's son-in-law, that swindler Gnecker, namely, 'The old man's losing his mind!' Everything else I've made up and invented."[50]

There is in fact a good deal of invention in "A Dreary Story." Feeling he will soon die, a much honored and much put-upon professor, Nikolai Stepanovich by name, sums up a lifetime of activity and comes to the conclusion that the life he has lived—his love of science; his behavior towards his wife, his daughter, and his ward Katya; his views on colleagues and students; his writings; his apparent success—is totally "senseless." Faced with the evidence of his spiritual bankruptcy, he can no longer stand the presence of his dear ones. He even breaks with Katya, his favorite, and flees to await death in a hotel room in provincial Kharkov.

Chekhov's allegations notwithstanding, the old professor's anguish and solitude bear a close resemblance to his own distress at the time. He, too, suffered from the lack of an idea, knew the vanity of success, and looked upon death with the cold serenity of an agnostic. His brother's premature death, far from bringing him closer to God, had convinced him that the absolute was unknowable and man's destiny opened onto a void.

There were those who made unfavorable comparisons with Tolstoy's *The Death of Ivan Ilyich,* published three years earlier, and both works do force their heroes to confront the idea of death. But in Tolstoy the confrontation, horrifying as it may prove to the hero, ends with the discovery of a supernatural light, while in Chekhov the professor receives no reassurance and must face the certitude of the coming night on his own. Here, as in other works, Chekhov the skeptic would seem to clash with Tolstoy the believer. Yet while the former went through life with a dignified and serene lack of faith, the latter was tortured by his faith, preaching abstinence from earthly joys for the salvation of the soul.

Much as Chekhov had foreseen, the critics were rather hard on "A Dreary Story." Nonetheless, the eminent Mikhailovsky, who until then had proved all but impervious to Chekhov's craft, praised it in the following terms: "If the story is so beautiful and so true to life, it is because the author has endowed it with his own sufferings." And Pleshcheev, in a letter to Chekhov dated September 27, wrote, "You have never written anything *so strong and deep* as this work. The tone of the old scholar is marvelously well kept up, and even the arguments with a subjective ring to them, your own, do not damage the whole."

As the early reactions to "A Dreary Story" came in, Chekhov was at work on a play, *The Wood Demon.* His initial intention had been to write it in collaboration with Suvorin, but when Suvorin proved too busy with another project, he decided to go it alone. Taking a tack diametrically opposed to *Ivanov,* he tried to avoid all "dramatic" turns of events, all *coups de théâtre,* and replace external with internal action; he wanted to win over his audience with psychology rather than stage business. In other words, he hoped to re-create on the stage the tour de force he had created on paper in "A Dreary Story."

The play was ready on October 5, 1889. Chekhov immediately submitted it first to the censor, then to the literary board of the Alexandrinsky Theater in Petersburg. The board rejected it "for want of effects, situations, and interesting characters." "Let me give you a piece of advice," Lensky told him. "Write a story. You have too much scorn for the stage and dramatic form; you don't value them enough to write a play. Writing plays is more difficult than writing fiction, and, if I may say so, you are too spoiled by success to embark on a thorough study of the theater." The playwright Vladimir Nemirovich-Danchenko, who had also read the play, seconded Lensky's view, but added, "I did not notice any scorn, though, simply lack of knowledge."

While surprised by the verdict, Chekhov put on a brave front and thanked Lensky for his letter, assuring him that, apart from curtain raisers like *The Wedding,* he would no longer write for the theater. Behind the bravado, however, he was deeply wounded. In a letter to Suvorin he likened the board's decision to "a court-martial brought against me and my *Wood Demon*."[51] What irritated him most was a rumor making the rounds in Petersburg that old Professor Serebryakov, one of the characters in *The Wood Demon,* was meant to caricature Suvorin. "How they would all rejoice if I slipped arsenic in your tea or turned out to be a Third Department [political police] spy. [. . .] It's all trivia, I agree. But it's the sort of trivia that makes the world fall apart."[52]

By then he had lost all confidence in the play, yet he reworked it according to Nemirovich-Danchenko's suggestions and submitted it to the Abramov Theater in Moscow, which finally decided in its favor. Opening night took place on December 27, 1889. The critics, unable to accept a play that ran counter to the rules and claimed to reproduce life in all its banality, loosed their fury on it. Chekhov got the message; he put the play in a drawer and refused permission to publish it. Years later he took it out again and turned it into one of his masterpieces, *Uncle Vanya.*

Nikolai's death, the poor critical response to "A Dreary Story," and the utter failure of *The Wood Demon* had begun eating away at his moral resiliency. There were some bright spots—he made friends with Tchaikovsky, for instance—but he tended towards pessimism and misanthropy. His contemporaries disappointed him, especially Tolstoy: he admired Tolstoy the artist, but could not accept Tolstoy the thinker. He faulted the old master's most recent work, *The Kreutzer Sonata,* for fighting a false battle. "There is one thing I am unwilling to pardon the author," he wrote to Pleshcheev, "namely, the audacity with which he treats topics about which he knows nothing and which out of obstinacy he does not wish to understand. For example, his opinions of syphilis, foundling homes, women's aversion to sexual intercourse, and so on are not only debatable, they expose him as an ignorant man who has never at any point in his long life taken the trouble to read two or three books written by specialists."[53] With his scientific background Chekhov could not accept Tolstoy's willful obscurantism. He was no more lenient towards Dostoevsky, of whom he wrote to Suvorin, "He's all right, but it's all so long and ostentatious. Pretentious, too."[54]

Nor did he feel close to woolly-minded liberals. He respected intelligence but mistrusted the intelligentsia. "Our sluggish, apathetic, cold-blooded intellectuals are full of idle philosophizing and unable to come up with even a decent banknote specimen; they are unpatriotic, gloomy, colorless, get drunk on a tiny glassful, go to fifty-kopeck brothels, grouse all the time, renounce *everything* (because a lazy brain finds it easier to reject than confirm), refuse to marry and bring up children, etc. Sluggish souls, sluggish muscles, general inertia, shaky ideas . . ."[55]

And finally, he was dissatisfied with himself. "You need equanimity in this world," he wrote to Suvorin. "Only people with equanimity can see things clearly, be fair and work. [. . .] The fire in me burns with an even, lethargic flame; it never flares up or roars, which is why I never end up writing fifty or sixty pages in one night or getting so involved in my work that I force myself to stay awake; it's why I never do anything outstandingly stupid or notably intelligent. [. . .] I have very little passion."[56] He was to repeat these last words often during his career. Several months later he gave Suvorin a somber self-portrait: "I long to hole up somewhere for five years and do some serious, meticulous work. I need to study, learn everything from scratch, because as a writer I'm a complete ignoramus; I need to write conscientiously, with feeling and intelligence, not five quires a month but one quire every five months."[57] And also: "In January I'm turning thirty. Hail, lonely old age; burn, useless life!"[58]

Then, all of a sudden, a spark lit up the gloom. Towards the end of 1889 Chekhov happened to pick up some notes Mikhail had taken at a course on criminal law. "We focus all our attention on the criminal before his sentence is handed down," he muttered. "Once he's in prison, we forget about him entirely. But what does happen in prison?" From that moment he could not get the idea out of his head. His place was not in Moscow. He would break with the world of gossip and tinsel and go off to Siberia; he would erase the faces made by jealous writers and confront true suffering; he would go to the Island of Sakhalin, a Russian penal colony in the Pacific just north of Japan. The more arduous the journey, the more it tempted him. At last he had a goal and could face the future with interest and pride!

VIII

From Sakhalin to Paris

All Chekhov's friends found his scheme absurd. How could a man in such fragile health, a man who lived for his art, undertake so risky and needless a journey? By way of self-justification he invoked his disgust with literary infighting, his need for a change of scene, his responsibility as a writer to experience Russian reality in all its horror, his interest in the possibility of doing a scientific study of the convicts in Siberia. Diverse as his arguments were, they reinforced one another in his mind.

There were those, however, who wondered whether he was not scurrying off to the other end of the world to overcome a disappointment of the heart. And there was at least one woman who was certain of it. Her name was Lydia Avilova.

Forty-three years after his death she claimed in her memoirs that Chekhov had been wildly in love with her and that he had fled to Sakhalin in desperation.[1] For want of proof she supported her case with no end of retrospective rapture. When she first met Chekhov, in 1889, she was the twenty-six-year-old wife of a civil servant, pretty, slim, and blonde, with a baby (two more were to follow), an active imagination, and a facile pen. She wrote lifeless stories and dreamed of insinuating herself into the literary world. At that first meeting—it took place at a Petersburg salon—she felt "something burst in her soul." The feeling was evidently not mutual, because when Chekhov returned to Petersburg the following year he did not make any attempt to see her. She wrote him a letter; he did not respond. Three years later he made a rather brash apology: "I once received a letter from you in which you asked about the idea behind a worthless story I had written. Since I did not know you well at the time and had forgotten that your married name was Avilova, I threw the letter away and pocketed the stamp. That is what I usually do with requests, especially when they come from the ladies."[2]

If an element of disappointment did in fact enter into Chekhov's desire to take flight, it had more to do with matters moral and literary than with matters of the heart. Dissatisfied with the direction his life and his work had taken, he felt compelled to turn his back on the daily grind, withdraw from the world, wrench himself into regeneration. To Suvorin, who tried till the end to dissuade him from the venture, he wrote: "I am going there absolutely secure in the thought that my journey will make no valuable contributions to literature or science. [. . .] I want to write at least one or two hundred pages to pay off some of my debt to medicine, towards which, as you know, I've behaved like a swine. [. . .] Besides, the journey, as I see it, means six months' continuous physical and mental labor, something I absolutely need, because I'm from the south and have begun to grow lazy. I need to discipline myself. Granted, my journey may be trifling, hardheaded, capricious, but think a while and tell me what I stand to lose by going. [. . .] You write, for instance, that Sakhalin is of no use or interest to anyone. Is that really so? Sakhalin could be of no use or interest only to a society that doesn't deport thousands of people to it and doesn't spend millions on it. Except for Australia in the past and Cayenne, Sakhalin is the only place where the use of convicts for colonization can be studied. [. . .] Sakhalin is a place of unbearable suffering, the sort of suffering only man, whether free or subjugated, is capable of. The people who work near it or on it have been trying to solve problems involving frightening responsibility; they are still trying. I'm sorry I'm not sentimental or I'd say that we ought to make pilgrimages to places like Sakhalin the way the Turks go to Mecca. Moreover, sailors and penologists ought to regard Sakhalin the way the military regard Sevastopol. From the books I've read and am now reading, it is evident that we have let *millions* of people rot in jails, we have let them rot to no purpose, unthinkingly and barbarously. We have driven people through the cold, in chains, across tens of thousands of versts, we have infected them with syphilis, debauched them, bred criminals, and blamed it all on red-nosed prison wardens. Now all educated Europe knows that we, not the wardens, are to blame, but it's still none of our business, of no interest to us. The much-glorified sixties [the period of reforms] did *nothing* for the sick and people in prison and thereby violated the chief commandment of Christian civilization. In our time a few things are being done for the sick, but nothing at all for the prisoners; prison management holds absolutely no interest for our jurists. No, I assure you, Sakhalin is of great use and interest, and the only sad part of it all is that I'm the one who's going and not someone more conversant with the problems and capable of arousing public interest. I myself am going there on a trivial pretext."[3]

Once he had made up his mind to do a methodical study of the convicts on Sakhalin, Chekhov made a point of perusing all the pertinent references. Maria and her friends spent hours in the Rumyantsev Library copying out key passages from the works he indicated, and Alexander did research for him in the Petersburg newspaper collections. With his head chock-full of reports and statistics, Chekhov came to think of himself as more geographer, geologist, meteorologist, and ethnologist than writer, and announced he was suffering from a new disease, *mania sachalinosa*.

Yet he still found time to publish his seventh book of stories, *Morose People,* which he dedicated to Tchaikovsky, and to send Suvorin a longish story entitled "The Demons" (later retitled "The Thieves"). It tells of two brazen, crafty horse thieves who dupe a foolish, bombastic medical attendant. When Suvorin dropped a mild comment as to how Chekhov had failed to come down hard enough on the thieves, Chekhov responded with a vehement statement about the need for an author to remain impartial in his treatment of characters: "You scold me for my objectivity, calling it indifference to good and evil, the absence of ideals and ideas, and so on and so forth. When I describe my horse thieves, you want me to state: stealing horses is evil. But nobody needs me to tell him that. Let juries judge horse thieves; my job is simply to show what they're like. So I write: if you have dealings with horse thieves, what you ought to know is that they're no beggars and have plenty to eat, that they make a cult of what they do, and that horse thievery is more than stealing, it's a passion. Oh, it would be fine to combine art and preaching, but personally I find it extremely difficult, all but impossible, for technical reasons. If I'm going to describe my horse thieves in seven hundred lines, I must speak and think as they do, feel as they do. If I added a speck of subjectivity, the images would come apart and the story would lack the compactness stories of that length need. When I write, I rely on the reader, assuming he will supply the subjective elements missing in the story."[4]

Whether convinced or not of the need for creative objectivity, Suvorin was clearly unconvinced of the need for the Sakhalin venture. Yet he was generous with his assistance, putting Chekhov up when he came to Petersburg for the preliminary procedures, and providing him with a *New Times* press card and entrée to influential friends in the government. The highest official Chekhov met during his stay there was Galkin-Vrasky, the director of the National Prison Administration.

Galkin-Vrasky gave him a friendly reception and appeared interested in the project, though he gave him neither advice nor letters of recommendation. What he did do the moment Chekhov was out of the door was to write a note to the Director of Prisons on Sakhalin forbidding Chekhov to question political prisoners.

Chekhov returned to Moscow just in time for a round of student demonstrations, the issues being complete autonomy for the university, the admission of Jews without quotas, and the abolition of police surveillance. There were stormy rallies, confrontations with the Cossacks, arbitrary arrests. Chekhov followed the events with interest, but did not show open sympathy for the rioters. Apparently he still felt as he had when he was a student, namely, that young people should see to their education, not to public affairs.

As the departure date drew closer—he planned to set out in early spring, when the Siberian rivers had thawed—he drew up a merciless inventory of his life and works. He reiterated his belief that the writer had no business lecturing the reader, and pointed out that he himself was a man like any other, a man whose principal quality happened to be the absence of animosity towards his fellow man. "If I can trust my clear conscience," he wrote to Leontyev-Shcheglov, "never in my life have I in word, deed, or thought, in my stories or farces coveted my neighbor's wife, nor his manservant, nor his ox, nor any of his cattle; nor have I ever stolen, or played the hypocrite, or flattered the strong, or sought any advantage from them, or engaged in blackmail, or lived at another's expense. True, I have wasted my life in idleness, laughed mindlessly, made a glutton of myself, and indulged in drunkenness and fornication, but all that is my personal affair and doesn't deprive me of the right to think that as far as morality is concerned I am distinguished from the ranks by neither pluses nor minuses, neither feats nor infamies: I am just like the majority."[5]

Soon after sending off this confession, Chekhov read a violent article in the literary journal *Russian Thought* accusing him of being "a writer with no principles." The article was by the editor of the journal, Vukol Lavrov. Chekhov was in the habit of turning the other cheek, but Lavrov's approach so infuriated him he could not help striking back. "Criticism usually goes unanswered, but in this instance it seems a question not of criticism but of libel, plain and simple. I might have let even libel go by, except that in a few days I shall be leaving Russia for an extended period, perhaps never to return, and I lack the strength to refrain from responding. I have never been an unprincipled writer or, what amounts to the same thing, a scoundrel. [. . .] I have written many stories and editorials that I should be only too glad to throw out for their worthlessness, but there is not a line I need be ashamed of today. [. . .] I have led a secluded life to date, shut up within four walls. [. . .] I have always made a point of avoiding literary soirées, parties, conferences, etc. I never show my face in editorial offices without an invitation, I've always tried to have my friends think of me more as a doctor than a writer—in short, I have been a modest writer, and the letter I am writing you now is the first immodest act I have committed in my ten years as a writer. [. . .] It goes without saying that after your accusation all professional relations between us and even conventional social relations are impossible."[6]

With that load off his mind he could go back to his travel plans. He laughed off his friends' worries about the dangers ahead, claiming that his only worry was the toothache he had been prey to for the past few days. He did, however, write to Suvorin, "Should I drown or have some other sort of accident, please keep in mind that everything I have and may have in future belongs to my sister. She will pay my debts."[7] Then he packed the heavy leather trunk Mikhail had given him with enough recently acquired gear to make him the perfect Siberian explorer: a sheepskin coat, a waterproof officer's greatcoat, a pair of boots, a revolver, and a long knife "for cutting sausages and chasing tigers." Suvorin had complied with his request for a fifteen-hundred ruble advance on the "travel impressions" he would be sending to *New Times*.

The departure date was set for April 21, 1890. On that

evening the entire family and several friends saw him off at
Moscow's Yaroslavl Station. Everyone chattered nervously in
the waiting room, trying to mask the sadness of the occasion.
Dr. Kuvshinnikov gave the traveler a flask of cognac and made
him swear not to drink a drop before reaching the Pacific.
Anton's mother and sister were in tears. Charming Lika Mizinova did her best to smile; that morning Chekhov had dedicated a photograph to her with the ironic inscription: "To the
wonderful creature who is making me flee to Sakhalin." At the
last moment Ivan, Levitan, and Olga Kundasova, the impetuous
astronomer who was still secretly in love with Chekhov, took
it into their heads to follow him into the train and accompany
him as far as Sergeevo, a village sixty-six versts outside of
Moscow. Chekhov's itinerary was as follows: Moscow to Yaroslavl by train, Yaroslavl to Perm by boat (along the Volga
and Kama), Perm to Tyumen by train, Tyumen to Lake Baikal
in the springless carriage known as a tarantass, and Lake Baikal
to the Pacific by boat and tarantass. It was enough to rattle the
bones of the most rugged of travelers—a journey of nearly ten
thousand versts, four thousand of which had to be covered in
a contraption only slightly more sophisticated than a cart.

On the boat from Yaroslavl to Perm Chekhov found a kind
of peace, or rather an absence of either joy or depression. The
countryside was dull, however, and his soul felt as if it were
"in aspic." "When a cold wind blows and ripples the water,
which now, after the spring floods, is the color of coffee dregs,
I feel cold, bored, and distressed. The concertinas along the
banks have a mournful ring to them, the figures standing motionless in torn sheepskin on the barges seem numb from endless
grief. The towns along the Kama are gray; their inhabitants
seem to be engaged in making clouds, boredom, wet fences,
and mud for the streets."[8] He did, however, enjoy seeing a
fellow passenger, a public prosecutor, read *At Twilight* in the
ship's library and discuss it with his companions.

From Perm he took the train to Yekaterinburg, where he
booked a room at the Hotel America: he needed a rest, needed
to soothe his "coughing, hemorrhoidal body." As soon as he

felt better, he went on by train to Tyumen, the end of the line (the Trans-Siberian Railway had not yet been built). There, on May 3, he first laid eyes on the great Siberian plain.

The next leg of the journey consisted in proceeding across the plain, as far as Tomsk, in a tumbledown tarantass ("the wicker basket" as Chekhov called it) harnessed to two horses and driven by an old coachman. Shut up in the tarantass, he saw himself as a goldfinch in a cage peering blankly at the world through bars. An icy wind chafed his cheeks, and he shivered with cold in spite of his new leather greatcoat. He wore two pairs of trousers to keep his legs warm. Each jolt went straight to the small of his back. "On and on we go," he wrote to his sister. "The milestones, puddles, birch stands flash by . . . We overtook some settlers just now, and then a group of convicts . . . We've met tramps with mess tins on their backs. These gentlemen stroll unimpeded along the length of the Siberian road. They'll slit some old crone's neck to make foot-windings of her skirt or tear the tin marker off a milestone—you never know when it will come in handy—bash in the head of a wandering beggar, or gouge out the eyes of a fellow exile, but they never touch travelers."[9]

Exhausted by the bumps and deafened by the monotonous ring of the bells, he wondered whether he had it in him to hold out to the end. The torture was to last twelve days, and at the end of three his back so ached that when he climbed out of the tarantass he could neither straighten up nor lie down. In time, however, his body grew used to the brutal discipline of the road, and his headaches, hemorrhoid attacks, and minor spasms of blood-spitting disappeared.

One morning an enormous mail coach collided with the tarantass. He lurched to the floor, and all the luggage toppled down on his head. Picking himself up, he was surprised to discover no bruises, but the shafts of the tarantass were shattered. The two coachmen called each other every name they could think of, then patched up the "wicker basket," after a fashion, with a few straps, and on he went to the next stop.

The heavy Siberian rains had begun to pour, and the Irtysh River overflowed, flooding the road. From time to time the traveler and his coachman were obliged to climb down from the tarantass and lead the horses across veritable lakes of mud.

In the villages where they stopped, Chekhov was amazed at how heterogeneous the population was: after serving out their sentences, Russians, Ukrainians, Tatars, Poles, and Jews lived in peace and harmony as peasants. They even seemed more civilized than on the other side of the Urals. "When you go into a room where there are people sleeping at night, you don't smell that musky, Russian smell. True, an old woman handed me a teaspoon she had just wiped on her backside, but they never sit you down to tea without a tablecloth, they don't belch or search their heads for lice in your presence, and when they serve you water or milk, they keep their fingers out of the glass."[10]

Although the breads and pies were delicious, nothing else was fit for the European stomach. His hosts kept pressing the specialty of the region on him, a "duck soup" consisting of a noxious broth with scraps of wild duck and raw onion floating in it. "Once I asked for a meat soup and some fried perch. The soup they served me was dirty, oversalted, and had callous skin for meat; the fish hadn't been scaled."[11] The tea was no better, "an infusion of sage and cockroaches—at least that was what it tasted like."[12]

Cold, heavy rain accompanied Chekhov as far as Tomsk, where he arrived exhausted on May 15. He rested there for a week, writing five short articles, based on his experiences, for *New Times*. He found the place uninteresting: full of drunkards and devoid of pretty women. He steered clear of the local intellectuals, but could not stop the deputy chief of police from reading him one of his stories or from showing him around the red-light district. "Just back from the brothels," he wrote to Suvorin. "Disgusting. It's two in the morning."[13] He took advantage of his stay in Tomsk to replace Mikhail's trunk, which had staved in, with a large, malleable leather bag. And fed up with the hired "wicker basket," he bought a light carriage of his own for 130 rubles with the intention of selling it at the end of the journey.

In this new conveyance he left Tomsk on May 21 for Irkutsk, fifteen hundred versts away. Two lieutenants and a military doctor accompanied him in their own carriage. The road was one big mud-filled rut, and the wheels sank into it "as into thick jam." The bumps played havoc with axles and shafts. There were expensive repairs to be made at each stop. "I pay more than I should, do the wrong things, say the wrong things, and keep expecting what doesn't happen," he wrote home.[14] There were times when repairs could not wait for the next stop, and he had to stand out in the elements or even trudge his way to the posting house. He would arrive with twitching calves and mud-spattered clothes, collapse on a lumpy mattress, and fall fast asleep, drunk with fatigue and fresh air.

After Krasnoyarsk the plain gave way to the dense Siberian taiga. It stretched out, endless, before him. Each time the carriage climbed to the top of a hill, Chekhov expected the forest to end; instead, he found wave after wave of fir trees, larches, and slender birches, as far as the eye could see. "You have the feeling you will never get out of it, this earthly monster," he wrote in his "Siberian Notes."[15] By then cold and rain had turned to sweltering heat and dust. The dust made its way into his mouth, his nose, his neck, his pockets, but nothing could dampen his spirit. "I've seen and experienced a great deal, all of it extremely interesting and new to me, not so much to Chekhov the writer as to Chekhov the man," he wrote to Leikin. "The Yenisei, the taiga, the posting houses, the coachmen, wild nature and wild game, the physical torments caused by the discomforts of the road, the pleasures of a good rest—it is all, the whole of it, so wonderful as to defy description."[16]

When on June 4 he finally reached Irkutsk, he plunged with delight into the comforts of civilization: a steam bath, a comfortable bed, clean clothes, a stroll through a friendly town that had its own theater and a park complete with sandy, tree-lined paths and bandstand. He immediately brought the family up to date on his adventures, but did not forget to ask for their homely news. Was Mother taking care of her bad leg as she had promised? Was Mikhail in love? How were Aunt Fedosia and her son? He asked for a Mass to be said on the anniversary of Nikolai's birth, June 17, and for his father to be fêted on his name day at home. Then he joked about being in love with Lika Mizinova: he had dreamed of her the other night. Besides, she was "a queen" in comparison with Siberian women, who did not know how "to dress, sing, or laugh." "They're like frozen fish. You have to be a walrus or a seal to make headway with them."[17]

In Irkutsk he sold his carriage at a loss—it had been damaged—and traveled on with the three officers in theirs. He was soon sorry: they either sang or went on about women. His only consolation was the beauty of the countryside. He was bowled over by the view of Lake Baikal, more landlocked sea than lake. "It's a mirror. You can't see the other shore, of course; it's ninety versts away. The banks are high, steep, rocky, and wooded. [. . .] It's quite like the Crimea."[18] Unfortunately, they had to wait three days for the boat. He put up in a "shed of a room," where he was prey to both fleas and cockroaches, and dined on buckwheat groats and bad vodka. "Going to sleep is disgusting. Every day I spread my jacket on the floor, fur up, lay my crumpled overcoat and a little pillow under my head, and fall asleep on the mounds, still wearing trousers and waistcoat . . . Civilization, where art thou?"[19]

They crossed the lake on the deck of a small paddleboat. Leaning over the rail, Chekhov was fascinated by the transparent turquoise water that opened up the deep to him—its rocks and mysterious flora. Soon, however, he was back on the road. Now the forests, plains, and hills slipped by without a hitch; the officers' carriage drove smoothly, the horses took less time to change at the posting houses, and the liberally tipped coachmen kept up a swift pace. They arrived in Sretensk on June 20, a scant hour before their boat, the *Yermak,* was due to depart. The most tiring, overland part of the journey was behind him. "May God grant everyone as safe a journey as I've had,"

Chekhov wrote to his mother. "I've not been ill once, and of all the things I took along I've lost nothing but a pocket knife, a suitcase strap, and a jar of carbolic oil. My money is intact. Few people manage to travel thousands of versts like that. I'm so used to traveling the road that I don't quite feel myself and can't quite believe that I'm not in a tarantass and don't hear the ting-a-ling of the bells. I feel strange going to bed and being able to stretch my legs out to their full length, knowing my face is free of dust."[20]

To be certain of some time to himself, he bought a first-class ticket for the *Yermak*. He had had enough of the three garrulous officers, who had also touched him for 150 rubles and made no sign of reimbursing him. Alone in his cabin he hoped to be able to write a few articles for *New Times,* but the boat shook "as if it had a fever." He therefore gave up the idea of getting any work done and sat admiring the landscape as it glided slowly by. "It's magnificent," he wrote to Pleshcheev. "The Siberian poetry doesn't begin until after Baikal. Before Baikal it's all prose."[21] His enthusiasm mounted even higher when the boat left the Shilka for the Amur. With the aid of a pair of binoculars he scanned the wild banks for herons and "all kinds of big-beaked rascals." When the boat put in at shore, he visited villages on both the Russian and the Chinese banks of the river. The recent discovery of gold in the region was an obsession with the populace. Deportees, peasants, even priests thought of nothing but prospecting. The ones who struck it rich drank only champagne, said Chekhov; they amassed fabulous sums only to lose them immediately at the gaming table. Total freedom reigned. No one observed the Orthodox fast days, women smoked, people spoke their minds without fearing spies. No captain of an Amur steamer would ever dream of turning in a runaway convict to the authorities. "I've fallen in love with the Amur," Chekhov wrote to Suvorin. "I'd be only too happy to live here a year or two. It's beautiful and spacious and free and warm. Switzerland and France have never known such freedom. The lowliest convict on the Amur breathes more freely than the highest general in Russia."[22]

On July 9, after twice changing ships, he passed through the Tatar Strait and watched, "with joy and pride," as the coast of Sakhalin appeared in the distance. Two days later the ship dropped anchor at Alexandrovsk, the island's administrative capital and center of its penal system. Chekhov disembarked immediately—together with a contingent of convicts, as it happened—and found lodgings with a medical colleague.

Alexandrovsk, a town of about three thousand inhabitants, was gloomy, clean, and still. The only sound in the streets was the clank of prisoners' chains as they made their way to or from work. Sakhalin had five prison colonies. When a convict had served his time, he was obliged to remain on the island as a settler. Wives who followed their husbands into exile were allowed to reside with them. Such was the information Chekhov received from General Kononovich, Alexandrovsk's military governor, who gave him an extremely warm reception. Kononovich also promised to aid him in his research and to open the prison archives to him. A few days later Baron Korf, governor-general of the Amur Region, authorized Chekhov to circulate freely over the entire territory, consult official documents, and interrogate all but political prisoners. He prided himself on his humanitarian feelings for those whom he called "the poor wretches," and claimed that convict life on Sakhalin was "easier than anywhere in Russia and even Europe. No one is deprived of the hope of regaining full rights," he said. "There is no such thing as a life sentence. An indefinite term at penal servitude is limited to twenty years. The labor is not onerous."[23]

Still, Chekhov was determined to carry out a rigorous study. He had gone to Sakhalin as an investigator, not as a tourist. His prime concern was to conduct a census of the prisoners, a project that had the added advantage of enabling him, under the guise of collecting statistics, to come into personal contact with even the most hardened of criminals. To this end, he drew up a thirteen-point questionnaire and ordered the prison printing office to put it on cards. Every morning at five o'clock, alone or with an armed guard, he would make the rounds of the prisons, barracks, huts, and mines, asking his questions of illiterate brutes who stared at him with blank faces—grim-looking murderers, grinning but suspicious robbers, simpletons. His soft-spoken yet direct approach quickly won their confidence, and within minutes they talked to him as to a friend. By the time he was to leave, he had filled in approximately ten thousand cards in his own hand.* It was extremely exhausting work. He developed a tic and suffered acute migraines, but refused to slow down. The more progress he made, the more clearly he saw that, contrary to Baron Korf's allegations, Sakhalin was rife with tyranny and lies.

Governor Kononovich had claimed to be a staunch adversary of corporal punishment, while "five hundred feet away there were daily whippings." Could he possibly have been unaware of them? Convicts chained to wheelbarrows worked on their stomachs in the mines. The Alexandrovsk hospital lacked the most elementary medicines, and patients slept on plank beds or on the floor. Prisoners were forbidden to enter churches. The guards reigned over their putrid charges with injustice, inhumanity, and complete impunity. Prison authorities had unlimited rights, prisoners none. As a result, prisoners soon lost their sense of human dignity; they robbed one another, informed on one another, played up to the guards, guzzled vodka, and played cards—"their only spiritual delight"—at night by candlelight. "Cardplaying has taken over all the prisons like an epidemic; they have turned into large gambling houses, and the villages and military posts are their subsidiaries."[24]

Motivated by a desire to descend to the lowest circle of Sakhalin hell, Chekhov asked to attend a whipping session. He looked on, sick with horror, as the accused was examined by a doctor (to determine whether he could stand the ninety lashes he had been sentenced to) and fellow convicts mingled around the torture site with a kind of morbid curiosity; he watched the victim being slowly and methodically strapped to the punishment bench; he heard the lashes being counted out by an im-

*The cards are now in the Lenin Library in Moscow.

passive official and the screams of pain accompanying them; he saw the naked body turn into a mass of swollen flesh.

"The torturer stood to one side and struck the victim in such a way that the lash hit the body diagonally," Chekhov writes. "After each five lashes he slowly moved to the other side, allowing the victim a thirty-second respite. The victim's hair soon stuck to his forehead. After only five or ten blows his flesh, covered with weals from former beatings, turned crimson and deep blue; his skin peeled with each blow. 'Your Worship!' we heard through the screams and tears, 'your Worship! Spare me, your Worship!' After twenty or thirty blows he started lamenting, as if drunk or delirious, 'I'm an unfortunate man, a broken man . . . Why are they punishing me?' Suddenly his neck stretched out unnaturally, and we heard vomiting . . . He did not say another word; he only moaned and wheezed."[25] Chekhov went out into the street well before the ninetieth blow, but the screams carried through the town. "For three or four nights thereafter," he wrote to Suvorin, "I dreamed of the torturer and the repulsive flogging bench."[26]

Other less spectacular forms of suffering also tried his sensibility. Women on Sakhalin were either convicts themselves (they accounted for slightly over 10 percent of the convict population) or the wives of convicts. In order to subsist, both groups practiced prostitution. The guards reserved the youngest and most attractive women for themselves, leaving the rest for the convicts. Mothers sold their daughters to rich settlers or overseers as a matter of course. "Given the enormity of the demand, neither age nor deformity nor even tertiary syphilis hinders a woman from indulging in prostitution. Youth is no obstacle either. In the streets of Alexandrovsk I had occasion to meet a sixteen-year-old girl who, I was told, had begun working as a prostitute at the age of nine. [. . .] There is a free woman on the outskirts of Alexandrovsk who runs an 'establishment' peopled entirely by her own daughters."[27]

Emaciated, lost, illiterate ragamuffins—such were most of the island's children. One day Chekhov entered a hut to find a stooped, freckled, barefoot boy of about ten. He began by asking the full name of the boy's father.

" 'I don't know,' he replied.

" 'You don't know? You live with your father and you don't know his name? Shame on you.'

" 'He's not my real father.'

" 'What do you mean?'

" 'He's just living with Ma.'

" 'Is your mother married or widowed?'

" 'She's a widow. She came here for her husband.'

" 'What is "for her husband" supposed to mean?'

" 'For killing him.' "[28]

On his way to a final inspection tour—of the southern part of the island—Chekhov informed Suvorin he was proud of what he had accomplished: "There's not a single convict or settler on Sakhalin who hasn't talked to me." And he added, "When I stop and think that I am separated from the world by ten thousand versts, I am overcome with apathy. I have the feeling it will take me a hundred years to get home."[29] He described the same sort of lethargy and letdown to his mother: "I miss you, and I'm tired of Sakhalin. For three months now I've seen no one but convicts or people with nothing to talk about but hard labor, whips, and convicts. A gloomy existence."[30]

At last it came time to leave. On October 13 Chekhov boarded the *Petersburg,* which, hugging the Asian coastline, would carry him back to Odessa. The return voyage took nearly two months, but compared with the journey across Siberia it was a luxury sightseeing tour. At one point he had thought of going back via the United States, but the cost proved prohibitive. He bypassed Japan because of a cholera epidemic there, afraid the disease's "green eyes" were on the lookout for him. He was greatly impressed by Hong Kong and its magnificent bay and outraged when his traveling companions vilified the English for exploiting the natives. "Yes, the Englishman exploits the Chinese, the sepoys, the Hindus, I thought, but in return he gives them roads, water mains, museums, Christianity. You do your own exploiting, but what do you give in return?"[31] He admired the junks milling in the harbor, the omnibuses, the funicular railway climbing the mountain; he rode in a ricksha, a bit sheepish at the thought of traveling on the backs of his fellowmen; he bought all kinds of Chinese baubles.

After leaving Hong Kong, the *Petersburg* was hit by a typhoon of such force that disaster seemed inevitable. The captain advised Chekhov to keep his revolver handy: he would want to commit suicide in case the ship went under—the waters were shark-infested. Miraculously, however, the ship pitched and rolled its way out of the storm, and Chekhov was proud to note he had not even been seasick. He was very much affected by the funeral service for two men who had died on board and whose corpses, as was the custom, were cast into the sea. "When you see a dead man wrapped in sailcloth flying head over heels into the water and when you think there are several versts down to the bottom, you are frightened and somehow start thinking that you are about to die too and that you too will be thrown into the sea."[32] The incident set his imagination to work, and he wrote a story, "Gusev," about a man who dies at sea, is thrown overboard, and attracts a voracious shark as he sinks into the depths.

If Singapore depressed Chekhov to tears, Ceylon struck him as a paradise on earth: it had palms, elephants, cobras, Hindu conjurers and miracle workers, and, best of all, beautiful dusky-skinned women with mysterious smiles. "When I have children," he confided to Suvorin, "I'll tell them, not without pride, 'Listen, you sons of bitches, I had relations in my day with a black-eyed Hindu girl, and guess where? In a coconut grove, on a moonlit night!' "[33] When he boasted of the same escapade to Alexander, his brother replied, "Regards to your anonymous wife and the children you engendered during your trip round the world. To think that somewhere in Ceylon there's a little Chekhov." Unable to bring home a Singhalese mistress, he gave in to an impulse and bought three mongooses with the intention of acclimatizing them in Russia.

The thirteen days that followed the Ceylon adventure seemed

a century to Chekhov: the ship called at no ports, and his only pleasure was to swim in the sea under the amused gaze of the crew. To be sure, he was moved by the sight of Mount Sinai and Constantinople, but he had had enough exoticism. His heart, his mind, and his stomach all yearned for Russia.

On December 1, 1890, in Odessa, he at last set foot on Russian soil again. Telegraphing ahead, he took the first train to Moscow. His mother and brother Mikhail traveled down to Tula to meet him. They found him at the station restaurant surrounded by a crowd of onlookers, the mongooses sharing a meal with him at his table. After hugs and tears of joy the Chekhovs boarded the train for the short stretch remaining to Moscow. There they went to Malaya Dmitrovka Street rather than Sadovaya-Kudrinskaya: the family had moved again that autumn in an effort to save money.

After more than seven months of strenuous peregrinations Chekhov was glad to be at home again, safe and sound, among friends, relatives, and books. "Hurrah! Well, here I am at last, sitting at my desk, praying to my slightly faded Penates, and writing to you," he announced to Suvorin. "I feel good inside, almost as if I had never left home. I am well and content to the marrow of my bones."[34] The feeling of well-being was reinforced by the idea that he had returned with a message for his compatriots. The selfsame Chekhov who had professed that a writer was not meant to teach suddenly saw himself the bearer of a quintessential truth: "God's world is good. Only one thing in it is bad: we ourselves." The Sakhalin data were so abundant, he joked, that he would marry any girl capable of classifying them. And how pathetic literary squabbles seemed after what he had been through! "Before my journey I found *The Kreutzer Sonata* an event; now I find it ridiculous and incoherent. Either I've matured or gone out of my mind—damned if I know which."[35]

Much as he would have liked to set to work on the Sakhalin report—and expose the abuses of the prison system, the degrading treatment of the convicts, the foul living conditions of the women and children—his new lodgings were scarcely conducive to it. A tiny, noisy courtyard house, it was constantly bombarded by hordes of friends, journalists, and curiosity seekers. To make matters worse, the mongooses had begun upsetting the neighborhood dogs and cats, and for want of cobras they went after trousers, dresses, shoes, foods, inkpots, flowerpots, gloves, hats, and ladies' hairdos. "They are cat-sized animals," Chekhov wrote to Leontyev-Shcheglov, "very cheerful and bright. [. . .] The first thing they do when they meet somebody is to rummage through his pockets and find out what's there. When they're left alone in a room, they start crying."[36] But before long they had wreaked such havoc that Chekhov gave two of them to the Moscow Zoo, hoping he could cope with the eccentricities of at least one.

In the end, he was too busy. The Chekhovs' financial situation had hit a new low. To bail them out he had to drop everything, put the finishing touches on "Gusev," and whisk it off to *New Times*. Immediately thereafter he started sketching a long story, "The Duel." "The work I do to earn my daily bread," he told Suvorin, "keeps me from working on Sakhalin."

Even more pressing were problems of health. Whereas he had been relatively fit during the journey, in Moscow he felt run down and suffered from headaches, coughing spells, and heart palpitations. "Every minute my heart stops for a few seconds and refuses to beat," he wrote, again to Suvorin.[37]

He grew bitter. Intruders irritated him; friends annoyed him. Even Mikhail, who had recently been promoted to the sixth rank in the civil service and enjoyed showing off in his new uniform, and his parents, who looked on with tender emotion, began to get on his nerves.

Early in January he escaped to Petersburg, to the Suvorins, but there, too, he was assailed by outsiders. "I'm working," he wrote to Maria, "but with the greatest of difficulty. As soon as I write a line, the bell rings and in comes someone 'to have a word about Sakhalin.' What a nuisance!"[38] He raced from reception to supper, "as tired as a ballerina after five acts and eight tableaux." The only reason he accepted all the invitations was that he wished to form a body of public opinion in sympathy with the children of Sakhalin. He counted on his hosts to collect textbooks for them, for example, and despite the reticence of the authorities he was able to amass some two thousand books.

If the journey to Sakhalin struck Chekhov's admirers as a feat of generosity, it brought sneers to the faces of certain writers and journalists who saw him as their rival. They said his visit to Siberia was an attempt to ape Dostoevsky; they accused him of using the convicts to make a name for himself. Their hate and envy made itself felt immediately. "I am surrounded by a dense atmosphere of extremely vague and imcomprehensible hostility," he wrote to Maria. "People give me meals and sing my praises, yet they're ready to devour me. Why? Damned if I know. If I put a bullet through my head, I'd give nine-tenths of my friends and admirers a great deal of pleasure."[39]

Chekhov was especially upset with an article by the *New Times* critic Burenin, who lumped him together with Korolenko and Uspensky as writers who had "begun to fade." "Mediocre talents like Chekhov," Burenin continued, "lose the habit of looking at life around them and bolt off God knows where, to Siberia and beyond, to Vladivostok, to Sakhalin!" The insinuation that his imagination had run dry leaving him desperate for new subject matter soon became the basis for a whisper campaign. Another rumor making the rounds at the time—that Chekhov's success was entirely orchestrated and financed by the millionaire editor of *New Times*—reached Leontyev-Shcheglov in the following formulation: "Chekhov is Suvorin's kept woman."

The rumor did not in the least affect Chekhov's fondness and esteem for his best friend. When Suvorin proposed a grand tour of Europe, Chekhov accepted enthusiastically. "We're on our way!!! I agree to go wherever and whenever you wish. My heart is jumping for joy. It would be silly for me not to go, because when will another such opportunity present itself?"[40] In reaction to his boyish exuberance Maria sighed sadly and said, "Why can't you stay in one place, Antosha?"

Before racing off in search of new horizons, Chekhov went to see the famous Duse, who was the toast of Petersburg at the time, in *Antony and Cleopatra*. "I don't understand Italian," he wrote to his sister, "but her acting was so beautiful that I felt I understood every word. A remarkable actress. I've never seen anything like it."[41] Next day he left for Europe with Suvorin and Suvorin's son Alexei.

Whereas several months earlier Chekhov had crossed Siberia in a tumbledown tarantass that quaked with every rut, he now traveled in a sleeping car "with mirrors, gigantic windows, and carpets." In his chocolate box on wheels he felt like Zola's heroine Nana. Pleasure gave way to wonder when they arrived in Vienna. Everything seemed the height of elegance and sophistication: the shops were "sheer vertigo, sheer mirage"; the enormous churches had such a light touch about them that they seemed "spun of lace"; the cabmen looked like dandies in their top hats and read newspapers—something inconceivable in Russia—while waiting for fares; every street had its own bookshop. "It's odd," he wrote to his sister. "You may read anything you like here, say whatever you please."[42]

Having bought some gifts for his family and some ties for himself, he left Vienna with the Suvorins for Venice. The city dazzled him with its fragile, floating, museumlike atmosphere, buildings of another age, narrow winding streets, and long black gondolas gliding noiselessly along the smooth canal water. "Never in my life have I seen a city more remarkable than Venice," he wrote to his brother Ivan. "The fascination, the glitter, the exuberance. [. . .] A Russian, poor and humbled, can very easily go out of his mind in this world of beauty, wealth, and freedom. You feel like staying here forever, and when you stand in church listening to the organ you feel like converting to Catholicism."[43] The young writer Dmitry Merezhkovsky, who also happened to be in Venice at the time, expressed the same jubilation. But Merezhkovsky was mostly attracted by the architecture and art collections, while Chekhov also noticed minutiae like the physiognomy of a bald-headed guide, the voice of a flower vendor, the sound of a mandolin at twilight, the continual tinkling of bells, or the congregations of pigeons in Saint Mark's Square. But his delight faded with the first rains. "*Venezia bella* has stopped being *bella*," he wrote to his sister. "There is a dismal boredom in the air; it makes you want to flee to the sun."[44]

The rest of the Italian leg of the journey—Bologna, Florence, Rome, Naples—was more disappointing. A conscientious tourist, he toured everything of value, but the diet was too rich, and satiation gradually set in. Racing from monument to museum caused his feet and back to ache; by the end of each day he felt he had swallowed an indigestible *Baedeker*. By the time he reached Rome, he had begun missing borscht and buckwheat groats. The Eternal City reminded him of Kharkov. In Naples he admired the bay and deplored the filthy streets. Yet he saw Italy as a country divinely blessed. "After all," he wrote to his sister, "even apart from its natural beauty and warm clime, Italy is the only country where you realize that art indeed reigns over everything, a conviction that is very encouraging."[45]

Not a day went by that Chekhov did not worry about the financial aspect of the journey. If he had been by himself, he said, he could have made do with four hundred rubles, but with Suvorin he had to live "like a doge or a cardinal," putting up in the best hotels and dining in the finest restaurants. He was afraid of running up a debt of a thousand rubles at the very least: once more he would have to work it off.

The next country on their itinerary was France, and from Nice they paid a visit to Monte Carlo. Fever-stricken, he lost five hundred francs at roulette. "Of course you'll say, 'What baseness! We're living in poverty and he plays roulette,' " he wrote to Mikhail. "That's perfectly just, and I give you my permission to slit my throat. But personally I'm quite pleased with myself. At least I can now tell my grandchildren that I played roulette and experienced the sensation the game arouses."[46] His sudden passion did not blind him to the corrupt atmosphere: everyone on the rock lived for money and cards alone; everything was for show. "I love luxury and opulence, but roulette luxury gives me the impression of a luxurious lavatory," he wrote in the same letter. "There's something in the air that offends one's sense of decency and cheapens nature, the sound of the waves, the moon."

If Monte Carlo, the "tart," upset him, Paris, "the birthplace of civilization," seduced him. And yet his first contact with her was rather harsh: on his way to the World Exposition he got caught up in a May Day workers' demonstration and was knocked about by the police.* Unperturbed, he kept to his original plan: after visiting the Exposition, he admired the Eiffel Tower ("Yes, the Eiffel Tower is very, very high") and the wax figures at the Musée Grévin, then attended a stormy session at the Chamber of Deputies. On that day the Minister of Internal Affairs was taken roundly to task for the May Day incidents at Fourmies, during which troops had opened fire on demonstrating strikers, killing nine and wounding sixty. For a Russian the idea that simple representatives of the nation could call the government in power to account was a bit startling. Clearly the Revolution of 1789 was not dead.

A few days before leaving Paris Chekhov went to the famous exhibition at the *Salon des Indépendants* and declared to his sister, "Russian painters are far more solid than French ones. Compared with the French landscape painters I saw yesterday, Levitan is a king."[47] True, he had broken his pince-nez and admitted to missing half the pictures because of nearsightedness, but as in Venice he was less interested in museums than in a thousand and one details of the bustling, noisy, cheerful street life: the droves of Frenchmen sitting outside the cafés at their little tables and "making themselves at home," the paucity of uniforms in public places and the resultant impression of freedom bordering on chaos. . . . "A wonderful people," he concluded. But when members of the Russian colony dragged him off on a tour of "Paris by night," he was sorely disillusioned: "*Anthropoi* girding themselves with boa constrictors, ladies kicking

---

*In the nineteenth century the Julian calendar used in Russia was twelve days behind the Gregorian calendar used in the West. For Chekhov, therefore, the demonstration occurred on April 19. Even while in Europe, Chekhov dated his letters according to the Julian calendar.

their legs up to the ceiling, flying people, lions, *cafés chantants,* dinners, and luncheons are beginning to disgust me."[48]

It was the first Easter he had spent away from home. The service at the embassy church was a poor substitute for the streets of Moscow, the Kremlin bells, the table groaning with Easter delicacies, the triple kiss of peace given to strangers with the greeting "Christ is risen." Suvorin, however, was in no hurry to pack his bags. Not until April 27 could Chekhov write to Ivan, "I'm leaving for Russia today. [. . .] I'm tired of traveling. I feel like doing some work." He signed his name in French: Antoine.

He arrived in Moscow on May 2, 1891, after six weeks abroad. On Sakhalin he had seen the depths of servitude, in the West the heights of civilization. Russia, to which he returned with a feeling of filial devotion, seemed to him poised between the two extremes.

IX
The Landowner

The day after his return to the fold, before he had had time to unpack his suitcases, Chekhov left Moscow with his family for a dacha in the nearby village of Alexin. In Anton's absence Mikhail had chosen the place, a small four-room house with a view of the Oka and the local railway bridge. From the outset Chekhov felt cramped there: it had "a sad and boring look about it." After two weeks he decided to strike camp and move the tribe to Bogimovo, a village only several versts away. There they had the entire ground floor of a large, elegant house with spacious rooms, sculptured columns, and a raised platform for musicians in the salon. The romantic grounds, crisscrossed with linden-lined pathways as far as the eye could see, were quite deserted and included a pond abounding in fish, a windmill, and even a small church, where the "aged parents" could say their prayers. It was an ideal hideaway for both rest and work.

As always, however, Chekhov was hounded by financial difficulties. His European journey had put him deeply into debt to Suvorin. Even though his sister Maria and his brothers Mikhail and Ivan now earned their own livelihood, he still had to care for his brother Alexander, who had been bemoaning his poverty since the birth of his latest child*—to say nothing of his father, who had left his job and was living at home again. Chekhov came up with a three-pronged approach to fill the family coffers: on Mondays, Tuesdays, and Wednesdays he would work on the Sakhalin book, the point of which was to show that the convicts, having lost all hope of seeing their native soil again, had thereby lost their sense of both morality and reality; on Thursdays, Fridays, and Saturdays he would continue work on his long story, "The Duel"; and on Sundays, for recreation, he would write short stories.

Up at dawn—that is, four or five in the morning—he made his own coffee, then set to work. He wrote at a windowsill rather than a desk, and whenever he raised his eyes, he looked out at the grounds. At eleven he went mushrooming or fishing. After lunch, which was served at one, he allowed himself a short nap, but the moment he opened his eyes, he picked up his pen and wrote till evening. He found it frustrating that "The Duel" gave him less trouble than *The Island of Sakhalin*. Often he cheated and spent a day scheduled for the latter on the former. "I'm writing my *Sakhalin,* and I'm bored, so bored," he admitted to Suvorin.[1] And forty-eight hours later: "There are times when I want to spend three to five years on it, slaving frantically, and times when I'm depressed and want to chuck it all."

After working hard all morning and afternoon, he enjoyed the relief of dinner with family and friends. Afterwards they would gather in the giant salon and talk on and on in the Russian manner about nothing in particular and with no sense of time. Needless to say, the house was full of people. Chekhov said it was like being a crayfish caught in a net with a bunch of crayfish.

*Mikhail Chekhov, the future actor of Moscow Art Theater fame.

There was Natasha Lintvaryova, a zoologist by the name of Wagner who was doing a study of spiders and talked himself breathless about heredity and the survival of the fittest, the Kiselyov family, Levitan the painter, and, last but not least, Lika Mizinova.

Within the last year or two the scintillating Lika had become a close friend of the clan's. She was ten years younger than Chekhov and worshiped him shyly, expecting him to declare his love from one day to the next. Chekhov, though attracted to her, behaved like an affectionate if flippant elder brother. Without admitting it to himself, he used the mocking tone to shield him from the charm of her fresh, winsome, yet melancholy ways. He would do everything possible to maintain the privacy, the inner solitude he needed for his work. What was a woman to him, no matter how desirable, when his life was all pen and paper? Though flattered by Lika's blossoming love, he neither encouraged nor discouraged her. He wrote her teasing notes, gave her preposterous nicknames, advised her to flee that cradle snatcher of a Levitan, nagged at her for eating too much starch, for smoking, for being idle and disorderly. "Golden, mother-of-pearl, lisle-threaded Lika," he wrote to her, "while you bellowed and dotted my right shoulder with tears (I've removed the spots with benzine) and ate your bread and beef morsel by morsel, we devoured your face and neck with our eyes. Oh, Lika, Lika, what an infernal beauty you are!"[2] Or, a few months later: "I love you passionately, like a tiger, and I offer you my hand."[3]

In fact, however, he was determined to keep his hand free for writing purposes. Even while the bewitching Lika lived under his roof, he remained a confirmed bachelor. "I have no intention of marrying," he wrote to Suvorin. "I wish I were a little old man with no hair sitting at a large desk in a good study."[4]

Evenings at Bogimovo were sometimes enlivened by a roulette wheel of Chekhov's own making; he also played the croupier. There were theatrical performances, *tableaux vivants*. The children were fascinated by the mongoose. One day it was reported lost in the woods, and the family was terribly upset—only to rejoice greatly when it reappeared. As usual, the local muzhiks came to be treated by the heaven-sent Doctor Chekhov. A peasant woman who had been seriously wounded in a fall from a cart interspersed moans about her imminent death with instructions to her husband about the oat harvest. "I told her to forget about the oats," he wrote to Suvorin, "we had more serious things to talk about, and she said, " 'But he's got such good oats!' I envy her her spirit. People like that have no trouble dying."[5]

The letter about the peasant woman accompanied the manuscript of the long-promised "Duel." As for the Sakhalin book, it had turned into forced labor. Thoroughly disgusted with himself, Chekhov wrote to Suvorin, "I have the feeling that my trousers don't hang right on me, that I'm not writing as I should, that I give my patients the wrong medicine. It must be a psychosis." And a little farther on: "I wish I had some carpets, a fireplace, some bronzes, and a little cultivated conversation. I'm afraid I'll never make a Tolstoyan! In women what I love above all is beauty, in the history of mankind culture, as expressed in carpets, carriages with springs, and keen minds."[6]

By early September he was back at the family lair in Moscow. His stay in the country and contact with nature and the peasants had only reinforced his mistrust of fuzzy-minded intellectuals. He even came down on Tolstoy, whose Afterword to *The Kreutzer Sonata* he had just read. "To hell with the philosophy of the great men of this world! All great wise men are as despotic as generals and as impolite and insensitive as generals because they are confident of their impunity. Diogenes spat in people's beards knowing that he would not be called to account; Tolstoy calls doctors scoundrels and flaunts his ignorance of important issues because he is another Diogenes, whom no one will report to the police or denounce in the papers. So to hell with the philosophy of the great men of this world."[7]

Soon, however, he was obliged to bow before the magnanimity and power of the venerable graybeard who reigned over all Russia from his Yasnaya Polyana retreat. As a result of a severe drought much of the country had been plunged into famine. Fearing riots on the land, the government censored the most alarming newspaper reports. It also forbade the collection of private funds to aid the victims, authorizing only the Red Cross and the Church to intervene. Tolstoy reacted immediately. Assured of impunity by his immense prestige, he issued repeated calls for public charity and collected large sums of money; he himself traveled to the disaster-stricken areas, and his daughters helped him to set up hundreds of soup kitchens. Chekhov found Tolstoy's one-man campaign awe-inspiring. "Tolstoy! That Tolstoy!" he wrote to Suvorin. "He's more than a man by today's standards; he's a Jupiter!"[8]

Eager to use his skills as a physician to help the thousands of starving peasants, Chekhov made contact with an old friend, Yevgraf Yegorov, head of the Nizhny Novgorod *zemstvo* or district council, but then a bad flu with pulmonary complications laid him low for weeks. His slow recovery coincided with a series of deaths: his Aunt Fedosia, Palmin the poet, and the saintly Zinaida Lintvaryova. Aunt Fedosia had succumbed to the family illness: tuberculosis. Chekhov no longer deluded himself about his own case, though he refused all serious, sustained treatment. "I'm beginning to think that my health will never return to its former state. Well, God proposes, man disposes. The treatment and care of my physical being fill me with something close to repugnance. I'll drink mineral water and quinine, but I refuse to let anyone sound me."[9]

As soon as he could stand on his own two feet—he still "looked like a drowned man"—he started helping Yegorov with his rescue operation. The plan was to buy up horses in the countryside, fatten them during the winter, and return them to the peasants in the spring in time for planting. The amount of capital required was considerable. Chekhov published announcements in journals, wrote hundreds of letters to friends and acquaintances, and paid visits to prospective donors. "I'm playing the charity lady,"[10] he wrote to an architect friend. Small amounts began trickling in. He kept a scrupulous account of them. Each time he could put together several rubles—a drop in the bucket—he forwarded them to Yegorov at Nizhny Novgorod.

In the hope of raising more substantial funds he went to Petersburg at the end of December. No sooner had he arrived than he was flooded with invitations. At luncheons and dinners he rubbed shoulders with colleagues whose company he did not know whether to seek or avoid. On New Year's Day, while attending a dinner in honor of the twenty-fifth anniversary of the *Saint Petersburg Gazette,* he saw Lydia Avilova again. Although they had not seen each other in three years, their conversation, as she would have it, immediately took a romantic turn. They had what seems a very un-Chekhovian talk about an encounter in a former life and their slow progress towards each other, across the centuries, until the present, when they stood face to face. If Chekhov ever did talk in such terms, he could only have done so in jest. But Lydia Avilova took it as genuine. When she introduced Chekhov to her husband, she discerned a cold courtesy in the way the men shook hands. Fifty years later she proclaimed in *Chekhov in My Life* that it was a "love story" no one suspected, though it lasted a full ten years.

Chekhov was so far from feeling himself involved in a "love story" that he did not even try to see the fiery young woman again during his stay in Petersburg. He did, however, show great interest in a ravishing Ukrainian actress, Maria Zankovetskaya. He promised to write a play for her, spent a night drinking champagne with her, and took her tobogganing on an icy hill just outside the capital.

But what about the famine? Contrary to appearances, Chekhov had not pushed it out of his mind. No sooner had he returned to Moscow than he left for Nizhny Novgorod. Working there with his friend Yegorov, he had the strange feeling of never having left Sakhalin. In both instances his goal was to put human dignity on a higher level. Despite the biting cold he traveled from village to village by sleigh. On one of the expeditions he got caught in a snowstorm, nearly lost his way, and was, by his own confession, "very much afraid." The situation was tragic. Even though the authorities, at a loss them-

selves, no longer opposed private initiative, donations had begun
to flag. "If there were as much talk and action about the famine
in Petersburg and Moscow as there is in Nizhny," he wrote to
Suvorin, "there wouldn't be any famine."[11] After a week of
zigzagging through the snowbound countryside he caught a bad
cold, which, combined with shooting back pains, forced him
to Moscow for treatment.

There he found the house much the worse for the mongoose's latest pranks, and with a certain feeling of guilt he
decided to let the mischievous little creature join its fellows in
the Moscow Zoo. He had barely time to catch his breath and
write a few letters when he was off again, this time with Suvorin, for Voronezh Province. Famine relief there had proved
more effective than in Nizhny Novgorod, but Suvorin's presence gave the journey an unpleasantly official character. As the
editor of *New Times,* as a dignitary who had the ear of the
government, Suvorin impressed the local authorities, and Chekhov had to attend sumptuously catered receptions and dinners
while the muzhiks in whose name they had come starved to
death in the surrounding villages. He was furious. His friend
seemed muddleheaded, ludicrous in the role of prestigious ad-
ministrator.

After ten days Chekhov could stand it no longer and returned to Moscow depressed at the thought of having wasted
his time in idle talk. Compared with his semifailure Tolstoy's
success appeared all the more prodigious. The utopian prophet
had organized his relief efforts more efficiently than the prag-
matic doctor. Actually, Chekhov thought of himself less and
less as a doctor. Yet he felt he lacked the living conditions, the
surroundings necessary for his art. "If I am a doctor, I need
patients and a hospital; if I am a writer, I need to live in the
midst of the people and not in the Malaya Dmitrovka house
with a mongoose. I need a bit of social and political life, a small
bit at least, and this four-walled life—without nature, people,
or Russia, without health or appetite—is no life at all."[12]

The solution? To buy a comfortable house in the country.
First of all, life in the country was less expensive, and his ex-

penses would go down. Second, the open air would help to restore his health. Third, the vain bustle of the city would be a thing of the past. And fourth, the isolation would enable him to concentrate on a longer work. Besides, no matter how deeply he buried himself, nothing could prevent him from going up to Petersburg in winter to see friends and the latest plays. "Oh, freedom, freedom!" he wrote to Suvorin. "If I live on no more than two thousand a year, which is possible only on an estate, I'll be absolutely free of all financial, debit-credit worries. Then I'll work and read, read . . ."[13]

With his predilection for the Ukraine, he asked a friend, Alexander Smagin, to find him something in the area of the Psyol River. They lost two prospects, one after the other, when the sellers vanished into thin air. Chekhov grew impatient; he began consulting the classified ads. Finding one for an estate only eighty versts from Moscow, he immediately dispatched Mikhail and Maria as scouts, and although the snow-covered countryside prevented them from forming a clear picture of the state of things, they returned favorably impressed. Chekhov was delighted and entered into negotiations with the owners before having visited the property himself. When he did make the visit a fortnight later, he, too, was favorably impressed. It turned out to be a large estate near the village of Melikhovo, 2½ hours by train from Moscow. About half of the 213 desyatinas (575 acres) was covered with low-quality timber; the rest consisted of meadowland, two ponds, "a nasty little river," and the grounds surrounding the house. The house itself was relatively new but poorly laid out and without toilets; the auxiliary buildings seemed in good condition. The room Chekhov chose for his study was lit by three windows and faced front. For the benefit of Alexander, Chekhov compiled a list of what came with the property: three horses, a piano, a cow, a tarantass, a sleigh, carts, hotbeds, two dogs. . . . The man selling it claimed that well run it would bring in two thousand rubles a year, which was why he was asking so much: thirteen thousand rubles.

Never in his wildest dreams had Chekhov imagined paying

such a price. Where could he find the money with only a pen as collateral? Once more Suvorin came to the rescue. Not only did *New Times* advance Chekhov the first four thousand rubles necessary to clinch the deal; it signed the five-year mortgage. While making the financial arrangements, Chekhov had talk after talk with lawyers, bankers, insurance agents, "and other such parasites." Their punctilious demands got his dander up. Bureaucrats made him feel like "an imbecile sticking his nose in other people's business." He was particularly indignant at having to pay a thousand rubles in miscellaneous expenses over and above the cost of the estate. But when all the papers were signed, the relief he felt! "How happy I am to be without a flat in Moscow! It's a luxury I can't remember having."[14]

On March 4 he set out for Melikhovo with his parents, his sister, his younger brother Mikhail, a mountain of trunks, suitcases, and bundles, and a large supply of medicine. The grounds and fields were still under snow. The house, which had long been deserted, looked "stupid and naïve" to its new inhabitants, but once heated up and dusted off, it felt as friendly as if it had belonged to them for years. The entire family took part in making the house livable. The day after they moved in, Chekhov wrote to Ivan and asked him to bring "a plane, a horse brush, a half-pood [sixteen pounds] of beef, twenty pounds of rye bread, five loaves of French bread, one of the pictures, and a small bronze tap." And the day after that he wrote to Suvorin, "I am sitting and luxuriating in my study with three large windows. About five times a day I go out to the garden and toss snow into the pond. Water is dripping from the roof, spring is in the air, but at night we have twelve or thirteen degrees of frost. For the time being I'm in a good mood. We're terribly busy—cleaning, washing, painting, redoing the floor here and there, moving the kitchen to the servants' quarters, building starling houses, fussing over the hotbeds, and so on. If I weren't busy with my own work, I'd spend all day outdoors."[15]

Amidst the cheerful bustle of banging hammers, curtains going up, and furniture moving this way and that, Chekhov received an unexpected letter from Lydia Avilova. She had written to him before, sending him stories for criticism, and he had responded out of kindness, finding fault with one thing, praising another. He did as much for most of the neophytes who asked his advice. But this time she had something more than literature on her mind. In indignant tones she related a scandalous rumor that was making the rounds of Petersburg and had finally come to the attention of her husband. The rumor had it that on the night they last met, two months before, Chekhov had got drunk and announced to his friends that he intended to seduce her, make her divorce her husband, and marry her.

Chekhov made a scathing reply. He could not allow the hysterical charmer to blame him for having "dragged her name through the mud." "What is this fantasy of yours?" he wrote to her. "My dignity forbids me to justify myself. Besides, your accusations are too vague to provide me with points for self-defense. As far as I can judge, it's all gossip. Am I correct? I ask you earnestly (if you trust me as much as the gossips) not to believe the bad things said about people in Petersburg. Or if you must believe them, believe them all, wholesale, the lot: my marriage into five million rubles, my affairs with the wives of my best friends, and the like. But for heaven's sake, do calm down. [. . .] Defending oneself against gossip is like asking a Jew for a loan; it won't work. Think of me what you will."[16]

At the beginning of the same letter Chekhov, never one to bear a grudge, had given his wrathful correspondent some literary advice that goes a long way towards defining his own conception of art: "When you portray the unfortunate and the down-and-out and wish to move your reader to pity, try to be colder. It will give a kind of backdrop to their grief, make it stand out more. All your heroes weep, and you sigh with them. Yes, be cold." In the event, it was like recommending that a pot of water over a fire should stop boiling.

Fortunately, the Petersburg libel melted away with the Melikhovo snows. Soon tufts of green grass peeked through, tiny rivulets cleared paths down to the river, and starlings rustled in the branches among the season's early buds. Despite the evidence to the contrary Chekhov could not bring himself to believe that his old dream had come true: at the age of thirty-two he, the grandson of a serf, had become a landowner. Like Tolstoy! And all these grounds, woods, stones—he owed them to his pen, not his parents. They were the gift of his characters, from the wildest to the most humble. Laughingly, he compared himself to Quinctius Cincinnatus, that austere and simple Roman, who preferred his farm to military honors. "We are living on our own estate," he wrote proudly to Alexander. "Like Cincinnatus, I spend all my time laboring, and earn my bread by the sweat of my brow. Mama fasted today and rode to church behind our own horse; Papa fell out of the sleigh it was going so fast! Papa still philosophizes. [. . .] Like all people from Taganrog he is incapable of any work but lighting oil lamps. He talks sternly to the muzhiks. [. . .] Imagine getting up at five o'clock secure in the knowledge you have nowhere to go and no one to come and see you. Think of hearing the starlings, the larks, the titmice." And he signed the letter: "Your Cincinnatus."[17]

While growing accustomed to his new position in life, he wrote somewhat less than usual. Moreover, his last major work, "The Duel," had cost him "a pound of nerves." It is set in a run-of-the-mill seaside resort and pits two opposing human natures: the weak and listless Laevsky—a failed intellectual and "Moscow Hamlet"—and the dynamic young zoologist von Koren, who considers him a parasite and takes him to task for blaming his moral collapse on the times and society.* Von Koren's disdain for Laevsky's combination of flaccidity and hypocrisy leads him to challenge Laevsky to a duel. Although neither man is even winged by the shots they exchange, their brush with death leaves its mark: Laevsky resolves to lead a more worthy life; von Koren becomes less intransigent in his judgments. Before leaving, von Koren calls on the man he meant to kill and tells him, "Don't think ill of me, Ivan Andreich. [. . .] It's true, as I now see to my great joy, that I

---

*A number of von Koren's statements are clearly inspired by Chekhov's conversations with Wagner, the zoologist, at Bogimovo.

was wrong about you, but it's human to stumble even when the road is smooth." And as Laevsky watches the boat take his enemy away, he thinks, "In the search for truth men take two steps forward and one back. Suffering, errors, and the tedium of life push them back, but a thirst for truth and a stubborn will drives them on. And who knows? Perhaps they will arrive at the real truth."

But the apparently optimistic ending cannot hide the bitter, violent strain running through the work. In the figure of Laevsky Chekhov settled his accounts with a large portion of the intelligentsia. He had nothing but contempt for brilliant but idle minds, empty hearts, loose tongues. The rage he felt for the Pharisees of culture was such that he wrote an article denouncing them and their arrogance and sent it to Suvorin with the request that it be published anonymously. The piece is called "In Moscow" and signed "A Grouch." In it Chekhov lambastes intellectuals fascinated by their navels and incapable of putting their high-minded, not to say highfalutin, ideas into practice. When one of their spokesmen describes his chronic disenchantment— "I twist and turn under the covers, I can't sleep, I constantly wonder why I am so tortured by boredom"—the Grouch counters anonymously, "Take a length of telephone wire and hang yourself on the nearest pole."

Was the remedy to be found in Tolstoy's evangelical preaching? No, replied Chekhov. He put his faith in science and the moral and material progress of mankind. And moral and material progress would not come, *pace* the sage of Yasnaya Polyana, from lowering civilized man to the level of the muzhik; it would come only from raising the muzhik to the level of civilized man. Chekhov found it absurd to preach chastity and temperance, curse doctors, anathematize works of art, absurd to attempt building a new world with agriculture and ignorance, absurd to turn one's back on the miraculous discoveries of science. The future was being made in laboratories, not *izbas*. By promoting obscurantism, Tolstoy denied a vital human force; he hindered the natural tendency of mankind towards the light, towards well-being. Though purporting to defend the downtrodden, he revealed inordinate pride in his manner of pronouncing, raging, condemning, absolving. Chekhov was shocked by so authoritarian an attitude; he felt no man had the right to judge his fellowman. "We must declare point-blank that nobody can make head or tail of anything in this world," he had written to Leontyev-Shcheglov several years before. "Only fools and charlatans know all and understand all."[18]

But even while his common sense revolted against Tolstoyan utopianism, Chekhov maintained a kind of tender deference to Tolstoy himself. "Every night I wake up and read *War and Peace*," he had written to Suvorin the previous year, "and feel the curiosity and naïve amazement of someone who has never read it before. It's remarkably good."[19] The more he admired Tolstoy the novelist, the more he challenged Tolstoy the moralist. It was almost as though by moving away from literature Tolstoy had betrayed not only his calling but Chekhov himself, the Chekhov who considered him Russia's greatest writer. While Tolstoy proclaimed, with Proudhon, "Property is theft" and suffered terrible pangs of conscience from owning an immense estate, Chekhov reveled in his newly acquired land and cheerfully confessed he enjoyed waking up a capitalist after a life of hard work. The former battled furiously against the stream of his day and age; the latter was content to float along, bearing witness.

X

Melikhovo

As was so often the case with Chekhov, insight followed hard on enthusiasm. No sooner did the weather turn fine than the faults of the Melikhovo "duchy" became glaringly obvious to him: the one-story, ten-room house was falling apart at the seams. It fairly swarmed with bugs and cockroaches. The mousetraps were full every morning. Since Chekhov was too tenderhearted to do the mice in, he would release them in a nearby copse, hoping they had learned their lesson and would steer clear of the house.

To make the premises more livable, he hired a team of carpenters, painters, and masons. Under his direction they mended the roof and floors, repainted and repapered the bedrooms, recemented the tile stoves, dug a new well, patched up the sheds and fences, put up a door to keep drafts out of the study, and, finally, installed a sumptuous, modern water closet. The whole family took part, Yevgenia Yakovlevna doing the housework,

Pavel Yegorovich weeding the pathways, Maria hoeing vege-
tables, and Mikhail directing work in the fields. Anton was in
charge of the orchard and the flower garden, and planted eighty
apple trees, sixty cherry trees, and any number of firs and elms,
rose- and lilac bushes. The sight of flowers filled him with
wonder and gratitude. The idea that an all-thumbs intellectual
like himself could encourage nature to blossom gave him a great
thrill. "Something amazing, something touching is going on in
nature, and its poetry and novelty make up for all the incon-
veniences of country life," he wrote to Suvorin. "Every day
brings new surprises, one better than the last. The starlings have
arrived; the babble of water is everywhere; the grass shows
green through patches of thawing snow. [. . .] Whenever I
see spring, I do so wish there were a paradise in the other
world."[1]

In addition to the two peasants who tilled the land for them
they had a cook and a maid. They were "living like lords," said
Chekhov, and all of them—parents, brothers, and sister—felt
as much a proprietary interest in the estate as he, the true owner.
Each room bore the stamp of the person who lived in it: Pavel
Yegorovich had a monastic cell complete with oversized church
books and the pungent aroma of incense; Yevgenia Yakovlevna's quarters were bright and airy, boasting starched curtains,
laundry baskets, and a sewing machine; Maria's virginal chamber consisted of a narrow bed, some vases, and an enormous
portrait of Anton looking down over her; and Chekhov's study
had tall, unobstructed windows, a daybed for naps, bookshelves
filled to overflowing, and a paper-strewn desk.

Yevgenia Yakovlevna doted on her famous son and devoted a major part of her time to cooking for him. Pavel Yegorovich, who had long since recognized Anton's primacy, still
had a hard time accepting his own inferior status, and Anton,
usually so indulgent, still bristled at Pavel Yegorovich's petty
despotism. While his mother's little quirks touched him, his
father's set his teeth on edge; he could not get over the idea that
someone who had failed at everything he had set his sights on
should continue, so late in life, to play the great man, to preach,

scold, and lay down the law with such beatific stupidity. Pavel Yegorovich kept a "log," duly noting, in a round hand, the arrivals and departures of guests and the ups and downs in temperature. With age he had grown even more pious, never missing a service, praying aloud in his room, intoning psalms, and, on holidays, swinging a censer through the house.

All three brothers were gainfully employed: Ivan was making his way as a schoolmaster, Mikhail as a civil servant, and Alexander, still a journalist, had reached the point of wanting to buy a small estate of his own. They all came to Melikhovo for summer holidays and also showed up for an occasional weekend. Fond of them though he was, however, Anton felt the greatest affection for Maria.

Decked out in heavy boots and a white kerchief, Maria did the work of four in the fields, yet she managed to safeguard her brother's privacy with a concern that verged on jealousy. Her love for him was absolute, uncompromising, and had an aura of self-sacrifice to it. It was doubtless the basis for her refusal to consider marriage. She could not imagine betraying the most important man in her life for a common sentimental attachment. Chekhov himself was affected by an analogous inhibition: Why take a wife when he had Maria? A little flirtation here and there, a summer romance, perhaps, but nothing more. "I have no desire to marry," he wrote to Suvorin, "nor is there anyone for me *to* marry. Who needs it? It would just get in the way. Falling in love, though, would not."[2]

Alexander, worried about his brother's future, took him to task for his negative attitude. "You live like an archimandrite," he wrote to him, "letting golden moments slip by without a trace, and soon all you'll have left is trips to the zoo to chat with your mongoose about the joys of celibacy." He went on: "One thing is clear—there is something wrong in your relationship with Maria. A single kind word from you, a warm tone of voice, and she is ready to do your every bidding. She is afraid of you and sees only your most noble and commendable side." A curious incident was soon to show how right he was.

During the summer of 1892 an attractive young man whom

the Chekhovs had met at the Lintvaryovs' made an appearance among Melikhovo's barrage of guests. His name was Alexander Smagin. After a bit of innocuous courting Smagin suddenly made an impassioned declaration of love and asked for Maria's hand. At loose ends or, rather, panic-stricken, Maria needed someone to turn to. Her father? No, of course not. Her mother? No, not even her. Anton. Wasn't he the sage of the family? And so, mustering all her courage, she confronted him in his study with the statement, "You know, Anton, I've decided to marry." Since Chekhov knew who the prospective groom was, he did not ask, but his features seemed to harden. Maria was frightened by his silence. "When he failed to respond," she wrote in her *Memoirs,* "I sensed he found the news unpleasant. He held his tongue, though, and what could he say? I saw he couldn't admit that it would be hard for him if I went off to another home, a new family." She returned to her room in tears, having failed to coax a word out of her brother. Nor did he broach the subject with her in the next few days. "I gave it a great deal of thought. The love and affection I felt for my brother made up my mind for me. I could consent to nothing that would cause him pain, upset his way of life, deprive him of the creative atmosphere I always tried to make for him. I informed Smagin of my decision, which caused him much suffering as well."

Chekhov heaved a sigh of relief. He had been very much alarmed. For the first time he had perceived the cardinal role his sister played in maintaining the equilibrium of his day-to-day existence. Without her his intimate world would crumble. He was moved not so much by jealousy as by an instinct of self-preservation. To be happy he needed discreet, industrious, loving Maria at his side; he needed to be assured that no suitor would distract her from her sisterly vocation. They were made for each other and had no need of outsiders for affection or respect; they were the perfect couple, unconstrained by complications of the flesh. In a letter to Suvorin Chekhov feigned surprise at the idea of a young woman of twenty-seven turning down what was after all a perfectly acceptable match. "My sister is not married yet, though the romance seems to be proceeding in letters. I don't understand a thing. There are conjectures that she's said no again. She's the only girl on earth who does not want to get married."[3] In reality, it suited him to believe that she was as much committed to the unmarried life as he was.

Most of the company never even noticed the piteous romance of Maria and Alexander. The stream of guests was such that no one could claim exclusivity: Anton's friends, Maria's friends, neighbors, curiosity seekers, local doctors, distant relatives with broods in tow—they slept four to a room, they slept in the halls, they slept in makeshift beds scattered throughout the house. "Oh, if you knew how exhausted I am," Chekhov wrote to Suvorin, "so exhausted it's made me all tense. Company, company, and more company. [. . .] Every itinerant intellectual feels bound and beholden to look in on me and warm up and sometimes even stay the night. The doctors alone are legion! It's nice to be hospitable, of course, but everything in moderation. After all, I left Moscow to get away from guests."[4]

Several favorites did stand out in the crowd, however: pretty Lika Mizinova, a young poetess by the name of Tatyana Shchepkina-Kupernik, Natasha Lintvaryova of the rippling laugh, and naturally the moody Levitan. Levitan was delighted with Melikhovo's typically Russian countryside and did several subtly melancholy paintings there. Hunting with Chekhov in the woods one day, he winged a woodcock and could not bring himself to finish it off: the bird's large black eyes kept staring up at them in wonder. Closing his eyes and knitting his brow, Levitan begged Chekhov to smash its head against the butt of the rifle. Chekhov refused at first, but eventually gave in and killed the bird. "And while two idiots went home and sat down to dinner," he confessed in a letter to Suvorin, "there was one beautiful, infatuated creature less in the world."[5]

At about this time Chekhov completed a long story entitled "The Grasshopper," which was clearly inspired by Levitan's liaison with Sofia Kuvshinnikova, the wife of the doctor friend who had seen Chekhov off to Sakhalin. Even though Chekhov took care to change the age and appearance of the characters, the resemblance to their models remained patent. Like her real-life counterpart, the pretty heroine of "The Grasshopper" is a young socialite bored with her husband, the too-sober, too-studious Dr. Dymov. She takes to hobnobbing with artists and deludes herself into believing she has a talent for painting. An expedition along the Volga with the painter Ryabovsky leads to an affair. At first she sees herself deceiving the most ordinary of men with a genius. Not until her husband's death, when everyone who knew and admired him comes forth, does she realize how wrong she was. In "The Grasshopper," as in so many other stories, Chekhov pits the modesty and dignity of a life spent in unsung labor against the tinsel of success.

If the general public greeted the story with acclaim, the art world was indignant. Levitan, who recognized himself in the painter, severed all relations with Chekhov and even considered challenging him to a duel; the grasshopper herself, feeling he had made an ignominious caricature of her, refused him entrance to her home. Conscious though he was of having used the lives of people of his acquaintance to give life to the story, he claimed ignorance of the motives behind the uproar. "Imagine," he wrote to Lydia Avilova, "a forty-two-year-old woman I know has recognized herself in the twenty-year-old heroine of my 'Grasshopper' (issues 1 and 2 of *The North*), and all Moscow is accusing me of libel. The main evidence is external: the woman paints, her husband is a doctor, and she lives with an artist."[6]

Chekhov was extremely disturbed by the breach with his friend, but he refused to plead guilty. In his eyes a writer had the right, the duty, to feed his work with the fare provided him by life. Without a constant osmosis between reality and fiction, literature would wither away. Besides, he was soon consoled for his lost friendship by an increasingly affectionate relationship with pretty Lika, whose frequent visits to Melikhovo had come to occupy an important place in his existence. Beneath his letters' customary irony ran a strain of sincerity. "I'm looking forward to seeing you," he wrote, "dreaming of your arrival as a Bedouin in the desert dreams of water." Or: "I miss you. I'd give five rubles for a chance to speak to you, if only for five minutes."

Or: "Come. You know how much I need you. Don't let me down, Likusya. Do come, please."

This renewed interest in Lika did not go unnoticed. Maria kept a close watch on the mating game. First Chekhov would take a step in Lika's direction, then, as if frightened, withdraw into the background. In early spring he wrote her a discouraging letter: "Alas, I've grown into an old young man, and my love is no sun: it hails no spring for me or for the little bird I love."[7] Two days later, however, he took a different tack: "Do write, Melita, if only a few lines. Don't consign us to premature oblivion. At least make believe you still remember us. Deceive us, Lika. Deceit is better than indifference. [. . .] Yours from head to toe, with all my heart and soul, to the grave, to self-oblivion, to intoxication and madness."

Responding to his call, Lika went to Melikhovo, but the dithering—whispered explanations, bumbled seduction attempts, bitter misunderstandings—continued as before. The ambiguity of it all upset her greatly, not the least because Chekhov seemed to delight in it. His letter of June 28 sums up his feelings—the pleasure he took in their relationship and the fear he had of marriage: "Noble, honest Lika, Ever since you wrote that my letters did not commit me to anything, I have breathed easier, and here I am, writing you a long letter free of fear that some old auntie will see it and make me marry a monster like you. For my part, I hasten to put your mind at rest. Your letters are fragrant flowers in my eyes, not documents. [. . .] In other words, you are free. [. . .] Take flight, take flight! Or no, Lika, what will be will be. Let my head spin from your fragrance and help me to tighten the lasso you have thrown round my neck. I can picture you exulting maliciously, laughing demoniacally as you read these lines . . . Oh, what rot I must be writing. Tear this letter up. Excuse me for writing so illegibly, and don't show the letter to anybody. [. . .] Well, good-bye, maize of my soul. I give your compact a cad's respectful kiss and envy your old boots their daily glimpse of you. Write to me of your doings. Be well and do not forget your victory over yours truly, King Midas."

But neither the banter with Lika nor the visits of outsiders kept Chekhov from his study for very long. At Melikhovo writing seemed almost a holiday. That season he completed several stories: "My Wife," "The Neighbors," and, most important, "Ward Six," the action of which takes place in a provincial hospital.

For all his success as a writer Chekhov had not lost touch with medicine, and he was even more in demand as a doctor in the country than in Moscow. Nearly every day peasants and workers—men, women, and children—came from a twenty-five-verst radius with their complaints. They lined up at dawn, and soon the sleepy house was a bustling clinic. Chekhov gave each of them a careful, methodical examination, entering his findings on cards and distributing free of charge the medications he had brought from Moscow. Rare were the patients who remunerated him for his services.

His reputation as a doctor spread so fast that in July 1892, when the region was threatened with an outbreak of cholera, the district council asked him to take charge of efforts to contain the disease. He accepted without hesitation and set to reading the latest works on the subject. His first move was to have isolation barracks built in the twenty-five villages and four factories in the immediate area. Unable to foot the bill himself, he turned "a beggar's eloquence" on friends, neighbors, and the area's rich factory owners. He jolted from village to village in a tumbledown carriage, teaching suspicious peasants to guard against the scourge and treating typhus, diphtheria, and scarlet fever into the bargain. In the space of several weeks he saw about a thousand patients. "My soul is weary," he wrote to Suvorin. "I'm bored. Not being your own master, thinking only of diarrhea, being startled at night by dogs barking and a knock at the gate (have they come for me?), riding abominable horses over uncharted roads, and reading only about cholera, waiting only for cholera, and yet feeling perfect indifference to the disease and the people you're serving—believe me, those are cooks that could spoil any broth."[8] And in an earlier letter to Suvorin: "The peasants are crude, unsanitary, and mistrustful, but the thought that our labors will not be in vain makes it all pass almost unnoticed. Of all the [local] doctors I am the most pitiable: my carriage and horses are mangy, I don't know the roads, I can't see anything at night, I have no money, I tire very quickly, and most of all—I can't forget that I ought to be writing. I have a great urge to drop this whole cholera thing and sit down and start writing."⁹

Of course he did not drop the "whole cholera thing." Thanks largely to his tenacity, cholera spared the district. Not that he himself took the credit: his skepticism precluded feelings of self-satisfaction. What satisfaction he did derive from the work he had done that summer in the provinces came from the discovery that there were a great many men of goodwill among the local landowners and officials. He had been surprised to find an entire class of generous, cultivated intellectuals, quite different from their big-city counterparts. Chekhov had no patience for those among the latter who considered using the situation as an excuse to foment political discontent. "If our socialists do in fact exploit the epidemic for their own ends, I shall feel utter contempt for them. Repulsive means for good ends make the ends themselves repulsive. Let them make dupes of the doctors and their assistants, but why lie to the people? Why assure them that they are right to be ignorant and that their crass prejudices are the holy truth? Can a beautiful future really expiate this base lie? If I were a politician, I'd resolve never to disgrace the present for the sake of the future even though I were promised a hundredweight of bliss for a pennyweight of base lies."¹⁰

With the onset of winter Chekhov's spirits tended to droop. The sight of empty, snow-covered fields and peasants muffled in rags reinforced his melancholy. "There is so little to do in the country in winter that anyone without a penchant for work of the mind will turn into a glutton and a drunk [. . .]. The monotony of the snowdrifts and bare trees, the long nights, moonlight, deathly silence day and night, the peasant women, young and old—it all makes one lazy and apathetic and enlarges the liver."¹¹ When short trips to Moscow failed to cheer him up, he tried Petersburg and Suvorin. Suvorin had fallen ill the previous autumn, and Chekhov, fearing the worst, wrote to Leontyev-Shcheglov, "The loss would be such that it would probably age me ten years."[12] Several months later he wrote to a completely cured Suvorin, "I have foul moods when I feel like talking and writing to somebody, and you're the only one with whom I correspond and have long talks."[13] Late in 1892, however, Chekhov decided to leave *New Times* for the more liberal *Russian Thought*. Suvorin was doubtless upset, yet their friendship survived.

On his return to Melikhovo, Chekhov sank back into the cold, white silence of winter, despairing of seeing the sun. As usual he dreamed of foreign parts: India, Japan, South Africa, Madeira, even—and why not?—Sakhalin. In Petersburg he had met a son of Tolstoy's, Lev Lvovich, and the two of them planned a spring trip to Chicago for the opening of the 1893 Columbian Exposition there. Chekhov eventually withdrew because of the expense, but poor health would have kept him from going in any case: his cough was acting up again. "It's nothing at all," he barked when Mikhail surprised him coughing blood. "Don't say anything to Mother or Maria." To Suvorin he justified his refusal to accept treatment in the following terms: "The enemy that kills the body tends to creep up on it imperceptibly, in a mask—when you have consumption, for example, and you think it's nothing. People aren't afraid of cancer because they think it's nothing. What's terrible is what you're *not* afraid of, not what *does* worry you. [. . .] I know I'll die of a disease I'm not afraid of."[14]

Tuberculosis and palpitations were not his only scourges. Chekhov suffered from a "vile, loathsome" illness he dared mention only to Alexander and Suvorin. "It's not syphilis," he wrote to the latter, "it's worse—hemorrhoids. [. . .] pain, itching, tension. I can't sit, can't walk; my whole body is so sore I feel like hanging myself."[15] The pain made him crotchety. He had more and more trouble putting up with his father's solemn blather, his mother's jeremiads, the daily routine: Mikhail had been on the verge of marrying when the wedding was called off, and he fancied himself the center of an unprecedented drama; Ivan was marrying into the gentry, "a nice girl with a long nose"; Alexander's children made a racket.

Not even books were able to shield him from the insidious amalgam of irritation and depression. He immersed himself in Turgenev, then wrote to Suvorin that he found him "charming but a great deal thinner than Tolstoy! I don't think Tolstoy will ever grow old. His language will become obsolete, but he will remain young."[16] Of all Turgenev's major novels only *Fathers and Sons* struck him as inspired. Moreover, he abhorred Turgenev's women: they were "impossibly affected and false." "When you think of Tolstoy's Anna Karenina," he wrote, again to Suvorin, "all Turgenev's gentlewomen with their seductive shoulders vanish into thin air."[17]

Confined to the estate and to books he had read many times over, he dreamed of travels, friends, lovers' trysts. "I have a *terrible* desire to live it up," he confessed to Suvorin. "The sea has a devilishly strong pull on me. A week in Yalta or Feodosia would be sheer bliss. Things are fine at home, but they'd be a thousand times better on a boat: I'd sit out on deck guzzling wine, talking literature, and in the evening—the ladies."[18]

No matter how he fantasized about escaping to the sun, however, he was chained to the hearth by feelings of filial piety. He may have had little to say to his narrow-minded parents, but he could not turn his back on them. Alexander encouraged him to go. "Give it all up," he wrote to him after several days at Melikhovo, "your dreams of the country life, your love for Melikhovo and all the feeling and work you've put into it. There's nothing unique about Melikhovo. What's the point in letting Aliatrimantran* gobble you up the way rats gobble candles?" And still Chekhov stayed on.

With the return of good weather his internal sky began to clear. He planted new trees, new rosebushes, and began making progress on the *Sakhalin* manuscript, which had been plaguing him for months. Even the threat of a new cholera epidemic failed to dampen his spirit. Again he did everything in his power

*A nickname the Chekhov brothers gave to their father.

to save the muzhiks. No sooner did he return from one village than he found a peasant waiting to take him to another. Literary labors were constantly interrupted by medical ones. He would curse the interruptions, but never shirked his duty. And that year, like the year before, the disease passed over, leaving no victims in the district.

Summer brought back the visiting hordes, and Melikhovo again became a place of strolls, games, and dalliances. Two dachshunds, Bromide and Quinine, trotted at Chekhov's heels, a gift from Leikin. "They're hideous," he wrote to Suvorin, "they have crooked legs and long bodies, but they are extraordinarily intelligent."[19] Every day at supper Yevgenia Yakovlevna fretted over whether the company was enjoying her cooking and Pavel Yegorovich dropped biblical sayings right and left, while Anton—now annoyed, now amused—did his best to raise the level of conversation. Afterwards everyone retired to the salon to smoke, chat, and listen to music. Lika would sing and accompany herself at the piano, and the dashing Ignaty Potapenko, a writer and newcomer to Melikhovo, would play the violin or sing Tchaikovsky and Glinka romances in a warm baritone.

Chekhov was friendly with everyone, but always seemed to be holding back. Potapenko wondered whether anyone so gregarious yet so removed could ever become a close friend. Even when Chekhov seemed entirely absorbed in what was going on around him, he was as like as not thinking of the manuscript open on his desk. Suddenly his eyes clouded over and he would leave the room to jot down a phrase that had come to him. Reemerging from his study, he would apologize by saying he had just "earned sixty kopecks." Nor was he above interrupting a serious conversation about, say, Marxism with an absentminded question like "Have you ever been to a stud farm?" and then returning to the topic at hand with only the slightest of blushes. He never spoke at length about himself and at all times tried to remain in the background. He seemed to be leaning back and watching life go past. Whenever possible, he preferred looking on to acting.

Such was definitely the case in affairs of the heart. Although he eagerly sought the company of pretty women, he was careful not to become serious with any one of them. Lika, whom he bombarded with letters ironic and ardent by turns, had no idea where she stood. That summer, the summer of 1893, she was unsure of whether to go to Melikhovo at all. "Come and see us, sweet, blond Lika," he wrote to her. "We'll talk, we'll argue, we'll make peace. [. . .] Come and sing, fairest Lika."[20]

And come she did, only to realize that all Chekhov's palaver was but a screen for his cold and reasonable intention not to marry her. Hoping to provoke him, she deliberately flirted with Potapenko, but Chekhov showed no jealousy. When Lika accompanied Potapenko at the piano, he looked on with a smile, as if nothing could have pleased him more.

Lika returned to Moscow unhappy and confused. "I'm burning the candle at both ends," she wrote to Chekhov. "Come and help me to burn it as quickly as possible. The sooner it burns the better." She could be even more direct: "There is only one man in the world who can keep me from this conscious self-destruction, but he has no interest in me. It's too late anyway . . . Don't forget the girl you left behind." And finally: "You know very well what I feel for you. That is why I'm not at all ashamed to write to you. I realize your attitude is one of condescension and indifference. My greatest desire is to cure myself of the hopeless state I am in, but it is very hard for me to do so alone. I beg you to help me. Please do not ask me to come and see you, and please do not try to see me again." And to escape the charm Chekhov held over her even at a distance, she became Potapenko's mistress.

But that autumn Chekhov turned his attentions to a woman he had met in Moscow, a young and sinuous actress by the name of Lydia Yavorskaya. Her flirtatious ways, slightly hoarse voice, and love of the unforeseen were diametrically opposed to the simplicity he usually admired; in fact, her artificiality seemed to be what attracted him. In any case, their affair was soon the talk of literary Moscow: he had promised to write a play for her; she wrote him letters ending "Love and kisses."

Lika quickly understood that Yavorskaya was out to take her place in Chekhov's affections. For one thing, she joined the clique that greeted him joyfully whenever he came to Moscow. All the women more or less in love with him knew one another and despised one another under the most friendly of exteriors. Trying a neglected hopeful's well-worn ruse, Lika wrote to Chekhov on November 7, 1893, "Madame Yavorskaya recently spent the evening with us. She said that Chekhov was charming and that she was determined to marry him. [. . .] She asked my assistance, and I promised to do what I could to ensure your mutual happiness. Drop a line to say whether you love her. To me, of course, not to her. Good-bye, executioner of my soul. Please write."

The ruse did not work. Chekhov's prompt response took the form of a five-line note referring to Lika as his "dear intermediary" but giving her no indication of his feelings for Yavorskaya. He was not averse to the idea of several young women lusting after him. He called them his "squadron" and himself their "admiral." They themselves had nicknamed him "Avelan" after the commander of the Russian squadron that had gone to Toulon in 1893 to conclude a Franco-Russian treaty. In Moscow he stayed at the Grand Hôtel, where Room Five was always waiting for him and where his admirers would come to call. "Girls, girls, girls," he wrote to Suvorin as part of the reason why he had never felt freer.[21] But Shchepkina-Kupernik claimed he always looked absentminded when he was with them, like a grown-up playing with children. When he saw a picture of himself staring morosely at the camera between the simpering Shchepkina-Kupernik and Yavorskaya, he entitled it "The Temptation of Saint Anthony." Although he maintained that the sexual instinct lay at the very foundation of love, he saw no reason to glorify the exploits of the flesh. Nor did he himself appear to have been prodigiously active sexually. "All thinkers are impotent at forty," he wrote to Suvorin, "while ninety-year-old savages keep ninety wives apiece."[22] And whether unwittingly or with tongue in cheek he invited Lika and Potapenko to Melikhovo for the 1894 New Year's celebrations.

By then *The Island of Sakhalin* had begun to come out serially in *Russian Thought*. Chekhov was relieved to put so thankless a task behind him. "Medicine can no longer accuse me of betrayal. I have paid my debt to scholarship and to what old writers used to call pedantry, and I'm glad that a rough convict's smock will now hang in my literary wardrobe."[23] He was now the foremost writer of his generation: critics praised him for both his art and his observation of contemporary mores; newspapers and journals badgered him for material; his books went through printing after printing and were translated into French, English, and German. No wonder readers turned to *Sakhalin* with great excitement. Most were disappointed. They had expected a dazzling, wild, dramatic book, a sequel to Dostoevsky's *Notes from the House of the Dead*; what they found was a sober and impartial—some said dry—report of his stay among the convicts. Dry or not, it immediately caught the attention of the authorities. A commission was dispatched to investigate Chekhov's claims, and the reforms it recommended went a long way towards alleviating conditions for the convicts. He could therefore rest assured that he had not labored in vain.

Unlike *The Island of Sakhalin,* "Ward Six," a long story published the previous year and perhaps his darkest work of fiction, attracted a large and enthusiastic audience. The ward in question is the mental ward of a provincial hospital, where the weak and listless chief physician, Dr. Ragin, has long since withdrawn with a supply of vodka, pickled cucumbers, and daydreams. Completely self-absorbed, he willfully ignores the corruption, violence, filth, and misery surrounding him; all he can say to his patients' tales of woe is "What difference does it make?" A despotic guard by the name of Nikita keeps the patients in line by bashing their heads in at regular intervals. By the time Ragin tries to take himself in hand, it is too late: his eccentric behavior has enabled the outside world to declare him insane, and he ends up an inmate of the ward, the blows of the dread Nikita now raining upon him as well. Only as he dies does he apprehend the crimes he has committed by countenancing horrors he should have denounced.

top: Chekhov and his family in Taganrog, 1874. Standing: Ivan, Anton, Nikolai, Alexander, and an uncle, Mitrofan. Sitting: Mikhail; Maria; Anton's father, Pavel Yegorovich, and his mother, Yevgenia Yakovlevna; an aunt and her son.

bottom left: Chekhov in 1890 with family and friends in front of the Sadovaya-Kudrinskaya Street house in Moscow where he lived from 1886 to 1890. Sitting beside him is his brother Mikhail.

bottom right: Anton (standing) and his brother Nikolai, 1881, in Moscow.

Chekhov, 1888.

right: Chekhov in Yalta, 1899.

below: Chekhov, Gorky, and Tolstoy.

lower right: Chekhov and Gorky in Yalta, 1900.

Chekhov, about 1900.

Chekhov and Tolstoy at Gaspra in the Crimea, 1901.

Chekhov in his study in Yalta, 1900.

left: Chekhov and his wife, the actress Olga Knipper, 1901.

below: Chekhov in 1904 with his dogs, in front of his Yalta villa.

Chekhov's house in Melikhovo.

Chekhov's villa in Yalta.

Chekhov's bedroom in Yalta.

Chekhov in a group portrait with the company of the Moscow Art Theater.
He is reading them the text of *The Seagull*.

Stanislavsky and his wife, M. P. Lilina, in a scene from *Uncle Vanya*.

Chekhov served up so strong a mixture of realism and pathology in "Ward Six" that it provoked a good deal of controversy. Some saw it as a veiled critique of Tolstoyan thought, the nonresistance of evil; others called it a tract aimed at the regime, with Ward Six symbolizing Russia, Nikita tsarist power, and the disillusioned doctor the ineffectual Russian intelligentsia. Chekhov, true to his customary discretion, refused to explain what he meant by the story. The writer's task, he felt, was to create a work, not interpret it.

Although "Ward Six" was tremendously popular, Suvorin felt it "contained no alcohol." What he meant can be inferred from Chekhov's modest response: "Keep in mind that the writers we call eternal or simply good, the writers who intoxicate us, have one highly important trait in common: they are moving towards something definite and beckon you to follow, and you feel with your entire being, not only with your mind, that they have a certain goal, like the ghost of Hamlet's father, which had a motive for coming and stirring Hamlet's imagination. Depending on their caliber, some have immediate goals—the abolition of serfdom, the liberation of one's country, politics, beauty, or simply vodka [. . .]—while the goals of others are more remote—God, life after death, the happiness of mankind, etc. The best of them are realistic and describe life as it is, but because each line is saturated with the consciousness of its goal, you feel life as it should be in addition to life as it is, and you are captivated by it. But what about us? Us! We describe life as it is and stop dead right there. We wouldn't lift a hoof if you lit into us with a whip. We have neither immediate nor remote goals, and there is an emptiness in our souls. We have no politics, we don't believe in revolution, there is no God, we're not afraid of ghosts, and I personally am not even afraid of death or blindness. If you want nothing, hope for nothing, and fear nothing, you cannot be an artist."[24]

Chekhov's refusal to call himself an artist fooled no one. Readers were again intrigued by his next long work, "The Story of an Unknown Man," which he had begun five years earlier but stashed away in a desk drawer for fear of what the censors might do to it. When he finally submitted it, however, it passed without a cut and appeared intact in *Russian Thought* in 1893. A first-person account of a revolutionary terrorist who hires himself out as a manservant to the son of a high official he intends to assassinate, it is valuable primarily for the psychological portraits of characters like Orlov, a cynical man of the world, and his mistress, the vulnerable but passionate Zina. Little by little the terrorist's murderous zeal is sapped by his love for Zina. For attributing such a failing to a leftist idealist, Chekhov earned the wrath of the liberal critics. They reproached him for showing up his hero as a man who lacked the courage of his convictions.

If readers found Chekhov's next major story, "The Black Monk," even more puzzling, it was for different reasons. One afternoon at Melikhovo, when everyone but Mikhail was taking a nap, Chekhov flew out of his room with a contorted face and told his brother, "I've just had the most awful dream! I was visited by a black monk." Obsessed by the vision, he tried to purge it by writing. For the first time he had entered the realm of the supernatural.

As Chekhov saw it, "The Black Monk" was the study of a neurosis. Kovrin, a mediocre philosopher whose nerves are frayed by mental fatigue, has a hallucination of a black monk soaring above the fields. It leads him to believe he is one of God's chosen, a servant to eternal truth. He glows with pride at his superiority to ordinary mortals until his wife and her father insist that he undergo treatment. Normal again, he suffers terribly from being restored to the common run of mankind: "I kept losing my mind, I had delusions of grandeur, but I was cheerful, lively, even happy. I was interesting and original. Now I am more reasonable and sedate, but I'm like everybody: I'm a mediocrity. I'm bored with life." He is furious with his wife for forcing treatment on him and leaves her to pursue his dream. But at the very moment his monk reappears, the tubercular Kovrin dies coughing blood.

Some considered this strange story a masterpiece of the fantastic while others saw it as a sneer at intellectuals who claimed the secret of universal happiness and denied a common law. When a friend informed Chekhov that Tolstoy, normally so sparing of praise, had reacted to the story by exclaiming, "Charming! Oh, how charming," Chekhov felt he had been given a high mark by a universally admired teacher. In fact, however, he had been moving further and further away from the teachings of the sage of Yasnaya Polyana. He could accept such Tolstoyan tenets as love of the downtrodden, hatred of violence, and a desire for justice, but he drew the line at glorifying the "holy Russian muzhik." As he wrote to Suvorin, "I have peasant blood flowing in my veins, and I'm not the one to be impressed with peasant virtues. [. . .] Tolstoy's philosophy moved me deeply and possessed me for six or seven years. It was not so much his basic postulates that affected me—I was familiar with them before—it was his way of expressing himself, his common sense, and probably a sort of hypnotism as well. But now something in me protests. Prudence and justice tell me there is more love for mankind in electricity than in chastity and abstention from meat. War is an evil and the court system is an evil, but it doesn't follow that I should wear bast shoes and sleep on a stove alongside the hired hand and his wife, and so on and so forth. But that's not the issue; it's not a matter of pros and cons. The point is that in one way or another Tolstoy has departed from my life; he's no longer in my heart and he's left me, saying, 'Behold, I leave your house empty.' I am now free of all tenants."[25]

Immediately after "The Black Monk" *Russian Thought* published a Chekhov story in a completely different key. Anna, the heroine of "A Woman's Kingdom," has inherited her father's factory. At twenty-six she is the prisoner of her money and social status. She dreams of marrying one of her workers, Pimenov, but gives in to pressure from the world she is destined to inhabit. "She saw clearly that everything she had thought and said about Pimenov and marriage to a simple worker was rubbish, nonsense, folly. [. . .] Her dreams of Pimenov were honest, lofty, noble, yet at the same time she felt that Lysevich and even Krylin [her lawyer and a high official] were closer to her than Pimenov and all the workers together." Another story of naïve ideals falling before grim reality.

A strain of pessimism now ran from one work to the next: Worsening health—early morning coughing attacks left him exhausted for hours—was not conducive to euphoria. In February 1894 he abruptly decided to go south. He arrived in sunny Yalta on March 5, happy to find the white villas along the seashore, the tall cypresses, the eternally blue sky—all as he had remembered them. He put up at the Hotel Russia, hoping to sequester himself long enough to make inroads on a play, but was soon distracted by friends, journalists, and itinerant actors. Even as he chatted with them, he fretted over lost hours.

Early in his stay he received a desperate letter from Lika. She was in Berlin on her way to join Potapenko in Paris and take voice lessons there. She complained of being "rejected" by Chekhov a second time, at loose ends, even desirous of ending it all. Steeled by experience, Chekhov refused to go along with the tragic tone. "Thank you for the letter. Although you frighten me by saying you'll soon be dead, although you tease me by saying I've rejected you, thank you all the same. I know full well you won't die and no one has rejected you." Whereupon he told Lika that he had helped an amateur company to put on *Faust,* that he had had a meal of roast lamb with a schoolmistress, that he missed his "ladies," that his ideal was "to be idle and love a buxom girl," and that he begged his charming correspondent to marry him when she was a rich and famous singer so he would not have to work. He concluded by enjoining her to return to Russia quickly. "Talk to Potapenko. He'll be going to Russia in the summer too. The trip will be cheaper with him. Ask him to buy your ticket and forget to pay him back (it won't be the first time)."[26]

Because not even Yalta's warm weather and salt sea air could restore his health, he returned to Melikhovo after only four weeks. There he once more succumbed to the charm of the Russian countryside in spring. He would go out into the garden in his dressing gown, daydream at the edge of the pond, plant flowers, mark out new paths, and go horseback riding, with Bromide and Quinine trotting close behind. The smell of freshly mown hay intoxicated him, he wrote to Leontyev-Shcheglov, and added: "Spend an hour or two on a haystack and you'll imagine yourself in the arms of a naked woman."[27] And to Suvorin: "I think that living close to nature and doing nothing are indispensable elements of happiness."[28] He had a small wooden house built behind the cherry orchard at a cost of 125 rubles. With its two rooms and attic he called it the "doll's house," and he used it as a retreat when the main house, packed with guests, became too noisy. It was there he eventually wrote *The Seagull*.

But that summer he could not wait to leave. He tried to interest Suvorin in a trip along the Volga—they could visit old monasteries and cemeteries—or a trip to Feodosia or Switzerland. Any trip would do. "A force, a foreboding is urging me to hurry. Though maybe it's not a foreboding but a feeling of regret at seeing life drift by so monotonous and dull. A protest of the soul, so to speak."[29]

Since Suvorin proved less than enthusiastic, he turned to Potapenko, who in the meantime had returned from abroad without Lika. Potapenko was not particularly forthcoming about the affair, and Chekhov did not question him about it. They enjoyed each other's company and looked forward to the trip down the Volga. Then at the tumultuous Nizhny Novgorod fair they met the loquacious and self-centered Tolstoyan Sergeenko, and his presence so marred the good time they were having that Chekhov packed his bags and returned to Melikhovo.

Learning there that his Uncle Mitrofan was on his deathbed, he immediately took the train to Taganrog, and if his first thought was to care for Mitrofan and his family, he was also grateful for an excuse to pick up and leave again. No sooner did he arrive, however, than he was sorry to have made the trip. He had little left in common with his family, and since the local papers had reported the presence of the "famous writer," there was constantly someone at the door. After six days at his uncle's bedside he realized there was nothing he could do, and he fled to Feodosia, where Suvorin received him royally in his villa. But the weather was cold, he seemed to be coughing his lungs out, and not even the friendly talks with Suvorin could distract him from his boredom. So he sailed to Yalta, only to learn of his uncle's death. "I loved my departed uncle with all my heart, loved and respected him," he wrote to his cousin Georgy.[30] Recalling the good and pious man his uncle had been, he thought of his miserable childhood in sleepy Taganrog and the distance he had traveled since. Soon he was ready to push on. The moment he set foot anywhere the ground seemed to burn up beneath him. He felt constantly compelled to push on.

From Yalta he went to Odessa, from Odessa—via Vienna—to Abbazia, a spa on the Adriatic. Suvorin accompanied him in the escapade. Chekhov felt guilty about the expense and kept the journey from his family, even his usual confidante Maria. In Vienna he wrote to Lika, "Please don't write to anybody in Russia that I'm abroad. I left in secret, like a thief, and Masha thinks I'm in Feodosia. They'll be upset if they find out I'm abroad; they've had enough of my trips for some time now. I'm not quite well. I cough pretty much continuously. It looks as though I've let my health go the way I let you go."[31]

Three days later he wrote to Lika from Abbazia that bad weather was chasing them away and that they hoped to find some sun in Nice. On the way there they stopped at Trieste, Venice, Milan, and Genoa. From Milan he sent a long, remorseful letter to his sister, informing her of his flight and inquiring whether she had money enough to take care of the family's needs. He then summed up his impressions by mentioning that in Vienna he had bought a jockey cap with ears and in Venice three silk neckties and a glass painted in "the colors of paradise," while in Milan he had gone to a dramatization of *Crime and Punishment*—with actors better than their Russian counterparts—and visited a crematorium, and he was now looking forward to a stroll through the Genoa cemetery. Suvorin expressed surprise at his companion's morbid tastes. Although Chekhov denied the importance of death, it was constantly on his mind.

Several letters from Lika, postmarked Switzerland, caught up with him at Nice in early October. She had decided to swallow her pride and tell him all about her recent disappointments in love. After Chekhov had "rejected" her, she had given in to Potapenko and followed him to Paris. But he had soon tired of her and returned to his wife. The happy family had gone off to Italy, while she remained behind, pregnant with Potapenko's child. "It is clear I am condemned and my loved ones will despise me," she wrote to Chekhov, alone and distraught. "I should so like to talk to you. I am so unhappy. There is nothing left of the former Lika, and no matter what I think, I cannot truly say it is entirely your fault." Next day he had another letter from her begging him to come and see her. "Come if you do not fear being disappointed by your old friend Lika. So little of her remains. [. . .] Yes, these six months have really changed my life. But I don't expect you to take my part. You have always been indifferent to people and their foibles and imperfections."

Chekhov was outraged at Potapenko's behavior and wrote to his sister that the man was a swine. But he was careful not to fly to Lika's aid. His response to her letters had a cold ring to it: "Unfortunately, I can't go to Switzerland. I'm with Suvorin, who needs to go to Paris. I'll be in Nice for another five to seven days, in Paris for three or four, and then go back to Melikhovo. [. . .] You were wrong to have written I was indifferent to people. Don't pine, cheer up, and look after your health."[32]

By October 19 he was back in Melikhovo. Although he must have been annoyed with himself for having treated Lika as he did, he was annoyed with her for having called him "indifferent" to his fellowman; besides, he feared that seeing her again would provoke a rush of pity in him, and he did not wish to end up with a lachrymose woman on his hands, a woman he no longer loved.

She, for her part, would not give in. "I shall soon have been in Paris for two months," she wrote in late December, "and still not a word from you. Might you be angry with me?

Without you I feel completely lost and rejected. I'd give half my life to be at Melikhovo, sitting next to you on the sofa and talking, having dinner, and in general living as though this year had never existed, as though I'd never left Russia and everything was as it used to be."

But it was no use. Once he had decided against a rescue operation, he stopped writing to her or speaking of her to his sister. (Because Maria went on corresponding with her, she later learned that Lika had given birth to a girl, seen Potapenko again in Paris, and hoped to return to Russia soon.) What is more, he soon forgot his resentment against Potapenko the "swine" and even took up with him again. Poor Lika had lost on all fronts. In an attempt to understand her brother's attitude Maria wrote in her memoirs, "I do not know what went on in his head, but I think he was struggling to overcome his feelings for Lika. Certain sides of her nature were foreign to him. She lacked character and was too fond of the bohemian life."

In the end, Lika's powers of seduction proved inadequate; Chekhov never moved beyond the stage of gallant remarks. He was not particularly sensual by nature and had little trouble mastering his physical desires. The preliminaries were what interested him most in love; he saw them as a self-sufficient game. In a moment of sincerity he confessed to Suvorin that he had had few affairs and was as much like Catherine the Great, known for her insatiable sexual appetite, "as a nut is like a warship."[33] The fickle Potapenko, his rival for Lika's affections, gives a sensible explanation of Chekhov's caution. "He resisted leading a private existence," he writes in his *Memoirs*. "He felt it robbed the creator in him of too much strength and concentration."

Soon after Lika returned to Russia her baby died, and again Potapenko took refuge in the bosom of his family. As for Chekhov, he began to wonder whether the ups and downs of the unfortunate episode might not have the makings of a play. One thing was clear: the older he grew, the more life appeared to him as an excuse for writing. By some mysterious alchemy the people he met and the incidents he experienced turned into words strung together on a page.

XI

The Seagull

One cold January evening in 1895 when the family had just about finished supper, the Melikhovo dogs started barking and there was a knock at the door. Maria went to see who it was. The lamp she held up to the visitors revealed the beaming Tatyana Shchepkina-Kupernik and a rumpled and embarrassed Levitan behind her. For more than two years the painter had borne Chekhov a grudge for portraying him as a cynic and lecher in "The Grasshopper," but Shchepkina-Kupernik had persuaded him to forget his quarrel with Chekhov, and there he was—half angry, half happy—in Melikhovo. Chekhov, clearly moved, came out to meet him, and, after a moment of silence, shook his hand. The two men tacitly agreed to avoid all mention of the past. During the banal conversation that followed, Levitan's eyes grew moist and Chekhov's gleamed with childlike gaiety. "It was a return to someone who had once been dear to me," Levitan wrote to

Chekhov from Moscow, "to someone who has never ceased being dear to me."

They met again before long, in Moscow, at Levitan's studio. Much as Chekhov admired the painter's latest canvases, he found something artificial about them. "He has lost his youthful touch and paints with bravura. I think he's been done in by women. The dear creatures give a man love and take little in return: only youth. Painting a landscape is impossible without spirit or rapture, and rapture is impossible on a full stomach. If I were a landscape painter, I'd lead an all but ascetic life: I'd have intercourse once a year and food once a day."[1] Joking apart, Chekhov set great store by ascetic discipline. "If monasteries accepted the irreligious and permitted abstention from prayer, I'd become a monk," he wrote a year later to Suvorin.[2] How to reconcile his day-to-day life with literature? Was a normal life at all compatible with the life of the pen? Questions like these had tormented Chekhov since he started writing seriously.

At about this time he completed a long story called "Three Years" tracing the downfall of a family in the corrupt atmosphere of mercantile Moscow. Though dissatisfied with the result, he was incapable of emending or expanding it, and submitted it to *Russian Thought* as it was. When the censors came down hard on the text, cutting a number of passages that dealt with religion, he wrote to Suvorin: "It takes away any desire you have to express yourself freely; whenever you write, you get a feeling there's a bone stuck in your throat."[3]

Not that he intended to let the bone in his throat affect his production. But for every new idea he had, he had any number of patients, and seeing them meant traveling to the four corners of the district. Besides, he was building a new school in the neighboring village of Talezh, where he served as honorary superintendent; he had been named first a juror, then the jury foreman, of the Serpukhov court; he lacked the backbone to ignore the aspiring writers who sent him manuscripts, begging for his comments; and finally, he had taken it into his head to enrich the library of his native Taganrog, and regularly dispatched bundles of books received from publishers or bought with his own savings.

When Suvorin expressed dismay at seeing his energies so dissipated and advised him, once more, to settle down and take a wife, his reply was quite clear: "Very well, then, I will marry if you so desire. But under the following conditions: everything must continue as it was before, in other words, she must live in Moscow and I in the country, and I shall go and visit her. I'll never be able to stand the sort of happiness that lasts from one day to the next, from one morning to the next. I turn ferocious in the company of Sergeenko, for example, because he's very much like a woman ('an intelligent and responsive woman') and because it occurs to me when I'm in his presence that my wife could be like him. I promise to be a splendid husband, but give me a wife who, like the moon, does not appear in my sky every day. I won't write any better for being married."[4] Several months later, however, he added, "I'm afraid of a wife and a domestic routine that will hamper me, that I can't quite combine with my lack of order; still, it's better than drifting on the ocean of life and tossing in the frail barque of debauchery. I don't care for mistresses anymore, and I'm gradually growing impotent with them."[5]

Chekhov may have lost some of his interest in women, but women were still interested in him. And the most enterprising among them was indisputably Lydia Avilova. Although Chekhov had not written her a single letter in 1894, she was convinced that he was still secretly infatuated with her. While he was passing through Petersburg in February 1895, she invited him to supper, tête-à-tête—her husband was away. Unfortunately, some friends dropped in on her unannounced that evening, and they not only dug into the hors d'oeuvres she had prepared for him but also completely monopolized her distinguished guest when he arrived. At last she succeeded in showing the former the door and turned her charms on the latter.

In her memoirs she claims that Chekhov made her a kind of retrospective declaration of love on that occasion. " 'Remember our first meetings? And do you know—do you know that I was deeply in love with you? Seriously in love with you? Yes, I loved you. It seemed to me there was not another woman in the world I could love like that. You were beautiful and sweet and there was such freshness in your youth, such dazzling charm. [. . .] But I knew that you were not like other women and that one's love for you must be pure and sacred and must last all one's life. I was afraid to touch you.' "6

Unfortunately, the letter Chekhov wrote Lydia Avilova the day after is so prosaic in tone that it belies her assertions: "You are wrong to say I was unconscionably bored with you. I wasn't bored, though I was a bit depressed at seeing in your face how tired you were of your visitors."7 The day after that he wrote her another, even drier, letter that contained the following candid remarks on some stories she had asked him to read: "To sum up, you are talented, but too heavy or, to put it vulgarly, flabby; you belong to the ranks of flabby writers. Your style is as precious as an old man's."8 The letter was signed "Yours, Chekhov," and the recently published *Stories and Tales* enclosed with it bore the cold inscription "For L. A. Avilova from the author." The author soon returned to Moscow, making no attempt to see the woman he was supposed to have spent years pining for.

Uncertain of what to make of his flight, Avilova decided to try a poetic tack. She ordered a watch fob in the form of a book with "*Stories and Tales* by A. Chekhov" engraved on one side and "page 267, lines 6 and 7" on the other, a reference to the sentence from "The Neighbors": "If ever you have need of my life, come and take it." She commissioned her brother to deliver the fob to the offices of *Russian Thought,* and waited anxiously for the response. There was none. Chekhov did not even acknowledge receipt of the gift. Avilova was mortified. She went to Moscow and wrote to Melikhovo asking Chekhov to join her. Again there was no response. Chekhov had left word with the editors of *Russian Thought* that he had gone to Taganrog.

He had done no such thing, of course; he was holed up in Melikhovo watching for signs of spring. At last, after months of snow, torpor, and solitude, he could write to Suvorin, "The larks are singing in the field, the thrushes calling in the wood. It's warm and pleasant."[9]

As usual, the first fine days saw an influx of visitors. Soon the whole family was reunited. Mikhail, now in Yaroslavl, had made new progress up the civil-service ladder; Ivan had started gaining a reputation for himself in Moscow pedagogical circles; Maria taught at the Raevsky Institute, but was now taking medical courses on the side to help her brother care for the peasants; and Alexander, who had not only held on to his job at *New Times* but was also publishing stories under the name of Sedoy, proudly announced to Anton that he had opened a bank account and was planning to rent a dacha of his own.

Lika visited Melikhovo three times that summer. She no longer appeared to have designs on Chekhov, and they were able to enjoy each other's company again. Chekhov was as happy to welcome her back to the fold as he had been to welcome back her seducer Potapenko, whom he now considered nothing but a hail fellow well met.

As for Levitan, the other close friend with whom he had recently been reconciled, he had tired of his "grasshopper" and moved on to a certain Anna Turchaninova, a woman of considerable fortune and years. Suddenly in July 1895 Chekhov received a letter from Turchaninova saying that the painter, who was living on her estate at the time, had attempted suicide. Although he had merely wounded himself, she wrote, he was so depressed that only Chekhov could save him. What she did not write was that he had been driven to the act by the violent arguments she had had with her daughter over his favors. Ever the true friend, Chekhov immediately rushed to her Novgorod estate, where he found Levitan looking deathly pale, his head wound round with a bandage. Fortunately, the bullet had no more than grazed his scalp. For five days Chekhov did what he could to raise his friend's spirits. That he succeeded is clear from the letter he received from him after returning to Melikhovo: "I don't know why, but the few days you spent here were the most peaceful of the summer for me."

Scarcely two weeks after accomplishing the Levitan mission, Chekhov set off on another. This time it was more of a pilgrimage, however, for he was going to visit Tolstoy at his Yasnaya Polyana estate. Most Russian writers and many foreign ones made the journey—some out of deference, others out of curiosity. Though a great admirer of the author of *War and Peace* and *Anna Karenina,* Chekhov had felt reticent about bowing before the redoubtable prophet, the Tolstoy who insisted on denying scientific progress to promote progress of a spiritual nature. In the end a Tolstoyan by the name of Ivan Gorbunov-Posadov overcame his objections, and on August 8, 1895, he had his first encounter with the sage.

They met on the beech-lined path leading to the house. Tolstoy was wearing a white smock and had a towel over his shoulder: he was on his way to bathe in the river. He invited Chekhov to join him. The two men undressed and jumped in, and they had their first conversation in a state of nature, paddling neck-deep through the water. Tolstoy's simplicity won him over to the point that he all but forgot he was face to face with a monument of Russian literature. Later they went for a spin along the Tula road, Tolstoy extolling the bicycle despite his seventy-seven years.

That evening Gorbunov-Posadov gave a reading from the newly completed first draft of *Resurrection* before a group of family and friends. The warm welcome Chekhov had received from his host gave him the courage to point out that, while he had nothing but admiration for the trial scene, he felt that Katya Maslova, the novel's heroine, was unlikely to receive a sentence of only two years: Russian courts tended to be particularly harsh when hard labor was involved. Tolstoy accepted Chekhov's criticism and changed the passage accordingly.

After their first meeting Tolstoy gave the following report about Chekhov to his son Lev in a letter dated September 4, 1895: "He is full of talent and doubtless has a fine heart, but he doesn't yet seem to have a definite point of view on life." As for Chekhov, he regretted that the characters in *Resurrection* were more or less spokesmen for the author, though he recognized

Tolstoy as a man of exceptional moral stature. "When you talk to Lev Nikolaevich," he said, "you feel you are entirely in his power. I have never met anyone so engaging and, so to speak, harmoniously conceived. He is a nearly perfect man."[10] To Suvorin he wrote, "My visit with the Tolstoys lasted a day and a half. He made a marvelous impression on me. I felt as free and easy as if I'd been at home. The talks I had with Lev Nikolaevich were equally free and easy."[11] Several days later he added, "Tolstoy's daughters are very nice. They adore their father and have a fanatical belief in him. That means Tolstoy really is a great moral force. If he weren't sincere and above reproach, his daughters would be the first to treat him skeptically. Daughters are cunning little things; you can't pull the wool over their eyes . . . You can dupe a fiancée or a mistress as much as you please: in the eyes of a woman in love even an ass seems a philosopher; but daughters are quite another matter."[12]

After a round of stories—"The Wife," "Anna on the Neck," "White Brow," "The Murder," "Ariadne"—Chekhov suddenly felt the lure of the theater again. On October 21, 1895, he made the following joyful announcement to Suvorin: "Believe it or not, I'm writing a play, which I'll probably not finish until the end of November. I can't say I don't enjoy writing it, though I'm flagrantly disregarding the basic tenets of the stage. The comedy has three female roles, six male roles, four acts, a landscape (the view of a lake), much conversation about literature, little action, and five tons of love." He called the play in question *The Seagull*.

Less than a month after drafting the first lines, he was able to inform a writer friend, Yelena Shavrova, "I have finished my play. [. . .] It's nothing special. All things considered, I'm a mediocre playwright."[13] Despite the self-disparagement, however, he polished the text relentlessly, and that at a time when he was poring over plans and estimates for the Talezh school, writing hither and yon to save the journal *The Annals of Surgery* from extinction, collecting funds for the needy, and, as in the past, seeing numerous patients without charge. Grabbing time whenever he could find it, he eventually succeeded in producing a final version and having it typed in two copies on a "Remington." In the letter accompanying the copy that went to Suvorin Chekhov wrote, "I started it *forte* and ended it *pianissimo,* against all rules of dramatic art. [. . .] I'm more dissatisfied than satisfied and, reading through my newborn play, I'm more convinced than ever I'm no playwright. [. . .] Be sure you don't let anybody read it."[14]

Must a writer plunder the misfortunes of others to achieve the ring of truth? In *The Seagull* Chekhov had again yielded to a natural inclination to borrow important plot elements from the lives of friends: it was clearly inspired by Lika and Potapenko's tawdry affair. Nina, the melancholy but passionate heroine of *The Seagull* is, like Lika, seduced and abandoned by a Potapenko-like writer named Trigorin; she bears him a child who dies in infancy. Yet the true interest of the play lies less in the somewhat banal plot than in the finely tuned dialogue, rich in allusions and suggestive pauses. Action is replaced by psychological climate. Emotion is expressed not so much externally, through a gesture or a shout, as in the innermost recesses of the psyche. What grips the audience is not sudden turns of events but the muted evolution of feelings. In short, the author no longer strikes a blow; he casts a spell.

The relationship of the play to Lika's situation was apparent at its first reading, before friends. Indeed, those present drew a further parallel between the character of the actress Arkadina and Potapenko's wife. The reaction at the second reading, in Lydia Yavorskaya's Moscow flat, was the same. When Suvorin, too, brought up the issue, Chekhov responded bitterly, "My play (*The Seagull*) has flopped before its first production. If I really do seem to have portrayed Potapenko in it, then of course it mustn't be staged or published."[15]

But Chekhov's friends were concerned about more than the references to Lika and Potapenko. No matter how they admired him, they could not help feeling that this time he was on the wrong track. How could a writer keep the audience's interest with inner struggles and disquisitions on the soul? Anything that did not directly feed the plot, move to action, was pointless. That Chekhov was hurt by their remarks is clear. "It seems I'm not meant to be a playwright," he wrote to Suvorin. "I haven't any luck. But I don't despair, because I keep writing stories—and in that domain I feel at home. When I write a play, I feel uncomfortable, as if somebody is poking me in the neck."[16]

It took great willpower for Chekhov to overcome his distaste and go back to work on the play, but in the first weeks of 1896 he completely rewrote it. Potapenko, to whom he candidly sent the new version, found nothing to object to: he was now the model husband and showed little concern for the whole Lika episode. When Chekhov visited Petersburg that January, the Potapenkos took him to a theater recently acquired by Suvorin to see Edmond Rostand's *The Distant Princess* in a translation by Shchepkina-Kupernik. "I go to Potapenko's every day," he wrote to his sister. "He's full of life. His wife is too."[17]

Chekhov put up at the Hôtel d'Angleterre and spent his time seeing friends and going to literary dinners. He loved the excitement of the capital and would have been only too glad to stay on, but he had to return to Melikhovo to attend a wedding: his brother Mikhail was marrying "a sweet and generous woman who is also an excellent cook."

Immediately after the ceremony he hurried back to Petersburg. On January 27 he went to a masquerade party at Suvorin's theater, where Lydia Avilova pursued him under the cover of a black domino. As she tells it, she went up to him and spoke to him of love. Although he must have recognized her, he pretended to take her for someone else. When she asked whether he had received her gift, he replied enigmatically that she would find out in his play, which was due to open shortly in Petersburg.

On his way home he stopped off in Moscow, where he and Suvorin paid a visit to Tolstoy. Lev Nikolaevich railed against the new Russian Symbolist poets, calling them "decadents"; his wife seemed angry, too, but with the religious painter Gay. Chekhov found it oddly refreshing to watch two of Tolstoy's daughters playing a peaceful game of cards through it all.

In the country Chekhov went back to work, though the work was not entirely literary. Unwilling to settle for mere cosmetic improvements on the estate, he had launched a crusade with the local authorities to have road repairs made, a telegraph and post office opened, a bridge rebuilt, the neighboring church restored, and the new school at Talezh completed. The latter project was particularly dear to his heart, and although he organized fund-raising campaigns, concerts, and amateur theatricals to finance it, he often had to put his hand in his own pocket; besides drawing up plans for the building, he bought the materials and supervised the carpenters and masons. The school was ready in August 1896. During the inauguration ceremony three priests blessed the walls and the peasants offered Chekhov an icon, several loaves of bread, and two silver salt-shakers.*

By building schools, establishing libraries, and treating the sick, Chekhov felt he was serving his country better than by decrying the initiatives of the new tsar, Nicholas II, who despite his youth seemed ill disposed towards a more liberal stance than that of his father, Alexander III. While in Moscow that June, however, Chekhov went to see the tombs of the Khodynka victims, the more than a thousand people trampled to death during the coronation ceremonies because of a poorly managed police force. The popular view—namely, that the disaster boded ill for the imperial couple—was of course inimical to Chekhov the rationalist.

After giving *Russian Thought* the tale of a couple with crossed destinies, "House with a Mansard," he tackled a much longer work. "My Life" combines memories of a Taganrog youth with the recent school building experience, but it is primarily the story of a young man's rebellion against his hidebound, bourgeois father. Having made a clean break with the social background he abhors, he tries to become a worker, a housepainter, and although he soon realizes that despite his best endeavors he will never be fully accepted by the folk, he considers failure

---

*Bread and salt are the traditional Russian symbols of hospitality.

preferable to the supposed successes of his former, privileged, friends. "My Life" was read as a diatribe against Tolstoyan thought, and in it Chekhov does reject assimilation into the masses as the remedy for the ills of provincial life; he does not, however, offer a remedy of his own. As a skeptic, he has no use for philosophical conclusions. He merely lays out the facts and lets his heroes make the endlessly painful search for a truth that leads to equanimity.

A similar concern for objectivity is evident in *The Seagull*. There too the author disappeared behind his characters. He could not, however, disappear from the censor, at whose hands he feared crippling cuts. He even asked Potapenko to be prepared to intervene on his behalf. But on August 20, 1896, after only minor modifications, the play passed muster, and on September 8 Chekhov received a telegram from Potapenko informing him that it had been accepted by the Petersburg Alexandrinsky Theater, that the cast would be brilliant, and that the opening would take place on October 17.

Heartened as he was by this first victory, Chekhov still worried over how the play would fare with the public. Even those who appreciated its poetry felt it was too static. Chekhov's response was that he had tried to depict life as it is, with its combination of absurdity and enthusiasm, vulgarity and grief, banality and mystery. But was the general audience up to the challenge?

On October 7 Chekhov left for Petersburg, and the day after his arrival he sat through a rehearsal in the Alexandrinsky's dark hall. What he saw and heard there filled him with dismay, and his forebodings grew daily. In a letter to a Melikhovo neighbor he described nightmares of being married off to a woman he did not love and being called names in the newspapers.[18] Yevtikhy Karpov, the director of the theater and the production, failed to grasp the subtleties of the play, and the actors declaimed with a grandiloquence that clashed head-on with the author's taste for understatement. Time and time again Chekhov stopped them and begged them to be more natural: "The point is, my friends, there's no use being theatrical. None whatever. The whole thing is very simple. The characters are simple, ordinary people." But the actors claimed to know better and went on with their bombast. Leaving the theater after a rehearsal, Chekhov confided to Potapenko, "Nothing will come of it. It's boring, dull; it has nothing to say to anyone. The actors aren't interested, which means the audience won't be either." And to Maria he wrote, "Petersburg is boring; the season won't begin until November. The people are mean, petty, false; a spring sun takes turns with fog. The production will go by without a murmur, sadly. My overall mood is so-so."[19] He advised her against coming to Petersburg for opening night. Suvorin, with whom Chekhov was staying, noted in his diary that his guest had starting coughing blood again.

All at once, five days before the play was due to open, Maria Savina decided that the role of Nina did not suit her and that she would have to be replaced. Out of the turmoil stepped a young actress named Vera Kommissarzhevskaya, ready to take over. Kommissarzhevskaya was fragile, petite. With her large, dark eyes, childlike face, and musical voice she created a Nina that unnerved the rest of the company. Potapenko, dazzled, said she had "illuminated the stage like a ray of sunlight," and Chekhov wrote to Mikhail, "Kommissarzhevskaya is astounding."[20]

Next day, however, the actors fell back into their bombastic ways. By then Chekhov had given up all hope of doing anything with them and began to talk of withdrawing the play altogether. Not until he was made to see the complications the move would entail did he change his mind.

On October 17, the day of the premiere, he went to call for his sister at the station. She and Lika had taken the night train. He looked tired and ill, and was racked with fits of coughing. "The actors don't know their lines," he told Maria. "They don't understand a thing. They're awful. Only Kommissarzhevskaya is any good. The play will be a flop. There was no reason for you to come."

In *The Seagull* a group of people who have gathered at an estate on the shores of a lake wrestle with ways to escape their

humdrum existence: an actress by the name of Arkadina is obsessed with growing old; her brother, Sorin, simply wants more
out of life; her lover, the writer Trigorin, longs to taste of
passions other than writing; her son, Treplev, aspires to new
forms in art; and their neighbor, the fresh, young, impulsive
Nina, dreams of a career as an actress and "true, resounding
fame." Nina rejects Treplev's love and falls for the well-known
Trigorin, Treplev attempts suicide but fails, and Nina leaves
for Moscow to join Trigorin. Two years pass. In the last act
one character after another confesses that his fantasies have been
dashed against the rocks of everyday life: Sorin, who feared
growing as stale as an old cigarette holder, is now paralyzed
and disillusioned; Trigorin has sunk even deeper into his conventional writing career; and Nina, who loses not only Trigorin
but also her baby by him, has taken up with a provincial touring
company. Treplev tells her he still loves her, and when she
rejects him he makes another attempt at suicide. This time he
does not fail.

The play is a testimony to the absurdities of the human
condition. All grandiose plans are doomed to failure, and it
takes a superhuman effort to throw a footbridge across the abyss
separating dream from reality. In Act Four Sorin tells of a story
he wishes to propose to Treplev: "L'homme qui a voulu," "The
Man Who Meant To." "When I was young," he says, "I meant
to be a writer—I never was. [. . .] I meant to get married—
I never did. I meant to live in town—and here I am ending my
days in the country." Even more than the image of a seagull
brought down by a thoughtless hunter,* the ideal of "the man
who meant to" sums up the central theme of the work. The
one thing all the characters in this hothouse atmosphere have
in common is a premonition of their defeat in love and art.
They dream their passions, they speak them, but they do not
live them.

As for the two writers in their midst, Chekhov supplies

---

*A clear reference to the woodcock winged by Levitan and finished off by
  Chekhov.

each with aspects of his own creative anxiety. The famous Trigorin ought to be thrilled with his popularity; instead, he comes to think of writing as a rut he has fallen into, something to put up with, like an infirmity brought on by age. Speaking in Trigorin's name, Chekhov says with agonizing sincerity, "What a mad life. [. . .] I look up and see that cloud in the shape of a grand piano, and I say to myself, 'I'll have to use that somewhere in a story: A grand piano of a cloud drifted by.' [. . .] I can't let a sentence, a word go by—yours or my own—without locking it up in my literary larder. It may just come in handy. [. . .] I never give myself a moment's peace, I'm devouring my own life. [. . .] Yes, I enjoy it while I'm writing. I enjoy proofreading too, but . . . as soon as it's published I hate it. I realize it's not what I had in mind, it's all wrong, I never should have written it, and I get all depressed and disgusted with myself. And then the public reads it and says, 'Yes, charming, clever . . . Charming, but a far cry from Tolstoy.' Or 'A fine piece of work, but Turgenev's *Fathers and Sons* is better.' 'Charming and clever, clever and charming' till the day I die. And then, as they file past my grave, my friends will say, 'Here lies Trigorin. A good writer, but not so good as Turgenev.' "

Treplev, Chekhov's second incarnation, accuses Trigorin of clinging to the hackneyed devices of Realism instead of moving art forward. But even as he dreams of provoking a literary cataclysm, he recognizes his inability to break with the tradition he condemns. The night he kills himself he thinks, "After all that talk about new forms in art, I'm starting to slip into a rut myself. [. . .] I'm cold. As in a cellar. Everything I write is dry, lifeless, gloomy. [. . .] I'm still rushing about in a maze of dreams and images with no knowledge of who or what any of it is for. I have no faith. I don't know what my calling is." These lines might have been taken from a letter to Suvorin. They reflect a chronic despondency.

Several hours before the first performance of *The Seagull* that despondency grew to such proportions that Chekhov was unsure whether to go to the theater. The evening had been billed as a benefit for the highly popular comic actress Yelizaveta Levkeeva.* Levkeeva was to appear in the three-act comedy that was to follow *The Seagull,* and most of the audience had come out for her. So when the curtain went up on Chekhov's disillusioned dreamers, the house froze: it was there for laughs, not penance. And when Vera Kommissarzhevskaya came to Nina's monologue—"Men, lions, eagles and quail, antlered deer, geese, spiders, silent denizens of the deep"—an initial burst of laughter turned into whistling and booing. The scanty applause at the end of Act One was lost in vociferous abuse, and by Act Two the hullabaloo was deafening; people guffawed at the most touching moments or turned their backs to the stage and struck up conversations. The actors were first bewildered, then frantic. Between acts writers and journalists, rejoicing in the failure of an otherwise successful colleague, outdid one another in vicious comments: "Trashy symbolism!" "Why doesn't he stick to his stories?" By then an appalled Chekhov had taken refuge in Levkeeva's dressing room.

The last two acts only contributed to the final disaster. When the curtain came down, the audience raised a storm of indignation and Chekhov ran from the theater with rounded back and raised collar. Making his way through the crowd, he heard an irate little man exclaim, "I can't understand these directors. It's an insult, putting on a play like that!" He went to the Romanov Restaurant, had supper, and then walked himself to exhaustion through the snowbound streets.

Meanwhile, his sister and Lika waited up for him in their hotel room. He had promised to meet them there after the performance, and as the minutes passed they grew more and more anxious. They dispatched Alexander to look for the runaway, but he came back empty-handed and left them himself after scribbling the following: "I didn't know your *Seagull* until I saw it this evening at the theater. It's a fine play, a wonderful

---

*It was a theatrical tradition in Russia to give the first performance of a play as a benefit for a well-known actor, and often, as on October 17, two plays were performed on the same evening.

play full of deep psychology and thought; it touches the heart."
At one o'clock Maria went to the Suvorins', who were putting
her brother up in a separate apartment. But he was not there
either. Her nerves strained to the breaking point, she was forced
to listen to Suvorin's peremptory ideas on how to make *The
Seagull* stageworthy and to his wife's society chitchat.

Towards two Chekhov showed up at last, but when Suvorin informed him that Maria was there, he refused to see her,
claiming extreme fatigue. Suvorin recorded Chekhov's words
in his diary as follows: "I roamed the streets, I sat. I couldn't
simply forget about the performance. If I live seven hundred
years, I'll never give a theater another play. When it comes to
theater, I'm doomed to failure."[21]

The very next day he took the train for Moscow. He wanted
to avoid meeting anyone; he was fleeing his friends as well as
his enemies. He did, however, dash off a note to Maria—"Yesterday's episode did not surprise or particularly upset me. I was
prepared for it by the rehearsals, and I don't feel too bad"—
and one to Mikhail—"The play was a flop, a washout. There
was a heavy, tense atmosphere of perplexity and shame in the
theater. The actors were abominable, stupid. The moral is: Writing
plays is wrong." In a third note, this one to Suvorin, he wrote,
"I shall never forget yesterday evening, but I still slept well and
am leaving in a perfectly bearable mood. [. . .] P.S. *Never
again* will I write or put on plays."[22] He also asked Suvorin to
hold up publication of a collection of his plays that was to
include *The Seagull*.

Potapenko saw him off at the station. Waiting for the train,
Chekhov made a few forced jokes and refused to buy a newspaper for fear of finding a venomous review. "His eyes were
full of bitterness," Potapenko later wrote. Chekhov was so
taken up with the misadventure that he left his luggage on the
train. It was delivered to him the next day.

The note to his sister had concluded, "When you come to
Melikhovo, bring Lika along." Nothing could have pleased
Maria more, and the two of them returned to the house ready
to nurse a broken man. But Chekhov soon set them straight:

"Not another word about the play." So they talked about it only between themselves.

Although Lika, the real seagull, might well have been shocked at seeing her sad experience with Potapenko transferred to the stage, the Lika character was so generously idealized by Chekhov that she accepted it as a flattering portrait. And in fact he had made of her a sensitive, wounded creature struggling gracefully to survive. Several weeks after the performance she wrote to him, "Yes, everyone here says that *The Seagull* is taken from my life and that you have called a certain person to account."

Another woman had followed the opening of *The Seagull* with passion: Lydia Avilova. She had not forgotten the promise Chekhov had made her nine months earlier, when he said she would find out whether he had received her gift. Line after line went by, and still no reference to the issue tormenting her. At last, in Act Three, she saw Nina give Trigorin a medallion she had had engraved with the writer's initials, the title of one of his books, and the reference "page 121, lines 11 and 12." But the numbers did not correspond to the ones Lydia Avilova had had engraved on the watch fob for Chekhov. She stopped following the actors and concentrated on her own concerns. By the time she had returned home, she was at her wit's end, yet she had to wait until her husband retired for the night before looking up the passage in Chekhov's works. What she found made no sense, and she went to bed disappointed. Lying there awake, she had a sudden inspiration: what if the quotation came from her own stories, from the volume she had sent to Chekhov! She threw off the covers and ran into the study, opened the book to page 121, and found lines 11 and 12: "It is improper for young women to attend masquerades." After a short period of perplexity she concluded that he had divined her amorous intentions, her pride blinding her to the more logical view that what he had in mind was a blunt, if humorous, rejection of her. Once more he had attempted to deflect the amorous claims of a woman by making light of his relationship with her.

So little did the fob mean to him that he eventually gave it to Vera Kommissarzhevskaya, the admirable Nina of the first

Seagull, who immediately wondered whether he did not feel a certain partiality for her. But he also told Lika he was going to give her a medallion with the inscription "Catalogue of Plays by Members of the Society of Russian Dramatists, 1890, page 73, line 1," and when she looked up the reference she found it to be the title of a farce, *Ignasha the Fool, or An Unexpected Folly,* a direct allusion to Ignaty Potapenko. Lika, like Lydia Avilova and Vera Kommissarzhevskaya, wished to see Chekhov as a passionate nature, while Chekhov was content merely to inhale their fragrance. All he asked of them was that they should be beautiful, charming, and gay, and accept his brand of circumspect affection.

The *Seagull* fiasco proved a shattering experience both morally and physically. Days passed, and he could not forget the hall exploding in laughter over a work that had so much of himself in it. When Suvorin called him a coward for having fled the scene of the crime, he was furious. "If I'd been a coward, I'd have run to all the newspapers and actors and nervously begged their indulgence, nervously made futile changes, and stayed on in Petersburg for another two or three weeks, going to the play, worrying, breaking out in cold sweats, complaining . . . When you came to see me the night after the performance, you yourself said the best thing for me to do was leave, and the next morning I had a good-bye letter from you. What's so cowardly about that? I acted as sensibly and coolly as a man who has made a proposal, received a rejection, and has no choice but to leave. Yes, it hurt my pride, but it didn't come out of the blue; I expected failure and was prepared for it, as I warned you in all sincerity. At home I took some castor oil and had a cold wash, and now I'm ready to write a new play."[23]

Despite his bravado he smarted under the critics' barbs. The only praise, apart from a favorable notice in the *Saint Petersburg Gazette* signed with Lydia Avilova's initials, came from Suvorin in *New Times.* The other papers went for it with gleeful savagery. One found it "totally absurd"; another denounced its "confusion and disorder"; a third maintained that "each of the acts was overrun by characters who are hopeless, tedious, false, and incomprehensible." Moreover, their view was shared by Tolstoy. According to Suvorin's diary, Tolstoy called *The Seagull* a pastiche of Ibsen and added, "He has brought together elements with no interconnection and no discernable goal. [. . .] Chekhov is the most gifted [Russian] writer, but *The Seagull* is a very bad play."[24]

All the bad press and negative remarks did not keep the second performance, which took place several days later, from scoring a great success. Chekhov had in fact followed Suvorin's suggestions and made a few changes in the text. More important, the audience no longer came expecting a farce. The turnabout in public opinion prompted Vera Kommissarzhevskaya to write to Chekhov: "I'm just back from the theater. We've won. The play is a great success, a hit. How I should like to see you now and even more how I should like you to hear everyone shouting 'Author!' " Potapenko sent the following telegram: "Colossal hit! Encores after each act, repeated encores and acclamations after the fourth. Actors ask me to pass on their delight."

Many letters from friends crossed Chekhov's desk in the next few days. They proffered congratulations and urged him to return to Petersburg and take part in his triumph. The compliments that touched him most came from Anatoly Koni, a prominent jurist and astute observer of human psychology. "*The Seagull*," he wrote in a letter dated November 7, 1896, "is a work whose conception, freshness of ideas, and thoughtful observations of life raise it out of the ordinary. It is life itself on stage with all its tragic alliances, eloquent thoughtlessness, and silent sufferings—the sort of everyday life that is accessible to everyone and understood in its cruel internal irony by almost no one." Chekhov wrote back that the letter meant so much to him because he had more confidence in Koni than in "all the critics put together."[25]

In fact, however, the wound still festered. As time went on he came to believe that what had happened on opening night amounted to a plot against both the play and himself, that many people he had considered friends had joined with his enemies in effusions of ill will, and that with the exception of several stalwarts the entire community of journalists and writers had conspired to do him in. An article in the November issue of *The Spectator* seemed to confirm his suspicions. "The playwright and actors have been subjected to a kind of mockery," it wrote. "Part of the audience rejoiced malevolently; indeed, a good half of the hall seemed to be occupied by Chekhov's enemies. [. . .] The nastiest among them belonged to the brotherhood of scribblers, who had come to settle some personal accounts."

It was with great reluctance that Chekhov allowed *The Seagull* to see print. In a letter to Suvorin he characterized his state of mind as follows: "I feel nothing for my plays but disgust, and I have to force myself to read the proofs. You may say again that this is not very intelligent, that I'm being silly, proud, egocentric, and so on and so forth. Yes, I know that, but what can I do? I'd be glad to rid myself of this silly feeling, but I can't, I simply can't. The trouble is not that my play was a failure—after all, most of my earlier plays also failed, and each time it was like water off a duck's back. It wasn't the play that was unsuccessful on October 17; it was my own person. One thing struck me as early as the first act, to wit: the people with whom I'd been open and friendly up to October 17, the people with whom I'd enjoyed carefree dinners, in whose defense I'd broken lances (Yasinsky, for example)—they all wore peculiar expressions on their faces, extremely peculiar expressions. [. . .] I am calm now, my mood is back to normal. But I can't forget what happened any more than I could forget being punched in the face."[26]

As a result Chekhov felt even more alienated from his fellow writers. At one point he even thought of making a clean break with the intelligentsia and joining the army. After hearing of a possible conflict between Russia and England over the Near East in December 1896, he wrote to Suvorin, "If there's a war in the spring, I shall go. In the last year and a half or two so many things have happened in my personal life (we've recently even had a fire in the house) that the only thing left for me is to go to war like Vronsky*—not to fight, of course, but to tend the wounded."[27]

The war never broke out, and Chekhov remained holed up in Melikhovo hard at work on a long story, "The Peasants," a ruthless picture of the Russian muzhik. While denouncing the iniquities of village life on paper, he spared no pains to improve actual conditions in the surrounding villages. "How good it would be," he noted in his diary, "if each of us left behind a school, a well, or something similar, so our lives would not slip into eternity without a trace."

That winter he undertook the construction of a new school building in the neighboring hamlet of Novoselki. For Novoselki as for Talezh he collected contributions, supplied a large sum himself, and played the architect. Manuscripts vied for space on his desk with scale drawings and estimates.

At the same time, he agreed to take part in a national, government-sponsored census. From January 10 to February 3 he made the rounds of the *izbas* in the district, bumping his head on the lintel of one low door after the other. He was also charged with supervising fifteen other census takers and with writing the final report. Hundreds of cards piled up in drawers. After it was over, he noted laconically in his diary: "They've given me a medal for the census."

The project that excited him the most was a "people's palace," a cultural center for the citizens of Moscow, complete with theater, library, museum, and reading and meeting rooms. His old ideal of humanitarian education seemed to be coming to life. In Moscow to look at the plans, he was devastated to find the cost of the operation so high as to be impracticable. The project was soon abandoned.

On February 19, 1897, he was back in Moscow for a sumptuous banquet at the Hotel Continental to celebrate the anniversary of the emancipation of the serfs. Afterwards he jotted

---

*Allusion to Anna Karenina's lover who, after his mistress's suicide, volunteered for the Serbo-Turkish War.

in his diary, "Boring and ridiculous. Eating, drinking champagne, making noise, and giving speeches on the people's self-awareness, freedom, and so forth, while slaves in frock coats, serfs even now, bustle about the table and coachmen stand waiting outside in the cold—it's like lying to the Holy Spirit."

After more than a fortnight of receptions, suppers, and feasts, Chekhov returned to Melikhovo and his story "The Peasants." He was exhausted and had started coughing blood again, but refused to think of himself as ill. A month later he took the train back to Moscow to meet Suvorin and travel on to Petersburg.

He arrived in Moscow on March 21 and checked in at the Grand Hôtel. He had just sat down to dinner with Suvorin at the restaurant of the Hermitage that evening when blood started gushing out of his mouth. Not even judicious applications of ice could stop the flow. Never one to make a spectacle of himself, Chekhov let Suvorin have him moved to the Slav Bazaar, where Suvorin was staying. There Suvorin sent for a doctor they both knew, Nikolai Obolonsky. Next morning Chekhov insisted on moving back to the Grand Hôtel—he had a number of letters to write and people to see—but when the hemorrhaging started up again Dr. Obolonsky packed him off to a clinic run by a specialist in pulmonary disorders, Dr. Alexei Ostroumov.

Embarrassed by having made a "scandal" at the restaurant, Chekhov persisted in denying the gravity of the case. Suvorin noted in his diary following a visit to the clinic: "He laughed and jested as usual, while spitting blood into a large vessel." To take Chekhov's mind off his illness, Suvorin mentioned that the ice on the Moscow River had begun to break up. No sooner were the words out of his mouth than Chekhov's face clouded over. Only then did Suvorin recall that his friend had recently told him, "When a peasant has consumption, he says, 'There's nothing I can do. I'll go off in the spring with the melting of the snows.' "

Once he had entered the clinic, Chekhov gave up all illusions concerning his health, but he asked his brothers and sister to keep the doctors' diagnosis, extensive pulmonary tuberculosis, from his parents, and he still liked to think that despite his lungs he had a number of years left in him. Dr. Ostroumov prescribed a radical change in his way of life: he was to avoid the city, look after himself carefully, and, most important, stop practicing medicine. "It will be both a relief and a great deprivation for me," he wrote to Suvorin. "I am giving up all my district duties and buying a dressing gown, and I shall bask in the sun and eat and eat. My doctors have ordered me to eat about six times daily; they are indignant at finding I eat so little. I am forbidden to do much talking, to go swimming, and so on and so forth. All my organs besides the lungs have been found healthy; I've hidden from the doctors the fact that in the evening I am occasionally impotent."[28]

The news of Chekhov's tuberculosis spread swiftly through Moscow. He was inundated with visitors and worn out by their chatter. "I must marry," he wrote to Suvorin. "A shrew of a wife might reduce the number of visitors by half. Yesterday they came in a steady stream—a calamity. They came in pairs, each one telling me not to speak and then asking me questions."[29] His bedside table was covered with bouquets of flowers and jars of caviar, bottles of champagne and parcels from novice writers in search of recommendations. Chekhov read the manuscripts attentively, making a great effort to respond to each with a letter. A young woman studying to be a teacher had sent him several stories. He returned them with a rather sharp critique. When she wrote back saying she had expected "more heart and magnanimity" from him, he pointed out the difficulty of keeping up a correspondence while bedridden, yet patiently offered her new advice.

The indefatigable Lydia Avilova happened to be passing through Moscow at the time, and when she learned that Chekhov had been taken to a clinic she too hastened to visit him. She was allowed in for three minutes but forbidden to let him speak. Not only did she claim to have had a frank conversation with him, she returned the next day bearing flowers. That day Maria sat at his bedside as well. "Anton Pavlovich lay on his back," she writes in her *Memoirs*. "He was not allowed to speak. After greeting him, I went over to the table to hide my emotion. There I saw a drawing of his lungs. They were outlined in blue, but the upper parts were filled in with red. I realized they were diseased."

Two days later, still immobile, Chekhov received a visit from Tolstoy. The doctors and nurses did not dare turn away so illustrious a personage. Chekhov, modest as ever, was impressed with such solicitude from on high. The venerable master sat in the oilcloth armchair next to his companion's narrow bed and, forgetting in his hauteur that he was talking to a man whose very life was in danger, launched into a passionate disquisition on the immortality of the soul. "We had a most interesting conversation," Chekhov wrote ironically to his friend Mikhail Menshikov a few weeks later, "interesting mainly for me, because I listened more than I spoke. We discussed immortality. He recognizes immortality in its Kantian form and assumes that all of us (humans and animals alike) will live on in a principle (such as reason or love), the essence and goals of which are a mystery to us. As for me, I can imagine that principle or force only as a shapeless, gelatinous mass with which my *I,* my individuality, my consciousness will merge. I have no use for that kind of immortality, I do not understand it, and Lev Nikolaevich was astonished I didn't."[30]

When the patient, exhausted, fell silent, the master, inexhaustible, took another tack: he started explaining his conception of art. He told Chekhov he had temporarily set *Resurrection* aside and gone through more than sixty treatises on aesthetics in preparation for writing one of his own. He felt that art had no justification unless it served morality or religion. When he saw Chekhov gathering strength to object, he went on in a louder voice: contemporary art, dedicated as it was to putrefaction, deserved absolute condemnation. The categorical prophet with the majestic beard and flashing eyes would not be gainsaid, and Chekhov no longer tried to contradict. But in a letter to a writer friend, Alexander Ertel, he noted, "His idea is not new; it has been reiterated in various forms by clever old men in every century. Old men have always been inclined to think the end of the world is at hand and to assert that morals have sunk to the *ne plus ultra,* that art has grown shallow and threadbare, that people have grown weak, and so on and so forth. Lev Nikolaevich is out to convince everybody in his book that art in our time has entered upon its final phase, that it is stuck in a blind alley from which it has no way out."[31] Even after the renowned gadfly had departed, Chekhov had trouble recovering his equanimity; he slept fitfully and started hemorrhaging again at dawn.

At last the doctors let him move about, however, and he began roaming through the corridors and garden. One day he went as far as the neighboring Novodevichy Monastery, where he stood and meditated over the grave of his friend Pleshcheev, buried there four years earlier. "The idea of death gives birth to something larger than fear," he said to Suvorin, who noted it in his diary. "People take you to the cemetery and come back to drink tea and make hypocritical remarks."

From now on he would live the life of a semi-invalid, yet he worried about the future more for his family than for himself. Would he have the strength to provide them with what they needed? When Suvorin joked that for once he would know the joys of idleness, he countered, "I despise idleness just as I despise all weakness and frailty in the impulses of the spirit."[32]

Although he soon looked forward to getting back to work and proving to himself that the crisis he had just pulled through had made no dent in his creative faculties, he was not released from the clinic until April 10. Next day, escorted by his brother Ivan, he arrived back at Melikhovo. He was glad to see his parents, his papers and book, the countryside shimmering in the clear spring sun. Maria informed the local peasants not to count on her brother for treatment, and he agreed to give up long walks and strenuous gardening, limiting himself to pruning one rosebush a day and feeding hemp seed to the sparrows. Yet certain duties he felt he could not ignore. His sister's admonitions to the contrary, he continued to send book parcels to the Taganrog library, supervise construction on the Novoselki school, examine Talezh schoolboys, receive visitors, and keep up an active correspondence with friends, writers, and supplicants of all varieties.

In addition to the cares of everyday life, however, Chekhov had to contend with the uproar caused by "The Peasants," which had recently appeared in *Russian Thought*. The censors, horrified by Chekhov's merciless portrayal of the Russian peasantry, had made major cuts. Even so, the reading public was flabbergasted by his daring. The story traces the discovery of country life by a young city woman. Olga is married to a peasant turned hotel waiter. When he falls seriously ill and loses his job, she takes him back to his native village. What she sees there seems to belong to a completely different world, a world steeped in poverty, superstition, filth, ignorance, crude manners, cruelty, and idleness. She finds ten to twelve people crammed together in a fly-infested hovel, eating little more than black bread and water; she finds men brutally beating women and drowning despair in vodka. The meek and gentle cannot survive such bestiality, and after her husband dies Olga takes her daughter and starts begging her way back to Moscow.

"The Peasants" caused a literary scandal and was accompanied by violent polemics in the press, but in the end critics upheld the work. "The success of 'The Peasants,'" wrote the critic for *The Northern Herald,* "brings back the times when a new novel by Turgenev or Dostoevsky would appear." Soon Chekhov received a number of enthusiastic letters. Leikin, for example, wrote: "I've read 'The Peasants.' It's wonderful! I read it in one night, one sitting, and couldn't fall asleep for a long time after." The playwright and director Alexander Sumbatov-Yuzhin went even further: "It is one of the greatest works to appear anywhere for many years. [. . .] It is suffused with the tragedy of truth, an irresistible force reminiscent of Shakespeare's spontaneity of design. It makes one think of you more as Nature herself than as a writer. [. . .] In 'The Peasants' I sense the weather on a given day, the position of the sun, the way the slope goes down to the river. I see it all without needing to have it described."

Others, however, especially the Populists and the Tolstoyans, accused Chekhov of being too eager to show the peasants in a bad light. Of course Chekhov could have replied that after five years of daily contact with peasants as a doctor he was better qualified than most to record their degradation, but here, too, he followed his rule of abstaining from the debates his writings provoked. As he well knew, the work had deeply troubled even those who shouted the loudest.

The triumph of "The Peasants" more than made up for the *Seagull* disaster, but the upsurge in his popularity—Alexander assured him he had never been so loved by the public—proved a source of anxiety as well as comfort. True, he had any number of new ideas for stories and plays, but his illness had taken its toll, and there were times when he sat and dreamed over a blank page for long periods of time. Then, too, with the coming of good weather came visitors, and Melikhovo was soon full to overflowing. His married brothers—with their wives and children—would stay a week at a time, and although he was always happy to see friends like Levitan, Lika, and Alexander Ivanenko, there were beggars and spongers to put up with as well. "Imagine," he once said to Leontyev-Shcheglov, "we've had more than ten visitors from Moscow these past few days. I might as well be keeping an inn. They all have to be wined, dined, and bedded down!"

If nothing else, the racket kept him from working. Often he had to wait for the guests to retire for the night before he could set to work. According to Leontyev-Shcheglov, his complexion was sallow, his face drawn, his eyes feverish; he coughed a great deal, and his husky voice only half masked what he was going through. Even when the evenings were mild, he wrapped himself in a traveling rug.

His rare escapades to Moscow or the environs completely wore him out. After visiting the estate of the merchant millionaire Sergei Morozov (the meeting was Levitan's idea), he wrote to Suvorin, "The house is as big as the Vatican, the servants wear white stitched waistcoats with gold chains over their stomachs, the furniture is in bad taste, the owner has a blank expression on his face, and I fled."[33]

Though he wrote little, he read a great deal. Maupassant delighted him, and despite his imperfect knowledge of French he thought of translating several of his stories. He was also attracted by the bizarre quality of Maeterlinck's plays and even proposed that Suvorin should open his theater to *The Blind*. "The public may be semimoronic, but you could keep the play from flopping by outlining the plot on the poster." In the same letter he writes, "I've got piles of company. Alexander has foisted his boys on me without leaving the proper under- or outerwear. They're living here now, and nobody knows when they'll go. They seem to be staying till the end of the summer, though maybe they're here for good. How nice of their parents."[34] He made much the same complaint to Leikin: "The place is crawling with guests. I'm short on room and bed linen and the patience to chat with them and play the gracious host."[35]

By August what little patience he had left was so sorely tried that he started thinking of following his doctors' advice and moving south before the winter frosts set in. When Vasily Sobolevsky, a friend and coeditor of *Russian News,* wrote to him from Biarritz, Chekhov dropped everything and decided to join him. "Please write and tell me whether to take the Berlin or Vienna train from Moscow, which train to take from Paris, and what hotel you're staying at . . . The reason I ask is that I've never been to Biarritz and feel a little intimidated. As you know, I speak all languages but foreign ones; when I'm abroad and try my German or French on ticket collectors they tend to laugh at me, and I find getting from one station to the other in Paris like a game of blind man's buff."[36]

All that was left was to settle the finances. After some juggling of figures Chekhov concluded that royalties from *The Seagull,* which had begun to be staged here and there, plus the large advance he had received for "The Peasants" would keep him for several months. Leaving Melikhovo on August 31, 1897, he had a feeling he was leaving behind not only the hubbub of daily life but his illness as well.

XII

Yalta

"Until Berlin I had a fine trip in pleasant company; from Berlin to Cologne the Germans nearly smothered me with their cigars; from Cologne to Paris I slept."[1]

In Paris he went straight to the Suvorins, and they spent several days together sightseeing. He overcame his fatigue enough to make the rounds of the fashionable cabarets (at the Moulin-Rouge he witnessed a belly dance to the accompaniment of tambourines) and shops (at the Magasins du Louvre he bought a candle, a cane, two ties, and a shirt). Then, having declared the city "picturesque and attractive," he took the train south to the resort town of Biarritz.

Immediately after checking into the Hôtel Victoria, he was caught up in the bustle along the streets and sea wall. His main acquisition was a silk hat for protection from the sun, and he spent his days lolling in a tiny wicker cabin on the beach, drinking in the spectacle of the surf and either reading the paper or observing the beautiful and lightly clad women with multicolored parasols and poodles in tow or the strolling, guitar-playing minstrels. He felt "hundreds of thousands of versts removed from Melikhovo" and not the slightest bit homesick. His only regret was that there were so many Russians, and to feel more a part of France he decided to take French lessons from a nineteen-year-old girl by the name of Margot. Within two weeks, however, the weather turned windy and rainy, and he moved on to Nice in search of the sun.

In Nice he put up at the Pension Russe, 9 rue Gounod, where he found himself in the company of forty fellow countrymen, many of them ailing. His room, on the second floor, was not only enormous; it also had wide bay windows with southern exposure, a bed "like Cleopatra's," and a private bath. The Russian cook made more-than-ample meals of borscht and *bifteck-pommes frites*. Chekhov adopted an ironic attitude towards his table companions—the quick-tempered widow who, for fear he would nab the best piece of meat, looked daggers at him as the dishes went by, the dried-up old maids and chattering, gossiping matrons, whom he confessed dreading to resemble one day.

Whenever he could, he escaped to the outdoors, where the sun, flowers, palm trees, and calm, blue sea—everything conspired to make him feel lazy. He would stroll up and down the Promenade des Anglais, stop at a café, read the papers, listen to open-air concerts—anything to keep his mind a blank. He kept up with his French lessons, but to no avail, and his lack of fluency hindered him from forming friendships with the locals. He did, however, befriend several noteworthy Russians, including Maxim Kovalevsky, a jurist, historian, and sociologist who, after being dismissed from the University of Moscow for progressive political ideas, had sought refuge in France; Valerian Yakobi, a painter with a bilious wit; and shy, mild-mannered Nikolai Yurasov, the Russian vice-consul. He played cards with them and accompanied them to the Taverne Gothique for oysters or the Casino Municipal for entertainment.

Even such innocent pleasures left him with a feeling of

remorse. Although he never stopped jotting down story topics in his notebooks, he lacked the will to develop them. "I usually find writing a slow, nerve-racking process," he wrote to the Russian editor of the multilingual magazine *Cosmopolis,* Fyodor Batyushkov, "but here in a *hotel room,* at a strange desk, when the weather is beautiful and beckons me out of doors, I have even more trouble writing."[2] Working in such conditions, he said, was like sewing on someone else's machine. He also complained that the copious meals made him drowsy. Yet he pushed on, forcing himself to complete three stories one after the other: "The Pecheneg," "The Homecoming," and "In the Cart." The effort wore him out, and he thought the results mediocre, but in the end he sent them off to *Russian News* anyway.

When after a brief respite he started coughing blood again, he feigned indifference. "There are times when I cough blood," he wrote to Yelena Shavrova, "but it bears no relation to how I feel, and I go prancing about like an unmarried calf. [. . .] Oh, how fortunate I'm not married yet. How convenient!"[3] Nonetheless, his doctors ordered him to move to a room on the ground floor and return to the *pension* before dark. Despite their precautions the hemorrhaging continued, though it was less serious than the bout in Moscow. "Because of the blood," he wrote to Suvorin, "I'm under house arrest, so I'm writing to you and trying to think of what else to say. I find living alone boring and sad."[4]

To counteract the effects of forced confinement, he began reestablishing epistolary contact with friends, in some instances the very ones he had fled. How were things getting on at Melikhovo without him? Maria, whom he had left in charge, began receiving detailed instructions: if she needed money, she could request an advance from *Russian Thought*; she must not forget to give a ruble to the cowherd for Christmas, and three rubles to the village priest; she must remember to thank a neighbor who had contributed bricks to the Novoselki school and to tell Father how happy he had been to receive a copy of the Melikhovo "log."

He resumed his seriocomic letters to Lika, one of which

indignantly informed her of an extravagant gesture instigated by Levitan: a gift of two thousand rubles in "aid" from the wealthy Sergei Morozov. "I didn't ask for the money, I don't want it, and I've requested Levitan's permission to return it, though in such a way as to offend no one, of course. He's against it, but still I'll send it back. I'll wait another two weeks or a month and return it with a thank-you note. I have money."[5] His next letter to her contained a friendly inquiry about who was wooing her and whether it was true she was planning to open a dressmaking establishment. "I have no desire to lecture you; I shall only say that work, no matter how modest a studio or shop may seem to others, will give you independence, peace of mind, and confidence for the days ahead." He also promised to come and pay court to the girls who sewed for her.

As for Lydia Avilova, she had not been the least discouraged by Chekhov's departure, nor did she shrink from renewing their correspondence. Once more she sent him several of her stories for his comments. "When I wrote to him, I could not help feeling that I was forcing myself on him, but I could not stop our correspondence any more than I could have put an end to my life."[6] Chekhov, annoyed but as civil as always, responded with an astute combination of compliments and criticism: "Your lack of experience and confidence, your laziness stands out between the lines of every story. [. . .] You don't work on your sentences. You must. That's what makes art."[7] When she chided him for showing only the dark side of life, he responded, "Unfortunately, it's not my fault! That's just the way it comes out. While I write I don't feel I'm being gloomy; in any case, I'm always in a good mood when I'm at work. Gloomy, melancholy people are said to write happy things, cheerful people to use their writings to chase away melancholy. Well, I'm one of the cheerful ones; at least I lived the first thirty years of my life, as we say, a happy man."[8] And the letter ends: "I'm not doing anything, I'm not writing and have no desire to write. I've grown very lazy."

For one thing, there was nothing in the new surroundings to stimulate his imagination. But more important, he was unable to turn his precise perceptions into literature from one day to the next; he needed distance from people and places before he could evoke them in his stories. The mysterious process whereby raw material was transformed into elements of literature could take months or even years. When Batyushkov asked him to send *Cosmopolis* a new work inspired by his stay abroad, he responded, "Only in Russia, thinking back, can I write such a story. I can write only by thinking back; I have never written straight from nature. I need to let a subject strain through my memory until only what is important or typical remains as on a filter."[9]

Chekhov was indifferent to Nice as a place but fascinated by its populace. He found the French remarkably refined, cultured, just, and kind, or as he phrased it, "Here every dog has the whiff of civilization." In a letter to Ivan he expressed his amazement at coming across a priest playing ball in the street with some schoolboys, at seeing his overworked chambermaid smile at him "like a duchess"; he found it comforting that everyone said "Bonjour" to everyone else in shops and trains and that even a beggar was addressed as "Monsieur" or "Madame."[10]

Chekhov's admiration for France's place at the forefront of European culture and for the Frenchman's spirit of independence increased when a number of newspapers reopened the Dreyfus affair. Could it be that Captain Alfred Dreyfus, court-martialed in 1894 for espionage on behalf of Germany and sentenced to life imprisonment on Devil's Island, was innocent? Had he not been the victim of the blind anti-Semitism prevalent at the time in the upper echelons of the army? Was not the true culprit Major Esterhazy, a Hungarian, whom Dreyfus's brother had recently denounced as the true culprit?

Chekhov, aware that the conscience and very unity of the country were at stake, followed the twists and turns of the debates with great passion. "I've been reading the papers all day," he wrote to Sobolevsky, "studying the Dreyfus affair. In my opinion Dreyfus is innocent."[11]

A month later, on January 13, 1898, Chekhov read Zola's

"J'accuse," an open letter to the president of the Republic condemning the government for trying to cover up the truth. He was very much excited by it. "The Dreyfus affair has got up steam and is on its way," he wrote to Suvorin, "but it's still not going at full speed. Zola is a noble soul, and I [. . .] am delighted by his outburst. France is a wonderful country and has wonderful writers."[12] And to Batyushkov: "The overwhelming majority of the intelligentsia is on Zola's side and believes Dreyfus innocent. Zola has been growing by leaps and bounds. His letters of protest are like a breath of fresh air, and every Frenchman now has the feeling that, thank God, there is still justice on this earth and that if an innocent man is convicted there is still someone to defend him."[13]

In February Zola himself stood trial. He was eventually sentenced to a year in prison and struck from the rolls of the Legion of Honor. But the more he came under attack the more Chekhov admired him. He devoured the press reports with the fervor of a native Frenchman. "You ask me whether I still think Zola is right," he wrote to a friend, the artist Alexandra Khotyaintseva. "Well, let me ask you whether you have so poor an opinion of me as to suspect me for a moment of being *against* Zola. One of his fingernails is worth more to me than the whole bunch of generals and highborn witnesses judging him now in court."[14]

If Chekhov had had his way, he would have brought all his Russian friends round to his point of view, but he was especially upset by the position of his dearest friend, Suvorin, whose *New Times* had come out against Dreyfus and Zola. Hoping to reverse that position, Chekhov wrote him a long letter—a legal brief, fervent plea, and exhortation to intellectual honesty all in one: "You write that you are irritated by Zola, while everyone here has the feeling a new and better Zola has been born. His trial has been as effective as turpentine in cleansing him of his incidental grease spots, and the French now see him shining in all his true radiance. There is a purity and moral integrity in him that no one suspected." He goes on to summarize the case from its beginnings, on the one hand accusing

the rightist press of stirring up anti-Semitism in France to prevent the truth from coming out, and on the other congratulating
Zola for having plunged into the fray to rectify an egregious
legal error. "The main thing is that [Zola] is sincere, that is, he
bases his judgments only on what he can see, not on phantoms,
as the others do. Even sincere people can err, that goes without
saying, but their errors cause less harm than sober-minded insincerity, prejudices, or political motivations. Let us assume that
Dreyfus is guilty—even so Zola is right, because the writer's
job is not to accuse or persecute but to stand up even for the
guilty once they have been condemned and are undergoing
punishment. 'What about politics and the interests of the state?'
people may ask. But major writers and artists should engage in
politics only enough to protect themselves from it."[15] All in all,
he found Zola a perfect example of a free man after his own
heart. He reserved the right for a writer to belong to no party,
to strike out at both right and left according to the dictates of
his conscience.

When the *New Times* hate campaign against Dreyfus and
Zola continued unabated, Chekhov put it down to Suvorin's
inability to withstand the pressure brought to bear on him by
his political cronies. "I like Suvorin very much," he told Leontyev-Shcheglov, "very much indeed, but people lacking in character are capable of acting like the worst scoundrels and tend
to do so at the most crucial moments in life." After deciding
to call off his polemics with Suvorin, he wrote to his brother
Alexander, "*New Times* has been behaving abominably about
the Zola case. The old man and I have exchanged letters on the
subject (in a rather moderate tone, however) and have both
lapsed into silence. I don't want to write to him and I don't
want any more letters in which he tries to justify the newspaper's
tactlessness by his love for the military."[16]

Disappointed though he was, Chekhov never considered
severing ties with Suvorin. There had been disagreements before, but just when a rift seemed imminent, Chekhov, naturally
pliant, would smooth things over. This time he had lost his
illusions, and he could never quite recover his respect for the

man. Their friendship continued, but more out of habit than esteem.

While the newspapers shook Chekhov's inner world, his day-to-day, Pension Russe existence, restful to the point of monotony, remained unperturbed. There were times when he felt like an unassuming French pensioner warming his bones in the sun. The only alarm was a bad toothache, bad enough to require surgery, but the hemorrhaging had ceased and he even dreamed of taking a trip to North Africa ("Algiers, Tunisia, and so forth") with Kovalevsky. When at the last moment Kovalevsky fell ill and had to beg off, Chekhov was terribly frustrated and returned to his sedentary life feeling, as he put it, closer to eighty-nine than thirty-eight.

Then Potapenko came to town, turning the Pension Russe on its head. Potapenko was a gambler. He had arrived on the Riviera on March 2 to make a fast million at roulette so he could write as he pleased without having to beg for advances. Soon he had Chekhov sharing his childlike enthusiasm and believing in the possibility of amassing a fortune at the casino. The whole secret was to leave nothing to chance. Chekhov and Potapenko purchased a small roulette wheel and shut themselves up for hours spinning the ivory ball and keeping track of the numbers that came up in the hope of discovering a winning formula. Day after day they went off to Monte Carlo to try their luck. Potapenko, impulsive by nature, staked large amounts on each number; Chekhov was more prudent. Even so, the ups and downs of fortune took a great toll of his nerves, and although he would return from the casino as if from a battlefield he let two weeks go by before admitting the excitement was harmful and putting an end to his visits there. As for Potapenko, he went back until he had lost everything, at which point he borrowed return fare from Chekhov and left Nice. The very day of his departure, March 28, Chekhov wrote to his sister, "I miss Potapenko."

Meanwhile, the painter Iosif Braz had arrived in Nice to do a portrait of Chekhov at the bidding of the wealthy collector

Pavel Tretyakov. For two weeks Chekhov spent all his mornings posing, a torture he agreed to in a weak moment. Moreover, he was unhappy with the result.* "I am sitting in an armchair with a green velvet back," he wrote to Alexandra Khotyaintseva, "in profile. In a white tie. People say the tie and I are very lifelike, but I think the expression on my face [. . .] makes me look as though I'd just sniffed some horseradish."[17] To his sister he wrote, "There's something about it that isn't me and something about me that isn't it."[18] He found it too photographic. "If I have turned pessimist and start writing sad stories," he joked, "that portrait is to blame."

With spring in the air he felt a violent, almost painful desire to return to Russia. He dreamed of Melikhovo and questioned Maria on the progress of the thaw. By early April he was giving her advice about the garden: "Don't prune the rosebushes before I get back. Clip only the stalks that rotted during the winter or are doing very poorly, but be careful: don't forget that ailing stems sometimes recover. The fruit trees need liming. The cherry trees could use some lime underneath as well."[19]

When Maria wrote back that it was not warm enough for him at Melikhovo, he decided to wait out Russia's cold spells in Paris. A week after he got there Suvorin arrived. Their meeting, though slightly reserved, was cordial, and Chekhov agreed to leave the Hôtel de Dijon and join Suvorin at the Hôtel Vendôme. Since his health had improved somewhat, Chekhov went to several plays and exhibitions, toured Versailles, took part in the life of the Russian colony, and met Alfred Dreyfus's brother, Mathieu, and the pro-Dreyfus journalist Bernard Lazare, who dedicated a copy of his pamphlet on the affair to him.

Chekhov devoted a large part of the time he spent in Paris to his native town of Taganrog. Back in Nice, he had bought more than three hundred French classics and shipped them to the Taganrog Public Library. In Paris, he put together a rich file on the Dreyfus case, also for the Public Library. And having

---

*Braz's portrait now belongs to the Tretyakov Gallery in Moscow.

made the acquaintance of the sculptor Mark Antokolsky, he persuaded him to donate his equestrian statue of Taganrog's founder, Peter the Great, to the town.

Through it all, however, he looked forward to the telegram from his sister telling him the weather was right, the roads negotiable. At last it arrived, and none too soon: Paris itself had turned rainy and cold. On April 26 or 27 he wrote to Alexander, "Shine your boots, put on a decent set of clothes, and come and meet me at the station. That's what etiquette calls for, after all, and I think I have a right to it, being a rich relative. Don't tell anybody about my arrival." On May 2 he took the Nord-Express for Petersburg, and on May 5 he was in Melikhovo. His father's log entry reads: "Antosha has returned from France. He has brought back many gifts." His mother wrote to Mikhail, "He arrived at five in the evening. He has lost a lot of weight."

Shortly after settling down in Melikhovo, Chekhov received a letter from Vladimir Nemirovich-Danchenko asking for permission to stage *The Seagull*. Nemirovich-Danchenko was a long-standing friend, a noted playwright and teacher of dramatic art. He had just joined with the actor and director Konstantin Stanislavsky to found what would soon be known as the Moscow Art Theater. The new company was made up of young actors from Stanislavsky's amateur group and Nemirovich-Danchenko's courses. They were full of spirit and dreamed of throwing over the bombastic practices of the day and replacing them with a simple, natural approach. Nemirovich-Danchenko found *The Seagull* perfect for their purposes and had long since admired the play in any case, but Chekhov could not forget the disastrous welcome it had received the year before in Petersburg. From Nice he had written to Suvorin, "I used to find nothing more enjoyable than sitting in a theater; now whenever I sit in a theater, I have a feeling somebody in the balcony is about to yell 'Fire!' I don't like actors either. Writing plays has spoiled it all for me."[20]

If only for his peace of mind, therefore, he refused to give Nemirovich-Danchenko permission to stage *The Seagull*. Stories were his security; the theater was more of an adventure.

Having returned at last to the solitude of his study, he was loath to reenter the world of actor egos, backstage intrigues, and audience caprices. But Nemirovich-Danchenko would not take no for an answer and courted him with such warmth and charm that he finally gained Chekhov's consent.

Even with Chekhov on his side, however, Nemirovich-Danchenko still had to win over Stanislavsky, who feared the work to be "unstageworthy." "Chekhov's play," Nemirovich-Danchenko wrote to Stanislavsky on June 21, "has the pulse of contemporary Russian life beating in it. That is why I find it so attractive." He had his way. But the young actors who gathered for rehearsals on an estate outside Moscow were worried about interpreting so difficult a play, a play that, even when performed by experienced actors, had earned the wrath of the first-night Petersburg audience. Clearly Stanislavsky and Nemirovich-Danchenko had their work cut out for them.

While they strove to crack the mysteries of *The Seagull,* Chekhov was hard at work at Melikhovo. He felt in better health than usual and, defying doctors' orders, had gone back to his former activities. "As I have told you," he wrote to the Archimandrite Sergei, an old friend of the family, "I have been ill. I have even been to clinics, been found to harbor bacilli, and so on, but now everything is fine, I feel perfectly well or at least don't think of myself as ill, and I live the life I used to live; I am once more involved in medicine and literature, taking care of the peasants and writing stories, and every year I build something."[21]

That year he had taken it into his head to build a school in his own village, in Melikhovo, but since the list of children waiting to enroll was already long he rented a hut, bought some desks, and engaged a schoolmaster.

Within several weeks of his return to Melikhovo he proudly announced to Victor Goltsev, editor of *Russian Thought,* "My machine has started running again."[22] And despite the numerous friends who came to see him that summer he kept his nose to the grindstone. Using the scribblings he had saved up in his notebooks, he wrote four stories one after the other: "Ionych,"

"The Man in the Case," "Gooseberries," and "On Love." The
last three share a setting and two characters: Burkin, a teacher,
and Ivan Ivanych, a veterinary surgeon. Chekhov had long
dreamed of putting together a series of stories having common
settings and characters and forming if not a novel then at least
a unified, interconnected cycle. But the Burkin/Ivan Ivanych
project never went beyond the three episodes. However secure
he felt in works of short and medium range, he could not seem
to guide his characters through the long-range trek required by
the novel. A horror of digressions, pomposity, of all kinds of
excess made him come quickly to the point, and much as he
admired certain "weighty" works, he himself was a partisan of
lightness in art.

After the sudden creative streak came a period of decline.
By the end of July Chekhov was complaining to Lydia Avilova,
"We have so much company I can never get round to answering
your last letter. I feel like writing at length, but my hand refuses
to respond when at any moment someone may come in and
disturb me. In fact, just as I was writing the word 'disturb,'
a little girl came in and announced that a patient had arrived. I
must go. [. . .] I've lost all taste for writing and don't know
what to do. I'd be glad to go back to medicine and take up a
post somewhere, but I'm no longer physically limber enough.
When I write or think about what I ought to write, I feel as
nauseated as though a cockroach had just been removed from
the soup I'd been eating—if you will excuse the comparison.
And it's not only the fact of writing I find disgusting, it's the
literary entourage. You can't escape it; you take it with you
everywhere, as the earth takes its atmosphere."[23] Yet given the
attentions he showered on writers who came to see him at
Melikhovo, the "entourage"—that "atmosphere" he so cursed—
was vitally necessary to him.

Early in September Nemirovich-Danchenko informed
Chekhov that the theater company had moved back to Moscow,
and Chekhov decided to attend a few rehearsals there. Watching
him enter the hall on September 9, 1898, was a great emotional
experience for the young actors. Their admiration for him shook

their self-confidence. Chekhov, who was as unsettled as they were, kept coughing, pulling at his beard, and fiddling with his pince-nez. After sitting through an act, however, he settled down. For the first time he felt his actors understood him. During the second rehearsal he made several suggestions about the acting and requested that Stanislavsky himself replace the actor playing the part of Trigorin.

Stanislavsky, who was also directing the play, had very definite ideas about the theater, one of which was to use sound effects—the croaking of frogs, the barking of dogs—to recreate a rural atmosphere. Chekhov had a good laugh at Stanislavsky's concern for realism. "The theater has its own conventions," he told him. "There is no fourth wall. Besides, the theater is art and reflects the quintessence of life; it wants nothing superfluous."

As the rehearsals went on, Chekhov took special notice of the beauty and talent of Olga Leonardovna Knipper in the difficult role of Arkadina. Olga Knipper was twenty-eight at the time and had a broad but active face, intelligent eyes, and rich black hair. She had just completed her studies with Nemirovich-Danchenko and decided in favor of a life in the theater. As soon as she laid eyes on Chekhov, she felt a vague premonition of things to come.

Chekhov also saw her in a rehearsal of *Tsar Fyodor Ioan-novich,* the verse drama by Alexei Tolstoy due to open the Art Theater's premiere season. He sat transfixed in the cold, damp hall as she performed the role of the tsar's wife, Irina, on a bare stage lit only by candles in bottles. Shortly thereafter he wrote to Suvorin, "I found Irina magnificent. The voice, the nobility, the sincerity—everything is so fine it brings a spasm to one's throat [. . .]. Had I stayed on in Moscow, I'd have fallen in love with that Irina."[24]

But the day after that memorable rehearsal he left for the Crimea. Autumn was in the air, and he had started coughing blood again. Like it or not, he had to follow his doctors' advice and spend the long winter months in a warm climate. A journey he had once looked forward to now seemed a journey into exile.

Again he had the impression of betraying the North, whose stark landscapes he so loved, for a South whose sun he needed if he was to survive.

Immediately after arriving in Yalta, he rented two rooms in a villa with a lush garden. But the grand hotels, the palms and cactuses, the bright blue sea—the whole resort atmosphere was too artificial for his taste. People who lived in Yalta lived outside the mainstream of life.

Chekhov's daily strolls along the seashore often took him to Sinani's bookshop, the center of Yalta's intellectual life. There he could find all the writers and artists who happened to be in town, and there he met such celebrities as the young poet Konstantin Balmont, the bass Fyodor Chaliapin, and the composer Sergei Rachmaninov, whose *Fantasy for Orchestra* was inspired by Chekhov's story "On the Road" and dedicated to him. But there he was also subject to celebrity seekers. "I'm as bored as a sturgeon," he wrote to Tatyana Shchepkina-Kupernik. "There are women everywhere—with plays and without—but I'm still bored."[25] To get away from it all, he often took meals with the directress and teachers at a local girls' school and was soon a member of the board of directors. As he walked through the corridors, little girls in white uniforms curtsied respectfully to him.

One day, after he had been in Yalta about a month, he dropped in at Sinani's and was handed a telegram from Maria. It was addressed to Sinani, not to him, and read: "How did Anton Pavlovich Chekhov receive the news of his father's death?" The date was October 13. His father had died on the previous day.

The idea of informing him directly of the death had been too much for Maria; she assumed he would find out about it from the press. He immediately sent her a telegram expressing his grief. Although he still harbored feelings of rancor against the petty tyrant of his youth, he was shaken by his sudden passing. "I grieve for Father, grieve for all of you," he wrote to Maria. "The thought that you must go through so difficult a time in Moscow while I am off in Yalta enjoying peace and quiet weighs heavy and will not leave me."[26]

Another, more subtle thought kept nagging at him as well: had not this man—whom he had tended to consider a pompous puppet, a windbag—marked him more than he knew? Were not his early religious skepticism, his all-embracing tolerance, and his taste for simplicity and modesty in human relations and in art—were not they all a reaction against his father's mean-minded bigotry, his high-handed authoritarianism, his insufferable prolixity? Did not some parents educate their children by serving as a foil, a counterexample? Perhaps he owed more to his father than to any other member of the family. Everything he lived and wrote had existed in embryo during the childhood he spent under his father's roof.

Before long he found out how the death had come about. Lifting a crate of books at Melikhovo, Pavel Yegorovich had suffered a serious hernia and was taken to a Moscow clinic, where he underwent a long, painful, and eventually unsuccessful operation. The news once more aroused Chekhov's regrets at not having been present. "It wouldn't have happened if I'd been at home," he wrote to Suvorin as both son and physician. "I'd not have let necrosis set in."[27] The state of his health was such that he could not simply pick up and travel to Moscow for the funeral, but he found it calming to learn that Pavel Yegorovich had been buried in the beautiful, peaceful cemetery of the Novodevichy Monastery.

Although Chekhov's mother was very attached to the house at Melikhovo, he felt it ill advised for her to remain there all winter with only Maria to look after her. Besides, he realized that with Pavel Yegorovich gone life in Melikhovo would never be the same, that it was "as if the end of his log marked the end of our Melikhovo existence."[28] And since for reasons of health he was condemned to live in the south, he decided he would do well to put Melikhovo up for sale and make a new nest for the family in the Crimea.

Even before his father's death he had toyed with the idea

of settling down there. He and Sinani had gone to see a charming four-room villa perched on a mountainside near the Tatar village of Kuchukoy. Then he saw a piece of land at Autka, twenty minutes from Yalta. He was thrilled by the location: it overlooked the sea. On a sudden impulse he resolved to buy it and put up his own house there. All that remained was the financing. He obtained an advance of five thousand rubles on his royalties from Suvorin, took out a seven-thousand ruble mortgage at a local bank, and by the end of October he had signed the contract and engaged a young architect by the name of Lev Shapovalov to draw up the plans. Construction was to begin in December.

When Maria came down to Yalta to inspect her brother's acquisition, she could not hide her disappointment: to her the Autka land was an abandoned vineyard overrun with weeds, too far from the water and too close to the Tatar cemetery. She went back north firm in the conviction that their mother would never leave her dear Melikhovo. But Chekhov immediately began bombarding the two of them with enthusiastic letters. To Maria he gave detailed descriptions of the orchard and the vegetable beds, of a flower garden he would plant, of a sunny paradise far from the madding crowds; to his mother he explained that the kitchen would be magnificent and have "running water and every American comfort," that there would be a laundry, a wood and coal cellar, bells for the servants, and even a telephone. Moreover, mass at Autka was at ten o'clock in the morning, her favorite time, and she could gather mushrooms all autumn in the crown woods.

But even as he sang the praises of Autka, Chekhov had Kuchukoy in the back of his mind, and one day, in the midst of their Autka correspondence, Maria received a letter that fairly stunned her: "Let me start off with a piece of news. Something pleasant and unexpected. Don't go thinking I want to get married and have proposed. I couldn't help myself; on the spur of the moment I bought Kuchukoy. I bought it for two thousand rubles and have already signed the papers, and in a few days I shall drive over with a mattress and some sheets and take possession. [. . .] I am now the owner of one of the most beautiful and unusual estates in the Crimea. [. . .] Don't tell anyone or the newspapers will get wind of it and say that I've bought an estate for a hundred thousand."[29]

Maria promised to be discreet, but his extravagance worried her. During his absence she had become the pillar of the family; she ran Melikhovo, cared for her mother, oversaw the construction of the village school, and kept a tight rein on expenses. But Anton's career was her main concern. As the date of the *Seagull* opening approached, she began to dread a new disaster and the repercussions it would have on her brother's already frail health. Without informing him, she went to the Art Theater and begged its founders tearfully to postpone the production. Gently they explained to her that they had invested a considerable sum of money in it and that it had gone through twenty-six rehearsals; in other words, the time for pulling out had passed.

On the evening of December 17, 1898, the actors were in a terrible state, fearing that if they failed they would cause their beloved Chekhov a mortal blow. They had all taken valerian drops, a sedative commonly used in Russia. The curtain opened on a hall that was only three-quarters full. Stanislavsky, who, following his own conception of the play, sat with his back to the audience, could not conceal the trembling in his leg. "When the curtain fell on the first act," writes Nemirovich-Danchenko in his memoirs, "something occurred which can occur in the theatre only once in a decade: the curtain closed, and there was silence, complete silence, both in the auditorium and on stage; it was as though everyone held his breath, as though no one quite understood. [. . .] This mood lasted quite a long time, so long indeed that those on stage decided the first act had failed, failed so completely that not a single friend in the audience dared applaud. A nervous chill close to hysteria seized the actors. Then, suddenly, it was as if a dam had burst or a bomb had exploded—all at once there was deafening crash of applause from everyone, friends and enemies."[30] By the last act the performance had progressed from success to triumph. Taking their final bows, the actors hugged one another and wept with joy.

Stanislavsky did a victory dance onstage. The applause was deafening. Before it was over, the audience had risen to its feet and called for a telegram to be sent to the author.

The telegram arrived at Yalta the next morning. It read: "Have just performed *Seagull,* colossal success. [. . .] Numerous curtain calls. [. . .] All are wild with joy," and was followed by another: "Newspapers with astonishing accord report *Seagull* brilliant, great success. Critics enthusiastic." Elated, Chekhov responded, also by telegram, "Tell everyone am infinitely, deeply grateful. Am exiled at Yalta like Dreyfus on Devil's Island. Your telegram has made me happy and well."

After a several-day hiatus—Olga Knipper had come down with bronchitis—*The Seagull* began playing to packed audiences. All-night queues in front of the ticket office were a common occurrence. The play's determined admirers included many young people who would perch on folding stools and read by the light of the streetlamps or dance to keep warm. The lucky few who ended up with tickets ran off to work exhilarated.

Soon Chekhov was buried under an avalanche of congratulatory letters and telegrams, partial compensation for having been present at the play's fiasco instead of its triumph. But that triumph meant more than revenge to him. The young writer Maxim Gorky, who had recently struck up a correspondence with Chekhov, assured him "with tears of emotion" that he had "never seen a play so wonderful and *heretically brilliant* as *The Seagull,*" and he added, "So you don't want to write for the theater? You must, damn it!" Chekhov was touched by Gorky's mock injunction. Could he be right? The Art Theater actors were so respectful of the author's intentions that he no longer needed to be cautious about striking out in new directions. Thanks to the Moscow Art Theater Chekhov had found both a suitable audience and suitable interpreters. He felt a new harmony between what he wanted to give to the world and what the world expected from him. Now all he needed was the strength to carry on his work.

Unfortunately in late November he started coughing blood again. His personal physician, Dr. Isaak Altschuler, saw him regularly but was unable to make him follow a regular course of treatment. He was too taken with his patient's combination of docility and courage, with his habit of speaking slowly and softly, his manner of disposing of spittle in paper cones. Chekhov, for his part, still refused to admit the gravity of the illness. When at the end of the previous October a number of newspapers issued reports on the alarming state of his health, he flew into a rage and sent a denial to the press. About one such report in the Petersburg *News* he wrote to Suvorin, "I don't know who felt it necessary to frighten my family by sending in that cruel and, by the way, completely erroneous telegram. My temperature has been normal all along; I haven't even taken it— there's been no need. I do have a cough, but it's no worse than before. I've been eating like a horse, sleeping like a log, drinking vodka, drinking wine, and so on."[31] But a month later he wrote, "I've been coughing blood for five days now, and it hasn't subsided until today. But that's just between you and me; don't tell anybody. I've stopped coughing, my temperature is normal, and the blood frightens others more than it does me. That's why I try to keep it a secret from my family."[32]

Chekhov's Yalta existence took its rhythm from these bouts and remissions. Whenever he grew weak, he withdrew into his room, but the moment he felt better he made extra demands on himself so as to make up for lost time. In addition to writing he supervised work on the Autka house, saw patients, toured schools, took part in the activities of the local Red Cross chapter, and raised money for the young famine victims of Samara. As Dr. Altschuler said of him, "His kindness and his desire to be of service to small causes as well as large were exceptional."

Although he quickly made new acquaintances in Yalta, he missed his family and friends. Only Ivan had gone down to visit him, and he had stayed for no more than a few days at Christmas. His mother and sister, who had moved to a rented flat in Moscow, obstinately refused to make the journey. And while he continued to extol the Crimea's sun and blue skies to them, he himself dreamed of snow, busy streets, restaurants, and theaters. "I do so long to go to the capital!" he wrote to

Vladimir Tikhonov, a fellow writer. "I'm bored here, I've turned into a philistine, and I have a feeling it won't be long before I set up house with a pockmarked peasant woman who will beat me on weekdays and pity me on holidays. We writers have no business living in the provinces. [. . .] Yalta differs only slightly from holes like Yelets or Kremenchug; here even the bacilli sleep."[33]

If it had not been for his friends' letters, he would have felt completely cut off from the world. He answered them at length and with gusto. His correspondence with Maxim Gorky was a case in point. Without ever having met Chekhov, Gorky wrote him a spontaneous letter in praise of his works. At the time Gorky was a thirty-year-old self-taught writer from a poor Nizhny Novgorod family. Gorky, a pseudonym, means "bitter" (his real name was Alexei Peshkov), and his early stories had attracted attention by exposing the flaws inherent in bourgeois society. Before long the two men had exchanged books and were regularly exchanging letters.

Gorky's admiration for Chekhov was unbounded, and he admitted to having shed tears over certain of his stories. As for Chekhov, he lauded his young confrère's "immense talent" by saying, "When you describe a thing, you see it and touch it with your hands. That is true art!" At the same time he warned Gorky not to yield to a certain facile tendency he perceived in him, a tendency to overwrite. "This lack of restraint is especially evident in the nature descriptions you use to break up your dialogues. When I read them—these descriptions—I feel I'd like them shorter, more compact, only about two or three lines long. Frequent references to languor, murmuring, plushness, and the like give your descriptions a rhetorical quality and make them monotonous; they discourage the reader and become almost tiresome. The same lack of restraint is evident in your descriptions of women. [. . .] I don't know you, I don't know where you come from or who you are. But I feel you ought to leave Nizhny for two or three years while you're still young and rub shoulders with literature and the literary world—not to learn the ropes from us and become a professional but to submerge yourself in literature totally and grow to love it."[34]

Several months later he gave Gorky even more pointed advice about style. "You have so many modifiers that the reader has a hard time determining what deserves his attention, and it tires him out. If I write, 'A man sat down on the grass,' it is understandable because it is clear and doesn't require a second reading. But it would be hard to follow and brain-taxing were I to write, 'A tall, narrow-chested, red-bearded man of medium height sat down noiselessly, looking around timidly and in fright, on a patch of green grass that had been trampled by pedestrians.' The brain can't grasp all that at once, and the art of fiction ought to be immediately, instantaneously graspable."[35] Thus, from their first letters the two men set up an open literary relationship with much deference on the part of the younger party and a hint of condescension and patronage on the part of the elder.

The oddest of Chekhov's epistolary relationships remained the one he kept up with Lydia Avilova. On the one hand he refused to acknowledge much less accept her love; on the other he seemed unwilling to cast her off once and for all. After the visit she paid him at Dr. Ostroumov's clinic she continued inviting him to come and see her and complaining bitterly about his indifference. "If my letters are sometimes harsh and cold," he responded, "my frivolous nature is to blame."[36]

When *Russian Thought* came out with a new Chekhov story entitled "About Love," Avilova—as she tells it in *Chekhov in My Life*—was thrown into a state of "violent agitation." She ran home clutching the magazine and indulging in all sorts of fantasies. Having read through the story feverishly, she made up her mind it represented a thinly disguised account of the feelings that tied her to the author. At last, she thought. He has used the character of Alyokhin and the theme of unrequited love to explain why he had failed to declare his passion. "I was no longer crying but sobbing hysterically. So he did not think I was to blame. He did not blame me but justified me. He understood me. He grieved with me. [. . .] If my family prevented me from being happy with Chekhov, then Chekhov prevented me from being happy with my family. I had to tear myself in two."[37] Inflamed by the story, she set her sights on Chekhov again and, the better to provoke him, adopted a sarcastic tone. She wrote him a letter of irate gratitude for the honor of starring in one of his stories and compared him to an author who had indulged in repugnant excesses so as to be able to describe them realistically in his novels. "In other words, a writer, like a bee, takes his honey where he finds it. He's bored with writing, tired of it, but he has the knack, so he goes on giving cold, apathetic descriptions of feelings his soul, crowded out by talent, can no longer experience. And the colder the author the more sensitive and touching the story. May his readers weep over it. That is what art is for."

Chekhov worded his response as prudently as if the addressee were slightly unbalanced. "You are wrong about the bee. First it sees bright, beautiful flowers; only then does it gather honey. As for the rest—the apathy, the boredom, the idea that people with talent live and love exclusively in the world of their images and fantasies—all I can say is that the soul of another is unfathomable. [. . .] I clasp your hand. Keep well and happy. Yours, A. Chekhov."[38]

Avilova, furious that Chekhov would not play her game, wrote back accusing him of trying to bring their correspondence to an end. Instead of jumping at the chance to do so, Chekhov beat a feeble retreat. "I have read your letter and can only throw up my hands. [. . .] If you see things in my letters that aren't there, it must be because I don't know how to write letters. [. . .] In any case, don't be angry with me and do forgive me if there really were cruel and unpleasant things in the last few. I had no intention of offending you."[39]

Three days later he wrote to Lika in the same friendly tone thanking her for having sent a photograph of herself. The letter ended: "Keep well and happy. Don't forget the man who used to worship you. A. Chekhov." Much as he dreaded the havoc feminine wiles would wreak on his peace and quiet, he was not altogether willing to give up the place he occupied in the affections of his pretty correspondents.

When at about this time his brother Mikhail pressed him yet again to marry, he responded with a clear statement of his views on the issue. "Marriage for love is the only kind of marriage that's interesting. Marrying a girl only because she's nice is like buying something you don't need at a market merely because it is pretty. The point around which family life revolves is love, sexual attraction, one flesh. Everything else is dreary and unreliable, no matter how cleverly it is calculated. Therefore, the main thing is to find a girl you love, not one you think is nice."[40] Not only had Chekhov not yet found that girl, he feared finding her. How complicated it would make his life! And was he still capable of falling in love? Run down by his illness, he had voluntarily withdrawn from the world. Since then his strongest emotions had arrived in the post. But even in the depths of lassitude he felt sudden explosions of desire to, say, build a new house or write a story even better than the last or be loved by a gentle, cheerful, intelligent woman—like the one who had played Arkadina in *The Seagull,* Olga Knipper.

For the time being he had to be satisfied with the joys of architecture and writing. The Autka house had begun to take shape, *The Seagull* was still enjoying its triumphant run in Moscow, and his books were selling well. In fact, Suvorin had undertaken an edition of his collected works.

But Chekhov felt Suvorin was dragging his feet. At the rate he was going, Chekhov jested, the final volume would not be out until 1948. When the well-known publisher Adolf Marx learned from Sergeenko that Chekhov was disgruntled with Suvorin, he offered to purchase everything Chekhov had written and to put out a definitive edition forthwith. Instead of the usual royalties, based on the number of books sold, he offered Chekhov a lump sum, and the prospect of receiving a small fortune was what finally decided Chekhov in favor of Marx's proposition. He saw it as a way of paying off his debts, covering the Autka construction costs, and saving his mother and Maria from want. True, Maria begged him not to sign away all his rights and proposed to edit his works herself (as Tolstoy's wife had begun doing for her husband), but he replied she had nothing to worry about: he had every intention of driving a hard bargain. Marx offered fifty thousand rubles, Chekhov asked eighty; they finally agreed on seventy-five.

Yet the contract, signed on January 16, 1899, was patently unfavorable to Chekhov. It stipulated that in exchange for the seventy-five thousand rubles (just under $40,000 or over £ 8,000 at the time), of which the sum of twenty thousand was payable upon signature and the rest payable in four installments during the following two years, Chekhov agreed to give Marx the rights, in perpetuity, to all his works, present and future, excepting plays. In the case of future works the author retained the right of first publication, after which the works became the property of the publisher upon payment of a supplementary remuneration calculated on the basis of each sixteen printed pages of text.

Although a letter to Maria makes it clear that Chekhov knew the arrangement was not without its drawbacks, he claimed that now at least he could be assured that his books would be published with care and that he would no longer need to do his own bookkeeping, in other words, that at last he could work in peace. The real reason he accepted such exclusive terms, however, was that he knew he did not have long to live. Marx was to be the savior of his last years. "There's a big piece of news in my life, an event . . . Am I getting married? Guess. Am I getting married? If so, to whom? No, I'm not getting married; I'm selling all my stories to Marx, selling my rights to them. Negotiations are under way, and in two or three weeks I may well be a man of means."[41] To other friends he announced cheerfully, "I've become a Marxist."

To be sure, he was somewhat conscience-stricken at backing out of his agreement with Suvorin: they had worked together for thirteen years. For the sake of propriety he kept Suvorin informed of his negotiations with Marx, though he took no account of Suvorin's objections. Summing up the motivations behind the decision, he emphasized that only the need for a large sum had led him to bind himself permanently to Marx and that he had fought Marx tooth and nail for the right to retain the rights to his plays. "Even so, I'm unhappy," he admitted. "I feel as if I've married a rich woman. [. . .] There is a saying among people in business that you fight while you're together, but part on good terms. We are parting on good terms, you and I, but we were also on good terms while together. I don't think we had a single misunderstanding between us the whole time you published my books. And some pretty big things we did too."[42]

According to the terms of the contract, Chekhov had six months to furnish Marx with a copy of every one of his stories, from the oldest to the most recent. The task was enormous, especially as many of the numerous early stories appeared in magazines that had ceased publication. He compared it to making a precise list of the fish he had caught during the previous twenty years. The few stories he was able to track down himself he subjected to a careful selection procedure, reworking the style where it now felt limp. His "forced labor," as he referred to it, was made particularly burdensome by the paucity of libraries and other archival resources in Yalta. Utterly helpless, he enlisted the aid of Maria and Alexander, who consulted the periodical collections in Moscow and Petersburg and had copies made of all the stories they were able to uncover.

For help with the stories originally published in the *Saint Petersburg Gazette* he wrote to Lydia Avilova, whose brother-in-law was the managing editor. The letter, asking her to find a copyist, concludes on a conciliatory note, a muted reference to the preceding turbulent letters: "At least write that you are not angry with me, even if you have no desire to write to me otherwise."[43] But Avilova was only too glad to render service to the great man, whom she still assumed to be in love with her. In fact, she undertook much of the work herself and did a meticulous job of it, for which Chekhov was duly grateful. The letters he wrote to her during this short period of collaboration were more relaxed, more confiding; he no longer seemed afraid of her: "Why am I in Yalta? Why is it so awfully boring here? It is snowing, a storm, the wind is beating against the windowpanes, heat is drifting over from the stove, and I have no desire to write and am writing nothing. You are very kind. I have said it a thousand times before and say it once again."[44]

The winter was exceptionally cold for the Crimea, and all work on the Autka house ceased until the weather turned. It was quite a sizable edifice, with two stories facing north and three facing south, a tower, a veranda, and a glassed-in entrance, but it lacked a unified style and Chekhov called it the "sardine tin." He tended to let himself be carried away by a project and was then disappointed with the results, and the greater his expectations the more he suffered.

Now he threw himself into the task of laying out the garden—the paths and lawns and flower beds. Two Turks in red fezes prepared the soil while he went from hole to hole planting trees, bushes, and roses. "It's a sheer delight," he wrote to Maria. "I've planted twelve cherry trees, four pyramidal mulberries, two almonds, and a few others. They are good trees and will soon bear fruit. The old ones are starting to bud, the pear tree is blossoming, and the almond tree has put out pink flowers. Birds stop for the night in the orchards on their way north and sing in the morning—thrushes, for instance."[45]

If Chekhov spent great sums on his Autka house, he was none the less liberal when it came to charity. No sooner did he receive his first payment from Marx than he contributed five hundred rubles towards the construction of a school in a nearby village. Having happened on the trail of Gavryushka, one of the peasants who had waited on customers in the Taganrog shop, he offered to pay for his daughter's schooling. Young writers in need knew they could count on his aid. And when his brother Alexander took it into his head to build himself a little dacha of his own outside Petersburg, Anton forwarded him a thousand rubles and took to signing his letters "Your Brother the Moneybags" or "The Rich Philanthropist."

The more famous he grew, the more strangers came to him not only for financial assistance, stylistic advice, or letters of recommendation to publishers but also for his opinion on various topics of the day. When a wave of student riots swept from Petersburg throughout the country and a number of young people were expelled from the university or thrown into jail after violent clashes with the police, Chekhov began to receive letters asking him for public statements on their behalf. Having refused all his life to participate in politics, he took refuge behind the rule that the artist had no business interfering in public affairs. "Are we to judge? Isn't that the job of gendarmes, policemen, and officials specially assigned by fate? Our job is to write and nothing else. Any fighting, fuming, and judging we do we must do only with our pens."[46]

At the same time, however, he spoke and wrote openly about the government's brutal measures of repression. Indeed, with age he had grown more and more disgusted with the excesses of the autocratic regime. He was a convinced liberal and disapproved of violence, from above or below. For that reason he was never attracted by Gorky's militant socialism. Mass movements alarmed him; they held out no hope of peaceful evolution. "I have faith in individuals," he wrote to an old friend, the country doctor Ivan Orlov. "I see salvation in individuals scattered here and there, all over Russia, be they intellectuals or peasants, because they're the ones who really matter, no matter how few they are. No man is a prophet in his own country, and the individuals I am talking about play an inconspicuous role in society. They do not dominate, yet their work is visible. Think what you will, but science is inexorably moving forward, social consciousness is on the increase, moral issues are beginning to take on a more disturbing character, and so on and so forth, and all this is going on independently of the intelligentsia en masse, despite all obstacles."[47]

As was to be expected, Suvorin took a hard line against the student rioters. He wrote two articles condemning them roundly and approving the tsar's decision to name an investigatory commission, the goal of which was clearly to stamp out the movement. As a direct result of the articles the intelligentsia boycotted his *New Times,* Gorky published a virulent "open letter," and rumors that Suvorin had received ten thousand rubles from the government started making the rounds. Not only did the *New Times* circulation drop, several members of the editorial board tendered their resignations. Soon even the Russian Writers Mutual Aid Society had summoned Suvorin to appear before a court of honor to explain his actions or have his membership suspended.

Besieged on all sides and ailing to boot, Suvorin wrote to Chekhov for advice. Chekhov responded to Suvorin's attempt at self-justification by criticizing the two articles. He accused Suvorin of having treated a grave issue lightly and championed a government that had patently overstepped its rights. He pointed out that rights and justice were the same for the state as for the individual and "the concept of the state should be founded on definite legal relationships. If it is not, it is a bogeyman, an empty sound producing an imaginary fright."[48]

Several weeks later he returned to the issue. "When people lack the right to express their opinions freely, they express them irately, in anger, and often—from the point of view of the government—in a form that is ugly, appalling. Grant freedom of the press and freedom of conscience and you will have the quiet you so desire. True, it may not last too long, but it will at least suffice for our lifetimes."[49]

Chekhov did not, however, agree with the idea of "trying" Suvorin before the court of honor: a trial might be suitable for, say, military officers, but it would scarcely do for writers, whose role in life was to express their opinions freely without fearing the judgment of their peers. (Suvorin did in fact refuse to appear before the court.) Besides, Chekhov felt, the true blame for the disrepute into which *New Times* had fallen lay entirely with its editorial board. "People have come to believe that *New Times* receives a subsidy from the government and from the French general staff. And *New Times* has done everything in its power to maintain this undeserved reputation. [. . .] In most people's opinion you are a man who has great influence on the government, a cruel and implacable man. And once more *New Times* has done everything in its power to preserve that misapprehension in our society as long as possible."[50]

When Suvorin's wife blamed Chekhov for deserting her husband in his hour of need, Chekhov responded, "You accuse me of perfidy, you write that Alexei Sergeevich is good-hearted and altruistic and that I am not responding in kind. But as a person who sincerely wishes him well, what else could I have done? Tell me. Today's mood did not materialize all of a sudden; it took shape over a period of many years. The things being said now were said long ago, everywhere, and you and Alexei Sergeevich have been kept in ignorance of the truth much as royalty is. I am not speculating; I am telling you what I know. *New Times* is going through a difficult period, but it has remained a force and will continue to remain a force. After some time has gone by, everything will go back to normal, and nothing will have changed, everything will be as it was."[51]

Chekhov was correct: the Russian public had a short memory. Once the storm had passed, *New Times* sailed on as majestically as before, with Suvorin firmly at the helm.* And although the student incident and the Marx affair did broaden the gulf between the two men, Chekhov could not bring himself to stop writing to him; he even invited Suvorin to come and see him in Yalta. Suvorin, whose pride had been sorely hurt by then, never came.

Gorky, however, was happy to make the journey. From their first Yalta meeting he was under Chekhov's spell, and Chekhov, for his part, took quite a fancy to Gorky. They spent days on end discussing art, literature, politics; they talked about the masterpieces of Western civilization and the plight of Russian teachers. "If you knew how badly the Russian village needs a nice, sensible, educated teacher! [. . .] A teacher must be an artist, in love with his calling; but with us he is a journeyman, ill-educated, who goes to the village to teach children as though he were going into exile. He is starved, crushed, terrorized by

---

*Suvorin lived and prospered until the age of seventy-eight. He died in 1912.

the fear of losing his daily bread. [. . .] Whenever I see a teacher, I feel ashamed for him, for his timidity, and because he is badly dressed. It seems to me I am myself to blame for the teacher's wretchedness."[52] A number of ailing and broken schoolteachers came through Yalta, and Chekhov dreamed of building a sanatorium for them.

With Gorky, a man of the people, Chekhov could talk easily about such projects. He felt more at home with Gorky's spontaneity and fierce idealism than with the sophistication of his Petersburg and Moscow colleagues. "He looks like a tramp from the outside," Chekhov wrote to Lydia Avilova, "but inside he's quite elegant—and I'm very glad. I want to introduce him to some women—it might be useful to him—but he balks at the idea."[53] To the critic and eminent thinker Vasily Rozanov he described Gorky as "a simple man, a vagabond who did not begin to read until he was an adult and now, as if born again, drinks in everything published, reads it all passionately and without prejudice."[54]

As for Gorky, he was amazed that a writer of genius like Chekhov could be so human. "Chekhov is an exceptional person," he wrote to his wife, "so kind, gentle, and considerate. People are wild about him and won't leave him in peace. [. . .] I enjoy talking to him immensely; in fact, I can't remember having had such pleasant talks with anyone." But he also told her that Chekhov's illness had made him somewhat capricious, even misanthropic, and that despite the numerous admirers surrounding him he was profoundly solitary, pensive, and disillusioned. One day he said to Gorky between two coughing fits, "Living with the idea that one must die is far from pleasant, but living and knowing that one will die before one's time is utterly ridiculous."

Even as spring began to make itself felt, Chekhov was seized by his chronic desire to flee Yalta. "I'm bored with the role of the man who, instead of living, vegetates 'for the sake of his health.' I stroll along the embankment and through the streets like a priest without a permanent parish."[55] On April 10 he left for Moscow without asking Dr. Altschuler's opinion.

At first he stayed with his mother and sister in their Malaya Dmitrovka flat. The usual visitors came swarming, and the samovar was kept boiling from eight in the morning till ten at night. Chekhov had some urgent proofreading to do for Marx, but he could not find it in his heart to throw anyone out. Now and then he would draw Maria aside and whisper, "Look, I've no idea who that man is and I never went to school with him. I know he has a manuscript up his sleeve, and if he stays to dinner he'll read it to us. This is really impossible."

Within four days he had moved into a flat of his own just down the street. It was near the Strastnoy Monastery, and he loved listening to the bells. But before long the company caught up with him there as well. "By the second day of the [Easter] festivities I was so exhausted I could scarcely move," he wrote to Dr. Altschuler. "I felt as lifeless as a corpse."[56]

In the midst of it all he was touched by a warm letter from Gorky. "I am happy to have met you," Gorky wrote on April 23 from Nizhny Novgorod, "terribly happy! I think you're the first free and completely unbeholden man I have ever seen. How good it is that you are able to consider literature the primary, foremost thing in life. But even knowing how good it is, I don't think I am capable of living like you—I have too many sympathies and antipathies. It's annoying, but I can't help myself. Please don't forget me. I'll be perfectly frank—I'd like you to point out my faults from time to time and give me advice, in other words, to treat me like a friend in need of instruction."

Chekhov was also touched by the visit Tolstoy paid him in Moscow, though the actors who happened to be present drowned out all attempts at serious conversation. Fortunately, the next day Chekhov was invited to dine at the Tolstoys', and there the two men were able to talk to their hearts' content. When the topic of the younger generation came up, Tolstoy pronounced Gorky "remarkable," though with one reservation: "Everything can be fabricated except psychology, and Gorky is full of psychological fabrications. He describes things he has not felt."

A week later Chekhov saw Lydia Avilova, who was passing through Moscow with her three children on the way to their estate. She suggested they should meet at the station, between trains, and Chekhov, wishing to show his gratitude for the work she had done on his behalf, acquiesced. But the moment he found himself in her feverish, possessive presence, he responded as usual by drawing back, and was visibly eager to see her leave. Avilova, still swathed in romantic illusions, compared their separation to the farewell scene in Chekhov's "About Love," but the passionate embrace that forms the climax of the scene never materialized. Chekhov merely said good-bye to the children in their compartment and walked out into the corridor, and when Avilova followed, asking him to visit her in the country, he told her that he would not go to see her even if she were to fall ill, that they would never see each other again. Then he shook her hand and left. "The train began to move slowly," she wrote in *Chekhov in My Life*. "I saw Chekhov's figure sailing past the window, but he did not look back. I did not know then and I never dreamt that I was seeing him for the last time."[57]

The same day, May 1, Chekhov attended a private performance of *The Seagull* at the Art Theater. He praised the actors, while criticizing the rhythm of the fourth act. A week later, on the day of his departure for Melikhovo, he agreed to be photographed with the cast. The picture shows him sitting at a table, pretending to read the manuscript of *The Seagull* to the deferentially hovering actors. One young woman stands out from the group. She is the only one in profile and appears lost in thought; she is Olga Knipper. Two days before, Chekhov had given her a picture of the "doll's house" at Melikhovo with the inscription: "My house, where *The Seagull* was written. To Olga Leonardovna Knipper with best wishes." She was secretly moved.

XIII

"Greetings, Last Page of My Life"

While Chekhov was away in Yalta, his sister had made friends with Olga Knipper. She admired her dignified acting style and impulsive nature. "I advise you to keep an eye on Knipper," she wrote to her brother. "I find her very interesting."

Olga Knipper, the daughter of an engineer of German descent, had received a standard bourgeois education: music lessons, drawing lessons, and foreign languages. When her father died, however, expenses had to be drastically reduced, and what Gorky called "the crazy Knipper family"—the widowed mother, who gave singing lessons; two rowdy uncles, who drank; and Olga—was crammed into a three-room flat in Moscow. Olga dreamed of going on the stage and, against her mother's better judgment, had studied acting with Nemirovich-Danchenko for three years. Her break came when Nemirovich-Danchenko included her in the company of the newly formed Moscow Art

Theater. She loved her profession and led a carefree if frenetic existence, learning her lines while her mother's pupils performed their scales and her uncles—one a doctor, the other a military officer—tippled vodka, played cards, or read Tolstoy and Chekhov aloud.

Not only was she a born actress, she had a great appetite for life in general. She could hold forth intelligently on art and literature, but showed an unabashed interest in dresses, hats, and even cooking. From the first she realized that Chekhov was not one to be attracted by a bloodless intellectual. She was flirtatious, impulsive, and demanding in his presence, and with her fair skin, silky dark hair, and laughing eyes—the picture of health. At twenty-nine she was only ten years younger than Chekhov, yet he saw her through the eyes of an old man: illness had aged him greatly.

Early in May 1899, just after returning to Melikhovo, he invited her to come and watch the Russian countryside blossom. She complied at once and was immediately won over by the simple and cordial atmosphere of the house, by Chekhov's mother, "a calm Russian woman with a good sense of humor," and by the innocent pride with which Chekhov discharged his hostly duties. "He loved everything that came from the earth," she wrote later in her memoirs. "We had three days filled with a sense of anticipation, with joy and sun." By the time she left, they were enthralled with each other and looking forward eagerly to the next visit.

In June Olga went to the Caucasus to spend the summer with her brother at Mtskhet. When Chekhov found out, he chided her in the bantering tone he had once used with Lika. "What is this supposed to mean?" he wrote. "Where are you? You so stubbornly refuse to keep us informed that we spend all our time guessing and are beginning to wonder whether you haven't forgotten us and married someone in the Caucasus. If so, then who is he? Don't tell me you've decided to leave the stage. The author forgotten—oh, how awful, how cruel, how perfidious."[1] Next day he scribbled a postscript to a letter his sister had written to Olga. It opened with the words "Greetings, last page of my life, great actress of the Russian land. I envy the Circassians who see you every day."[2]

Soon after showing off Melikhovo to Olga, Chekhov started making ready to part with it. True, it held many memories for him, but he was firm about moving to Yalta. He advertised it for twenty-five thousand rubles, and even though no takers were forthcoming he went on packing—books, personal effects, and the outdoor furniture.

Then in late June Olga wrote to propose a rendezvous in the south. Chekhov accepted with gratitude. They agreed to meet at Novorossiisk on July 18. From there they would go on together to Yalta. They followed the plan to the letter. In Yalta Chekhov went to the Hotel Marino while Olga stayed with mutual friends, the Sredins. Chekhov divided his time between the Autka house, which was now nearing completion, and outings with Olga. He was intrigued by her abrupt changes in mood. "Knipper is in Yalta," he wrote to his sister, "and in a melancholy mood. Yesterday she came to have tea with me and just sat there without saying a word."[3] It upset her to see how he lived, scurrying from place to place and eating poorly—grabbing a piece of bread and cheese or skipping meals entirely; it gratified her when he finally took time out for a meal of seafood and Crimean white wine.

On August 2 the couple left for Moscow: Olga was due back for rehearsals. They took a carriage to Bakhchisarai, the nearest railway station at the time, admiring cypress-lined rose fields, Tatar villages, and abandoned Muslim cemeteries. The air was fragrant, the conversation light and gay, and the two travelers lamented the end of a pleasant visit, a visit that had brought them closer, if not quite together.

In Moscow Olga's time was completely taken up with rehearsing, Chekhov's with preparing the first volume of his complete works. They rarely saw each other. Moreover, by mid-August the weather had turned rainy and cold, and Chekhov fell ill. "I don't know if it's the bacilli up in arms or the weather, but I'm so done in I can't keep my head up."[4] The only thing to do was retreat to Yalta. He arrived, still run down, on August 27. Maria and his mother joined him two weeks later, Maria having succeeded in finding a buyer for Melikhovo.*

The three of them settled into the new Autka house as best they could, but the plasterwork was not yet dry and the workers still reigned supreme. "The carpenters hammer from morning till night and keep me from writing," Chekhov wrote to Victor Goltsev, the editor of *Russian Thought,* "and the weather is so beautiful I have trouble staying inside."[5] The beautiful weather was what finally won over Chekhov's mother. Even with the inconvenience of living in an unfinished house she no longer missed Melikhovo, and when Maria left for Moscow she saw no reason to go along.

With time the Autka house grew more livable. Chekhov was particularly happy to have a study of his own again. The room had lily-of-the-valley wallpaper and a large fan-shaped window offering a fine view of the garden, the valley, the town, and the sea beyond. The fireplace was hung with a Levitan landscape, the walls covered with family photographs, watercolors, and portraits of Tolstoy, Turgenev, and Grigorovich, and the large desk strewn with papers, books, and wooden and stone figurines. Although a No Smoking sign occupied a conspicuous place above the desk, Chekhov never pointed it out when a visitor inadvertently lit up. He preferred coughing to giving orders. And if he had to excuse himself and lie down, his white, ascetic bedroom was just next door.

Despite the energy he devoted to editing his collected works, Chekhov found time that autumn to write two long stories, "The Lady with the Dog" and "In the Ravine," and to sketch out another, "The Bishop." Like "The Peasants," "In the Ravine" gives a relentlessly honest picture of rural life, while "The Lady with the Dog," inspired by the artificial ambience of Yalta,

---

*The contract signed by the lumber merchant who purchased it provided for payment in several stages. The first payment was late in coming; the following never came. Melikhovo was eventually resold to a Baron Stuart.

tells the story of an adulterous affair that begins as a holiday romance and gradually turns into deep though hopeless love. Chekhov brilliantly captures the slightly tainted charm of the place—the southern landscape, the dusty roads, the restaurants along the esplanade, the moonlight, the gentle murmur of the sea—as it goes to the lovers' heads. He tells their story in an effortless yet merciless vein, in such a way that each detail, no matter how insignificant, contributes to the muted harmony of the whole. The conclusion might serve for many of Chekhov's mature stories and plays: "It seemed as though a solution would not be long in coming, and then a wonderful new life would begin; and they both saw clearly that the end was still a long way off and that the most complex and difficult part was just beginning."

Gorky responded to the story with great enthusiasm. "Do you realize what you're doing?" he wrote to him early in January 1900. "You're killing Realism. And you'll succeed, too—for good, forever. It's a form that has outlived its time—really! No one can go further than you along its path, no one can write so simply about such simple things as you can. After the most inconsequential of your stories everything else seems coarse, written with a log instead of a pen. And the main thing is that everything else stops seeming simple, that is, truthful. [. . .] You're doing a great service with your short stories, making people feel disgust for this sleepy, moribund existence. [. . .] Your stories are elegantly faceted flacons of all life's scents."

If Chekhov borrowed a good deal from the lives of others for his work, "The Lady with the Dog" shows he could also borrow from his own experience. For was he not thinking of himself when he wrote: "He always seemed to women other than what he was, and they loved in him a man who instead of being himself was someone created by their imagination, someone they had eagerly sought all their lives; even later, when they saw their mistake, they went on loving him. And not one of them had been happy with him. Time passed, and he went on meeting women, having affairs, and parting, but he had never loved; call it what you please, it was not love. And only now, when his hair was gray, had he fallen really and truly in love—for the first time in his life."

Of course Chekhov's case was less clear-cut than that of his hero Gurov. His melancholy daydreams of charming Olga may have been due as much to a nostalgia born of loneliness or boredom as to love. "I've grown accustomed to you," Chekhov wrote to her from Yalta, "I miss you and can in no way reconcile myself to the idea of not seeing you until the spring."[6] And a month later: "I envy the rat that lives under the floor of your theater."[7] As the weeks separating them went by, however, his impatience started losing its edge, his letters their frequency. On December 8 he wrote her a note that included the following: "Dear actress, charming woman, I've stopped writing to you because I've set to work and don't allow myself to be distracted."

Yet he looked forward to seeing her, if only for the joys of contemplation and conversation. He suffered greatly from the isolation that kept him from his writer friends, his editors, the theater. To Maria, his principal confidante, he spoke openly of his frustration, his solitude, his feeling of living in exile. "There's snow on the mountains. A cold wind is blowing. Only a fool would live in the Crimea now. You write about the theater and the Literary Circle and all kinds of temptations as if to tease me, as if you didn't know how boring and oppressive it is to go to bed at nine, go to bed furious, aware you have nowhere else to go, no one to talk to, and nothing to work for since no matter what you do you won't see or hear the results. The piano and I are two artifacts spending our lives in silence and wondering why we were put here when there's no one to play us."[8]

As always, Chekhov's personal plight did not blind him to the sufferings of others. The deplorable conditions he observed among indigent tuberculosis victims who flocked to Yalta for treatment (or, as he put it, "whom Russia gets rid of by dumping them here") would not let him forget his intention to establish a sanatorium. "I am plagued by consumptives," he wrote to the Taganrog journalist Abram Tarakhovsky. "They turn to me for help, and I'm at a loss to know what to do. I've come up with an appeal, and we're soliciting donations. If we don't collect anything, I'll have to flee Yalta."[9] He sent the appeal to Gorky too, adding, "It's so painful to watch their faces as they beg, their pitiful blankets as they die."[10] Before long he had gathered enough to bring together thirty patients in a small convalescent home, but, as much a perfectionist in life as in art, he was far from satisfied. In the end it took two years to raise the forty thousand rubles necessary to open a bona fide sanatorium.* The only dark spot in the campaign came when certain "progressives" refused to contribute, claiming the undertaking was on too grand a scale to succeed.

Paradoxically, Chekhov did not for a moment think of entering a sanatorium himself. He accepted the gravity of his illness, but could not accept the idea of awaiting death in a state of hygienic confinement; he preferred living life to the hilt even at the risk of shortening it. He believed in medicine for his patients, but tended to reject it when his own health was at stake.

Not even the vicissitudes of the sanatorium campaign could fill the vacuum Chekhov felt at Yalta. As he wrote to the young actor Vsevolod Meyerhold, "The weather here is magnificent and warm, but that's only gravy, and what good is gravy without meat?"[11] The one thing that kept him going was the production of *Uncle Vanya* due to open that autumn.

Uncle Vanya, a reworking of *The Wood Demon,* had actually enjoyed considerable success earlier, in the provinces, but Chekhov was long wary about authorizing a Moscow or Petersburg production. He did not give in until the oldest and most prestigious theater in Moscow, the Maly, approached him with an interest in the play. But after reading the script, the Maly's literary board requested major changes. It felt, for instance, that the idea of an enlightened individual like Uncle Vanya becoming so enraged as to fire a revolver at a university professor was

*It is still in operation and now bears his name.

implausible to say nothing of indecent and that it would greatly offend the sensibilities of the intelligentsia. After a good laugh at the board's expense Chekhov reclaimed the manuscript and handed it over to the Art Theater.

During his last stay in Moscow he had attended several rehearsals of the play at the Art Theater and exhibited a vigilance and will astonishing in one usually so self-effacing. The slightest error in interpretation, the merest labored effect wounded him to the quick, and he had no qualms about telling off both director and cast. Because he paid more attention to the female members of the cast, they nicknamed him "the actress inspector."

Back in Yalta he anxiously awaited news of the production. Olga, who was playing Yelena in the production, wrote him asking for psychological insights into the character. He replied that Stanislavsky was wrong in assuming Dr. Astrov to be passionately in love with Yelena. Astrov was attracted by her beauty, but realized he would get nowhere with her; in the last act he spoke to her "as if speaking of the heat in Africa" and kissed her "for no particular reason, for want of anything better to do." "Oh, how I wish to go to Moscow, my dear actress!" he added. "But of course your head is spinning, you're contaminated, you're in a daze, you have no time for me."[12]

Opening night was set for October 26, 1899. It was sold out long in advance. The following evening, after Chekhov had gone to bed, the Yalta post office started phoning him the messages of telegrams as they came in. "I woke up each time and ran to the phone in the dark, barefoot and freezing; I would barely doze off when the phone started ringing again. It was the first time my fame kept me awake."[13]

All the telegrams pointed to a hit—prolonged applause, numerous encores—but Chekhov's highly developed sixth sense discerned an undercurrent of discomfort and dissatisfaction. The studied intermingling of praise and criticism in the actual reviews seemed to confirm his suspicion. But as time went on, the quality of the performance improved and the play scored a resounding triumph.

In *Uncle Vanya* Chekhov returns to familiar themes—the wear and tear of day-to-day routine on the spirit, the burden of provincial lethargy on the gentry, the inevitable failure of idealistic aspirations—but he is particularly concerned with the opposition between the selfish and those who try to help their fellowmen. The former category is represented by the famous but vapid and conceited Professor Serebryakov and his wife, the young and beautiful Yelena, the latter by devoted Uncle Vanya and his kindhearted niece Sonya—the two of whom run the estate Sonya has inherited from her mother, Serebryakov's first wife—and by the once idealistic Dr. Astrov.

Vanya, who has all but sacrificed his life to Serebryakov's career, finally realizes that the "brilliant professor" is nothing but a gilt-edged nonentity, a pompous parasite. When Serebryakov proposes they should sell the estate and invest the profits, Vanya gives vent to his hatred and despair by firing some unsuccessful shots at him. Yet the deed seems to have no consequences. The characters' dreams of love—Vanya's and Astrov's for Yelena, Sonya's for Astrov—melt into thin air. After an awkward reconciliation Serebryakov and Yelena return to Petersburg, leaving Vanya and Sonya to carry on their selfless work for the prosperity and renown of the "Herr Professor."

Once more mediocrity has triumphed and mocked magnanimity. All the protagonists are marked by defeat. Dr. Astrov, the most lucid of them all, goes on treating his patients even as he doubts his calling; the oversensitive Uncle Vanya now sees not only his past but also his future ruined out of a misguided sense of family responsibility; Yelena comes to recognize herself as a flimsy "episodic character"; the glorious Serebryakov, who is at the bottom of it all, complains of old age and accuses his wife of finding him disgusting. As for the ardent Sonya, she ends up with no illusions whatsoever, ready to resume her burdensome and tedious existence. She is the one to whom Chekhov vouchsafes the closing lines of the play: "You've known no joy in your life, Uncle Vanya, but wait, wait . . . We shall rest . . . We shall rest . . ." For Chekhov's fragile creatures resignation provides the best defense against the blows of fate. From the start they know they will be crushed no matter what. Perhaps they even unconsciously wish to make a humble sacrifice. Peace in tedium.

When, several weeks after opening night, Nemirovich-Danchenko complained of overwork and told Chekhov he was thinking of resigning from his executive position at the Art Theater, Chekhov, aware of the role it had played in making so difficult a play successful, responded fervently, "Oh, don't wear yourself out, don't lose your enthusiasm! That theater is your pride and the only theater I love, though I've never once been in it. If I lived in Moscow, I'd try and join the staff if only as a watchman, so I could help in my own small way and keep you, if possible, from losing your enthusiasm for so dear an institution."[14]

By late January Gorky had seen *Uncle Vanya* twice. "*Uncle Vanya* again," he wrote to Chekhov after the second time. "Again. And I'm going to book a seat in advance and make yet another trip to see it. I don't consider it a pearl, but I do think it's got more content than others see. The content is rich and symbolic, and the form makes it completely original, incomparable." After many such testimonials Chekhov felt certain his play was destined for a long and brilliant career.

Then Tolstoy gave his opinion. "Where is the drama?" he asked the actor Alexander Sanin, hopping mad. "What does it consist in? It doesn't go anywhere!" Nemirovich-Danchenko tried to defend his author, but Tolstoy replied curtly that *Uncle Vanya* lacked all semblance of a tragic situation and used guitars and crickets in its place. When Tolstoy's words reached Chekhov, he merely smiled a good-natured smile. Some time later, talking to the writer Pyotr Gnedich, he mentioned that the old master could not stand his plays. "There is one thing that consoles me, though," he added. "Tolstoy once told me, 'As you know, I detest Shakespeare. Well, your plays are worse than his.' " Whereupon Chekhov let out a peal of laughter so great that, if Gnedich is to be believed, his pince-nez popped off his nose.

Tolstoy's peremptory condemnation of *Uncle Vanya,* which

he also criticized for its moral laxity, did not keep Chekhov from welcoming the publication of *Resurrection* that winter as a major literary event. Not that he was without his reservations. "Everything in the novel," he wrote to Gorky, "everything but the rather vague and contrived relationship of Nekhlyudov and Maslova contributed to my amazement at the power and wealth and breadth and insincerity of a man who fears death, but refuses to admit it, and therefore grasps at texts from the Scriptures."[15]

Yet when he heard that Tolstoy had fallen seriously ill, he was as upset as if a close relative were in danger. "I fear Tolstoy's death," he wrote to Mikhail Menshikov, a well-known journalist. "His death would leave a large empty space in my life. First, I have loved no man as I have loved him. I am not a believer, but of all beliefs I consider his the closest to mine and most suitable for me. Second, when literature has a Tolstoy, it is easy and gratifying to be a writer. Even if you are aware you have never accomplished anything and are still not accomplishing anything, you don't feel so bad, because Tolstoy accomplishes enough for everyone. His activities provide justification for the hopes and aspirations that are usually placed on literature. Third, Tolstoy stands above us, his authority is enormous, and as long as he is alive bad taste in literature, all vulgarity in its brazen-faced or lachrymose varieties, all bristly or resentful vanity will remain far in the background. His moral authority alone is enough to maintain what we think of as literary trends and schools at a certain minimal level. If not for him, literature would be a flock without a shepherd or an unfathomable jumble."[16]

Tolstoy responded to Chekhov's veneration with almost paternal affection, and while he rejected the plays he praised a number of the stories, comparing Chekhov to Maupassant. "In Chekhov everything is real to the verge of illusion," he once said. "His stories give the impression of a stereoscope. He throws words about in apparent disorder, and, like an impressionist painter, he achieves wonderful results by his touches."[17]

On January 16, 1900, Chekhov learned that he, Tolstoy,

Korolenko, and seven other writers and scholars had been named to the Academy of Sciences: the government had decided to establish a Pushkin Section for Russian Language and Literature. Chekhov was deluged with congratulatory telegrams, and the Taganrog Municipal Council voted two Chekhov Scholarships into existence. But apart from the pleasure of standing beside Tolstoy among the new academicians, he thought the whole thing ridiculous. He began signing family letters "Your brother, the well-known academician, A. Chekhov" or "A. Chekhov de l'Académie," and to his sister he wrote that the old family retainer, believing him to have been promoted to the rank of general, required all visitors to refer to him as "your Excellency." The only practical advantage he saw to the new distinction was that it granted him the legal status of "academic immunity" and a special passport that could save him harassment at customs. "I'll be happier, though, when I lose the title after some misunderstanding," he wrote to Menshikov.[18]

The more his fame grew the more he suffered from being confined to Yalta. "The idleness, the stupid above-freezing winter, the utter lack of pretty women, the pig snouts on the esplanade—it can all fray and tarnish a man in no time. I'm tired; I feel winter has been dragging on for ten years."[19] This to Gorky, who had written to him a month before: "Word has it you're marrying an actress with a foreign name. I don't believe it. But if it's true, I'm pleased."

Chekhov remained silent on that point. For fifteen years he had been the subject of marriage rumors. This time, however, they seemed more believable than usual. Everyone could see that Olga Knipper and Maria Chekhova were inseparable. The letters Chekhov received from his sister overflowed with praise for her new friend, who often added a few friendly words of her own. Maria looked on bemused; she saw their bantering as a passing fancy. One thing was certain: Anton would never marry. Besides, his letters to Olga could be quite gruff. When she expressed anxiety at the idea of his going abroad, he retorted, "Why are you so gloomy? You live, work, hope, drink, laugh when your uncle reads to you—what more do you need? I'm different: I'm cut off from my roots, I don't live a full life, I don't drink though I enjoy a drink now and then, I like noise and I hear none—in other words, I'm in the position of a transplanted tree unsure of whether it will take root or wither."[20]

For relaxation he worked in the garden, trying to adapt Autka's dry, pebbly soil to birches and poplars beside the native cypresses, palms, and eucalyptuses. An avenue of acacias had grown very quickly. Of the seventy rosebushes he had planted the previous autumn only three had died. "If I weren't a writer," he wrote proudly to Menshikov, "I think I could be a gardener." When the Melikhovo dachshunds died, they were replaced by two mutts, who tagged along wherever Chekhov went. Chestnut was a good-natured oaf of a dog, while the brazen Little Ace showed off his rasping bark at the slightest provocation. A pair of cranes, which had also taken up residence in the garden, followed Chekhov step by step as he pruned his roses, and whenever Arseny the handyman came back from an errand in town, they would dance around him on their long angular legs, opening their bills and emitting hoarse cries. With the exception of cats, for which he felt a mixture of revulsion and fear, Chekhov loved all animals. As at Melikhovo he made a point of releasing the mice he caught in traps; here he took them to the Tatar cemetery next door.

Now that Marx was sending him the advances called for by their contract and he had started receiving considerable royalties from his plays, Chekhov no longer worried quite so much about financial matters. He deposited five thousand rubles in an account in Maria's name and, acting again on his instinct for property, bought a small three-room, seafront house in Gurzuf, twenty kilometers from Yalta. He justified the folly by claiming the family could use it on holidays, and for once Maria approved, adding impishly in her response that Olga Knipper approved too.

As spring approached, Chekhov began to miss Olga again. He had submitted a proposal to the Art Theater for a Crimean tour, and when after some initial hesitation Stanislavsky came round, the tour was set for early April. The entire company looked forward to showing Chekhov what it could do, in the hope of encouraging him to write a new play. "I'm happy, happy mostly for myself, because seeing you all, especially with full sets and costumes and electric lighting, is a dream that till the last few days I must admit I never thought would come true. Even now I give a start every time the phone rings: I'm sure it's a telegram from Moscow announcing that the tour has been canceled."[21]

A few days before the Art Theater was due to arrive in Sevastopol, Olga and Maria turned up in Yalta. The joy of seeing Olga again was clouded by the crowds of friends who came to call and a violent hemorrhage that banished him to his room. Olga was very concerned, but had to leave to meet the company. By April 9 Chekhov had recovered enough to take the boat for Sevastopol. He arrived the next day looking pale and weak, his body wracked by a dry cough. When asked about his health, he replied with a forced smile, "It's excellent. I'm in fine shape."

That evening, hidden in the back of the director's box, he attended a performance of *Uncle Vanya* by a company he had never seen act in public. It was a triumph. The audience clapped and cheered and called for the author. When he came out on-stage, his knees were weak and his pince-nez misted over, but he was happy. He approved of all the actors. Especially Olga.

Two days later he saw the Art Theater's production of Ibsen's *Hedda Gabler*. "Ibsen's not really a playwright," he told the actors when they asked for his opinion. Next day he left for Yalta, so disabled by his illness and the emotional strain of the events that he was unable to stay even for that evening's *Seagull*.

When the Art Theater disembarked at Yalta a day later, it was met by a crowd of theater lovers who had assembled at the port despite a raging storm. There was much joyous pushing and shoving among the mountains of luggage, much shouting of congratulations and presenting of bouquets, and this amidst gales of wind and before performances had even begun. On the following day the company made its way to Autka—some on foot, others in cabs—to attend a party Chekhov had thrown for them. The party was graced by a number of writers, artists, and musicians, men like Maxim Gorky, Ivan Bunin, Alexander Kuprin, and Sergei Rachmaninov, who had made the journey to Yalta especially to see the Art Theater. Small groups formed around tea tables, in the study, on the terrace, in the garden. The elegant Bunin amused his circle with stories of the Russian countryside, Gorky harangued his with views on art and politics. Olga and Maria circulated among them all with trays of refreshments, while a radiant Chekhov greeted each guest with a kind word.

The actors immediately started making daily pilgrimages to "their" author for either lunch or tea. The table conversations ranged from the serious to the hilarious. They all felt so at home with Chekhov that they came up with a plan whereby they would return to Yalta every year and even build a "collective residence" there.

The company opened with *Uncle Vanya*. The audience was made up of well-to-do holidaymakers and an admixture of teachers, provincial officials, and consumptives. Yevgenia Yakovlevna, who had never seen a play by her son, demanded to go, and unearthed a shiny black silk gown from the bottom of a trunk for the occasion. Throughout the performance Chekhov worried about what she would think—she was so simple and unaccustomed to the theater. To make matters worse, the town band was performing in the park next door and polkas wafted into the hall at the most inopportune moments. Still, the play was a great success and the author received a standing ovation. The response was even more tumultuous when the Theater performed *The Seagull* a week later; after numerous curtain calls Chekhov was handed a congratulatory message signed by more than two hundred well-wishers.

A rich admirer of the Art Theater invited the entire company to a farewell luncheon on the roof of her mansion. Then everyone exchanged presents. The actors gave Chekhov the bench and swing used in the production of *Uncle Vanya,* and Chekhov gave each actor a gold fob containing a miniature of the photograph of himself reading *The Seagull* to the cast. Nem-irovich-Danchenko's also had an inscription on the back; it read: "You gave life to my *Seagull*. Thank you."

The moment the Art Theater left, Yalta sank back into its lethargy. After the excitement the absolute calm seemed un-bearable. In early May, as soon as he possibly could, Chekhov raced up to Moscow to pay a visit to Levitan, who was re-portedly dying. He saw Olga too, but since she had to spend most of her time rehearsing he returned to Yalta after only ten days. Once back, he wrote, "Greetings, dear, charming actress, How are you? How do you feel? I had a hard time of it on the way home. In Moscow I had a bad headache and fever, but I hid it from you. Sorry. Now everything's fine."[22]

Everything was so fine, in fact, that he decided to go on a two-week sightseeing trip with Gorky and a few other friends through the Caucasus. They traveled along the famous Georgian military road, touring a number of monasteries and stopping in Tiflis. In the train that took them from Tiflis back to Batum who should Chekhov run into but Olga: she was taking a short rest in the region with her mother. He was thrilled to spend the next six hours with her, and before a change of train sep-arated them they had agreed to meet again at the beginning of July in Yalta.

This time she stayed with the Chekhovs from the day of her arrival. They had been friends and correspondents for more than two years; now for the first time they were living under the same roof. Olga's charm—her youth, her spirits, her whims—had an even stronger effect on Chekhov at close range. For a while he remained faithful to his storm-and-retreat tactics, mak-ing it impossible for her to predict his next move, but gradually he left off his gallant ruses and she realized with pride that she had won: flirtation had turned to love. At last she became his mistress.

Every evening they met secretly. Olga would wear the long white dress Chekhov so admired—it showed off her black curly hair—and hum Glinka's romance "Don't Tempt Me in Vain." After making love they would whisper together tenderly, holding hands. Then, after Olga had come down to earth, she would make some coffee and butter some bread and the two of them would regale themselves like fifteen-year-olds.

Discreet as the lovers tried to be, Maria and Yevgenia Yakovlevna could not have been long in guessing what had happened. If nothing else, the mere fact that Chekhov had stopped seeing visitors and was neglecting his desk was enough to rouse their suspicion. But Anton looked so happy that Maria was actually touched. Besides, experience had led her to believe that the infatuation would not develop into anything more serious.

The only event that cast a shadow over Chekhov's euphoria was the news of Levitan's death, which he received on July 22. Then there was an almost comic contretemps: the ill-timed visit of a former "seagull," the beautiful Vera Kommissarzhevskaya. Kommissarzhevskaya, who was now at the height of her career, happened to be on tour in southern Russia. Chekhov consented to see her on August 3 at Gurzuf. As they strolled along the seashore, Vera recited Nina's monologue from *The Seagull* and some poems by Pushkin in her mellifluous voice. When she asked him for permission to stay on another day, he was rather vexed, his only thought being to return to his beloved Olga. He fled the next day, leaving behind a photograph with the dedication: "To Vera Kommissarzhevskaya, August 3, a stormy day when the sea roared, from the tranquil Anton Chekhov."

Since Olga could spend only two more days in Yalta, each hour was precious. On August 5 the couple went to Sevastopol, where they spent the night together and Anton put Olga on the train to Moscow. They were now completely free in each other's presence; they had switched to the familiar form of "you" and were demonstratively affectionate. Clearly each could no longer imagine a life without the other.

Three days after Olga's departure, Anton wrote: "Greetings, my dear Olya, my joy! [. . .] I'm now back in Yalta, bored, moping, out of sorts. [. . .] I keep thinking the door's going to open and you'll come in. But you won't; you're at a rehearsal far from Yalta and from me. Good-bye, and may the heavenly hosts and guardian angels keep you. Good-bye, dear girl. Yours, Antonio."[23] And a few days later: "My dear, marvelous, magnificent actress, I'm feeling well and thinking of you. I dream of you and miss your presence here. Yesterday and the day before, I was at Gurzuf; now I'm back in Yalta, in my prison. The wind is cruel, the launch isn't running, there's a heavy swell, people are drowning, the rain refuses to fall, everything is parched, withering; in a word, since you've left, everything has been awful. I could hang myself without you. Be happy and well, my good little German."[24]

At first they exchanged affectionate letters more or less every other day. Then Chekhov became engrossed in a new project: *Three Sisters*. "I'm working on the play, but I'm afraid it will turn out to be boring. I'll finish it, and if I don't like it I'll put it aside, hide it until next year or whenever I feel like going back to it."[25]

The scintillating letters Olga wrote from up north made him jealous. After describing an unforgettable day in the country, she would suggest he come and spend the next summer "somewhere in the vicinity." "I kept thinking how much you belong to this ever so Russian nature, to the immensity of it all—fields, meadows, ravines, shady rivers." She would end an account of a get-together that went on until two in the morning with the words "I don't remember having laughed so much in my life," or conjure up a ball where she had danced herself breathless in a gown with a "plunging neckline."

These echoes of a young and charmed existence made Chekhov feel his age, illness, and isolation all the more acutely. "I'm afraid of disappointing you. My hair is falling out at such a rate that if I don't watch out I'll be a bald-pated grandpa in a week's time. [. . .] I'm terribly bored, do you understand? Terribly. All I eat is soup. The evenings are cold, so I stay home. There are no pretty girls, my money is gradually running out, my beard is graying . . ."[26]

Wretched as Chekhov's self-portrait was, it did not diminish Olga's love. For all his ailments she was determined to marry him. To Nemirovich-Danchenko she even went so far as to speak of the marriage as "settled." But she failed to take into account his aversion to married life.

Not only had he no intention of proposing, he started putting off his trip to Moscow. To justify the delays, he invoked slow progress on *Three Sisters* due to lack of inspiration and illness ("fever, coughing, and a head cold"). Besides, did she really want to see him? Hadn't she begun to forget him? "You're diabolically cold—as befits an actress, by the way. Don't be angry, darling. It just slipped out in passing."[27] And when she kept pressing him to leave Yalta and come to her, he replied bitterly, "I see no reason for going to Moscow. Why should I? To glance at you and leave again? Very interesting. Arrive, have a look at the hustle and bustle of the theater, and leave again. [. . .] You don't write often, and the way I explain it is that you're tired of me and beginning to be wooed by others."[28]

Now it was her turn to be upset. She accused him of being callous and veiling his feelings. Why the game of hide-and-seek, the constant dodging? Isn't it more satisfying, more honest to make one's love public?

But the more she insisted the more he backed off—anything but speak of the future or go to the crux of the matter. "How actually have I shown you a hard heart?" he asked her with more than a hint of bad conscience. "My heart has always loved you and been affectionate with you, and I've never hidden anything from you, never, and you accuse me of being hardhearted just like that, with no rhyme or reason. Judging from your letter, you want and expect an explanation, a long talk with serious faces and serious consequences, and I don't know what to tell you except what I've told you ten thousand times before and will as likely as not go on telling you for a long time to come, that is, I love you, that's all. If we're not together now, neither you nor I am to blame, it's the devil who planted the bacilli in me and the love of art in you."[29] And to patch up the quarrel, he wrote the next day about the character he had created for her: "Oh, what a part you're going to have in *Three Sisters*! What a part! Give me ten rubles and I'll make sure you get it; otherwise, I'll give it to another actress."[30]

On October 16 he announced triumphantly that the play was ready at last. "I had a lot of trouble with *Three Sisters*," he wrote to Gorky. "Three heroines, after all, each of which must be her own person, and all three the daughters of a general! The action takes place in a provincial town, a place like Perm, and the milieu is all soldiers, the artillery. The weather in Yalta is wonderful, the air is fresh. My health is restored. I don't even feel like going to Moscow." Yet a week later, yielding to Olga's appeals, he went.

Every day he attended rehearsals and performances at the Art Theater. He saw both *The Seagull* and *Uncle Vanya* several times. Though moved by the audiences' acclamations, he was as nervous as ever about the new play. Still, he consented to have his portrait painted by Valentin Serov and gallivanted about town with Olga, Gorky, or Chaliapin until all hours of the night. This reckless existence soon wore him down, and he started experiencing headaches, coughing bouts, and sudden high temperatures. Yet not for a moment did he consider cutting his stay short. The reason, of course, was Olga.

She would drop in on him at his hotel between rehearsals, bringing chocolates, flowers, a bottle of cologne, a funny trinket or two. Then out would come the samovar and bread sliced thin and spread with butter and honey. But much as Chekhov enjoyed watching her fuss about like a true housewife, he did not think of asking for her hand: free love, secret yet warm, was still enough.

Shortly after Chekhov had arrived in Moscow, Stanislavsky arranged for a reading of *Three Sisters* in the Art Theater lobby. The entire company was present. Its mood, excellent at first, darkened from one scene to the next. After the last act there was a heavy silence, a form of courteous consternation. Chekhov hid his embarrassment by smiling, coughing, and trying to catch the glance of one or another of the actors. The discussion that followed was dominated by comments like "It's not really a play yet; it's more of an outline" or "It's not ready to be acted; it has no roles, only hints." Some of the discussants wondered whether the play was a tragedy or a comedy, and one declared in a strong voice, "Although I cannot agree in principle with the author, I must admit . . ."

Chekhov could bear no more, and left. Stanislavsky, fearing he had been taken ill, rushed to the hotel. There he found Chekhov sulking over the actors' response to the play: "That 'in principle' was intolerable!" For a while Chekhov seemed determined to withdraw it entirely, but Stanislavsky finally made him see reason. Soon he was hard at work on major revisions of the first two acts. Yet when Vera Kommissarzhevskaya requested *Three Sisters* for a Petersburg benefit performance, he sadly refused, calling the play "boring, monotonous, and disagreeable."

Suddenly, on December 11, he upped and left Moscow without so much as completing the revisions. Again the urgent need for a change of scene had pushed him towards a mirage; what he found soon after arrival was a desert of boredom. Depressed at the prospect of another Yalta winter, he fled to Nice.

Olga could not help wondering whether the flight had been influenced by her insistent attentions. In any case, she was crushed. "I can't reconcile myself to our separation," she wrote to him. "Why did you leave when you belong here at my side? Not until yesterday as the train was pulling out and taking you away from me did I clearly understand that we were separating. I walked after the train for a long time as if unable to believe it, and then began to cry as I haven't cried in years."

The letter he wrote to her the following day, from Vienna, went some way towards reassuring her: "Tomorrow I'm leaving for Nice, but now I keep looking lustfully at the two beds in my room. I shall sleep and think. It's a shame I'm here alone without you, my pet, my own, a crying shame." A month before, he had written to Suvorin, "So you've heard I'm getting married. It's not true. I'm going to Africa to visit the crocodiles."[31]

Much as he despised the staid atmosphere of the Pension Russe, he took up residence there again. Everything was as he had left it: the French chambermaids with their regal smiles, the Russian cook with her Negro husband, the same horrible old ladies at the dining-room table. Still, he was enchanted with the mild weather: "There are roses and all kinds of flowers in bloom," he told Olga in his first letter from Nice. "I can't believe my eyes. The young people are all wearing summer coats; there's not a hat to be seen."[32] And the next day: "I have the feeling I'm on the moon. It's warm, the sun is beating down, I'm hot in my coat, everyone is in summer dress. The windows in my room are wide open; my soul seems open too. I'm copying over my play and wonder how I could have written such a thing and why."[33]

The first two acts had remained behind with Stanislavsky, who was already rehearsing them. Chekhov made only minor emendations in the third act, but reworked the fourth completely. Within a week of his arrival he sent the rest of the manuscript back to Moscow. "I've added a lot of lines for you," he wrote jokingly to Olga. "You ought to say thank you."[34]

Chekhov was worried about how things were proceeding at the Art Theater. Had the actors understood their characters? Was Stanislavsky overloading the production with those naturalist effects he was so fond of? "Describe at least one rehearsal of *Three Sisters* to me," he requested of Olga. "Does anything need to be added or removed? Are you acting well, my pet? Be careful now! Don't pull a sad face in any one of the acts. Angry, yes, but not sad. People who bear their grief inside them for a long time and are used to it only whistle and brood a lot. So brood a lot on stage when conversations are in progress, understand?"[35] And a few days later: "How vile of you not to write me any letters! You might at least write what's happening with *Three Sisters*. You haven't written me a thing about the play, not a thing, except that you went to rehearsal or today there wasn't any."[36]

Every detail of costuming and makeup was important to Chekhov. Moreover, because he feared that the actors would turn the many officer characters into caricatures, he recommended that they should avoid all comic effects. To ensure authenticity, he asked an acquaintance, a Colonel Petrov, to attend rehearsals and check the veracity of the costumes and the actors' behavior. The good colonel took his mission so to heart that he wrote Chekhov a long letter berating him for portraying an officer so immoral as to seduce a married woman. "Still, he's done what I asked him to do," Chekhov wrote to Olga; "in other words, the officers will be dressed like officers. [. . .] I miss Moscow and I miss you."[37]

The tone of Chekhov's letters remained as affectionate as ever, but still not the slightest allusion to marriage. "You know, Anton," she had written to him on the day of his departure, "I'm afraid to dream or, rather, to express my dreams out loud, but I have a feeling something beautiful and strong will come of our love. Whenever I start believing that, I feel like living and working, and life's petty cares cease to annoy me; I no longer wonder why I'm alive."

Chekhov refrained from commenting directly on the letter; in fact, he seldom spoke of the future: his illness precluded long-term commitments. He took one day at a time, prudently saving his strength. "I love you, though you don't understand," was the closest he came to a response. "You need a husband or, rather, a spouse with mutton chops and the cockade of an official. And what am I? Nothing special."[38] And in another letter dating from the same day: "Did I wish you a happy new year in my previous letter? I really didn't? I kiss both your hands, all ten fingers, and your forehead, and wish you happiness and peace and much, much love lasting a long, long time—say, fifteen years. What do you think? Can such a love exist? It can with me, but not with you." To highlight the frivolous mood of his letters, he signed them "Your Elder, Antoine," "Toto the Academician," "Antonius the Monk," and "Your Retired Doctor and Playwright on Reserve."

It was not long before Nice began to pall on him—if for no other reason than that the population included too many Russians eager to meet Anton Chekhov. But his writing was not going well either. "I do write, of course," he assured Olga, "but halfheartedly. *Three Sisters* seems to have worn me out, or else I'm simply tired of writing and out of date. I don't know.

What I ought to do is stop writing for five years or so, travel for five years, and then come back and sit down to work."[39]

Although he dreamed of going to Algeria, the sea was rough and the crossing risky. He settled on Italy, leaving Nice on January 26 with his friend Kovalevsky. On the train that night he confessed to Kovalevsky, "As a doctor, I know my life will be short." The two men toured Pisa, Florence, and, most conscientiously, Rome. "Oh, what a marvelous country this Italy is!" he wrote to Olga. "It's amazing! There's not a corner, not an inch of land that doesn't seem educational in the extreme."[40]

At the same time he was surprised to have no news of his play. Had it opened? And if so, did the silence mean it had flopped? Several days after the fact—as a result of his frequent changes of address—he learned that *Three Sisters* had opened on January 31, 1901. Nemirovich-Danchenko assured him by telegraph that the play was a great success, though the second act had felt a bit long. He was not quite telling the truth, however; both audience and critics had been put off from the start by the seemingly disjointed dialogue, the endless pauses, the absence of action, the characters' wavering inclinations. But Chekhov was not long in discerning a kind of charitable conspiracy behind the initial praise he received. Of all his friends, only Lavrov, the editor in chief of *Russian Thought,* gave him a forthright opinion: "A success? Not so brilliant as *The Seagull*'s, but for me more precious and meaningful."

Meanwhile, the weather in Rome had taken a turn for the worse, and the ruins were daubed with snow. Chekhov was sorry to abandon a projected trip to Naples, but felt bound to book passage on the first boat to Odessa. As soon as he reached Yalta, he wrote to his sister: "I arrived at night and haven't slept and know nothing about Moscow, the play, and so on and so forth."[41] And three days later he sent Olga the following wire: "Await detailed telegram. Health good. In love. Miss my dog.* Sending letters. How are your health spirits. Chekhov."

---

*Chekhov often used "dog" as a term of endearment for Olga.

Even before reading the reviews, he knew the play had been misunderstood. He expected as much. But he also had a premonition that in time *Three Sisters* would compel recognition from the very people who had criticized it as slow and colorless.

To bring alive the provincial backwater where the action of *Three Sisters* takes place, Chekhov recalled his stay at the drowsy garrison town of Voskresensk, where intellectuals and officers whiled away their time in routine and in philosophizing. He also thought back to the summers he had spent in Luka at the estate of the three Lintvaryov sisters. Thanks to a magic mental fusion of two groups of people who had never actually met, the young women welcomed the artillery officers into their home, and a unique work of art was born.

The three sisters, all Moscow-born, fervently hope to return and escape the vulgarity and pettiness of provincial life. Their leitmotiv—"To Moscow! To Moscow!"—runs throughout the play. Painful nostalgia, however, is the only point they have in common. The eldest sister, Olga, is rigid and melancholy, and suffers from an acute sense of obligation; she works as a schoolmistress and seems resigned to old-maidenhood. The middle sister, Masha (Olga Knipper's role), is curt but sensitive and full of passion; she has married a stupid, pretentious schoolmaster and blames the universe for her choice. Irina, the youngest, is spontaneous and gay, but full of illusions; she burns with a desire to have faith and do good. When an artillery regiment comes to town and a group of officers takes to frequenting the house, innocent but promising attachments begin to form. Awakened from their torpor, the three sisters regain a taste for life. Olga thinks of leaving her school, Masha falls in love and has an affair, and Irina goes to work and agrees to marry. But when the regiment moves on and the officers take leave of them, they come brutally down to earth, Olga returning to her lonely fate, Masha to her pathetic schoolmaster, and Irina, whose fiancé is killed in a duel, to a life of hard work and sacrifice. While the military band marches off, Olga clasps her sisters to her breast and says tenderly, "Dear sisters, our lives aren't over. We shall go on living. The music sounds so cheerful, so full of joy, that it almost seems as if any minute now we'll find out why we live, why we suffer . . . If only we knew, if only we knew."

The entire play centers on the issue of the meaning of life. It is suffused with the psychological tension between the sisters' anguished searchings and the officers' realism. "Look, it's snowing," one of them says. "What's the meaning of that?" Using bits and pieces of seemingly casual conversation, Chekhov creates an atmosphere so pregnant and poetic that it overflows the stage and engulfs the audience. We do not so much follow the action as delve into ourselves, experiencing with the characters the absurdity of the human condition. Without quite realizing it, we perceive the dull provincial town as an internal landscape, the three sisters' piteous adventures as our own; we too begin to wonder where we come from, where we are going, and what we are doing in this world. Long after we leave the theater, we hear Andrei, the unsuccessful brother, delivering his tirade against the townspeople: "All they do is eat, drink, sleep, and die. When others are born, they too eat, drink, and sleep. And to keep from dying of boredom they fill out their lives with stinking gossip, vodka, cards, and lawsuits. Wives deceive husbands; husbands lie and make believe they see nothing, hear nothing. And the brutal insensitivity of it all weighs so heavily on the children that the divine spark in them dies and they turn into pitiful, corpselike imitations of one another like their mothers and fathers before them." In other words, life is ugly and petty, happiness is only an illusion, and the only cure for despair is work, work without ambition or hope of recompense. Surely these were Chekhov's thoughts as he wrote the play. The more undermined he felt by his illness, the less reason he found for his fleshly presence in the midst of people who addressed him by name, called themselves his friends, dazed him with their compliments.

Still, he was happy to find Ivan Bunin at Yalta. Bunin had been invited by Maria and had been staying at the Autka house for several weeks. Perhaps her feelings for the lively, personable young writer went beyond mere friendship. In any case, when

Chekhov returned, he moved to a hotel. Bunin was ten years younger than Chekhov and looked upon him affectionately as his mentor. During his frequent visits to the house he noted Chekhov's almost morbid fear of appearing before anyone without a waistcoat and tie on, his exquisite courtesy even with intruders, his mania for order, his sad smile, his childlike joy at hearing a good anecdote.

One day when they were out for a ride, Chekhov said to Bunin, "Do you know how many more years I'll be read? Seven." "Why seven?" Bunin asked. "Well, seven and a half," Chekhov replied, adding later, "but I have even fewer years to live: six at most. And don't you breathe a word of it to those Odessa reporters."

Another young writer who met Chekhov at the time, Alexander Kuprin, was struck by his innocent, unassuming, melancholy manner. The black-ribboned pince-nez and goatee would have made him look like a German doctor or provincial schoolmaster had it not been for the intense, spellbinding light in his brown, blue-flecked eyes: "I saw the most beautiful, exquisite, inspiring face I have ever been privileged to see." Chekhov belied all the bohemian stereotypes of the artist: he preferred to write in the morning, rarely spoke of his work, and loathed all posturing. Nor did he complain of his health. He felt discretion to be a sign of breeding; decent people did not make a display of their misfortunes. The more he suffered, the more hale and hearty he tried to appear. If his mother or sister came across him sitting with closed eyes and strained features, he would immediately reassure her that it was nothing, he simply had a headache. Grimaces and shouting matches upset him terribly. As much as he delighted in seeing the theater resemble life, he despised seeing life resemble the theater.

Yet his fame was such that by noon each day Autka was filled with visitors. "All kinds of people came to see him," writes Kuprin, "scholars, writers, rural officials, doctors, officers, painters, admirers male and female, teachers, society people, senators, priests, actors, and God only knows who else." There were those who hoped to persuade him to come out in favor of one or another political cause, but he would give them his standard response: A writer must stick to literature. And if they insisted, he had another rejoinder: "Do you want me to tell you something? In ten years Russia shall have a constitution."[42]

Starting in the spring of 1901, however, the country was shaken by a wave of disturbances. When Tolstoy was excommunicated by the Holy Synod for supporting a number of persecuted sects—a move that increased rather than decreased his popularity—crowds marched through the streets of Moscow and Petersburg. More violent were the student riots that came in the wake of new laws restricting academic freedom. On March 4 mounted Cossacks charged the protesters in front of Kazan Cathedral in Petersburg, killing several and wounding many more in a little over a half hour. At the end of the month Gorky sent Chekhov a vivid eyewitness report. "I'll remember that battle as long I live! The fight was fierce, ferocious, on both sides. The Cossacks grabbed women by the hair and thrashed them with their whips. They beat a student friend of mine on the back like a pillow, beat her black and blue; they cracked another one's head open, poked a third one's eye out. [. . .] Life now has a tense, menacing aspect to it. You sense an enormous black beast lurking somewhere near at hand, in the shadow of the events, wondering whom to gobble up first."

Chekhov kept a close watch on the events, but, true to his principles, signed no petitions and wrote no articles in support of the students. To Olga he wrote: "I've been getting rather ominous letters from Petersburg and Moscow. I'm disgusted by what I read in the papers."[43]

All this time Olga was herself in Petersburg, leading a glamorous existence with the Art Theater. Although critics had turned their noses up at *Three Sisters,* audiences loved it. The receptions and dinners in honor of the company thrilled the budding star in Olga. "Yesterday we were guests of the Union of Writers," she wrote to Chekhov on March 5. "We all had flowers and gold decorations in the form of lyres at our place settings. I was at the place of honor. [. . .] I wore a black velvet dress with a small lace collar, and I'd had my hair waved at a hairdresser's. But do these details interest you?" Olga and her friends spent the next few days in Finland skiing, having snowball fights—enjoying themselves like a group of school-children on holiday.

Chekhov was looking forward to a visit from Olga after the Art Theater's spring tour to Petersburg, while Olga had asked him to come up to Moscow and visit her. She was sympathetic about his health, of course, but she had her self-respect to think of. All their friends were talking about the upcoming marriage; he was the only one who seemed to deny it. Did he really think she would meet him on the sly forever? She wanted to be loved openly, publicly; she wanted to share his life. In any case, she refused to go to Yalta for Easter and play the mistress under the suspicious eyes of his mother and sister.

This time there could be no doubt that if he failed to act he risked losing the only woman he had ever really loved. He had so little time left to live. Should he deprive himself of one last joy to remain faithful to his ideal of independence? Could he not, even as a married man, maintain the peace of mind he needed for his writing? Once when Bunin was in his study, he blurted out, "Did you know I was getting married?" But at once he made a joke of it, saying it was better to marry a German woman than a Russian one, because the German woman would take better care of him and keep their child from crawling all over the house and banging his spoon on the copper bowl. Bunin, who knew of the romance with Olga, was careful not to take sides, but when he thought of Olga's devotion to her career and Maria's devotion to her brother he concluded to himself, "It would be suicide, worse than Sakhalin."[44]

Little by little, however, Chekhov seemed to be growing used to the idea of marriage. On March 16 he wrote to Olga: "My health seems to be growing old-mannish, so you'll be acquiring more of a grandfather than a spouse in me. [. . .] I've given up literature entirely, and when I marry you I'll order you to give up the stage and we'll live together like planters. You don't like the idea? Very well, go on acting another five years or so, and we shall see."

Now Olga, too, was willing to compromise. She promised from Petersburg that because of his health she would risk blemishing her reputation and go to Yalta after all. She stayed for two weeks, but was unable to persuade Chekhov to name the day. Back in Moscow she wrote that the visit had left a bitter taste in her mouth.

At the end of his tether, Chekhov yielded to fate. "I'll be there early in May. [. . .] Give your word that not a soul in Moscow shall know of our wedding until after it takes place, and I'll marry you the day I arrive if you like. For some reason I'm terrified of the ceremony and congratulations and the champagne you have to hold in your hand with a vague smile." And he added, "Everything is fine with me, everything but a minor detail—my health."[45]

In fact, he had been coughing violently for a week, and in a letter written a few days before his "proposal" he painted a grim picture of the life they would have together: "My cough completely debilitates me. All thought of the future leaves me listless [. . .]. *You* think of it for me, be my guide. Whatever you say I will do, or else instead of living we shall swallow life at the rate of a tablespoon an hour."[46] A few days after the proposal he wrote: "I'm confined to my study and, for want of anything better to do, am completely involved in thinking and coughing. Don't be angry with me for behaving this way, darling; don't punish me with gloomy thoughts. Soon we'll be together, very soon. I'll leave Yalta on May 5 or, at the latest, May 10; it depends on the weather. Then we'll go down the Volga and do whatever your heart desires. I am in your power."[47]

On May 11 Chekhov arrived in Moscow. More hostile than ever to the idea of publicity in connection with his matrimonial plans, he did not let even Maria and Ivan know of his presence. Not until his sister had returned to Yalta did he write to her, and then only to let her know he had been to see a specialist, been informed that both lungs were badly affected,

and been ordered to take a koumiss* cure in the province of
Ufa. As if afraid Maria would guess his ulterior motives, he
went on in a bantering tone: "Going off alone is boring, the
cure itself is boring, but taking somebody along would be selfish
and therefore distasteful. I'd marry, but I haven't got my documents with me; they're all in Yalta, in my desk."[48]

The documents in question were not in his desk at Yalta.
Olga had reminded him to take them. There were no further
obstacles to the wedding. In a final move to preclude all sen-
timentality from the event, he asked Alexander Vishnevsky, a
member of the Art Theater company, to arrange a dinner in his
name on May 25, the day of the wedding, for a group of relatives
and friends of the couple. Having duly gathered at the restaurant, they waited patiently for Olga and Anton, unaware of
what was keeping them. While they waited, Olga and Anton
were married in a small church on the outskirts of Moscow.
The only people at their side were the four witnesses: for Olga,
a brother and an uncle; for Anton, two of the brother's student
friends. After the ceremony the newlyweds paid a quick visit
to Olga's mother and then went on to the station to take the
train for Nizhny Novgorod, the first stop on their honeymoon.
Before boarding the train, Chekhov sent off two telegrams: one
to Vishnevsky to announce that he had been married while his
guests were at the restaurant, the other to his mother: "Dear
Mama, Give me your blessing, I'm getting married. Everything
will remain as before. I'm going on a koumiss cure. [. . .] My
health has improved. Anton."

The couple spent a day in Nizhny Novgorod with Gorky,
who was under house arrest for having taken part in the March
riots. Then they went down the Volga and up the Kama and
the White River until they came to the village of Axyonovo,
where they booked two rooms at the sanatorium.

There was a telegram with blessings from Chekhov's mother
awaiting them, but nothing from his sister. He was worried;
she was undoubtedly furious with him for having concealed his

*A fermented beverage made by the Tatars from camel's or mare's milk.

265

intentions. Next day he wrote the following by way of self-justification: "By now you know I am married. I don't suspect it will alter my life or the way I live it in the slightest. Mother must be talking all kinds of nonsense, but tell her there won't be any changes whatsoever, everything will remain as before. I will live as I have lived and so shall mother, and my relations with you shall be as unfailingly warm and affectionate as ever. [. . .] My wife and I shall have to live apart from each other, but I'm used to that."[49]

Two days later Chekhov received a letter from his sister dated May 24. It was a response to his letter of the twentieth, in which he had jokingly alluded to a wedding in the offing, and it had taken so long to reach him because they had been on the move. As he had feared, Maria was quite short with him: "Let me state my opinion about your marriage. I personally find the whole wedding procedure odious. And you'd be much better off without all the additional excitement. If she loves you, she won't leave you; there is no sacrifice on her part nor the slightest bit of egotism on yours. How could you ever think such a thing! Egotism?! Besides, there's always time to tie the marriage knot. Tell that to your Knipschitz.* The most important thing is to make sure you keep well. Don't think I'm saying all this out of egotism. You have always been the closest and dearest person for me, and I wish you nothing but happiness. I want nothing more than for you to be healthy and happy. Anyway, do as you see fit. Maybe I am partial in this instance. You brought me up not to have any prejudices! [. . .] God, how hard it will be to be away from you for two whole months, and in Yalta to boot! If only you would let me come and see you during the cure, just for a week." And she closed with the postscript: "If you fail to answer this letter at once, I shall fall ill. Give *her* my best."

If Maria had reacted so strongly to the mere possibility of his marrying Olga, how she must have suffered when she learned he had actually gone through with it. Chekhov was filled with

---

*Another of Chekhov's pet names for Olga.

dismay. "I don't know whether I've done right or wrong," he wrote to her on June 4, trying to plead his cause, "but the main reasons I've married are: first, I'm over forty; second, Olga is from a good family; third, if I must leave her, I can do so without the slightest compunction, as if I'd never married in the first place—she is independent and supports herself. Another important consideration is that the marriage has not in the least altered either my own way of life or the way of life of those who have lived and continue to live with me. Everything, absolutely everything, shall remain as before, and I will go on living alone in Yalta." To prove how much he still needed her, he sent a telegram inviting her to come and join them for a cozy little honeymoon cruise *à trois*.

News of the marriage had plunged Maria into a state of tragic confusion: on the one hand, she was distressed both at the idea of the marriage and at having been kept in the dark about it; on the other, she was sorry to have sent Anton so harsh a letter. "I pace back and forth, thinking and thinking. One thought keeps bumping into the next. It's so dreadful for me to imagine you suddenly married! Of course I knew that Olya would eventually grow close to you, but the fact of your marriage has suddenly shaken my whole being and given me a great deal to think about in connection with you and me and our future relations with Olya. And they'll immediately change for the worse, I'm afraid . . . I feel more lonely than ever. But don't think there's any malice on my part or anything of the sort; no, I love you even more than before and wish you all the best, and Olya too, only I don't know what life will be like for her here with us and I can't yet be sure of how I feel towards her. I'm a little angry with her because she didn't tell me a thing about the wedding, and it couldn't have happened just like that, on the spur of the moment. I'm very unhappy, you see, Antosha, I'm depressed. I can't eat, everything makes me nauseous. All I want is to see you, you and nobody else."

Clearly Maria felt doubly betrayed: by her brother and by her best friend. The two people she had chosen as confidants had plotted their marriage without consulting her. The woman

had usurped her place in Anton's affections, and Anton had
allowed her to do so. Now that they had excluded her, she had
no one, nothing left to dedicate her life to. She could not resist
a dig at Olga when the newspapers finally informed the public
at large about Chekhov's marriage and a portrait of the couple
appeared in the *Daily News*: "Who is more famous, you or
Knipschitz?" she wrote to him. "They've shown her in her *Uncle
Vanya* costume and you in your pince-nez." And when Olga
sent her an affectionate but reproachful letter, she apologized
to her brother rather than to Olga: "It was the first time I'd
ventured to be frank," she wrote to him on June 16, "and I'm
sorry if I offended you and Olya. If you had married anyone
but Knipschitz, I'd probably not have written you a word about
it and simply hated your wife. But things are completely different: your wife was my friend; I felt close to her, we had been
through a lot together. So I started simmering with various
doubts and fears, needless and excessive perhaps, but I was
sincere and wrote everything I thought. [. . .] Don't be angry
with me, and remember that I love you and Olya more than
anyone else on earth."

After devoting the best years of her life to her brother and
perhaps even giving up marriage to stay by his side and care
for him, she had been left high and dry. Anton's assurances that
everything would be as before did not alter the fact that he had
thrust her aside. As long as Olga had been his mistress, Maria
had retained her privileged place in the family, but the moment
Olga became his wife that place passed to her. And contrary to
Chekhov's assurances, certain indefinable but irreplaceable bonds
of affection had been broken between Maria and him.

Despondent, Maria confided in Bunin, who had demon-
strated tact, intuition, and a fondness for her on more than one
occasion. "I'm in an awful mood," she wrote to him. "I keep
thinking of my life as a disaster. The reason in part is my
brother's marriage. It happened so abruptly! [. . .] For a long
while I was distraught and wondered how Olga could have let
someone so ill experience such a shock, but everything seems
to have turned out well in the end." And if that were not

heartrending enough, she went on, "Find me a rich and generous husband. I don't wish to go on writing now, but I'd very
much enjoy talking to you. Write to me more often. I'm terribly
depressed because of Antosha and Olechka."

Meanwhile, Chekhov was taking his cure at Axyonovo.
The sanatorium, though not particularly luxurious, was beau-
tifully situated between an oak wood and the steppe. But the
only company consisted of patients preoccupied with their health
and the local Bashkirs, whom he characterized as sluggish and
devoid of song, and not even Olga could liven things up for
him. A few weeks into the cure he wrote to Sobolevsky: "It's
like life in a penal battalion: unmitigated boredom. I can't wait
to clear out."[50] The treatment visibly improved his health; by
dint of forcing down four bottles of koumiss a day, he put on
weight and stopped coughing almost entirely. But although he
had originally planned to stay for two months, he begged off
after only one. On June 30 he announced to Bunin in a typically
farcical way: "Tomorrow I'm leaving for Yalta, where you may
send your congratulations on my legal marriage. You've heard,
have you not, that I've been married off? Well, I'm now engaging lawyers and suing for divorce."

On July 8, after a week's journey, he arrived in Yalta with
his wife. His mother and sister welcomed them with a mixture
of affection and discomfort, curiosity and apprehension.

XIV

Love by Correspondence

Now a wife with indisputable rights instead of a tolerated mistress, Olga soon made her presence in the Chekhov household felt. Her husband's disorderly way of life offended the Germanic taste for order in her. His mother and sister had coddled him, letting him take poor care of himself and even go without meals if he pleased; they did not dare criticize his bachelor ways. Olga treated him as a small child in a great man. With almost maternal authority she made him change his underwear more often, brush his clothes and shine his shoes, wash his hair regularly, and have it cut before it grew shaggy. Since his stomach constantly gave him trouble, she changed his diet, set regular mealtimes, and prescribed laxatives. Yevgenia Yakovlevna, who had always presided over the kitchen, was hurt by the new regime, as was Maria, who had nursed her brother with great affection for years. Both women saw themselves as upholding a tradition of gentle, loving care, and looked upon Olga as an intruder, a troublemaker. There were cutting remarks, blowups; Olga threatened to leave and take her husband with her. Nothing upset Chekhov more than such scenes, and he always managed to smooth ruffled feathers and iron out differences on both sides. Still, the undeclared war over his person proved a great drain on him.

On August 20 Olga left for Moscow and rehearsals. Chekhov was both despondent and relieved. When he received a letter from her containing an open confession of jealousy for her mother- and sister-in-law, he responded with a call for tolerance and understanding. "You write that Masha will never grow used to you and so on and so forth. How silly! You're blowing it all out of proportion, imagining things, and I'm afraid you'll be arguing with her soon. Here is what I recommend: be patient and hold your tongue for a year, only a year, and then you'll see. No matter what anyone says, no matter how things seem to you, don't utter a word. For anyone newly married the pleasant things in life depend on initial nonresistance. Be a good girl, darling, and do as I say! [. . .] I will never love anyone, any other woman, but you. Be well and happy."[1]

That summer he had given Olga a letter for Maria that was not to be opened until after his death. It was his will. "Dear Masha, I bequeath to you my house in Yalta for as long as you live, my money, and the income from my dramatic works; and to my wife, Olga Leonardovna, my house in Gurzuf and five thousand rubles."[2] It also included liberal sums for his brothers, cousins, the town of Taganrog, and the peasants of Melikhovo, as well as an exhortation to Maria to take care of their mother.

If Chekhov provided better for his sister than for his wife, it was because he knew his wife could always make her way as an actress. Being separated from her after three months of life together and being forced to express his love by the pen caused him great pain. They wrote to each other every day or two, and their letters combine sadness, affection, and desire with the most mundane detail: "Let me answer your questions. I've been sleeping wonderfully well—though it's terribly aggravating to sleep alone (I'm used to it though!)—eating a lot, and spending all day talking to visitors. I have kefir every day and enjoy it, and my 'innards' are still doing well, but I've forgotten to rub my neck with cologne. Yesterday I washed my hair."[3] And elsewhere: "I'm attached to you like a child; I feel uncomfortable and cold without you."[4] Or: "When you're not here, I'm as bored as if I were shut up in a monastery."[5] When Olga came up with the idea of having a cat in their new Moscow lodgings, he protested at first—he hated the beasts—and proposed a dog instead, but then added immediately, "You can have a crocodile if you like, darling. I give you free rein. I'm even ready and willing to sleep with a cat."[6]

Not a month had passed before he raced up to Moscow to be with his wife, even though the weather was already cold and wintry there. Maria and Olga had rented a large flat together, and he was happy to see them getting on better. But he had to share Olga with the theater as well: rehearsals lasted at least six hours a day and often went on till late in the night. In addition, Olga found the energy to attend all sorts of social functions. But when she came home, threw her arms around his neck, and called him her dear "Russian Maupassant," it filled him with an inordinate if fragile joy.

The Art Theater was working on *Three Sisters* again, and Chekhov as usual sat bundled up in the empty hall commenting on the performances. He particularly objected to the excessive realism of the production and asked Stanislavsky to eliminate the sound of doves cooing made by backstage actors as the curtain went up. One day he announced to the company that he was going to write a new play. " 'What fine quiet,' the chief person of my play will say. [. . .] 'How wonderful! We hear no birds, no cuckoos, no owls, no clocks, no sleigh bells, no crickets.' "[7] Stanislavsky wished to dazzle his audience with meticulous, authentic detail; Chekhov insisted upon paring down detail to the minimum and letting the characters take over. Stanislavsky saw the work from the outside; Chekhov saw it from within. Still, when *Three Sisters* opened the season on September 21, it was greeted with tumultuous applause. And when Chekhov appeared onstage at the end of the fourth act, sheer pandemonium broke loose. "The production of *Three Sisters* is superb, brilliant, much better than the play as written," he wrote to his friend, the Yalta doctor Leonid Sredin. "I did a little directing, gave some of the actors a few tips, and now people say it's going better than it did last season."[8]

But trying to keep pace with Moscow life ran him down, and he soon had to resign himself to winter in Yalta. "My wife, to whom I'm very much attached, is staying on alone in Moscow," he wrote to the editor Victor Mirolyubov. "I am leaving by myself. She is weeping, though I haven't told her to leave the theater. In a word, I'm in a pickle."[9]

By October 28 he was back in Yalta, condemned to a winter of love by correspondence. The very next day he poured out his passion in a letter. "Darling, angel, dog, sweetheart, please believe me when I say I love you, adore you. Don't forget me, write to me, and think of me a little more often. No matter what happens—even if you turn into an old crone, I will love you, for your soul, your character. [. . .] I kiss you very, very hard. I put my arms around you and kiss you again. My bed seems as lonely as if I were a mean, nasty old bachelor."[10] And a few days later: "The pleasure it would give me to talk to my wife, touch her eyelashes, her shoulder, laugh with her. Oh, darling, darling!"

Olga responded with equal passion. She told him that after he left she had not had the heart to make their bed, because as long as it remained unmade she could feel their intimacy in it. "I kiss you, Antonka. I kiss you lovingly, sweetly, tenderly. [. . .] How I long to snuggle up to you!" And: "I'm tired. I can't face getting up this morning. Each time I turn, I hope to see your dear face, your blond beard." And: "I love to think of you as you were in the morning, sitting on the bed with your back to me just after washing and before putting your jacket on. You see the guilty thoughts I have; well, I have guiltier ones I won't tell you about." Between lovelorn sighs Olga described rehearsals, worldly conquests, and dresses, while Anton spoke of visitors, indispositions, and the minor events of a lonesome existence: he had taken some castor oil, his inkwell had broken. . . .

In letter after letter both returned to the same question: "When shall we see each other again?" Olga was conscience-stricken, and Maria doubtless dropped remarks that fanned her guilt. As Chekhov's mistress, she had not felt obliged to look after him night and day; as his wife, however, she wondered whether she was right to pursue a career of her own when he needed her by his side. In the end, the desire to act—appear before the public, win its applause—got the better of her; she simply could not bring herself to give it all up.

Characteristically, Chekhov never made her career an issue. "We're committing a terrible sin by living apart" was as far as he would go. But on November 6 she confessed her agony: "I want to be near you and curse myself for not leaving the stage. [. . .] It makes me sick to think of you alone, unhappy, and bored, while I indulge in an ephemeral activity and refrain from giving my feelings free rein. What holds me back?!" Clearly she wanted him to take part in her decision, but he knew that she would be torn by remorse no matter what, and he had too much respect for the rights of the individual to advise his wife to exchange a brilliant Moscow existence for Yalta tedium. "You want to leave the theater? That's what your letter seems to say. Do you? Think it over thoroughly, darling, thoroughly, before you reach a decision. Don't forget I'll be spending the coming winter in Moscow."[11] Four days later he was a bit more specific: "It makes no sense for you to leave the stage for the boring life we lead in Yalta."

Chekhov's response dovetailed well with Olga's new feelings on the matter. "I had always hoped your health would permit you to live in Moscow at least part of the winter," she confessed to him on December 4, "but that's not how things have turned out, Antonchik. Without my work I'd bore you insufferably. I'd pace up and down and grumble at everything. I've lost the knack of living a life of leisure, and there is no point at my age in destroying everything I've built up so carefully."

All through the autumn months Chekhov had nurtured the hope of a January reunion with Olga in Moscow, but on December 9 he suffered a bad relapse, started coughing blood, and was forced to bed. All thoughts of Moscow went by the board. Two days after the crisis he reassured her—as always, attentive to her independence—from his sickbed: "I feel much better today. There was hemorrhaging only in the morning and it was very slight, but still I've got to stay in bed. I'm not eating anything, and I'm annoyed at not being able to work. [. . .] I don't expect you for the holidays, darling, you needn't come. Do your own work, and we'll find time to be together." Next day he repeated his recommendation: "Don't be worried, my pet, don't be angry, indignant, or sad. Everything will be fine, everything will end happily, everything will be exactly as we wish, my incomparable wife. Just have patience and wait." The day after that a touch of bitterness began to make itself felt: "You write that on the evening of December 8 you had a bit too much to drink. Oh, how I envy you, darling, if only you knew! I envy your vigor, your freshness, your health and mood; I envy you because you can drink without worrying about hemorrhaging and the like." But by December 17 he could write: "I have a compress on my right side and I'm taking creosote, but my temperature is normal and things are going well. Soon I'll be a man again."

The stronger he grew, the more he missed her. Suddenly he let out a cry of despair: "If only you knew how much I think of you, how much I regret your not being here when I have to put that huge compress in place and feel lonely and helpless. [. . .] I love you, my little doggy, love you very much, and I miss you terribly. It seems incredible that we shall ever see each other. I'm nothing without you. I kiss you hard, my pet, and embrace you a hundred times. I've been sleeping soundly, but I don't consider it sleep, because my sweet missus is not here with me."[12]

Olga responded immediately. "I give you my word it's the last year things will be like this," she wrote to him on December 23. "I'll do everything to make your life nice and pleasant, to keep you from being lonely. You'll see how good you feel when I'm there. You'll write and work. I suppose you condemn me inwardly for not loving you enough. You do, don't you? You condemn me for not leaving the stage, for being a bad wife! I can just imagine what your mother thinks about me! And she's right, she's right! Anton, dearest, forgive me, frivolous fool that I am. Don't think too badly of me. You're probably sorry you ever married me. Tell me. Don't be afraid to say it openly. I seem terribly cruel to myself. Tell me what to do!"

Chekhov responded to Olga's mea culpa with heroic detachment. Given the putrefaction spreading throughout his body, he did not feel justified in chaining a young, vibrant woman to his bed. "You are silly, darling," he wrote to her. "Not once the whole time I've been married have I condemned you for staying on the stage; on the contrary, I've been delighted to know you are at work, that you have a goal in life, that you are not simply whiling away your time, like your husband. [. . .] You mustn't be depressed and in the doldrums. Laugh. I embrace you and unfortunately that is all."[13] Next day, himself depressed at the idea of all the healthy people making ready for New Year's Eve celebrations, he wrote: "Tomorrow I shall purposely go to bed at nine to avoid seeing the New Year in. You're not here, so nothing's here, and I want nothing."

While Chekhov grew accustomed to an invalid's existence, spending more and more time sitting with his eyes closed, exhausted and motionless, in his armchair, Olga took full advantage of the Moscow holiday season. Each of her letters, after opening with inquiries about dear Anton's health and laments over their separation, went on breathlessly about rehearsals, performances, concerts, suppers, and balls where she was the center of attention. As if apologizing for his condition, Chekhov reminded her they had decided *together* that she would be better off in Moscow, and assured her his mother was not in the least cross with her. He only feared lest she should overtax herself. "Dear flighty wife," he admonished her, "do stay home for at least a week and get to bed on time! If you stay up every night till between three and six in the morning, you'll grow old before your time and be scrawny and vicious."[14] But she refused to listen to reason or even hide her escapades. "After the performance we went to the Hermitage for dinner and laughed and laughed," she announced coyly on January 11. "I flirted with Konstantin Sergeevich [Stanislavsky]. Are you upset? [. . .] Then—horrors!—we went to a cabaret."

Maria, who was sharing the Moscow flat with Olga, passed harsh judgment on her conduct. The zeal with which she had looked after her brother for so long had carried over to her relations with Olga; besides, by serving Olga as a kind of factotum, Maria became more a part of the couple's life. Austere, even rigid, by nature, Maria disapproved of Anton's leniency to say nothing of Olga's abuse of it. "I'm bored in Moscow," she wrote to him on February 2, 1902, "especially now that I'm ill and have been staying at home alone. I miss the house and you. I almost never see Olga. We nearly quarreled yesterday. I tried to stop her from going to the Morozovs' ball, but she went anyway and didn't come home until morning. Of course she was exhausted when she left for rehearsal today, and she's got a performance tonight."

From time to time Olga complained of being excluded from Chekhov's workshop: he wrote to her in great detail of his health, his diet, his love, yet jealously kept the literary side of his life to himself. Had he no confidence in her? Did he think her incapable of sharing the joys and woes of the artist in him? "How silly you are," he replied. "The reason I haven't written to you about my new play is not that I have no faith in you, as you say, but that I have no faith in the play yet. It's only just begun to dawn in my brain, like the earliest rays of sunrise, and I myself have no idea yet of what it's like, what will come of it—it changes every day. If we were together, I'd tell you about it, but I can't write about it because there's nothing to write. [. . .] In your letter you threaten never again to ask me about anything or meddle in anything. What's the point, darling? No, you're a good girl; your wrath will turn to mercy when you can see again how I love you, how close you are to me, how I can't live without you, my little silly. Stop moping, stop it!

Laugh! I'm the one who deserves to be moping, because I live in the wilderness, have nothing to do, no one to see, and am ill almost every week."[15]

But Olga refused to listen. She was sure he had loftier talks with Tolstoy, with Gorky, with Bunin, with all his writer friends. And of course she was right.

In fact, Tolstoy happened to be living in the Crimea. After a serious attack of malaria he had been advised by his doctors to leave Yasnaya Polyana for the sun of the Black Sea. He arrived in a private railway carriage and took up residence at Gaspra, some ten kilometers from Yalta, in an enormous wisteria-covered, double-turreted, Scottish-style castle placed at his disposal by the Countess Panina.

On September 12 Chekhov paid the first of several visits to Gaspra and the seventy-three-year-old magus. He had thought long and hard about what to wear, not wishing to appear either too elegant or too informal. In the end, he opted for a correct dark suit and soft felt hat. Tolstoy received him in his usual getup—though the peasant blouse and boots were accented by a white, broad-brimmed Panama hat—and with his usual informality.

Their meetings, always lively and cordial, took place on the terrace overlooking a profuse garden and the sea. Tolstoy would sit with a glass of cold tea at hand, his back stooped, his eyes piercing, his beard bobbing up and down as he talked and talked, irrevocably condemning this and extolling that, while Chekhov sat tapping the hat on his knees or adjusting his pincenez, waiting for a chance to put in a word or two. In the last analysis, the wild-eyed prophet and the courteous skeptic remained rather aloof from each other.

Even in literature they tended to disagree. Tolstoy would rant and rave about Shakespeare, who in his eyes had written one disastrous play after the other, and about the younger generation of Russian writers, who—again, in his eyes—were taken with fussy, empty experimentation. Nor did he let Chekhov off the hook, condemning his plays for failing to raise and solve moral issues. "Where do your characters take you? From the sofa to the junk room and back." As always, it was the stories he praised: "You are Russian, yes, very, very Russian." And in the mouth of a fervent nationalist that meant gratitude as well as praise. One of Tolstoy's sons, Sergei, later wrote: "It seemed to me that Father wanted to get really close to [Chekhov] and try to exert his influence on him, but he came up against a sort of passive resistance all the time and there was always a barrier between them."[16] And Bunin, in his *Memoirs,* quotes Chekhov as saying, "What I particularly admire in [Tolstoy] is the contempt he feels for all us other writers—or not even contempt: he simply considers us all nonexistent."

Tolstoy enjoyed teasing his visitor about his sense of modesty. "Did you whore a great deal in your youth?" he asked Chekhov outright one day. And when Chekhov tugged at his beard and mumbled a few muddled words, Tolstoy declared proudly that *he* had been an insatiable womanizer, using a spicy peasant word. Gorky, who had observed the two together, was especially struck by the contrast between Tolstoy's ardor, crudeness, and vanity and Chekhov's almost pathological self-effacement. Once at the sight of Chekhov walking on the Gaspra lawn Tolstoy whispered to Gorky, "Ah, what a beautiful, magnificent man: modest and quiet like a girl! He even walks like a girl. He's simply wonderful."[17] And after one of the days the three of them had spent together Tolstoy noted in his *Journal:* "I am glad I love Gorky and Chekhov."[18]

Gorky had come to the Crimea for his health, having obtained permission for the move from the authorities after his Nizhny Novgorod house arrest. Although they had expressly forbidden him to live in Yalta, he stayed with Chekhov for a week, with the result that a policeman stood guard in front of the house and the chief of police phoned Chekhov to learn of the suspect's whereabouts whenever Gorky left the premises. Eventually Gorky rented a house for himself and his family not far from Gaspra, and the more he and Chekhov met the more their friendship grew. "Alexei Mikhailovich [Gorky] has not changed," Chekhov wrote to Olga. "He is as decent, intelligent, and kind as always. There's only one thing about him—or, rather, on him—that feels wrong: his peasant blouse. I can't get used to it any more than I could get used to a chamberlain's uniform on him."[19]

As for Gorky's view of Chekhov, it could scarcely have been more positive. Gorky was especially impressed with Chekhov's modesty. "I think that in Chekhov's presence everyone involuntarily felt in himself a desire to be simpler, more truthful, more oneself. [. . .] He did not like conversations about deep questions, conversations with which our dear Russians so assiduously comfort themselves, forgetting that it is ridiculous, and not at all amusing, to argue about velvet costumes in the future when in the present one has not even a decent pair of trousers."[20] Gorky was all the more moved by Chekhov's unpretentious ways since he knew Chekhov had not long to live. With smiling stoicism he went on entertaining visitors, planting trees, writing, making travel plans—as if expecting to recover from one day to the next. Nor did he complain of his unusual, absentee marriage. The soul of discretion, he was the perfect person to confide in, though he himself confided in no one. And if he did go so far as to talk politics with Gorky, he always did his best to talk him into a less violent stance. While Gorky, a convinced Marxist, dreamed of a revolution capable of sweeping aside the bourgeoisie and handing power over to the people, Chekhov hoped for the slow but steady transformation of the tsarist regime into a regime of enlightened liberalism. Yet he did not have a particularly high opinion of his fellow countrymen. At times he even wondered whether they were worthy of the country that had given them birth. "A Russian is a strange creature," he once said to Gorky. "He's like a sieve—nothing remains in him. In his youth he fills himself greedily with anything he comes across, and after thirty years nothing remains but a kind of grey rubbish . . . In order to live well and humanly one must work—work with love and faith. But we Russians, we can't do it. [. . .] Russia is a land of insatiable and lazy people: they eat enormously of nice things, drink, like to sleep in the day-time, and snore in their sleep. They marry to have their houses looked after and keep mistresses to have prestige in society. Their psychology is that of a dog: when beaten, they whine shrilly and run into their kennels; when petted, they lie on their backs with their paws in the air and wag their tails."[21] Chekhov felt that life would not improve with a new tsar or a new century; he felt that life would improve only if people took an active, conscious part in improving it. And instead he found people growing duller and more detached from life.

The pointers on writing he gave to Bunin, whom he saw again that winter, bear a similar stamp. When Bunin confessed to him that his output was small, Chekhov boomed back, "You must work, you know, and never stop your whole life through." And on another occasion he told him not to begin writing until he felt as cold as ice. Of Leonid Andreev, whose early stories dealt with the fantastic in a rather pretentious style, he said to Bunin, "Read a page of Andreev, and you need to take a two-hour walk in the fresh air." He himself had little in common with Andreev's tormented personality. But to Olga, who was very much taken with the stories, he wrote, "Yes, he's a good writer. If he wrote more, he'd be more successful. There is a lack of sincerity, a lack of simplicity in him that makes him hard to get used to, but eventually the public will get used to him and he'll make a big name for himself."[22]

In the same letter Chekhov informed his wife that he had been under the weather and was taking castor oil. In fact, he was all but unable to work the whole winter. He did, however, complete "The Bishop," a story so imbued with the atmosphere of the church that it seems more the work of a man of faith and prayer than a confirmed skeptic. He also tried putting together an outline for *The Cherry Orchard,* but both characters and plot still eluded him. He spent a great deal of time reading his friends Bunin, Kuprin, and Gorky, and also reread Turgenev. He was annoyed with critics who drew parallels between his work and Turgenev's. "Only an eighth to a tenth of what he wrote will survive," he wrote to Olga. "All the rest will be buried in archives twenty-five to thirty-five years hence."[23]

Looking back over the years, Chekhov was amazed at how the day-to-day work had accumulated. His was a life marked less by events than by stories and plays; he seemed to have written his life rather than lived it. From time to time, however, a ghost from his real life came back to haunt him. One such ghost was Lydia Avilova.

The news of Chekhov's marriage had given her a bad jolt. "I broke into a cold sweat," she wrote in her memoirs, "and collapsed into the first available chair." Her only consolation was the idle chatter her "successful rival" appeared to be provoking: "Olga looks so funny next to Anton Pavlovich. Why, he's practically an old man—gaunt, frail. The last thing they look like is newlyweds." More malicious was the rumor that Nemirovich-Danchenko was wooing Olga openly, and for a while it kept Lydia from congratulating Chekhov on his marriage. When at last she did write, she also reminded him of what "their now dead love" had meant to her. Chekhov thanked her for her good wishes and added: "You want to know whether I am happy. First and foremost, I am ill. And now I know I am very ill. There, make of it what you please. I repeat I'm very grateful for your letter. [. . .] I've always wanted you to be happy, and if I could have done anything to make you happy I'd have been glad to do it. But there was nothing I could have done."[24] With the stroke of a pen Chekhov thus rid himself of the importunate Lydia and the love she had invented for her greater glory in the eyes of future generations.

Before long another ghost took to haunting Chekhov: Lika Mizinova. Lika had failed as an opera singer, decided against opening a dressmaking establishment, and now, at a loss to know what to do with herself, was drinking heavily. When Maria offered her the Moscow flat for a night, she had to air it thoroughly the next morning to get rid of the alcohol and cigarette fumes. "I pity Lika," she told her brother.

Olga was less indulgent. She wrote Chekhov a biting account of an encounter with the ex-"beautiful Lika" at a party: "Lika was drunk and kept pestering me to drink *Brüderschaft**

---

*A ritual whereby two people formalize their desire to be close friends (and use the familiar "you") by crossing arms and drinking out of each other's glass.

with her. I refused, because I loathe that kind of thing. I don't know her, I find her extremely strange, and feel no particular warmth towards her." Several weeks later she told him of Lika's betrothal to Alexander Sanin, an actor and director at the Art Theater, where Lika was a minor member of the company for a while. "I've known Lika for years," Chekhov responded. "She's a good girl in spite of everything, decent and intelligent. She'll have a bad time of it with Sanin; she won't love him [. . .], in a year she'll have a bouncing baby by him, and in a year and a half she'll start betraying him."[25] Now that he was married and ill, he had lost all interest in Lika and all taste for the gallant persiflage of his youth.*

The only woman Chekhov cared for now was Olga, and she had become something of a faraway princess for him: despite his supplications Dr. Altschuler refused to let him go to Moscow. Maria, moved by his despair, managed to wrangle a few days off for Olga from the Art Theater, and soon Anton had a letter from Olga saying she would be coming for "four days and five nights." She arrived in Yalta on February 22 for what she called their "second honeymoon." Time was so short that they made love wildly, whenever possible, as if under threat. No sooner had she left than he wrote: "Come back as soon as possible, darling. I can't live without my wife."[26]

The Art Theater was on tour in Petersburg at the time. Popular and critical acclaim was so great that it was invited to give a special performance of *Three Sisters* for Tsar Nicholas and his court. Olga was fast becoming the star of the company. Never had she received so many compliments, flowers, supper invitations—her head was spinning from it all. But alone in her room after the ovations had died down, she was filled with remorse at the thought of Anton, ailing and bored to tears in his cozy Yalta "prison." Then she would hasten to write and justify herself: "There are times when I detest the theater and times when I am madly in love with it. It has given me life,

---

*In fact, Maria notes that Lika and her husband were a devoted couple. They emigrated to France after the 1917 Revolution. Lika died in Paris in 1937.

great sadness, and great joy; it has given me you and made me a human being. Perhaps you think it a false life, a fiction; perhaps it is. But it is still a life. Before the theater I merely vegetated, I knew nothing of life, I had no understanding of people and the way they feel."

As usual Chekhov reassured her: he was happy for her, glad she was doing well. "So you're on your way to being a famous actress," he wrote in jest. "A Sarah Bernhardt. Will you send me packing? Or will you let me tag along as your accountant?" And in a postscript he added: "I have nothing against your being famous and earning twenty-five or forty thousand a year, only first do what you can for little Pamfil."[27]

"Little Pamfil" or the "little half-German" came up frequently in their correspondence. Both of them wanted a child. Shortly after the Yalta holiday Olga began sending reports of nausea. Chekhov advised her to drink less. Then on March 31 she reported a miscarriage. "When I left Yalta, I hoped to give you a Pamfil, but I couldn't be certain. I kept feeling sick, but thought I had an upset stomach. Much as I wished to be pregnant, I didn't realize I was. [. . .] As soon as the doctors were sent for, I guessed what was wrong, and started weeping bitterly. [. . .] Losing Pamfil broke my heart." She was taken to a hospital, where she underwent an emergency operation. Not even the kindness shown her by members of the company could bring her through the shock. Her only thought was to seek refuge with her husband in Yalta. But would he want to see her after she had failed him so? "Send me a telegram," she wrote to him several days later. "Don't forget me, don't despise me for my failure."

Chekhov did send her a telegram—he sent her several— asking lovingly after her health and assuring her he was looking forward to seeing her. The loss of the child meant less to him than his wife's physical and moral stability. When her boat docked in Yalta on April 14, she had to be carried to the cab on a stretcher. And of course Chekhov never dreamed of chiding her for her "failure." In fact, seeing her so frail and wan made him ill for several days.

In the midst of it all an important event had taken place in the Russian literary world. Gorky, who had recently been elected to the literary section of the Academy of Sciences, learned that the government had ordered the Academy to annul the results of the election in view of the fact that he was under police surveillance. Chekhov was extremely upset. A group of friends he consulted on the matter pressed him to resign in solidarity, a lawyer advised him not to do anything, and Tolstoy evaded the issue by asserting gruffly that he had never considered himself a member of the Academy. Chekhov could not make up his mind. When Korolenko asked for his stand on what he considered a scandalous abuse of power by the authorities, Chekhov had nothing more to say than, "My wife has a high temperature and is flat on her back. She's lost weight."[28] Several weeks later Korolenko came down to see him at Yalta, and the two men decided to resign from the Academy. Neither felt it advisable to send off the letter of resignation to the venerable assembly immediately, however; they thought it more prudent to wait and see whether it would reverse its sentence. Diplomacy was of the essence—and very much in Gorky's interest.

Meanwhile, the family situation had worsened: Anton's mother and sister had openly reproached Olga for continuing to lead her self-indulgent life while pregnant. Chekhov was so distressed by the dissension among them that he decided to leave for Moscow with Olga before she had completely recovered. The moment they arrived in Moscow, on May 27, she took to her bed.

Not long thereafter she fell seriously ill again. Her doctors diagnosed the illness as peritonitis and advised an operation. Chekhov did not leave her bedside, keeping track of her temperature and attending to her poultices. Now it was Maria's turn to be filled with remorse, and she wrote from Yalta that she was willing to come to her brother's aid. But on June 12, when an operation seemed inevitable, Olga's condition suddenly improved; the pain and vomiting ceased. Chekhov boasted to Nemirovich-Danchenko that of all the doctors treating her he alone had been right in forbidding her anything but milk and cream. Soon Olga was out of danger.

Relieved, Chekhov turned his thoughts to the summer holidays. Maria proposed Yalta, but Chekhov had so unpleasant a memory of the attempt at family happiness there in the spring that he declined. He chose instead to accept the invitation of the fabulously rich Savva Morozov* and go to Perm in the Urals, leaving Olga in the care of his mother. Again the compulsion to move on. The call of the unknown was so strong in him that he did not hesitate to leave behind an ill and passionately beloved wife in order to follow it.

The two men set off together on June 17, traveling first by train, then by boat along the Volga and the Kama. It took them a week to reach Morozov's vast estate at Vsevolodo-Vilva, just beyond Perm. Along the way, Chekhov sent back cheery letters and telegrams to the convalescent: "I'm in good, German spirits; the journey has been comfortable and pleasant; I've been coughing a lot less. I'm not worried about you because I know, I'm positive, that my dog is well; it could not be otherwise." Or: "I am healthy, well fed, and warm. Don't be cross, don't be bored, and keep your spirits up." Or: "By the time I arrive, you must put on weight and be as big and plump as the wife of a theater owner."[29]

Savva Morozov's estate consisted of a sumptuous manor house with an army of servants and vast grounds, a birch wood, numerous villages, and several chemical factories. Morozov had a long beard, the manners of an upstart, and pretensions to being a philanthropist and patron of the arts. He had just put up the money for the Art Theater's new premises, which boasted the latest in electric equipment, a revolving stage, and comfortable dressing rooms.

No sooner had they arrived than the exhausted Chekhov was subjected to a tour of the factory. He found it impossibly noisy and ill-smelling, and when he learned that laborers worked twelve-hour shifts he lodged a protest with his host. Morozov

*The brother of Sergei Morozov, the merchant millionaire, mentioned earlier.

was apparently shaken by Chekhov's arguments and eventually consented to reduce the work day to eight hours for skilled workers and ten hours for nonskilled workers.

That first evening Morozov threw a large banquet for local intellectuals and officials and the executive staff of his various enterprises. They all came, dressed in their Sunday best, shaking at the sight of him, imitating his mannerisms, agreeing with his every word. During the seven-course meal Chekhov took only a few spoonfuls of soup and drank only water; he said hardly a word. Most of the guests had no idea who "the writer" was, and they could only assume that he too looked upon Morozov as his benefactor.

In fact, Chekhov had a kind of love/hate relationship with the man. He admired his ambition, kindness, and magnanimity, but abhorred the staggering wealth he stood for and the obsequious ways he fostered in the people who caught scraps from his table. After inspecting the workers' medical facilities, he told Alexander Tikhonov, a young engineering student in Morozov's employ,[30] "He's a rich merchant. He builds theaters and plays the revolution game, but his pharmacy has no tincture of iodine and the medical assistant is a drunkard who has downed all the alcohol and treats rheumatism with castor oil. They're all the same, our Russian Rockefellers."*

When Morozov was obliged to go off on business, he asked Tikhonov to look after Chekhov. At first the young man found his famous charge reserved, even irritable, but before long they became friends. They took walks through the forest together, went fishing, discussed politics and literature. Occasionally an ironic remark on Chekhov's part offended the twenty-two-year-old's exalted sensibilities. One day, for example, Chekhov told him, "The reason students are rebelling is to make themselves look like heroes and have an easier time with the young ladies." When Tikhonov scowled, Chekhov put his arm around his shoulders and said with a sad smile, "What about you? Do

---

*Rumor had it that Savva Morozov had provided financial assistance to revolutionaries to show his broad-mindedness.

you write? . . . No? . . . Good. Students don't study anymore; they write novels or make revolution. But maybe it's better that way. When we were students, we drank beer and did almost no work—with the result that we're a bunch of washouts." On another occasion he told him, "The most important thing is never to lie. One fine feature of art is that it doesn't let you lie. You can lie in love, politics, and medicine, you can fool people and even God—such cases do exist—but you can't lie in art. [. . .] You know, there are people—and Tolstoy is one of them—who accuse me of writing exclusively about trivialities and having no positive heroes, no revolutionaries, Alexanders of Macedonia, or even, like Leskov, honest chiefs of police. But where am I supposed to find them? There's nothing I'd like better. We lead provincial lives: our cities are without paved streets, our villages poor, our people worn. When we're young, we all chirp fervently like sparrows on a dung heap, but we're old by the time we reach forty, and we start thinking of death. What kind of heroes are we?"

Morozov had had a new school built on the estate and decided to name it after Chekhov. But Chekhov felt so weak on the day of the inauguration ceremonies that he had to receive the officials stretched out on a couch in the manor house. When the steward of the estate gave a speech in honor of the distinguished writer, the distinguished writer responded by looking him up and down and saying, "Your fly is open." Chekhov was pleased by the general mirth that followed; he was glad to have compromised the grotesque solemnity of the occasion.

Like Gorky, Tikhonov was touched by the great Chekhov's simple, unaffected behavior and the courage with which he bore his illness. But the illness was now at an advanced stage. Chekhov's chest was sunken, his complexion pale, his beard flecked with gray. He walked with a cap pulled down over his eyes, taking tiny steps, like an old man, and stopping frequently to catch his breath. Moreover, he was never without a leather-covered flask, which he wore slung across the shoulder at his left hip, and whenever a coughing fit came upon him, he unscrewed the nickel-plated stopper, turned away, and spat a reddish, viscous substance into the flask. After regaining his breath, he would readjust his pince-nez and try to smile.

Tikhonov had the room next to Chekhov's. One night an ear-shattering cough pierced the wall. Moans followed. Tikhonov, frightened, ran next door barefoot, in his nightshirt, and saw Chekhov lying on his side, his body racked with convulsions and his head hanging over a blue enamel spittoon clutched in one hand. With each spasm a spurt of blood came pouring out of his mouth. Tikhonov later wrote that it was like watching "a bottle being emptied." When he called out, "Anton Pavlovich," Chekhov fell back on his pillows, wiped his bloodstained mustache and beard with a handkerchief, and turned in the direction of the intruder. "And there, by the light of a stearin candle," Tikhonov writes, "I saw his eyes without a pince-nez for the first time. They were large and defenseless, like the eyes of a child." His eyelids were wet with tears. At first he did not seem to recognize Tikhonov, but after a moment or two he managed to say, "I'm keeping you . . . awake . . . Forgive me, my boy . . ."

Several days later Chekhov felt well enough to leave for Moscow. Once there, he immediately thought of leaving, this time with Olga, who appeared to have recovered entirely. When Stanislavsky's mother offered them the use of the family's summer dacha at Lyubimovka, a village not far from Moscow, Chekhov accepted with gratitude. The surrounding countryside was picturesque, and there was a river running through the property. Although they still had many visitors to contend with, they were both delighted with the retreat. "The weather is beautiful, the river is beautiful. We are eating and sleeping like archbishops," he wrote to Stanislavsky, who was abroad at the time. "I thank you from the bottom of my heart. It's been a long time since I've spent a summer like this. I go fishing every day, five times a day, and the catch has been pretty good (yesterday we ate perch). I can't tell you how pleasant it is to sit by the water. In a word, everything is fine. The only trouble is I'm lazy and not getting anything done. I still haven't started my play. All I do is turn it over in my mind."[31]

The sunny, carefree interlude lasted until August 14, the date Chekhov had set for his Yalta departure. Although Olga was obliged to go back to Moscow for rehearsals, she was annoyed that he had not even suggested she should return to the Crimea with him. Suspecting Maria of having insisted he leave her behind, she wrote a letter demanding an explanation and told Chekhov to deliver it to her unopened. Conversations between husband and wife began to turn sour, and Anton refused to move his departure date forward by so much as a day. By the time he left, he was angry with her, his mother, his sister, and himself.

The first thing Chekhov had meant to do in Yalta was patch up the family quarrel, but Maria was offended by the tone of Olga's letter and showed it to him. His response was immediate. "Why did you scold Masha? I give you my word of honor that when Mother and Masha urged me to come back to Yalta they didn't ask me to come alone, they asked me to come with you. Your letter is very, very unfair, and what the pen writes can never be erased—that's all there is to it. Let me say it again: I give you my word of honor that Mother and Masha invited the two of us, not me alone, and that they have always had the warmest and tenderest of feelings for you."[32] He also informed her that he would soon be back in Moscow.

When in a week's time he had received no answer, he begged for one: "Don't torment me, darling, don't torture me needlessly. Let me hear from you a little more often. You're angry with me, but I'm sure I can't tell why. Because I went off? But I'd been with you since Easter without a break, I never left your side, and I never would have left if it hadn't been for my work and the hemorrhaging."[33]

At last Olga gave a sign of life, but she did so to present her side of the story. She pointed out curtly that Maria had had no right to show Anton her letter, that his mother and sister had not wanted him to stay with her while she was ill, and that there was no reason for him to race up to Moscow now that he had stopped loving her.

Chekhov tried hard to reason with her. "You mustn't be

so unfair, darling, really you mustn't. One must be pure, perfectly pure, in matters of fairness and unfairness, particularly because you are kind, so kind, and understanding. Forgive me for sermonizing, darling, I won't do it again. That sort of thing frightens me." And he added sadly, "Even though your letters have been cool, I keep pestering you with my affections and think about you endlessly. I kiss you a billion times. I hug you. Darling, write to me more often than once every five days. I'm your husband, after all. Don't leave me so soon, before we've had a chance to live together as we should and before you've borne me a little boy or girl. Once you give me a child, you can do as you like."[34]

This time Olga responded by accusing Anton of not really caring whether they ever got back together. "That can mean only one thing," she wrote bitterly, "that we've lived together long enough. So it's time for us to part? Very well, then." She also returned to the issue of her career, which she felt lay at the root of the "mess" they were in. But why should she give up the theater when he had so little need of her presence? "You are capable of living with me and never uttering a word. There were times when I felt in your way. You seem to need me only as an amiable woman; as a human being I feel alien and isolated from you." Other passages, too, demonstrate how well she understood her husband's curious character. Under the pleasant exterior she saw a man who could be quite indifferent to the lives of others, who was never satisfied with the place he happened to be living in or the moment he happened to be experiencing, who could treat his wife like an object and fail to probe her intimate feelings, who felt not the slightest jealousy for the admirers surrounding her, and who complained about constant visitors when in fact he was delighted to have them.

Olga's avalanche of reproaches was too much for Anton. "Who told you that I don't want to return to Moscow, that I've left for good and am not going back this autumn?" he challenged. "Didn't I write you in plain and simple language that I'd definitely be coming in September and live with you until December? Well, didn't I? You accuse me of not being frank, yet you forget everything I write or say to you. I am at a loss to know what to do with my wife or how to write to her. You write that you tremble when you read my letters, that it's time for us to part, that there's something you fail to understand in all this . . . It seems to me, darling, that the guilty party in all this mess is neither you nor I but someone else, someone you have had a talk with. Someone has instilled in you a mistrust of my words and feelings; everything strikes you as suspicious—and there's nothing I can do about it, nothing at all. I won't try to dissuade you or convince you I'm right, for that's useless. [. . .] Dearest darling, you are my wife, when are you ever going to understand that? You are the person who is closest and dearest to me; I've loved you infinitely, I still love you, and you describe yourself as an 'amiable' woman who is alien and isolated . . . Well, have it your way, if you must."[35]

Tired of quarreling, Olga finally put her gloomy thoughts behind her. She was sorry about the squabble, but they were both made of flesh and blood and both had their excuses. In any case, she swore no one had talked her into mistrusting him; she had simply been unable to bear the separation after the wonderful times they had had together at Lyubimovka. Besides, she realized she had occasional black moods. "How terribly, terribly bad I am! [. . .] When I think of you, I always picture myself on my knees, asking your pardon." To make it clear that she hoped for a general reconciliation, she informed Anton she was looking forward to Maria's return and had put flowers in her room.

Meanwhile, Chekhov anxiously inquired whether her doctor had given her permission to have children yet. "Oh, darling, darling, time is wasting," he wrote to her. "By the time our baby is a year and a half old, I'll be a bald graybeard with not a tooth in my head."[36] Her answer was that the doctor had given her a clean bill of health. "Are you happy?" she added. "I'll be presenting you with a handsome baby boy next year."

Even the war of the letters did not make Chekhov regret having stayed on in Yalta. For one thing, his mother and sister ignored his bachelor quirks; for another, he had a chance to reminisce with Suvorin, who came to call early in September. Again Chekhov showed that his reservations about the politics of *New Times* had not dulled his gratitude or affection for the man behind them. After Suvorin's departure he defended him to the editor of a local newspaper: despite Suvorin's faults, Chekhov told him, he was the first to raise journalists' salaries and improve their working conditions; he had aided numerous writers in need; he had contributed to the general spread of culture.

By defending Suvorin, Chekhov had no intention of defending the powers that be. When on September 18 he learned of Zola's death, he wrote to Olga, "I'm sad today: Zola is dead. It's so unexpected and wrong somehow. I never cared much for him as a writer, but as a man I thought very highly of him, particularly during the past few years when the Dreyfus case was at its peak."

Another "case" had obsessed Chekhov recently: the Gorky case. After waiting several months for Gorky to be reelected to the Academy, he came to realize that the decision to annul his election was irrevocable. The time had come to take a position against the encroachment of state power on literature. For the first time he felt morally bound to intervene in politics. On August 26, 1902, he sent a letter of resignation to Alexander Veselovsky, the head of the literary section of the Academy. He began by pointing to a contradiction arising in his mind from the fact that the decision to annul his friend Gorky's election came from the Academy and, since he was a member, from his person as well ("I offered [Gorky] my heartfelt congratulations, yet I declared his election null and void"), and ended by stating that his conscience refused to accept the contradiction: "After long deliberation I could come to but one decision, a painful, regrettable decision, namely, to respectfully request that you divest me of my membership in the Academy." The day before, he had sent a draft of the letter to Korolenko, who had already tendered his resignation, with the following commentary: "Well, there it is. It took me a long time to write. The weather was very hot, and I was unable to write anything better. I probably couldn't have done better in any case."

The letter was reproduced in a number of clandestine newspapers and circulated abroad. Most Russian intellectuals approved the courageous move. Chekhov was no longer a member of the Academy, but he was all the more famous. His public expected new and brilliant works from him, and he suffered acutely from not being able to provide them. He felt he was coming to the end of the road; he was tired, he was sluggish, his head was empty.

From Moscow Olga badgered him to get to work on his play much as a mother reminds her son to take his castor oil or wash his hair. She seemed convinced that all a writer had to do was settle down before a blank page and words would sprout from his pen. Nemirovich-Danchenko and Stanislavsky applied persistent pressure of their own.

Chekhov put up his standard defense: he had no drive, no confidence in his powers of invention, and he was constantly plagued by visitors. More significant, his interest in the details of life had dwindled. Age and illness had widened the gap between him and his fellowman. He had always maintained a certain distance from his friends; now he was detached from them and no longer felt a need to confide in anyone, even Olga. The more agreeable he appeared, the less he gave of himself. In one of his notebooks he wrote: "Just as I shall lie alone in my grave, so I live alone." Bunin, who knew him well at the time, remarked: "No one, not even those who were closest to him, knew what went on deep inside him. His self-control never deserted him, even during our most intimate conversations. [. . .] Had he ever had a passionate, blind, romantic love in his life? I don't believe so." Bunin never understood how people could talk of Chekhov's tenderness, melancholy, warmth; he was certain Chekhov would have been repelled by the idea. And in fact Chekhov's art is endowed with the lucidity and impassivity of a scientist. Such are the qualities Gorky had in mind when he wrote to Chekhov about *Uncle Vanya*: "You are colder than the devil with people. You are as indifferent to them as snow, a blizzard."[37] And his old school chum, Sergeenko, observed that although Chekhov had many friends, "he was a friend to no one, that is, he was never involved with anyone to the point of forgetting himself."

Thus, while remaining the most open and obliging of men, while receiving hordes of petitioners, while giving aid to young writers, needy teachers, and down-and-out consumptives, he was never one for loving humanity blindly. His concern was never without its egotism. Gifted with an extraordinary intuition, he could grasp a person's psychology in a flash. But instead of letting it engage the depths of his being, he used it to people his works. He had a quick eye and a cool head, and lived, as it were, under a glass jar. Even the people who thought they touched him most would run up against its transparent wall. He was as mistrustful of great joys as of great sorrows. He was a man of the golden mean. His only passion was his art—literature. When he wrote, time stopped for him, and out of the void came pages covered with scribble—new lives, a new story. What could be more miraculous? Yet he refused to think of himself as superior. He loathed braggadocio in others and could never, even at the pinnacle of his fame, forget the limits of his talent. Not that he was all modesty or humility; he was simply possessed of a clear mind and a good upbringing. He never ceased pruning and polishing his stories and plays, but never believed they would survive him. "Even though he occupied an eminent place in literature," wrote Bunin, "he was not conscious of his worth." And Kuprin recalled: "No one could leave him without being overwhelmed by his immense talent and one's own mediocrity."

Correcting the proofs of his collected works—the sixth volume was due to appear in 1902—Chekhov came to the conclusion that the basic principles behind his writing had remained stable throughout his career. They consisted of simplicity and sincerity, sparing but precise descriptions, and nonintervention on the part of the author. By pleading a cause or suggesting a solution to the problems that confront his characters, the author takes unfair advantage of his reader. The reader must draw his own conclusions. On the basis of the evidence. With complete freedom.

The older he grew, the more clearly he saw the relationship between his literature and his life: no spectacular events, no high-flown phrases, no heroic poses, just a subdued, poignant, intimate music, a few gray areas, a few questions with no answers—the benign absurdities of day-to-day existence bearing us closer and closer to the final abyss. His plays were meant less to make audiences cry, as Stanislavsky thought, than to encourage them to reflect on the human condition. As he said to Tikhonov, "All I wanted was to tell people honestly, 'Look at yourselves. Look at what bad, boring lives you lead.' That's the most important thing for people to understand. And when they do understand it, they will certainly create a new and better life. I won't see it, but I know that everything will be different, that nothing will be like the lives we now lead." In his notebooks he phrased the same idea in a slightly different form: "Man will become better when we have shown him to himself as he is."

Such, vague as it was, was his only hope—he had no use whatsoever for political upheaval. And when his characters speak of that hope, they do so by way of consolation, as if it were mildly unreasonable. "Life is hard," says Lieutenant Colonel Vershinin in *Three Sisters*. "To many of us it seems stagnant and hopeless. But we do have to admit it's getting clearer, brighter, and in all probability the time is not far off when it will be absolutely radiant." Meanwhile, there was the tsar, the bureaucracy, the police to contend with. As Chekhov put it, "Nowhere do the authories wield such overwhelming power as among us Russians, and humiliated as we are by our secular thralldom, yet we fear freedom."

Chekhov wished to make his next play an illustration of passivity as a Russian trait, but he felt he could never write the play in Yalta: he needed Moscow, Olga, the glitter of the theater to infuse a fresh taste for work and life into him. Dr. Altschuler, summoned for the purpose of giving his stamp of approval to the journey, lacked the heart to forbid it. Next day Chekhov wrote to Olga: "He finds my health considerably improved and says that, judging by the change which has taken place since the spring, my illness is responding well to treatment. I'm doing so well he has even granted me permission to go to Moscow. Only he says I may not go now, I must wait for the first frosts." And two days later: "Don't forget now, dog. When I get to Moscow, we'll buy some perfume, a big bottle of Houbigant or two or three small ones, and send it to Altschuler. [. . .] In Moscow I'll do nothing but eat, drink, caress my wife, go to the theater, and—in my free time—sleep. I have decided to be an Epicurean."

Olga responded with the enthusiasm of a newlywed. "So we're going to be together soon, my darling little Antosha! Hurrah! We can hope again and be happy. Things won't always be so dismal. The kisses I'll give you!"

So as not to leave his mother alone in Yalta, Chekhov sent her to his brother Mikhail in Petersburg. Maria went with her, apprehensive of living together with Anton and Olga after the summer's spat. On October 12 Chekhov packed his bags and set off in a light coat: Olga had agreed to take his fur coat to the station if the weather was cold. She had also readied his standard remedies—cod-liver oil and creosote—and promised him a glass of beer and a hot bath for his arrival.

Visiting Moscow was almost as much of a treat as visiting Olga. Chekhov immediately began making the rounds of the stores, restaurants, and theaters. He saw Chaliapin, Diaghilev, Rossolimo, Bunin, Suvorin, and Gorky, whose first play, *Lower Depths,* was in rehearsal at the Art Theater. Chekhov was pleased with the Art Theater's new home; he appreciated its simplicity of decor and ingenious stage equipment. He attended a performance of Tolstoy's *Power of Darkness* and saw *Uncle Vanya* and *Three Sisters* again. The latter, he felt, had now reached perfection.

But the kaleidoscope of sensations wore him out, and soon he started coughing again. After only six weeks he was forced to return to Yalta. The constant comings and goings between north and south, urban flurry and rural tedium, marriage and celibacy, between the illusion of life and preparation for death were hard on his nerves. The day after he arrived he wrote to Olga: "Don't be bored, my treasure. Work, go everywhere, sleep as much as you can. How I want you to be happy and well! During this last stay you grew even more precious to me. I love you more than before. Going to bed and getting up without you is very annoying, ridiculous somehow. You've really spoiled me."[38]

It was so cold in Yalta that Chekhov thought it best not to venture out. Nor was there much to tempt him. And when Nicholas II came to town for the consecration of a new church, Chekhov did not even attend the ceremonies. Early in January he contracted pleurisy, but allowed Dr. Altschuler to treat him without a fuss. The only thing that gave him pleasure through the long winter months was the news that Gorky's *Lower Depths* had taken Moscow by storm. He was also gratified to learn that *The Seagull* had at last scored a victory on the stage of the Alexandrinsky Theater, where six years before it had gone down to ignominious defeat. "The success of *The Seagull* on the Imperial stage is quite remarkable," read a rave review in *The World of Art*. "It bears witness to the fact that Chekhov's years of struggle are over. As a playwright Chekhov has become a classic, and the state theater has now officially recognized him as such."

The moving spirit behind *The World of Art,* Sergei Diaghilev, who would soon make a name for himself as a choreographer, did everything he could to persuade Chekhov to write for the journal. During one of their last meetings, in Moscow, the two men had discussed the future of religion in Russia. When Diaghilev renewed the dialogue by mail, Chekhov responded: "It is safe to say that the educated segment of our society has moved away from religion and is moving further and further away from it, whatever people may say or whatever philosophical and religious societies may be formed. I won't venture to say whether that is good or bad, but I will say that the religious movement you write about is one thing and all contemporary culture something else again, and there's no point in trying to derive the latter from the former. Present-day culture is the beginning of work in the name of a great future, work which will perhaps continue for tens of thousands of years with the result that finally, if only in the distant future, mankind will perceive the truth of the real God, that is, not make conjectures or search for Him in Dostoevsky but perceive Him as clearly as they perceive that twice two makes four."[39]

Chekhov's notebooks contain more on the subject. "Between 'God exists' and 'There is no God' stretches an immense space, which the honest sage has great difficulty crossing. The Russian knows only one of the extremes; what lies between is of no interest to him. In other words, he generally knows nothing or very little." As he moved closer to death, he grew more and more skeptical, and bristled at the sermons Tolstoy turned out for the edification of humanity. Chekhov found their explanations of God an insult to the author of *War and Peace* and *Anna Karenina,* and was even prepared to see signs of creeping senility in them.

Meanwhile, Chekhov kept coming across signs of declining vitality in himself. Because he found it impossible to concentrate on an exacting task, he continued keeping Olga informed of the petty events of the day. And always the same lament, always the same hope: "I have a feeling that if I could lie even half the night with my nose buried in your shoulder I'd start feeling better and stop moping. I can't live without you, no matter what. [. . .] Take a dacha for the summer, the kind of place where I can write."[40] He also told her the time would come when he would live all the year round with her. "Then you'll have a little son who'll break the dishes and pull your dog's tail, and you'll watch him and take comfort."[41] Olga still felt she was equally responsible for their separation, and he still did his best to assuage her guilt: "Darling, you keep writing you still have pangs of conscience about living in Moscow rather than in Yalta with me. But what can we do, dearest? Try and be sensible: if you lived with me in Yalta all winter, your life would be ruined and I'd feel pangs of conscience, which would hardly be better. I knew I was marrying an actress, after all; what I mean is, when I married you, I was fully aware you'd be spending winters in Moscow. I don't feel a millionth bit hurt or cheated; on the contrary, I think things are just fine or as they should be, so don't bother me with your conscience anymore, sweetheart. In March we'll be together again and won't feel lonely the way we do now. [. . .] I've begun working again. I'm probably not going to write to you every day. You will forgive, won't you?"[42]

To say that he had "begun working again" was a bit of an exaggeration. His story "The Bride" had bogged down for a while, but was now moving forward slowly. Now the problem was not so much that his imagination had run dry as that he found putting words on paper physically exhausting. "What a multitude of themes I have in my head and how I long to write, but I have a feeling something's missing—either in the surroundings or my health."[43] A few weeks later he was more specific: "I write six or seven lines a day. I couldn't do any more if my life depended on it. My stomach is upset literally every day."[44] Then all at once he made a terrible confession: "Let me be frank with you, darling: it would give me great pleasure to stop being a writer!"[45]

Thanks to a mixture of pride and will—and "a spoonful of soup every hour"—he pushed on with "The Bride," and on February 27, after five months of intermittent efforts, he completed the manuscript and sent it off to *Everyone's Magazine,* where several of his late stories appeared. In it the young Nadya rebels against her comfortable but stuffy family by deciding at the last minute not to accept a conventional marriage and fleeing to Petersburg and a life of self-sacrifice. Nadya's dreams of a time when "one can bravely look one's destiny in the eye" and be happy and free echo the end of *Three Sisters.*

Did Chekhov suspect that "The Bride" would be his last story? His works comprise hundreds of them—some extremely short, others long, some forthrightly frivolous, others heart-rending. Together they form an unsurpassed panorama of Russian life. From muzhik to priest, professor to cabby, student to merchant—all social ranks have their place in Chekhov's human comedy. Reading Chekhov's stories is like taking a whirlwind tour through late nineteenth-century Russia with a cool, lucid guide who shows all but avoids commentary. The unity of style from beginning to end is amazing. "Concision is the sister of talent," Chekhov declared to his brother Alexander as the first decade of his writing career came to an end,[46] and he never forgot it. Nor did he ever give the impression of having exhausted his resources.

Now that he had sent off "The Bride," he could devote all his creative energy to *The Cherry Orchard*. But the lines would not come. When Olga berated him, he blustered: "Laziness has nothing to do with it. I'm not my own enemy, after all. If I had the strength, I'd write not one but twenty-five plays."[47] Two days later, however, he was in a more optimistic mood: "If my play doesn't turn out the way I've conceived it, you can give me a punch in the nose. Stanislavsky has a comic role, and so have you." And a few weeks later he had some positive news for her: "*The Cherry Orchard* is coming along. I'm trying to work it so there will be as few characters as possible. That way it will be more intimate."[48] Then on April 9 he declared: "I'm going to write the play in Moscow. Writing here is impossible."

But Dr. Altschuler quickly squelched the idea of a Moscow rendezvous by proclaiming Chekhov unfit to step out of the house. Crestfallen, Chekhov begged Olga to ask the Art Theater for a few days off so that she could come down and see him in Yalta, but she sadly replied that they were about to leave on tour for Petersburg. Chekhov was bound by his doctor's decisions; she was bound by her director's.

With the advent of warm weather Dr. Altschuler relented enough to let his patient stroll along the esplanade. Chekhov preferred to putter in the garden with his dogs. But even after a few moments of examining trees or looking on as the handyman trimmed the rosebushes, he would have to sit down on a bench and catch his breath.

Spring had also brought Bunin, Gorky, and Kuprin back to the Crimea. They paid Chekhov frequent visits, trying to cheer him up with their chatter. Chekhov followed it with an indifference bordering on lethargy, his cane between his legs, his eyes looking out into the distance. Life seemed to have lost its excitement for him. Odd remarks escaped from his lips at times. "I'd like to become a tramp, a pilgrim," he said to Bunin, "and tour the holy places, spend time at a monastery near a forest, on a lake, and sit on a bench at the gate on a summer evening . . ." After a while he would start showing signs of impatience, and his visitors knew it was time to be on their way.

"My head aches," he wrote to Olga on April 11, "I've been coughing, the visitors stay forever. Yesterday a bearded gentleman sat at my table for four and a half hours." His only desire was to see his wife again—and as soon as possible. By then he could stand neither Yalta nor the visitors nor Dr. Altschuler. And all of a sudden he went over the top: on April 22, without consulting a soul, he fled to Moscow.

XV

"How Hard It Was for Me to Write That Play!"

Following close on the heels of Yalta's sun, Moscow's cold kept Chekhov in his room for several days. He was delighted with the new Petrovka Street flat Olga and Maria had rented, but it was on the third floor and there was no lift. When they touched on the problem in a letter, he had all but ignored it. But climbing the stairs proved sheer torture; it took a half hour of huffing and frequent stops. So Chekhov preferred to invite friends in. But as soon as word of Chekhov's return went out, the intruders came to call as well: Chekhov still felt it his duty to receive every stammering young author and old hack, every copy-hungry reporter, manuscript-hungry publisher, every cackling literata. The faithful Bunin later recalled "his silence, his cough, his lowered eyes, his sad, pensive, serene, almost solemn face. [. . .] Like most people who think intensely, he had a tendency to forget what he had said several times over."

To raise Chekhov's spirits, Tolstoy sent him an inscribed photograph and a list of the thirty stories he considered Chekhov's finest to date—fifteen "first quality" and fifteen "second quality."* He had bound them together in a single volume and read them over frequently. "Chekhov is Pushkin in prose," he was known to say.

By then connoisseurs and general reading public alike had agreed that Chekhov was a master of the highest order. What does he add to Gogol, Dostoevsky, Goncharov, Turgenev, and Tolstoy to justify his contemporaries' highest praise? Two qualities, essentially: sincerity and moderation. His illustrious predecessors are, each in his own way, passionate, tempestuous. They capture their readers by reaching for extremes; furthermore, their descriptions are highly lyrical, their language magic. Chekhov is the first to speak softly, confidentially. Unlike Turgenev, whose narration is slow, harmonious, "artistic," Chekhov uses a spare style in which each word has latent significance. And unlike all the rest, who support the reader emotionally, laugh and cry with him, Chekhov brings the reader face to face with events and people and then leaves him to his own devices, at most setting his nerves on edge with an occasional well-placed fillip of detail. Thus without a word of explanation he jolts the reader into a deep understanding of his characters. One does not read a Chekhov story or watch a Chekhov play in a state of passive ecstasy; one always collaborates in the process. In Chekhov there is no intellectual force-feeding; there is complicity.

As for his thought, it is pessimistic, true, but only for the present. Chekhov possessed an almost naïve belief in progress, the perfectibility of man, the advent of a better life. But Che-

---

*In Tolstoy's judgment the "first quality" stories were: "Children," "The Chorus Girl," "A Drama," "At Home," "Sadness," "The Runaway," "In Court," "Vanka," "The Ladies," "The Malefactor," "Darkness," "Sleepy," "The Wife," "The Darling," "Little Boys"; the "second quality" stories were: "A Trangression," "Heartache," "The Witch," "Vera," "In a Foreign Land," "The Cook Gets Married," "Oh, the Public!" "The Mask," "A Woman's Fortune," "Nerves," "The Wedding," "A Defenseless Creature," "Peasant Women," "The Commotion," "Worries."

khov the materialist and nonbeliever also recognized a deep and abiding grain of mysticism in himself, an anxious premonition of something he could not quite define. What gave his works the ring of truth was their combination of human warmth and scientific spirit. Despite his modesty Chekhov was aware he had originated a new way of thinking and writing in Russia. "The paths I have opened up will remain sound and intact," he said to Gorky. "That is my only worth."

For some time Gorky and a number of close friends had been urging Chekhov to negotiate a new contract with his publisher Marx. Within a few years Marx had made more than two hundred thousand rubles on the sale of Chekhov's works, and he soon started republishing them as a supplement to his magazine *Niva* without paying Chekhov a kopeck. There was no question of breaking the contract by reimbursing Marx for the seventy-five thousand rubles Chekhov had received by signing it, but Marx could at least be asked to reconsider what was clearly a one-sided agreement and, given the enormous profits involved, set aside, say, one third of the sales income for the author. If Chekhov had not received liberal royalties for the productions of his plays, he would have been in financial straits. After long opposing the idea, Chekhov went to Petersburg to see Marx. He came up against a wall. Marx refused him point-blank. Talking about money had always made Chekhov uncomfortable; figures plunged him into an almost childlike state of confusion. Face to face with a determined adversary like Marx, he could not bring himself to make demands, raise his voice, bang his fist on the table. Describing the meeting to his sister, he wrote: "I talked to Marx, but nothing came of it. He gave me a large number of finely bound books (about four poods' worth [144 pounds or 65 kilograms]) and offered me five thousand rubles for my treatment, which I naturally refused."[1]

All through the winter Chekhov had dreamed of taking Olga to Switzerland and Italy, but he could not set out on so strenuous a journey without medical approval. He decided to consult Dr. Ostroumov, at whose clinic he had recuperated several years earlier. Ostroumov found him in very poor shape. The right lung was badly affected, and emphysema had spread to the left lung. All travel abroad was out of the question. In fact, Ostroumov advised against traveling as far as Yalta. "You are seriously ill," he told Chekhov. The day after the examination Chekhov wrote to his sister in Yalta, "He listened to my heart and did a lot of tapping and palpating. [. . .] He gave me five prescriptions and told me not to spend the winters in Yalta—he thinks winters are bad there—and ordered me to live in a dacha near Moscow. Now what do you make of that?"[2]

Chekhov was thrilled. Completely ignoring Ostroumov's dire diagnosis, he rejoiced at the thought that from now on he would spend winters in Moscow—not on the Crimean coast but in Moscow—with his wife and his literary cohorts near at hand. No longer would he have to make his way there furtively; he would be following doctor's orders. He immediately wrote to Maria about the possibility of selling Gurzuf and Kuchukoy, and set about looking for a suitable dacha in the environs of Moscow.

As a doctor, however, he could not help wondering about his colleagues' contradictory opinions. Should he believe Altschuler, who sang the praises of the Crimea's climate, or Ostroumov, who denounced its nefarious consequences? "I don't know what to think," he wrote to his friend Dr. Sredin. "If Ostroumov is right, then why did I spend four winters in Yalta?"[3] And to Lavrov he wrote: "As soon as I'm settled in Moscow and start feeling at home there, the doctors will send me back to the Crimea or on to Cairo."[4]

Just as the theater season was coming to a close, a friend of Olga's invited the Chekhovs to spend a few weeks at an estate outside Moscow near Naro-Fominskoe. They were only too glad to accept and overjoyed to find they had been allotted a house of their own large enough to accommodate ten people. "There's a river, open space for strolling, an old chapel, and plenty of fish," Chekhov announced to his sister, who was in Yalta. "Write and let me know about the fruit trees, the rosebushes, and all the plants. How is the eucalyptus doing? And the Japanese iris?"[5] He and Olga scoured the region hoping to find a dacha to rent for the autumn, but the few alluring prospects proved beyond their means. During a two-day respite in Voskresensk with Savva Morozov, Chekhov told Madame Morozova, "Everything I've written to date is past history. How am I going to write from now on? I haven't a clue. It troubles me no end."

Though eager to get back to *The Cherry Orchard,* already a year in the writing, he was distracted by the page proofs of "The Bride" awaiting him in Naro-Fominskoe: he felt they needed extensive revision. It was exhausting work, but he refused to deliver a less than perfect text to the publisher. He looked upon revision as a kind of intellectual hygiene. The honor of the profession was at stake.

When at last he returned to the play, he found it hard going. He had been living with the characters for too long, and they had lost their freshness. One stormy day the wind burst into Chekhov's study through an open window and carried off several manuscript pages. Eventually they were retrieved from the garden, but the ink had run so badly that they were entirely illegible. One of the visitors present tried to console Chekhov with the thought that he would have no trouble reconstructing such recently written material. "You know, I don't remember it at all," Chekhov replied with a smile. "I'll have to write the scenes from scratch."

For all its proximity to Moscow, Naro-Fominskoe belonged to another world—calm, orderly, and luxurious. But not even Naro-Fominskoe was impervious to rumblings from the outside, and it was there that Chekhov learned of a particularly bloody pogrom at Kishinyov. The official press kept mum, but rumor had it that the massacre was the work of reactionaries protected by the police. Chekhov wished to find out more, and asked Suvorin to send him the pertinent copies of *Liberation,* a clandestine Marxist newspaper. Although the risk involved was far from negligible, Suvorin, the archconservative, complied. After perusing the antigovernment articles conscientiously, however, Chekhov dismissed them as "drier than an encyclopedia." He was even critical of Gorky's open letter about the events, describing it to Suvorin as "attractive, like everything he writes, but more fabricated than written: it has no youth, no Tolstoyan assurance to it, and it is too long."[6]

Yet Chekhov sympathized with the pogrom victims from the bottom of his heart. When the famous Yiddish writer Sholom Aleichem asked him to contribute a story to a collection to be published in Warsaw for their relief, Chekhov replied: "I have been writing nothing or very little these days, so I can make you only a conditional promise: I shall be glad to write the story if my illness does not prevent it. As for stories of mine that have already been published, they are entirely at your disposal, and I shall be nothing if not deeply gratified to see them translated into Yiddish and printed in a miscellany for the benefit of the Jewish victims in Kishinyov." To show how urgent he realized the matter to be, he added in a postscript: "I received your letter yesterday, June 18."[7]

At about this time he agreed to become a manuscript reader for *Russian Thought*. Did he do so because he was determined to go on serving literature despite his waning strength and if only by commenting on the work of others? In any case, the position added yet another burden to an already overburdened life.

While Olga blossomed in the company of houseguests, Anton wilted. All their fashionable chitchat was worth less to him than the rustic truths of Maxim the gardener. As a result, Anton and Olga left the Naro-Fominskoe dacha two weeks before the end of the two-month stay they had originally planned. The logical move would have been to Moscow, but in defiance of Dr. Ostroumov's recommendations they headed for Yalta.

They arrived on July 9. Chekhov resolved not to leave until he had completed *The Cherry Orchard*. To spur himself on, he set an absolute deadline: it would be ready by October, for the new season. He was terribly run down and had to muster prodigious discipline and will—day after day, line after line—to keep himself going. He hoped that Yalta's natural beauty and mild climate together with the peace and quiet of life *en famille* would help him to concentrate, but although the garden was full of flowers, the sun bright, and the sky blue, family life was still stormy. Maria was so happy to see her brother that she resented sharing him with her sister-in-law. Olga continued to criticize his dress and keep an eye on his diet, and now required him to take a cold bath every day in her presence. No matter how mild her domestic tyranny, it could scarcely meet with Maria's approval.

Olga was also constantly at Anton to work more on the play: the Art Theater was counting on it for the new season. Like a guilty schoolboy, he had promised to have it ready in time, but Stanislavsky and Nemirovich-Danchenko were still worried and queried Olga by mail whether he was making progress, whether they could expect him to keep his word. Chekhov responded directly: "My play isn't ready. It's moving slowly, which may be accounted for by my indolence, the nice weather, and the difficulty of the subject matter."[8] But Stanislavsky was too astute to accept Chekhov's offhand explanation. The true reason for the delay was his illness and the inroads it had made on his creative faculties.

"Don't think ill of us," Stanislavsky wrote to Olga. "We are concerned for Anton Pavlovich and his dear ones. We only think of the play when we wonder what is to become of our theater. No matter how one looks at it, our theater is Chekhov's theater; without him we'd be in dire straits." Olga's early August response to Stanislavsky's plaint was optimistic: "He's working every day now, though yesterday and today he's been ill and hasn't done any writing. [. . .] We don't have many visitors, and if his health were better he'd be getting a lot more done." She interrupted her letter to have a look at what Chekhov was up to, and returned to note: "Don't worry. He's just sat down to work."

Chekhov felt he would have suffered less had he been writing a story. Over and over he had sworn to give up writing for the theater, which, as he had pointed out to Pleshcheev many years before, was "a mistress who, though sophisticated, was noisy, insolent, and tiring."[9] Yet he had always gone back to it, fascinated by the very difficulty of the undertaking. He was also fascinated by the direct, almost blood, relationship between the playwright and his audience. He saw it as a kind of battle between the two, the playwright challenging the audience to forget its troubles and take on those of his characters. The battle for the mind of another, the victory over a large auditorium full of people, was much more intoxicating than the subtle satisfactions of the prose writer in the solitude of his study. Besides, through Olga he was in constant contact with the hurly-burly of theater life, and while writing *The Cherry Orchard* he had specific actors in mind and heard his lines coming from their mouths.

In late August Olga informed Nemirovich-Danchenko that Chekhov was feeling better and working "with enthusiasm." On September 1 Chekhov himself confirmed the report: "Don't worry. My play will be ready soon if I can keep working as I have done. I've had trouble, a good deal of trouble, with the second act, but I think it's all right now. I'm going to call the play a comedy." Olga was due to leave for Moscow on the nineteenth, and he hoped he could give her the completed manuscript to pack in her bags, but illness got the better of him and on September 15 he confessed to Stanislavsky's wife that he had too severe a headache to think of writing or even dictating. "So Olga won't be taking the play with her," he said. "I'll send all four acts as soon as I can work all day again." To Stanislavsky's wife, too, he made it clear that he had written "a comedy, not a drama—even a farce in spots."

After Olga had left, the house seemed so empty he lost all desire to get back to work. "I'm so far from everything that I've started losing heart," he wrote to her. "I feel I'm finished as a writer, and every sentence I write strikes me as worthless and of no use whatever."[10] Next day, however, he brightened up a little, and, despite the headache, an upset stomach, and extreme general debility he went back to the manuscript, working late, by candlelight. "The last act will be cheerful; in fact, the whole play is cheerful and lighthearted." Daily letters kept Olga abreast of his two-front battle—with words and with illness. On the twenty-fifth he wrote: "The fourth act is coming along smoothly and seems to work well, and the only reason I haven't finished it sooner is that I've been ailing." Next day he sent her the following telegram: "Four acts completely ready. Copying. Shall send you. Health improving. Warm. Kiss you. Antoine." And the day after that he wrote: "My characters have turned out lifelike, that's true, but whether the play amounts to anything I can't tell."

The more he copied, the more his enthusiasm waned. He found psychological flaws, drawn-out scenes, inexcusably awkward dialogue, and resolved to rectify them all. Meanwhile, Olga grew more and more impatient: When would she receive the manuscript? The whole company was on pins and needles, and here he was shilly-shallying, polishing and polishing. . . . On October 2 he sent her a humble letter in self-defense: "I am still weak and coughing. I write every day, not much, but I write. When I send the play and you've read it, you'll see what could have been done with the theme under favorable circumstances, in other words, if I were healthy. Now it's disgraceful." Next day: "Don't be cross about the play, darling. I'm copying it slowly; I can't write any faster." And four days later: "I keep dragging on and on, and that makes the play seem immensely long, colossal. I'm horrified and have lost all relish for it." Then, on October 12, victory at last: "Well, pony, long live my patience and yours! The play is finished, absolutely finished, and tomorrow evening or at the very latest on the morning of the fourteenth it will be on its way to Moscow." And he added impulsively a few paragraphs later: "Darling, how hard it was for me to write that play!"

Sending off the manuscript made Chekhov apprehensive. What would the Art Theater think of it? Had he not bitten off more than he could chew? Why had he let it go in such an obviously imperfect state? Five days passed, and still no word from Moscow. True, it took two days for mail to reach him at Yalta, but still! No news from Nemirovich-Danchenko was certainly bad news.

At last on October 19 he received a 180-word telegram

from Nemirovich-Danchenko spelling out why he considered *The Cherry Orchard* Chekhov's finest—most novel, most original, most poetic—play. He immediately wrote to Olga that he had been sick with anxiety the whole day. Two days later a telegram from Stanislavsky set his mind to rest once and for all. Stanislavsky told him how moved he was while reading the play, echoed Nemirovich-Danchenko's sentiments about its place in Chekhov's oeuvre, and concluded: "My sincere congratulations to an author of genius." Both directors sent new telegrams after the company had had its first reading of the work: "Tremendous impression. [. . .] Intense emotion. [. . .] Exceptional success, brilliant. [. . .] Engrossed from first act. [. . .] Wept during last. [. . .] Your wife absolutely delighted. [. . .] No play has ever met with such unanimous enthusiasm."

Anyone would have perked up after praise like that, but Chekhov was disturbed by its very exuberance. "I had a telegram from Stanislavsky today," he wrote to Olga. "He calls my play a work of genius, thereby overestimating it and robbing it of a good half of the success it might have under favorable circumstances."[11] He was also annoyed with Nemirovich-Danchenko for having released a summary of the play to the press—and an inaccurate summary at that. In general, he felt that once the Art Theater received the manuscript it had begun to treat him rather cavalierly. Why had he not been informed whether *The Cherry Orchard* would open during the present season? Why had no one responded to the casting preferences he had submitted? But soon a cast was agreed upon and the first rehearsal set for November 10.

As the date approached, however, Chekhov grew even more jittery and suspicious. Confined to Yalta by his coughing fits and intestinal disorders, he was unable to take direct part in the production and feared what the well-meaning but sometimes less than subtle Muscovites would do to the play. When Olga asked whether he would give permission for it to be translated into French, he replied insecurely, "What a wild idea! The

French will make nothing of Yermolai* or the sale of the estate; they'll only be bored. There's no point to it."[12] He also bombarded Olga and Stanislavsky with missives—now supplicatory, now minatory—containing his views on sets, staging, and the psychology of one or another character. Yet he was certain that no one took the slightest notice of them in his absence. "It began with misunderstandings, and with misunderstandings it shall end—such appears to be the fate of my play."[13]

From the beginning Chekhov longed to go to Moscow and set matters straight, but his health had declined so radically that as early as October 2 he wrote regretfully to Olga: "Altschuler had a long talk with me yesterday about my illness and said some highly unflattering things about Ostroumov for giving me permission to spend the winter in Moscow. He begged me not to go to Moscow or live in Moscow. He said that Ostroumov must have been in his cups."

Deep down Chekhov knew Altschuler was right. His illness was now such that he could not ignore it for an instant. Dressing made him short of breath; the weight of an overcoat was unbearable; after a few steps in the garden his ears began to buzz; coughing fits constantly interrupted his writing; the mere sight of food—not to mention medication—turned his stomach. His mother and sister kept a close, sad watch over him, urging him to follow Altschuler's recommendation and eat eight eggs a day. He refused.

Everything seemed burdensome, even his correspondence with Olga. Apart from the theater his health was their only topic. As usual, she exhorted him to take care of himself—to eat well and be fastidious in his personal hygiene. Her obsession with bodily cleanliness irritated him. He wrote to her that Altschuler had been horrified to learn she made him take cold baths, and that the only consequence of his having given them up was that ferns and fungi had started sprouting out of his body.

*Yermolai Lopakhin, one of the main characters in the play, is a former serf who buys his former masters' estate.

When Maria left for Moscow in mid-October, Anton grew even more distraught. To calm his nerves, he went through the *Russian Thought* manuscripts sent to him for perusal and played solitaire. Now and then he tried to talk Altschuler into giving him leave to travel, but Altschuler remained firm. Even Olga advised against his coming to Moscow: the weather was awful. And still he balked. Memories of Moscow would come over him in waves. To Nemirovich-Danchenko he wrote: "I'd so like to go to the Hermitage and have some sterlet and a bottle of wine there. There was a time when I could drink a bottle of champagne solo without getting drunk and then have some cognac and still not be affected by it."[14]

Several days later he took up the theme again. "I don't feel like writing," he wrote to Olga, "I feel like going to Moscow, and I'm still awaiting your permission. [. . .] I feel quite well, I think. My stomach is the only problem. I need a change; I need a more dissolute way of life; I need to eat everything—mushrooms, cabbage—and drink everything. What do you think?"[15] He seemed convinced that the moment his feet touched Moscow soil he would regain his strength. Reasonable arguments only exasperated him. "Dear Pony, Forgive me for showing you my nasty temper all the time. I'm your husband, and all husbands are said to have nasty tempers. [. . .] Quickly, quickly, ask me to come and be with you in Moscow. It's sunny and warm here, but I've been perverted: I can't appreciate the local charms as I should. I need the Moscow slush and storms; I can't live without literature and the theater. I *am* married, you know. I feel like seeing my wife. [. . .] To Moscow, to Moscow! That's not *Three Sisters* talking, it's *One Husband*. I embrace my little turkey. Yours, A."[16]

So feverish was his desire to be gone that two days later he reiterated it to Stanislavsky: "I can hardly wait for the day and hour when my wife will at last let me come. I'm beginning to wonder whether she isn't up to something. The weather here is calm, warm, wonderful, but when I think of Moscow and the Sandunovsky Baths it all seems boring and pointless. Sitting in my study, I keep one eye on the telephone—my telegrams are delivered by phone—waiting from one minute to the next to be summoned to Moscow."

Eventually the telegram came, and on December 2, 1903, utterly indifferent to the consequences of the venture and determined to make the most of it, Chekhov rushed off to Moscow without consulting Dr. Altschuler.

XVI

"Ich Sterbe"

Having learned of his patient's escape, Dr. Altschuler cried suicide, but the sight of Moscow under snow did in fact invigorate Chekhov. He loved the dry cold, the motley street crowds, the church bells resounding through the clear, crisp air. His only problem was how to make his way up the endless stairs leading to the third-story flat. To conserve strength he made it a rule to turn down all invitations. Nonetheless, he did attend a benefit performance for Chaliapin at the Bolshoi Theater and a New Year's party held in his honor by the Art Theater.

The New Year's party featured comic skits improvised by the actors, the high point of the evening being a duel—between the strapping Chaliapin, dressed as an Oriental prince, and a minuscule regular in the company by the name of Sulerzhitsky—which ended with the enemies making peace and singing a duet in Ukrainian. Next everyone moved to the lobby for a supper with endless, ebullient toasts, and finally—in a whirl of tailcoats, uniforms, and shimmering, low-cut gowns—the dancing began. Olga was swept off at once. Chekhov and Gorky, who were sitting to one side like a couple of good-natured conspirators, tried hard to carry on a conversation over the laughter, music, and general brouhaha. Before long they were both coughing raucously, and Chekhov, giving Gorky a melancholy smile, managed to rasp, "People might say of us, 'They exchanged some highly interesting coughs.' "

Most of Chekhov's evenings, however, were spent at home in the Petrovka Street flat. Bunin was his most constant companion, because Olga was forever off to the theater, a concert, a charity event. Occasionally Nemirovich-Danchenko came to fetch her. He was always elegantly dressed and swathed in the aromas of fine cigars and fine scent. Olga, young and radiant, would turn to her husband and say, "You won't be too bored without me, will you, darling? I know you're happy with Bouquichon."* Whereupon Bunin would kiss her hand and she would run off, escort in tow.

Chekhov felt completely at ease with Bunin. He could wash his hair in front of him while going on about his family, his childhood, his conception of art, the books he had just finished reading. "Olga Leonardovna usually came home at about four in the morning—though on occasion as late as dawn—smelling of wine and perfume," Bunin recalled in his memoirs. " 'Why aren't you asleep yet, darling? It's bad for you. Oh, are you still here, Bouquichon? Well, at least he wasn't bored.' I would quickly get up and leave."

But there were also times when Chekhov ventured out with Olga on his arm. Olga had ordered a new fur coat and mink hat for him, and they strolled along in measured steps, stopping often to peer into shop windows. He was proud to walk beside her.

He also attended most of the *Cherry Orchard* rehearsals, helplessly looking on as Stanislavsky turned his play into the

*Chekhov's nickname for Bunin.

opposite of what he had intended. Alone in the hall, the fur coat buttoned chin high, struggling to stifle each cough, he attempted—first timidly, then with greater and greater irritation—to put his viewpoint across to Stanislavsky. But Stanislavsky seemed determined not to understand. As far as he was concerned, a writer had no business interfering with the director. "The buds had just begun to appear," Stanislavsky wrote to an actress friend on December 26, "when the author arrived and made a mess of things."

Underlying the friction between Stanislavsky and Chekhov was a fundamental disagreement about how to approach the work psychologically. Chekhov, as he had made it amply clear, conceived of it as a comedy, a comedy on its way to farce, while Stanislavsky considered it a social drama portraying the downfall of the impoverished gentry class in the face of an enterprising but vulgar new class of upstarts. From the first rehearsals he had impressed upon the actors that their goal was to make the public lament the loss of an honorable way of life.

No matter how Chekhov protested, therefore, he had arrived too late to sway Stanislavsky. "I don't know what's going on," he said to one of his visitors. "Either the play is no good or the actors don't understand it. It can't be performed the way they're staging it."

With time Stanislavsky himself started worrying about how the audience would react to the play. Then he hit upon the idea of adding a bit of glamour by opening on Chekhov's forty-fourth birthday, January 17, 1904, and celebrating the birthday, twenty-five years of literary endeavor, and the premiere all at once.* If the audience did not applaud the play or the actors, they would certainly applaud the author.

Gorky and Andreev also decided to take advantage of the occasion, but their goal was to persuade Marx to reconsider his contract with Chekhov. They drafted a letter saying that Russia was about to fête the twenty-fifth anniversary of Chekhov's literary debut, that Chekhov was ill and in straitened circum-

---

*In fact, as Chekhov later pointed out, he had published his first story in March 1880 and the "anniversary" was a bit premature.

stances despite all he had done for his country, and that it was Marx's patriotic and cultural duty to emend the terms of the contract. The letter was then signed by a number of writers, artists, and university professors.

When Chekhov found out about the letter, however, he categorically opposed its being sent. "I signed the contract of my own free will, and I have no desire to repudiate it," he said to one of the writers. "If I sold my works too cheap, I am the only one to blame. I made a stupid mistake, and Marx is not responsible for other people's stupidity. Next time I'll be more careful." To another writer he said, "I ought to have published my works myself. But how could I have guessed then that I'd still be alive five years hence? At the time seventy-five thousand rubles seemed an inexhaustible amount. Now without the income from my plays I'd have nothing."

Chekhov may have suspected that his friends were planning to honor him at the opening of *The Cherry Orchard,* and since he had a horror of all such celebrations he stayed home on the evening of the seventeenth. To the company's great regret the curtain rose without him. But at the end of Act Two Stanislavsky and Nemirovich-Danchenko sent him a note saying that actors and audience alike had been calling for him. He arrived at the theater just after Act Three had ended, and was dragged onstage at once. Behind him stood the actors and a group of representatives from the Moscow literary world; before him sat a clapping, cheering throng.

The ceremony began with an assortment of gifts and flowers piling up in front of the horrified guest of honor. Then came the speeches, pompous and interchangeable. Journalists, actors, and chairmen of literary societies outdid one another in praise of a man who execrated praise. Chekhov stood there pale and blinking in the spotlight, wondering what to do with his hands, trying not to cough. "Take a seat," a voice from the audience called out when he started looking unsteady, but there was no seat for him to take. Besides, he felt it only polite to remain standing: it was the least he could do for all these people who had gathered to honor him. Yet he himself always made fun of the Russian propensity for long speeches and overblown toasts. Had he not stayed away from the celebration honoring Grigorovich, the man who "discovered" him? Had he not told Nemirovich-Danchenko that he was less afraid of death than of the oration someone like Goltsev would make over his grave? And here was Goltsev, editor in chief of *Russian Thought,* carrying on about him as if he were six feet under. Chekhov listened to the speeches and to the telegrams from all over Russia staring out into space and wiping his pince-nez. He could not wait for it to be over. At last Nemirovich-Danchenko took the floor and concluded in the name of the Art Theater: "Our congratulations may have exhausted you, but one thing should be of consolation: what you see here is only a sample of the immense affection which educated Russians feel for you. Our theater owes so much to your talent, your gentle heart, your pure soul that you have every right to say: This is my theater."

After the last ovation Chekhov left the stage completely drained, without a word of thanks. The festivities had lasted an hour. Stanislavsky acknowledged that although they had gone well they had left a bad taste: there was something funereal about them. For Maria, however, the evening was a triumph, recompense for twenty years of love and self-denial, and if Olga shared Anton's glory in the limelight she was content to look on from the wings. As for Chekhov, he came to realize he was sincerely touched by the outpourings of admiration and affection. "They were so happy and effusive in their wishes and it was all so unexpected that I'm not over it yet," he wrote to Batyushkov two days afterwards.

The cheers turned out to have been more for the author than for the play. The press was cool, the papers on the right berating Chekhov for choosing a hackneyed theme and the papers on the left criticizing him for inserting all sorts of gags into a "social tragedy." No one seemed to see the comedy in *The Cherry Orchard.* "Why do the posters and newspaper advertisements insist on calling my play a drama?" he wrote to Olga several months later, evidently still upset at the misunderstanding. "What Stanislavsky and Nemirovich-Danchenko see in the play is not at all what I wrote, and I'm willing to bet anything that neither one nor the other has ever read it through carefully."[1]

In fact, what makes *The Cherry Orchard* a masterpiece is the contrast between the tragic quality of the subject matter and the comic quality of the characters acting it out. In *The Cherry Orchard,* even more than in its predecessors, absence of action creates dramatic tension. The audience, caught up in the magic of Chekhov's lazy, everyday dialogue, ceases to expect change; it even finds itself hoping that nothing will happen to disturb the characters' stodgy but harmless provincial existence, hoping that the cherry orchard will somehow be saved.

The cherry orchard belongs to an old family estate and is filled with memories. Its owners, dreamers like so many of Chekhov's characters, are on the brink of ruin and about to be dispossessed of the property. Lyubov Ranevskaya and her brother Leonid Gaev spend their time reminiscing and are incapable of action: Lyubov does not bother to visit a rich aunt who might bail them out; Gaev plays billiards all day. Lyubov's daughter Anya and her student friend Trofimov welcome the loss of the cherry orchard: they see all Russia as their orchard. On the day the estate is auctioned off in town, Lyubov invites everyone to a ball at the manor house to dance, drink, and flirt away the horror of what is to come. It comes in the person of the merchant Yermolai Lopakhin, a rough, resolute, resourceful man, who plans to chop down the cherry trees and subdivide the land into dacha plots. "I've bought the estate where my father and grand-father were serfs," he cries out to the assembled guests, "where I wasn't even let into the kitchen!" But even though he plans to destroy natural beauty from purely venal motives, he is no more to blame than the Ranevskayas or Gaevs, whose negligence has made his triumph inevitable. He represents the future, a future of hard work and cold reason, while the landowners embody the spirit of the once charming, but now decadent and doomed old Russia.

Sparer than the rest of the plays, *The Cherry Orchard* casts its spell by rendering the family atmosphere to perfection. Thanks to the seemingly artless dialogue, the audience feels it has known the family intimately for years and is now a guest in their humdrum paradise. When, as the play ends, the old retainer Firs is left mumbling to the accompaniment of axes chopping in the distance, the audience no longer knows whom to condemn, whom to pity. For all the fun he makes of his weak, indecisive heroes, Chekhov portrays their foibles with great affection. When Anya leaves the cherry orchard, she calls out, "Goodbye, house! Good-bye, old life!" to which Trofimov responds with the optimism of youth, "Hello, new life!" But it is Firs, forgotten by his masters, who has the last word: "My life's gone by as if I'd never lived it."

Chekhov must have felt something similar once *The Cherry Orchard* had opened. From one day to the next he had been forced to come down to earth and face the possibility that he would never write another play. To kill time he proofread the printed version and read more manuscripts for *Russian Thought*. He also received many visitors and, as usual, complained about having to receive so many visitors. "This place is a madhouse," he wrote to Dr. Sredin. "I never have an instant to myself. I'm constantly obliged to welcome or see out guests and have long conversations, and in my rare free moments I dream of going back home to Yalta, and a pleasant dream it is too."[2]

Many of the long conversations centered on the Russo-Japanese War, which had just broken out. While wary of the exaggerations served up by the press, Chekhov reacted like a patriot, predicting a speedy Russian victory and even talking— rather loosely—about joining up as a doctor. But when a visitor suggested he should write a play based on the events, he replied, "Twenty years have to go by. There's no way of talking about it now. The writer's soul must be at peace or he can't be impartial." And when Lydia Avilova, resurfacing yet again out of the past, asked him to send her a story for a miscellany she was putting together for the relief of the wounded, he discouraged her, saying that the only reasonable project would be an anthology of the finest texts in world literature inspiring compassion for war victims.[3]

In the same letter he announced his return to Yalta. He never quite understood what drew him back to his "southern Siberia," his blue-skied prison, but he could not do without it. Perhaps the constant changes of residence were an unconscious attempt to throw death off the scent. At any rate, he now knew himself to be so far gone that there was no need to consult either Altschuler or Ostroumov. But the latter had advised him to take a dacha in the environs of Moscow, and on the spur of the moment he decided to go and have a look at one in Tsaritsyno with Olga. They took an open sleigh. The weather was freezing cold but sunny. The whole idea was foolhardy, yet Chekhov enjoyed the ride—the white countryside, the fresh air, the sleigh bells—immensely.

Arriving home that evening, Chekhov found another letter from Lydia Avilova. She had changed her tactics, apologizing for having been tactless in the past and expressing the hope that he would let her explain her actions to him in person. "I feared I might die before telling you that I have always had the deepest respect for you and considered you the finest of men. What does it matter that I have lowered myself in your eyes. It could not have been otherwise, and it is the most painful experience in my life. [. . .] I do not ask you to forgive me; I only ask you to understand me."

Of course, Chekhov was on his guard. He had no intention of getting himself embroiled in a new round of letters with the impulsive, insidious Lydia. Why did she refuse to acknowledge that she had long since stepped out of his life? His response put an end to their correspondence once and for all. "Forgive me. I am frozen. I've just returned from Tsaritsyno. [. . .] My hand will hardly write, and I've still got to pack my bags. I wish you all the best and hope you will be happy and have a less complicated view of life, because life is probably a good deal simpler than you make it out to be. Does it really deserve all the anguished meditations we Russians waste on it? Nobody knows."[4]

On the following day, February 15, he said good-bye to Olga and left for Yalta. He arrived to find his brother Alexander and Alexander's wife, youngest son, nursemaid, and dog living in the neighboring dacha. They had come to spend a month in the Crimea. Though slightly disconcerted at first, he was soon reassured: Alexander had given up drinking and cutting capers, and had even turned into an interesting conversationalist. Anton was sorry to see him go.

Dr. Altschuler marveled at finding his patient in such high spirits as he showed him the odd assortment of gifts he had received at the celebration. Chekhov was especially fond of a new, improved fishing rod, while Altschuler admired an eighteenth-century silver inkwell. "Since you're so taken with it," Chekhov told him cheerfully, "you shall have it for your punishment after my death."

Before a week was up, however, he was despondent again. "If our Moscow flat weren't so ridiculously high up, I'd be pining for Moscow now," he wrote to Olga on February 23. And four days later: "Life is pretty boring, uninteresting. The people around are annoyingly uninteresting; they're not interested in anything, don't care about anything." He dreamed of the summer he would spend with his wife. "Where shall we live? I'd like it to be near Moscow and near the station so we can do without a carriage and without benefactors and admirers. Give some thought to the dacha, darling. You'll come up with something. You're so clever, sensible, and practical—when you're not cross. I so enjoy thinking of our ride to Tsaritsyno and back."

Word from Moscow about the growing popularity of *The Cherry Orchard* was not enough to raise Chekhov's spirits. Even though the play was making the rounds of the provinces as well, and to full houses, the only production he had any information about was the Art Theater production, and he was convinced it was all wrong. "An act that should last twelve minutes maximum drags on with you for forty minutes," he wrote to Olga. "All I can say is, Stanislavsky has ruined my play."[5] Yevtikhy Karpov, director of the original *Seagull*, quotes Chekhov in his memoirs as saying, "Is that my *Cherry Orchard*? Are those my characters? Apart from two or three roles they have nothing to do with me. I describe life. A gloomy, conventional life perhaps, but never tedious or whimpering. They make me into either a maudlin writer or a boring writer. I've written several volumes of cheery stories, but the critics have decked me out as a sniveler."

Chekhov's faith in the Art Theater did not begin to revive until he received a telegram from Stanislavsky on April 2 after the Petersburg premiere of the play reporting its success there to be "incomparably greater than in Moscow." Nemirovich-Danchenko confirmed the report, claiming he had never seen an audience react so intensely to the slightest nuance of a psychological drama. The pattern was familiar: most of Chekhov's plays had received guarded if not hostile reviews before making a sudden hit with the public. Although he might have been used to it after all these years, it always took him by surprise and left a residue of ill will. This time, however, he wrote to Olga to buck her up after a vicious attack on the Art Theater he had read in *New Times*: "No one can tear you to pieces anymore, no matter what. You've accomplished what you set out to do, so you can face present and future with all but complete equanimity . . ."[6]

By now Olga had no illusions about leaving the theater to administer to Anton and Anton had no illusions about living all year round with her: she belonged on the stage, and he could not stand to have a feminine presence constantly underfoot. Yet he wrote to her almost daily, calling her his "pony," his "wonderful better half," his "dear great actress," his "little dog." "I can't wait to see you, my joy," he wrote. "When you're away, I lead a humbledrumble existence. I say Thank God when each day is over—no ideas, no desires, just patience and pacing from one corner to the other."[7] And the next day: "I'm awaiting your orders about my journey, the dacha, and my life. I'm yearning, really yearning to give you a little beating and prove my power, yearning to stroll with you along Petrovka and Tverskaya." And a few days later: "I'm very bored without my wife and afraid to take on a mistress. [. . .] You ask me what life is. That's like asking what a carrot is. A carrot is a carrot, and there's nothing more to know."[8]

The latter comment represents Chekhov's attitude towards metaphysical issues in a nutshell. He rejected all religious or philosophical explanations of the other world. If God exists, we only belittle Him by presuming to grasp Him with our meager intelligence. "The only thing that dies in a man is what is subject to our five senses," he wrote in his notebooks. "Everything that lies beyond those senses—and is most likely immense, unimaginable, sublime—continues to exist."

Occasionally he felt a desire to write, but since he was too weak to keep at anything for long he would soon start looking for excuses not to. "I've been working," he wrote to Olga, "but I'm not getting anywhere. I have a feeling that nobody will read us because of the war." Like all his fellow countrymen, he pounced upon the papers daily and was deeply grieved by Russia's defeats. In time all he hoped for was an immediate end to the hostilities.

Though not actually writing, he went on hatching plays in his head. To the actor Pavel Olenev he proposed a comedy in three acts that could be produced abroad without going through censorship. He even promised him a completed manuscript by September. To Stanislavsky he spoke of a play in which the hero, a scientist disappointed by a phlegmatic or unfaithful wife, goes off to the far north and, in the last act, alone on the bridge of his icebound ship, sees his wife's shade hovering over him in the unearthly Arctic light.

Awaiting the return of the creative impulse, Chekhov spent hours on end staring out of his study window. The only work he could manage was to read and write short reports on *Russian Thought* manuscripts and copy over his notebooks in ink. "I've got five hundred sheets of unused material in them," he told the novelist Nikolai Garin-Mikhailovsky, "enough for five years of work. If I can make my way through it all, my family will want for nothing."

In mid-April he started coughing again and his intestinal pains increased. "I think the climate is largely to blame," he wrote to Sobolevsky, "a climate I love and despise as one loves and despises a pretty but capricious woman."[9] His deplorable state notwithstanding, he could not stand the thought of staying put. He set his departure date for May 1, and although he went to a dentist to have a tooth pulled he did not make an appointment with Dr. Altschuler. "I'll arrive in Moscow in the morning: the express trains have started running again," he wrote to Olga, all excited at the prospect of a new escape. "Oh, puppy, puppy, how I've missed you!"[10]

But Chekhov had an attack en route, and by the time he arrived in Moscow on May 3 he was hardly able to put one foot in front of the other. Olga had rented a new flat for him in a building with a lift, but he had scant opportunity to appreciate it: he took to his bed at once. Olga called in her family doctor, a German by the name of Julius Taube. Dr. Taube diagnosed a relapse of the pleurisy together with an "intestinal catarrh," which indicated beyond all doubt that the tuberculosis had spread to the abdominal region.

As time went on, Chekhov had more and more trouble breathing. He would shiver with fever, suffer acute shooting pains in his arms and legs, and lie awake at night, wondering whether his spinal column had been affected. Dr. Taube gave him morphine injections to sustain his heart, placed him on a strict diet, and ordered him to remain in bed. He also ordered him to be examined by a prominent Berlin specialist as soon as he was well enough to make the journey to Germany.

The moment he could hold a pen, Chekhov wrote to Dr. Sredin: "My wife at her ill husband's bedside—pure gold. I've never seen such a nurse. In other words, it's good, very good I got married. Otherwise I don't know what I'd do now."[11] And to Maria, who had returned to Yalta to care for Yevgenia Yakovlevna: "I'm still in bed. I haven't dressed even once, I haven't gone out, I'm still in the state I was in when you left. The day before yesterday I had a sudden attack of pleurisy for no reason whatever. Now everything's fine. [. . .] I've started breathing better and wheezing less. I'm satisfied with my doctor."[12]

In addition to writing all kinds of letters (including detailed instructions to Maria for the maintenance of the Yalta garden), he read and annotated manuscripts and arranged for more books to be sent to the library in Taganrog. The friends who came to see him found him stretched out on a daybed wearing a dressing gown. He would apologize to them for the informality of his attire and force himself to make jokes and appear interested in everything, but they were all struck by his hollow cheeks, waxen complexion, and dilated pupils. Dr. Rossolimo observed that like all tubercular patients he spoke of the disease with an almost reckless indifference. With his burning hands and flushed cheeks could he really believe in a cure?

One evening Chekhov was reminiscing happily with the writer Gilyarovsky, one of the first to encourage him to write, when Gilyarovsky mentioned he had recently returned from a visit to the steppe. All at once Chekhov grew pensive: "Oh, the steppe, the steppe! What a lucky man you are! That's where the poetry is." And he closed his eyes, smiled a childlike smile, and let his head drop onto the pillow. "I am certain he dreamed of the steppe," Gilyarovsky wrote.

Towards the end of the month Chekhov's temperature went down and he felt strong enough to get out of bed. On May 31 he announced triumphantly to his sister: "Just think. Today for the first time I put on shoes and a coat [. . .] and for the first time went out for a ride." Now there was nothing to hold him back from the journey Dr. Taube had counseled. On June 3, 1904, Anton and Olga took the train for Berlin.

Although he had left Moscow in a morbid mood, Chekhov perked up at once in Berlin. A change of place always did him good. From a comfortable room at the Hotel Savoy ("the best in Berlin") he wrote Maria letter after optimistic letter: his appetite had improved; he was putting a bit of flesh on his bones; his diarrhea had subsided; his legs no longer ached; in fact, he was on his feet all day, "running around Berlin," raiding the shops, riding through the Tiergarten. It was the first time he had ever been out of Russia with Olga, and he felt all the closer to her for their being "stranded" in a foreign city; he enjoyed discovering a new world and discussing new impressions with her. He claimed jestingly that he had not seen a single good-looking woman and that German women dressed "abominably." Yet, as he admitted to Maria, "people live a comfortable existence, the food is good, life is not expensive, [. . .] the streets are clean, order reigns."[13] In his optimism he even made plans to spend some time at the Italian lakes and return to Yalta in August via Constantinople.

Chekhov's confidence in the future was not shared by Dr. Karl Ewald, the specialist Dr. Taube had recommended. After giving Chekhov a careful examination, Dr. Ewald spread his arms in a gesture of helplessness and left without a word. The message was obvious. "It was cruel of him, of course," Dr. Altschuler later wrote, "but Ewald's attitude may be explained by the fact that he did not understand how anyone could have permitted a man so ill to undertake so long a journey—and for what?" After an interview with Chekhov the Berlin correspondent for *Russian News* reported to his editor: "I am of the opinion that Chekhov's days are numbered. He seemed mortally ill: he was terribly thin, coughed all the time, gasped for breath at the slightest movement, and was running a high temperature."

The same journalist saw the Chekhovs off at the Potsdam station, where after three days in Berlin they took the train for Badenweiler in the Black Forest. "He had trouble making his way up the small staircase at the station," he wrote, "and sat down for several minutes to catch his breath. But as the train began to pull out, he disregarded my plea and leaned out of the window to nod good-bye."

Badenweiler is a spa on the western edge of the Black Forest not far from Basel, a clean, calm, unexciting little town that seemed to Chekhov made for convalescence. Olga and he spent their first two days there in a boardinghouse, then moved into a private house that took in guests. The large, well-kept garden, all gravel paths and flower beds, afforded a beautiful view of the mountains. Chekhov spent the entire day—from morning until seven in the evening—seated or reclining in a comfortable chair. In Badenweiler the sun did not burn, he wrote to his sister, it caressed the skin. The spa physician, a Dr. Schwöhrer, proved perfectly competent and easy to get on with. Besides absolute rest he prescribed a diet of cocoa, oatmeal drenched in butter, and strawberry tea ("to aid the patient's sleep"). And while Chekhov could not help grumbling about Schwöhrer's "quackery," he boasted to Maria that he was growing stronger fast. On June 13 he went so far as to write to his mother: "My health is improving, and it's likely I'll be completely cured in a week." Olga was hopeful enough to leave him on his own and go to Basel to have her teeth examined.

After a week of euphoria, however, Chekhov once more gave way to anxiety, boredom, and the need for change. "I can't get used to this German peace and quiet," he wrote to Maria. "There's not a sound inside or out except when a band with no talent strikes up at seven in the morning and noon. There's not a drop of talent, not a drop of good taste anywhere to be seen, only great quantities of order and honesty. There's a good deal more talent in Russia, to say nothing of Italy or France." Now Dr. Schwöhrer seemed wanting too: "The same stupid cocoa, the same oatmeal."[14] Since there was no question of their leaving Badenweiler, however, they left the house they had been staying at for the Hotel Sommer, the best the spa had to offer. Chekhov would sit out on the balcony of his room for hours, watching people enter and leave the post office across the road. Or he would plan journeys, perusing timetables and requesting information on departure dates for boats en route to Odessa from Trieste or Marseilles.

Then Badenweiler was hit by a heat wave. Chekhov, his lungs half destroyed, suffered horribly. "It's caught me un-awares," he wrote to Maria, "and since all I have with me is winter clothes, I'm suffocating and dream of getting out of here."[15] In this letter, the last Chekhov ever wrote, he gives in to despair for the first time: "The food is very tasty, but it doesn't do me much good. My stomach keeps getting upset. I can't eat the kind of butter they have here. Apparently my stomach is ruined beyond all hope. About the only remedy for it is to fast, in other words, to refrain from eating entirely, and that's that. And the only remedy for short-windedness is to keep perfectly still." His letter to her crossed one of hers to him saying that since he was doing so well she and their brother Ivan had decided to go on a short tour of the Caucasus. "So take care of yourself, dear Antosha. Try to cough less and eat more. Gather your strength and come home."

On June 29 Chekhov had a sudden violent attack and Schwöhrer had to give him both morphine and oxygen, but his pulse returned to normal and he had a peaceful night. The respite was short-lived; next day he had a new attack. Two correspondents from the Russian press rushed to Badenweiler and wired back alarming reports on the state of Chekhov's health. Chekhov, meanwhile, soon over the second attack and perfectly lucid and calm, instructed his bank in Berlin to make all payments in his wife's name. When Olga asked him the reason for his concern, he replied evasively, "It's nothing really. Just in case . . ."

On July 1 he seemed to feel better and the correspondents' reports were more optimistic: his heart was doing well, the day had passed uneventfully. Towards evening he insisted that Olga, who had not left his bedside for three days, should take a walk in the hotel grounds. When she returned, she lay down on a narrow couch near the bed. He scolded her for looking so sad. To cheer her up, he started improvising a story. It took place in a fashionable watering place where the guests were all "well-fed bankers" and "rosy-cheeked English and American tourists." Every day they would work up an appetite by going on a hike, and every evening they would rush back to the hotel dreaming of the delicious meal awaiting them. One day they returned to learn that the chef had decamped and they would have no dinner. At this point Chekhov began to describe how each of the hungry gourmets reacted to the disaster. For all her anguish Olga could not help laughing.

Although the heat was still oppressive, Chekhov soon fell asleep. His breath came in spurts, but his face was calm. Then at half past twelve he sat up in bed and called for a doctor. It was the first time Olga had ever heard him do so. Suddenly she felt very much alone in their large German hotel where everyone was asleep for the night. After a moment of indecision she recalled that there were two Russian students in the room next door. She ran and woke them, and one of them immediately rushed off to fetch Dr. Schwöhrer. "I can still hear the sound of the gravel under his shoes in the silence of that stifling July night," she later wrote.

Fever had made Chekhov delirious. He went on about a sailor or asked about the Japanese, his eyes shining. But when Olga tried to place an ice bag on his chest, he suddenly regained consciousness and said, "Don't put ice on an empty stomach."

The windows were wide open, but he could not stop panting; his temples were bathed in sweat. Dr. Schwöhrer arrived at two o'clock. When Chekhov saw him, he sat up, leaned back against the pillows, and, in a final reflex of courtesy, mustered his weak German and said, "*Ich sterbe.*"* Schwöhrer immediately gave him a camphor injection, but his heart failed to react. He was about to send for an oxygen pillow when Chekhov, lucid to the end, protested in a broken voice, "What's the use? Before it arrives, I'll be a corpse." So Dr. Schwöhrer sent for a bottle of champagne.

When it came, Chekhov took a glass and, turning to Olga, said with a smile, "It's been so long since I've had champagne." He emptied the glass slowly and lay down on his left side. A few moments later he stopped breathing. He had passed from life to death with characteristic simplicity.

It was July 2, 1904, three o'clock in the morning. A large

black-winged moth had flown in through the window and was banging wildly against the lamp. The muffled sound soon grew maddeningly distracting. Dr. Schwöhrer withdrew after a few words of consolation. All at once there was a joyous explosion: the cork had popped out of the champagne bottle and foam was fizzing out after it. The moth found its way out of the window and disappeared into the sultry night. Silence returned. When day broke at last, Olga was still sitting and staring into her husband's face. It was peaceful, smiling, knowing. "There were no human voices, no everyday sounds," she wrote. "There was only beauty, peace, and the grandeur of death."

Before leaving Badenweiler, Olga arranged for the remains to be transported to Moscow, where the burial was to take place on July 9. That day a group of friends gathered at the station to meet the train carrying the body. They were flabbergasted to learn that his coffin had traveled in a dirty green van with the words FOR OYSTERS written in large letters on the door.

Gorky was furious. "I feel like screaming, weeping, brawling with indignation and wrath," he wrote to his wife. He knew that Chekhov would not have cared whether his body traveled in a basket of dirty laundry. What he found unforgivable was that Russia could have treated him so shoddily, and he later called the oyster van an enormous smirk of triumphant vulgarity. Yet was the absurdity of it all so very far from the absurdity of life as depicted many times over in Chekhov's stories and plays?

A military band that had assembled on the platform struck up an appropriate melody, and a funeral procession began to take shape. Many of the mourners were surprised that the government had seen fit to bury Chekhov with such military pomp, but they praised it for recognizing the significance of the occasion. Only gradually did they realize they were following the coffin of a General Keller who had been killed in Manchuria and happened to have arrived at the same moment as their beloved writer.

Chekhov's procession, which set off with no more than a hundred people, was led by a fat constable on an imposing white horse. Olga walked behind the coffin, which rested on the shoulders of several students. The weather was cold. The two men in front of Gorky, lawyers "dressed like newlyweds" in shiny shoes and bright ties, chatted about the intelligence of their dogs and the relative merits of their dachas. A woman wearing a purple dress and carrying a lace parasol said nonchalantly to the old man in horn-rimmed spectacles next to her, "What a nice, witty man he was!" Even his admirers failed to grasp the significance of the loss Russia had just sustained, thought Gorky.

As the procession moved on, it increased noticeably in size. A group of students formed a human chain to keep the idly curious at bay. Trams and carriages had been held up all along the route. The procession made a few stops of its own—one in front of the Art Theater, another in front of the *Russian Thought* building—for brief religious services. Chekhov's mother, sister, and brothers arrived in Moscow in the midst of it all and rushed to catch up with the procession, but the police did not recognize them at first and refused to let them join it until Maria cried out, "Let me go to my brother! Let me go to my brother!"

By the time it had reached the Novodevichy Monastery, the crowd was so vast that it blocked the gates, and the pallbearers, immediate family, and close friends had to jostle their way through. The crowd rushed in immediately after them, breaking crosses, overturning fences, trampling flowers. With tears in his eyes Chaliapin turned to Gorky and said, "And this is the rabble he lived and worked for."

The grave had been dug next to his father's. There were no speeches. Once the coffin had been lowered into the grave, the crowd, quiet at last, began to sing the traditional "Eternal Memory." Next Olga and the family and close friends of the deceased filed past the open grave throwing fistfuls of earth on the resonant coffin lid. Only then was the grave filled in. It immediately disappeared under an avalanche of bouquets and wreaths. Numb with grief, three women kept their eyes fixed on the mountain of flowers: mother, sister, and wife.*

Next day a religious service was held at the cemetery. A choir sang as the setting sun gilded the linden trees shading the grave. The family was surrounded by friends. After the ceremony Kuprin bent down and kissed the hand of Chekhov's mother without saying a word. "What a calamity has struck us," she said. "Antosha is no more."

Such was the only funeral oration pronounced over the grave. Given his dread of bombast, Chekhov would have appreciated the discretion.

*Chekhov's mother outlived him by fifteen years. His sister became the director of the Chekhov Museum in the Yalta house and died in 1957 at the age of ninety-four. His wife continued her brilliant acting career and died in 1959 at the age of eighty-nine.

Notes

I. The Family Circle

1. January 2, 1889.
2. April 7, 1887.

II. Schools and Escapes

1. February 22, 1892, to Vladimir Tikhonov.
2. August 29, 1888.

III. The Allure of Moscow

1. April 8, 1879.
2. February 8, 1877.
3. May 10, 1877.
4. July 29, 1877.
5. April 8, 1879.
6. November 4, 1877.
7. June 9, 1877.

IV. A New Clan Leader

1. February 1, 1886, to Victor Bilibin.
2. August 21 or 24, 1883.
3. March 1881.
4. March 1886.
5. January 7, 1889.

V. Journalism and Medicine

1. May 13, 1883.
2. August 29, 1888.
3. January 12, 1883.
4. April 1883 (sometime after April 17).
5. February 20, 1883.
6. Ibid.
7. February 1883 (between February 3 and 6).
8. May 13, 1883.
9. October 1883 (between October 15 and 28).
10. Ibid.
11. August 1 or 2, 1883.
12. December 25, 1883.
13. February 24, 1884.
14. August 23, 1884.
15. June 27, 1884.
16. January 31, 1885.
17. Ibid.
18. April 11, 1884.

VI. First Successes, First Failures

1. May 10, 1885.
2. September 14, 1885.
3. May 10, 1885, to Mikhail Chekhov.
4. May 9, 1885.
5. Maria Chekhova, *Memoirs of a Distant Past* (in Russian).
6. October 1, 1885.
7. October 12 or 13, 1885.
8. January 4, 1886.
9. January 18, 1886.
10. February 21, 1886.
11. February 28, 1886.
12. February 14, 1886.
13. February 20, 1886.
14. February 14, 1886.

15. Ibid.
16. March 28, 1886.
17. April 4, 1886.
18. April 6, 1886.
19. April 25, 1886.
20. February 1, 1886.
21. February 28, 1886.
22. March 11, 1886.
23. June 9, 1889.
24. Vladimir Korolenko, "Anton Pavlovich Chekhov," *Memoirs* (in Russian). All further quotations of Korolenko come from this source.
25. March 1886.
26. April 6, 1886.
27. May 10, 1886.
28. January 17, 1887.
29. September 21, 1886.
30. December 13, 1886.
31. April 10–11, 1887.
32. April 7, 1887.
33. April 25, 1887.
34. May 11, 1887.
35. May 14, 1887.
36. September 11, 1887.
37. September 29, 1886.
38. September 13, 1887.
39. October 10–12, 1887.
40. December 30, 1888.
41. October 6–8, 1887.
42. October 24, 1887.
43. November 20, 1887.
44. November 24, 1887.

VII. "My Life Bores Me"

1. December 3, 1887.
2. Ibid.
3. January 9, 1888.
4. January 22, 1888.
5. February 4, 1888.
6. February 3, 1888.
7. February 9, 1888.
8. March 14 and 15 or 16, 1888.

9. March 25, 1888.
10. Ibid.
11. April 1888 (sometime after April 26).
12. April 18, 1888.
13. May 30, 1888, to Suvorin.
14. Ibid.
15. Ibid.
16. July 22–23, 1888.
17. July 18, 1888, to Leontyev-Shcheglov.
18. Ibid.
19. August 13, 1888.
20. October 14, 1888.
21. September 24, 1888.
22. October 10, 1888.
23. Ibid.
24. October 9, 1888.
25. September 11, 1888.
26. May 3, 1888.
27. October 4, 1888.
28. May 30, 1888.
29. October 27, 1888.
30. October 20, 1888.
31. October 9, 1888.
32. November 3, 1888.
33. November 7, 1888.
34. December 19, 1888.
35. December 30, 1888.
36. February 18, 1889.
37. February 17, 1889.
38. February 18, 1889.
39. December 23, 1888.
40. March 16, 1889.
41. January 2, 1889.
42. May 8, 1889.
43. May 14, 1889.
44. May 7, 1889.
45. May 31, 1889.
46. June 26, 1889.
47. June 24, 1889.
48. August 13, 1889.
49. August 3, 1889.
50. October 17, 1889.
51. October 13, 1889, to Suvorin.

52. October 17, 1889.
53. February 15, 1890.
54. March 5, 1889.
55. December 27, 1889.
56. May 4, 1889.
57. December 20, 1889 (approximately).
58. December 7, 1889.

VIII. From Sakhalin to Paris

1. Lydia Avilova, *Chekhov in My Life: A Love Story,* trans. David Magarshack (London: J. Lehmann, 1950). The original appeared in the Soviet Union in 1947.
2. March 19, 1892.
3. March 9, 1890.
4. April 1, 1890.
5. March 22, 1890.
6. April 10, 1890.
7. April 15, 1890.
8. April 29, 1890.
9. May 14–17, 1890.
10. Ibid.
11. Ibid.
12. Ibid.
13. May 20, 1890.
14. May 28, 1890.
15. Published by *New Times* in June and August 1890.
16. June 5, 1890.
17. June 7, 1890.
18. June 13, 1890, to his sister.
19. Ibid.
20. June 20, 1890.
21. June 20, 1890.
22. June 27, 1890.
23. *The Island of Sakhalin,* Chapter 2 (in Russian).
24. Ibid., Chapter 21.
25. Ibid.
26. September 11, 1890.
27. *The Island of Sakhalin,* Chapter 21.
28. Ibid., Chapter 17.
29. September 11, 1890.
30. October 6, 1890.
31. December 9, 1890.

32. Ibid.
33. Ibid.
34. Ibid.
35. December 17, 1890, to Suvorin.
36. December 10, 1890.
37. December 24, 1890.
38. January 16, 1891.
39. January 14, 1891.
40. March 5, 1891.
41. March 17, 1891.
42. March 20, 1891.
43. March 24, 1891.
44. March 26, 1891.
45. April 1, 1891.
46. April 15, 1891.
47. April 21, 1891.
48. April 24, 1891.

IX. The Landowner

1. August 28, 1891.
2. May 17, 1891.
3. June–July 1891.
4. May 10, 1891.
5. August 18, 1891.
6. August 30, 1891.
7. September 8, 1891.
8. December 11, 1891.
9. November 18, 1891.
10. December 14, 1891.
11. January 22, 1892.
12. October 20, 1891.
13. November 22, 1891.
14. March 3, 1892.
15. March 6, 1892.
16. March 19, 1892.
17. March 21, 1892.
18. June 9, 1888.
19. October 25, 1891.

X. Melikhovo

1. March 17, 1892.
2. October 18, 1892.

3. Ibid.
4. December 8, 1892.
5. April 8, 1892.
6. April 29, 1892.
7. March 27, 1892.
8. August 16, 1892.
9. August 1, 1892.
10. Ibid.
11. November 22, 1892.
12. October 30, 1892.
13. August 7, 1893.
14. August 24, 1893.
15. April 26, 1893.
16. February 13, 1893.
17. February 24, 1893.
18. July 28, 1893.
19. Ibid.
20. August 13, 1893.
21. November 11, 1893.
22. Ibid.
23. January 2, 1894.
24. November 25, 1892.
25. March 27, 1894.
26. March 27, 1894.
27. July 5, 1894.
28. May 9, 1894.
29. July 11, 1894.
30. September 9, 1894.
31. September 18, 1894.
32. October 2, 1894.
33. January 21, 1895.

XI. The Seagull

1. January 19, 1895.
2. December 1, 1895.
3. January 19, 1895.
4. March 23, 1895.
5. December 10, 1895.
6. Lydia Avilova, *Chekhov in My Life: A Love Story,* trans. David Magarshack (London: J. Lehmann, 1950), pp. 69–70.
7. February 14, 1895.
8. February 15, 1895.

9. April 18, 1895.
10. Quoted by B. G. Shchetinin in the "Literary Anthill" column of the *Historical Herald,* 1911.
11. October 21, 1895.
12. October 26, 1895.
13. November 18, 1895.
14. November 21, 1895.
15. December 17, 1895.
16. December 13, 1895.
17. January 9, 1896.
18. Letter to Vladimir Semenkovich, October 13, 1896.
19. October 12, 1896.
20. October 15, 1896.
21. Suvorin's *Diary* appeared in the Soviet Union in 1923. An abridged French translation by M. Lichnevsky, *Journal intime d'Alexis Souvorine,* appeared in Paris four years later.
22. October 18, 1896.
23. October 22, 1896.
24. Entry dated February 11, 1897.
25. November 11, 1896.
26. December 14, 1896.
27. December 2, 1896.
28. April 1, 1897.
29. April 7, 1897.
30. April 16, 1897.
31. April 17, 1897.
32. April 7, 1897.
33. June 21, 1897.
34. July 12, 1897.
35. July 4, 1897.
36. August 19, 1897.

XII. Yalta

1. September 5, 1897.
2. December 15, 1897.
3. October 29, 1897.
4. December 16, 1897.
5. November 2, 1897.
6. Lydia Avilova, *Chekhov in My Life: A Love Story,* trans. David Magarshack (London: J. Lehmann, 1950), p. 124.
7. November 3, 1897.
8. October 6, 1897.

9. December 15, 1897.

10. October 2, 1897.

11. December 4, 1897.

12. January 4, 1898.

13. January 23, 1898.

14. February 9, 1898.

15. February 6, 1898.

16. February 23, 1898.

17. March 23, 1898.

18. March 28, 1898.

19. April 1, 1898.

20. March 13, 1898.

21. May 27, 1898.

22. June 6, 1898.

23. Between July 24 and 26, 1898.

24. October 8, 1898.

25. September 28 and October 1, 1898.

26. October 14, 1898.

27. October 17, 1898.

28. October 14, 1898.

29. December 8, 1898.

30. Vladimir Nemirovich-Danchenko, *My Life in the Russian Theatre,* trans. John Cournos (Boston: Little, Brown, 1936), pp. 186–87.

31. October 27, 1898.

32. November 29, 1898.

33. January 5, 1899.

34. December 3, 1898.

35. September 2, 1899.

36. July 10, 1898.

37. Avilova, *Chekhov in My Life,* p. 125.

38. August 30, 1898.

39. October 21, 1898.

40. October 26, 1898.

41. January 22, 1899.

42. January 27, 1899.

43. February 5, 1899.

44. February 18, 1899.

45. March 14, 1899.

46. April 17, 1899.

47. February 22, 1899.

48. March 4, 1899.

49. April 2, 1899.

50. April 24, 1899.

51. March 29, 1899.
52. Maxim Gorky, *Reminiscences of Tolstoy, Chekhov, and Andreev,* trans. S. S. Koteliansky and Leonard Woolf (London: Hogarth Press, 1934), pp. 92–93.
53. March 23, 1899.
54. March 30, 1899.
55. April 2, 1899.
56. April 24, 1899.
57. Avilova, p. 143.

XIII. "Greetings, Last Page of My Life"

1. June 16, 1899.
2. June 17, 1899.
3. July 21, 1899.
4. August 19, 1899.
5. September 15, 1899.
6. September 3, 1899.
7. October 4, 1899.
8. November 11, 1899.
9. November 26, 1899.
10. November 25, 1899.
11. Late in 1899.
12. September 30, 1899.
13. October 30, 1899.
14. November 24, 1899.
15. February 15, 1900.
16. January 28, 1900.
17. A. B. Goldenveizer, *Talks with Tolstoi,* trans. S. S. Koteliansky and Virginia Woolf (London: Hogarth Press, 1923), p. 51.
18. January 28, 1900.
19. February 3, 1900.
20. February 10, 1900.
21. March 17, 1900.
22. May 20, 1900.
23. August 9, 1900.
24. August 13, 1900.
25. August 23, 1900.
26. September 8, 1900.
27. September 15, 1900.
28. September 22, 1900.
29. September 27, 1900.
30. September 28, 1900.

31. November 16, 1900.
32. December 14, 1900.
33. December 15, 1900.
34. December 17, 1900.
35. January 2, 1901.
36. January 11, 1901.
37. January 24, 1901.
38. January 2, 1901.
39. January 21, 1901.
40. February 2, 1901.
41. February 16, 1901.
42. Alexander Kuprin, *Memoirs* (in Russian).
43. March 18, 1901.
44. Ivan Bunin, *Memoirs* (in Russian). All further quotations of Bunin come from this source.
45. April 26, 1901.
46. April 22, 1901.
47. May 2, 1901.
48. May 20, 1901.
49. June 2, 1901.
50. June 23, 1901.

XIV. Love by Correspondence

1. September 3, 1901.
2. August 3, 1901.
3. August 28, 1901.
4. August 24, 1901.
5. August 31, 1901.
6. August 30, 1901.
7. Constantin Stanislavsky, *My Life in Art,* trans. J. J. Robbins (Boston: Little, Brown, 1924), p. 420.
8. September 24, 1901.
9. October 19, 1901.
10. October 29, 1901.
11. November 7, 1901.
12. December 18, 1901.
13. December 29, 1901.
14. January 7, 1902.
15. January 20, 1902.
16. Sergei Tolstoy, *Tolstoy Remembered by His Son,* trans. Moura Budberg (London: Weidenfeld and Nicolson, 1961), p. 121.
17. Maxim Gorky, *Reminiscences of Tolstoy, Chekhov, and Andreev,*

trans. S. S. Koteliansky and Leonard Woolf (London: Hogarth Press, 1934), p. 66.

18. Lev Tolstoy, *Diary,* November 29, 1901 (in Russian).
19. November 17, 1901.
20. Gorky, *Reminiscences,* p. 98.
21. Ibid., pp. 105–106.
22. December 7, 1901.
23. February 13, 1902.
24. Between May 25 and September 1901.
25. March 12, 1902.
26. February 28, 1902.
27. March 17, 1902.
28. April 20, 1902.
29. June 18, 19, and 22, 1902.
30. Tikhonov later became a writer and published memoirs under his pen name, Alexander Serebrov. The memoirs, which form the basis for the quotations below, came out in Moscow in 1955 as *Time and People* (in Russian).
31. July 18, 1902.
32. August 17, 1902.
33. August 24, 1902.
34. August 27, 1902.
35. September 1, 1902.
36. September 10, 1902.
37. Between November 20 and November 30, 1898.
38. November 30, 1902.
39. December 30, 1902.
40. December 25, 1902.
41. December 14, 1902.
42. January 20, 1903.
43. January 23, 1903.
44. February 5, 1903.
45. February 16, 1903.
46. April 11, 1889.
47. March 4, 1903.
48. March 21, 1903.

XV. *"How Hard It Was for Me to Write That Play!"*

1. June 7, 1903.
2. May 24, 1903.
3. June 4, 1903.
4. July 1, 1903.

5. May 29, 1903.
6. June 29, 1903.
7. June 19, 1903.
8. July 28, 1903.
9. January 15, 1889.
10. September 20, 1903.
11. October 21, 1903.
12. October 24, 1903.
13. November 25, 1903.
14. November 2, 1903.
15. November 7, 1903.
16. November 21, 1903.

XVI. "Ich Sterbe"

1. April 10, 1904.
2. January 20, 1904.
3. February 7, 1904.
4. February 14, 1904.
5. March 29, 1904.
6. March 31, 1904.
7. April 10, 1904.
8. April 20, 1904.
9. April 20, 1904.
10. April 22, 1904.
11. May 22, 1904.
12. May 22, 1904.
13. June 8, 1904.
14. June 21, 1904.
15. June 28, 1904.

Index

349